POLITICAL MESSAGING IN MUSIC AND ENTERTAINMENT SPACES ACROSS THE GLOBE

VOLUME 1

Edited by

Uche Onyebadi
Texas Christian University

Series in Politics
VERNON PRESS

Copyright © 2023 by the authors.

All rights reserved. No part of this publication may be reproduced, stored in a retrieval system, or transmitted in any form or by any means, electronic, mechanical, photocopying, recording, or otherwise, without the prior permission of Vernon Art and Science Inc.
www.vernonpress.com

In the Americas:
Vernon Press
1000 N West Street, Suite 1200,
Wilmington, Delaware 19801
United States

In the rest of the world:
Vernon Press
C/Sancti Espiritu 17,
Malaga, 29006
Spain

Series in Politics

Library of Congress Control Number: 2022937728

ISBN: 978-1-64889-570-8

Also available: 978-1-64889-432-9 [Hardback]; 978-1-64889-471-8 [PDF, E-Book]

Product and company names mentioned in this work are the trademarks of their respective owners. While every care has been taken in preparing this work, neither the authors nor Vernon Art and Science Inc. may be held responsible for any loss or damage caused or alleged to be caused directly or indirectly by the information contained in it.

Every effort has been made to trace all copyright holders, but if any have been inadvertently overlooked the publisher will be pleased to include any necessary credits in any subsequent reprint or edition.

Cover design by Vernon Press using elements designed by pikisuperstar/Freepik and rawpixel.com/Freepik.

TABLE OF CONTENTS

ACKNOWLEDGMENT vii

FOREWORD ix
Lyombe Eko
Texas Tech University, USA

PREFACE xiii
Uche Onyebadi
Texas Christian University, USA

CHAPTER 1
Z/Sarsuwelas: Music, theater, and the mediation of political dissent in the Philippines 1
Rodelio Cruz Manacsa
University of the South (Sewanee), Tennessee, USA

Zeny Sarabia-Panol
Middle Tennessee State University, USA

CHAPTER 2
Bringing Spirituals onto the Classical Music stage in the service of African American Civil Rights 33
Julia Schmidt-Pirro
Independent Scholar, Savannah, GA, USA

CHAPTER 3
"I Am More Than My Body!": Politicizing the *Female Masquerade* performance in the West Indian Carnival 61
Cherry-Ann M. Smart
Information Smart Consulting, Jamaica, W.I.

CHAPTER 4
Military Rhetoric: Making sense of political messaging in Reggae music 87
Kameika S. Murphy
Stockton University, USA

CHAPTER 5
Revisiting the role of Popular Culture in supporting the anti-Apartheid Movement (1970s-1980s) 111
Archie W. Simpson
Centre for Small State Studies, University of Iceland, Iceland

CHAPTER 6
Political music in Brazil: An examination of *Punk Rock* in Brasília, 1979-1985 137
Silvio César Tamaso D'Onofrio
Universidade de São Paulo, Brazil

Marta Fernanada Tamaso D'Onofrio
Universidade de São Paulo, Brazil

Henrique César Tamaso D'Onofrio
Fundação Armando Álvares Penteado, Brazil

CHAPTER 7
Political Messaging in Indian Cinema: Core or Periphery? 163
N. Usha Rani
University of Mysore, India

CHAPTER 8
Musicians and Political songs in the struggle for freedom in Zimbabwe 183
Bhekinkosi Jakobe Ncube
University of Johannesburg, South Africa

CHAPTER 9
Stylistic vernacular jingles in political messaging: An analysis of Igbo language jingles in Nigeria's General Elections (2019) 207
Cecilia A. Eme
Nnamdi Azikiwe University, Nigeria

Benjamin I. Mmadike
Nnamdi Azikiwe University, Nigeria

CHAPTER 10
**Performative sites of resistance: A challenge to
oppression through artistic entertainment** 227
Rachael Cofield
Florida State University, USA

Douglas L. Allen
Emporia State University, USA

CHAPTER 11
**Chile's *Nueva Canción* and the Pinochet Regime:
Censoring political messages in music** 253
Kelly Grenier
University of Kentucky, USA

CHAPTER 12
**Zimbabwe: Music, performance, and political lyrics
as "cure" for post *Bhalagwe* trauma** 279
Mphathisi Ndlovu
Stellenbosch University, South Africa

Khanyile Joseph Mlotshwa
University of KwaZulu-Natal, South Africa

CONTRIBUTORS 305

INDEX 311

ACKNOWLEDGMENT

Evidently, being the editor of an academic publication is a merited honor. But, it is an accomplishment that must acknowledge and celebrate everyone who contributed in whatever measure towards its production.

So, I am immensely indebted to all chapter authors from various parts of our world, most of whom I did not know prior to the commencement of this project, and I still have not met in person even at this point. Nonetheless, they believed in this book project and did their best to contribute towards its success. I also appreciate and treasure the support of my family, friends, colleagues and mentors.

And, in a special way, I express my profound gratitude to God who continuously provides me with the inspiration and energy to succeed in multiple endeavors.

Uche Onyebadi, Ph.D.
Texas Christian University
Texas, USA

FOREWORD

Lyombe Eko
Texas Tech University, USA

Music and entertainment consist of culture-specific narrative re-presentations and reenactments of the human condition, and of lived experience. While music is said to be a universal language, it, like entertainment, is produced, disseminated, and consumed within the contextual parameters of specific historical periods, political, and cultural geographies. One of the oldest instances of the instrumentalization of music and performance in history is recorded in the Hebrew Torah (1 Samuel: 18). After David had killed Goliath the giant, the women of all the cities of Israel came out singing, playing tambourines, dancing, and celebrating David's military prowess, while denigrating the achievements of King Saul, a man of unstable temperament. This nationwide political performance drove King Saul into murderous jealousy that ultimately unraveled his reign.

A more recent political performance of the rituals of political messaging occurred in China in 1989. Protesting students in Tiananmen Square erected a 10-metre-tall (33 ft) statue of the Goddess of Democracy and Freedom, and demanded more freedom and democracy in China. The students proceeded to recite parodic chants and mocking rhymes of Paramount Leader, Deng Xiaoping, and Premier, Li Peng. Tiananmen Square became a stage where for close to three months, dissatisfied students performed rituals of dissent, and presented counter-narratives and discourses of political defiance that CNN and other media outlets broadcast live to television audiences around the world. This was political theatre and messaging at its best. Three months after the demonstrations and metaphorical worshipping of the Goddess of Democracy began, the Chinese People's Liberation Army, the armed wing of the Chinese Communist Party, crushed the student demonstrations with extreme violence leading to heavy loss of student life.

As these examples demonstrate, political messaging through music and entertainment has been part of human society from time immemorial. That is because music and entertainment are spaces where diverse mentalities, collective memories, cultural expressions, and identitarian assertions are set forth. This two-volume collection of case studies and analyses of instrumentalizations of music and entertainment for purposes of political messaging from Afghanistan to Zimbabwe, demonstrate that the phenomenon is cross-cultural, global, and of contemporary relevance. It is mostly prevalent in geographies or territorialities of repression, jurisdictions where explicit and overt criticism of the government, the president, political leaders, political parties, ethnic groups, religions, or prophets can lead to dire legal and extra-legal consequences. As such, musicians, comedians, artists, and entertainers have to tread carefully to avoid offending the powers that be, those who have the ability to use the coercive power of the state to persecute and victimize their critics. Public political communicators in these kinds of authoritarian contexts embed their messages in humor, metaphors, analogies, and other literary techniques. This is the process of communicational couching, the subtle embedment and dissimulation of political messages–counter-discourses, counter narratives, and counter-communication–within the lyrics of music and entertainment content for purposes of eliciting desired responses from audiences. The trick is not to arouse the ire of the powers that be. Music and entertainment in which subtle or overt political satire and messages are embedded and couched do double duty as instruments of resistance and subversion.

The chapters in this two-volume book take the reader on an insightful scholarly safari of heuristic analyses of the instrumentalization of music and entertainment for purposes of political messaging in multiple politico-cultural geographies around the globe. The case studies span a broad spectrum of realities and politico-cultural contexts. They range from the appropriation of highbrow Western classical music in the United States, where it was presented anew as a weapon of activism in the struggle for civil rights, to the emergence of morbid "Pashto Terror Songs" in the killing fields at the Pashtun Belt which lies at the intersection of Pakistan and Afghanistan, the world's contemporary crucible of incessant war, gender inequality, and massive human rights violations. Analyses of the instrumentalization of classical music as an act of resistance in the cauldron of racism and racial discrimination in the United States, stand in stark contrast with the morbid songs of terror that have emerged from the "merchants of death" at the Pakistan-Afghanistan border. These two case studies serve as "book ends" that bracket diverse case studies of the deployment of music in the service of critical political communication in multiple political and cultural geographies around the world. The chapters within these "book ends" provide points of access to diverse narratives and case studies of the deployment of popular music and entertainment as instruments of resistance and subversion in a variety of politico-cultural contexts. The chapters are an eclectic and insightful collection of analyses that span multiple political and cultural geographies of communication around the globe. Written by a diverse group of scholars from all continents, they amount to re-presentations, novel presentations of instances of the instrumentalization of music and entertainment as the thin edge of the wedge of resistance, defiance, subversion, and identitarian affirmation. Taken together, the chapters present anew, good, bad, and unorthodox political and social uses to which music and entertainment are put, given their diversity and almost inexhaustible carrying capacity.

In oppressive politico-cultural contexts, music and entertainment are often the only avenues for the expression of dissent, the only instrument for the communication of counter-discourses and messages of resistance. As the chapters demonstrate, music and entertainment give voice to the marginalized "Other" from the Caucasus to the Caribbean. They not only describe and explain reality, they are satirical weapons that judge lived experience in specific politico-cultural contexts. This is because in critical and satirical political communication, to sing is to sting, to portray is to betray, to perform is to deform, to narrate is to berate, to describe is to ascribe, and to act is to attack. The case studies of political messaging in entertainment contained in these volumes do it all. They range from the performance of resistance in the Philippines– deployment of music and theatre as context-specific forms of dissent– to the transformation of entertainment spaces into places for projecting socio-political messaging and bringing into existence alternative, affirmative visions of society in the United States. The collection also includes analyses of Rastafarian military symbolism in performances of Reggae, the music of resistance par excellence, as well as the content of *cinéma engagé* or engaged political films in India. The unifying theme of the case studies in both volumes is the problem of autocracy; political and cultural repression, militarism, corruption, and societal injustice.

These diverse chapters offer new insights and avenues that make political communication varied, relevant, global, and open to new approaches. As such, they are bound to stimulate more global, interdisciplinary engagements and research endeavors in political communication and freedom of expression. This compendium enables us to view politics through the prism of music and entertainment. Their premise is that politics and political messaging are too important to be left to professional politicians, political scientists, and journalists. Music and entertainment in which subtle or overt political satire and messages are embedded or couched are as relevant objects of analysis as other forms of political communication.

Lyombe Eko (Ph.D.) is a Professor of Media Law, Comparative & International Communication in the Department of Journalism and Creative Media, College of Media and Communication, Texas Tech University, Lubbock, TX – USA. He is the author of *The Charlie Hebdo Affair & Comparative Journalistic Cultures* (https://link.springer.com/book/10.1007%2F978-3-030-18079-9#authorsand affiliationsbook).

PREFACE

Uche Onyebadi

Texas Christian University, USA

Contemporary political communication research is still overly concerned with investigating institutions and structures, processes, political participation and civic engagement, voter education, political cognitions and behaviors, etc. No doubt, these are legitimate, epistemological research subjects. However, these important areas of inquiry only emphasize the transmission, reception, and effects dimensions of the *political* content of this eclectic discipline, almost precluding its instrumental, functional, and *communicational* components. Decades earlier, Denton and Woodward (1998, p. 10) had also noted that "the crucial factor that makes communication 'political' is not the source of the message, but its content and purpose." Therefore, the need for an expansion of the intellectual and research frontiers of political communication cannot be clearer or more compelling.

While advocating the expansion of the present and restricted boundaries of political communication inquiry, Professor Wayne Wanta, a political communication scholar of international recognition and former president of the Association for Education in Journalism and Mass Communication (AEJMC), noted that what is *communicated* through music, for instance, possibly has longer-lasting and stronger influence on audiences, than a typical evening news bulletin. This is because, "The average person would never recite verbatim a news text from an evening newscast" (Wanta, 2019, p. xii), while the same person will not only commit the lyrics of a politically charged piece of music to memory, but will easily recall the words and probably act on them.

Quite notably, political communication research is gradually witnessing an evolution from what was solely the *political* to the inclusion of the *content and instrumentalization* of the *communication* through a variety of platforms. This movement has been greatly enabled by the advent of the Internet and all forms of social media which empower people to share political ideas across the spectrum. Contemporary political audiences are no longer passive recipients of political messages from contestants for political office, the legacy news media, political advertisements, and institutional or individual stakeholders in society. Members of this audience now horizontally discuss and share ideas about politics and its concomitant issues, and can use their platforms and self-selected membership of often exclusive political organizations, to motivate and campaign for concerted action on any political issue of interest to them.

This book, *Political messaging in Music and Entertainment Spaces Across the Globe*, is conceptualized as supporting this unique push toward the extension of the horizon of political communication research, by focusing and emphasizing political messaging (content) through music and entertainment spaces (platforms), and from a global perspective. It offers researchers and students of political communication a compendium of well-researched, valuable, and rich insights into how political messaging is constructed, instrumentalized, and disseminated through forms that are outside the orbit of mainstream research in the discipline.

The globalist perspective that underlies this book is a recognition of the fact that the forms of entertainment and music used for political messaging are not limited to constructs and experiences in the United States and other developed nations in the Western world. For instance, Bassem Raafat Mohamed Youssef, an Egyptian surgeon-turned comedian, conceptualized and hosted a satirical news program titled *El-Bernameg* (2011-2014), to expose the ills of successive governments in Egypt. Not only was the program successful and widely acclaimed in the country, he was nicknamed the *Jon Stewart* of Egypt. Stewart is a notable American satirist and former host of the popular *Daily Show* program on US Comedy Central television. However, when the Egyptian authoritarian leadership deemed him as too critical of government's highhandedness and corruption, Youssef had to escape into exile in the United States, as it became clear to him that his life was in danger.

In their article, *Producing Journalistic News Satire: How Nordic Satirists Negotiate a Hybrid Genre*, Koivukoski and Ödmark (2020) noted how Finnish and Swedish news satirists use their platforms to encode strong political messages to their audiences. Baym (2005), discussed how Jon Stewart's "fake news" *Daily Show* impacted audiences through discussing political issues in a satirical manner. Needless to point out that Volodymyr Oleksandrovych Zelensky, the man whose comedy show titled *Servant of the People* where he played the role of a fake Ukrainian president, ended up being sworn in as the 6th Ukrainian president in May, 2019. Finally, the global impact of the late Bob Marley's political lyrics as well as the politically charged music of the late Nigerian musician, Fela Aníkúlápó Kuti, also attest to the powerful political messaging that is disseminated through music.

Having edited two books that address political messaging through the instrumentality of music[1], and being cognizant of the severely limited books in this genre that include Love (2006), Street (2012) and Garratt (2019), it became obvious to me that music alone cannot sufficiently provide the

---

[1] Music as a Platform for Political Communication (2017) and Music and Messaging in the African Political Arena (2019).

pedestal upon which the latitude of research on the *communication* aspect of political communication can be firmly established. As Michael D. Carpini (2000) noted, the entertainment space offers some people the opportunity to learn and form opinions about political affairs. The concept of *Music and Entertainment*, which encompasses comedy, drama, literature and other forms of art and popular culture, is therefore a more virile and broader platform for political messaging as advocated in this book.

As the title suggests, chapter contributors to *Political Messaging in Music and Entertainment Spaces Across the Globe* come from various countries and continents. The focus is equally transnational. Interest generated upon publishing the call for chapter contributions was remarkable, such that the editor and publisher decided to publish the title in two volumes.

Below are insights into each chapter:

Chapter Summary [Volume 1]

Chapter 1: *Z/Sarsuwelas*: Music, theater, and the mediation of political dissent in the Philippines

Rodelio C. Manacsa
Zeny Sarabia-Panol

Political messaging via the theater and music, the authors contend, is an indirect, mediated process. They examine how Filipino activist artists appropriated the Spanish colonialist tradition of artistic Zarzuela and created an indigenous version, the Z/Sarsuwelas, as an instrument to fight injustices in society and resist the excesses of the political class and overlords in the Philippines.

Chapter 2: Bringing Spirituals onto the Classical Music stage in the service of African American Civil Rights

Julia Schmidt-Pirro

In the 1800s and early 1900s America, classical music was considered the exclusive enclave of Caucasian musicians and composers. However, three African Americans - Marian Anderson (1897–1993), Paul Robeson (1898–1976) and William Grant Still (1895-1978) – shattered this mystique by essentially turning their folk songs – the Spirituals - into classical music and concerts that attracted acclaim and recognition across the entire spectrum of classical music in the country. In this chapter, the author examines how the works of these African American classical music icons provided the templates used for the civil rights activism of later years.

Chapter 3: "I Am More Than My Body!": Politicizing the Female Masquerade performance in the West Indian Carnival

Cherry-Ann M. Smart

West Indian carnivals are usually associated with musical performances, dancing and merriment. What is often ignored, or sidelined, is the politicization that lies underneath the glitz and razzmatazz the carnivals often showcase. In this chapter, the author sheds light on the Trinidad and Tobago carnival, highlighting the politicization, abuse of power and inequalities against the Female Masquerade participants in the extravaganza, and the political messaging embedded in such disrespect and disregard.

Chapter 4: Military Rhetoric: Making sense of political messaging in Reggae music

Kameika S. Murphy

Underlying Reggae music is something the author identifies as "military symbolism" in performances. When these symbolisms are understood within the context of the Rastafarian philosophy that guides Reggae music, and the model of resistance that historically emerged out of the 1831 Baptist War of emancipation in Jamaica, it becomes clear that Reggae is a space for political messaging, not just a forum for musical entertainment. This is the author's contention as expressed in this chapter.

Chapter 5: Revisiting the role of Popular Culture in supporting the anti-Apartheid Movement (1970s-1980s)

Archie W. Simpson

South Africa's system of apartheid was officially introduced in the country after the May 1948 election victory of the Afrikaner Nationalist Party led by Daniel François Malan. That system of official racial segregation turned out to be a festering sore on the conscience of the international community. This chapter examines how all forms of popular culture were used by nation-states, individuals and organizations across the world to fight the obnoxious apartheid system, leading to the 1994 general elections that heralded the end of apartheid policy. And, with the victory of the African National Congress in the election, Nelson Mandela became the first black president of South Africa.

Chapter 6: Political music in Brazil: An examination of Punk Rock in Brasília, 1979-1985

Silvio César Tamaso D'Onofrio
Henrique César Tamaso D'Onofrio
Marta Fernanda Tamaso D'Onofrio

Brazil was governed by authoritarian regimes in the 1970s and 1980s. Censorship was perhaps at its peak in the country in this period. In this chapter, the authors took a historical view of how Punk Rock bands in the country used the platform of the music genre known as Rock of Brasília, to continue performing their art and spreading their political ideology and messaging, in spite of the restrictions imposed by their government.

Chapter 7: Political Messaging in Indian Cinema: Core or Periphery?

Usha Rani

This chapter traces the evolution of the political content of the film industry in India, "based on the premise that film producers in states in the country where communist political parties are in power, tend to produce politically engaging films." The author uses two states – West Bengal and Kerala – to test this hypothesis. These are states where communist-leaning political parties have been dominant in power. The author concludes that while political communication was at the heart of films produced in these states decades earlier, that is no longer the case in the content of films produced in the states in modern times. Political messaging is now at the periphery of the contents of those films.

Chapter 8: Musicians and Political songs in the struggle for freedom in Zimbabwe

Bhekinkosi J. Ncube

When Zimbabwe became independent in 1980, expectations within and outside the country were that the political agitations that resulted in independence and freedom would recede into history. The story, however, turned out to be different. The author of this chapter takes a look at the use of protest music and political agitation in post-colonial Zimbabwe to challenge the shortcomings and excesses of the country's president, Robert Mugabe (now deceased). Here, the musician in focus is Desire Moyo who goes by the stage name, Moyoxide.

Chapter 9: Stylistic vernacular jingles in political messaging: An analysis of Igbo language jingles in Nigeria's General Elections (2019)

Cecilia A. Eme
Benjamin I. Mmadike

Using vernacular radio jingles in political messaging appears to be a most effective instrument to ensure that the messages are clearly understood by their intended audiences because of the presence of shared meaning between the encoders and decoders of the messages in a local setting. It is against this backdrop that the authors investigated the stylistic components of vernacular radio jingles in Nigeria's 2019 general elections, restricting themselves to the examination of how three main political parties in the country used such jingles for political campaign messaging in a designated state in the eastern region of Nigeria.

Chapter 10: Performative sites of resistance: A challenge to oppression through artistic entertainment

Rachael Cofield
Douglas L. Allen

According to its authors, the objective in this chapter is to "challenge societal oppressions by transforming entertainment spaces into places for projecting socio-political messaging and bringing into existence alternative, affirmative visions of society and place." The authors brought this to fruition by specifically evaluating the political messaging in the performances of two marginalized communities: the queer burlesque dancers of Metropolitan Studios in downtown Atlanta (USA) and Black members of the Florida A&M University band. They conclude that, "Such performances seek to project more affirmative counter-narratives into society and display more inclusive, justice-oriented articulations of space and performance."

Chapter 11: Chile's Nueva Canción and the Pinochet Regime: Censoring political messages in music

Kelly Grenier

Chile's former dictator, Augusto Pinochet, wielded absolute power in many respects. One area where he most noticeably cracked down on dissenting voices and imposed strict censorship was on what is generally referred to as political music and its musicians. Perhaps acknowledging the power of music, the former dictator paid particular attention the country's Nueva Canción movement. In this chapter, the author examines Pinochet's censorship by focusing attention on the Nueva Canción and arguably its foremost artist, Violeta Parra, and how the government hounded musicians who opposed Pinochet into exile.

Chapter 12: Zimbabwe: Zimbabwe: Music, performance, and political lyrics as "cure" for post *Bhalagwe* trauma

Mphathisi Ndlovu
Khanyile J. Mlotshwa

State-sponsored terrorism against an indigenous group of people is not a new historical phenomenon. But, what happened in Zimbabwe between 1983 and 1987, was as phenomenal as it was unprecedented. An estimated number of 20,000 Zimbabweans of Matabeleland origin were killed in this pogrom known as the Gukurahundi massacre. The authors revisited this gruesome event through the songs of Zimbabwean musician, Bongani Mncube, who used his platform to memorialize the killings that subsequent Zimbabwean governments have failed to officially acknowledge.

Chapter Summary [Volume 2]

Chapter 1: Stirring up "Good Trouble": Black songs of protest and activism in 21st century US

Dorothy M. Bland
Marquita S. Smith

The Black Lives Matter (BLM) and the other social justice movements that originated from the US and spread all over the world, stimulated the creativity of Black musicians in the US in using their platforms to join the protest for racial equality. However, such politically charged music and songs of protest pre-date the BLM and protest against the 2020 killing of George Floyd by a Minneapolis police officer. The authors of this chapter look back at protest music in 21st century United States, and also paid particular attention to three prominent entertainment awards/shows of the modern era - the Black Entertainment Television, the 35th annual Stellar Awards, and the 15th installment of the BET Hip Hop Awards – to highlight the contributions of Black artists in stirring up "good trouble" in the fight against racial oppression and injustices in the country.

Chapter 2: Speaking for the "Other": Reinforcing the Jezebel stereotype in Alexander McCall Smith's No. 1 Ladies' Detective Agency

Ann White-Taylor

Who speaks for the oppressed? And, are those speakers truly authentic in their self-styled, self-imposed mission to speak for others without belonging to the group they claim to represent? This chapter shines light on Alexander McCall Smith's, No. 1 Ladies' Detective Agency book series to challenge the political stereotypes about African women who are usually characterized as morally bankrupt and "bad girls" in society. The author provides a counter narrative in the works of several writers of African origin that challenge the negative stereotype of African women by people who pretend to be qualified to "speak for" the maligned ladies, but indeed denigrate them.

Chapter 3: Human Rights and redemptive-corrective justice in Bob Marley's music

Kevin Barker

A lot of literature exists on the music of the late global Reggae music icon, Robert "Nesta" Marley. However, not much has been written about his philosophy of redemptive justice against the backdrop of his Rastafarian beliefs. This chapter addresses this important but understudied area, and highlights the iconic artist's conception of justice. According to the author of this chapter, Marley clearly articulates and communicates his conceptualization of human rights and redemptive-corrective justice in his Reggae music.

Chapter 4: Framing contesting Nationalisms, Resistance, and Triumph in Ethiopian popular music

Dagim A. Mekonnen
Zenebe Beyene

No matter the particular regime in which they find themselves, either in a military dictatorship or a democratically elected government that acts more like a military junta, Ethiopian musicians have never ceased to produce songs with political themes and lyrics that celebrate nationalism and challenge the establishment. More recently, however, such themes have veered into ethno-nationalism sentiments. This chapter therefore focuses on, and analyzes, the songs with such centrifugal ethno-nationalistic themes and political messaging that threaten to further fragment the manifestly unstable Ethiopian polity.

Chapter 5: Interpreting Feminism through sounds of resilience in the U.S.: An analytical approach to music from the 19th to the 21st centuries

Ngozi Akinro
Jenny J. Dean

The authors of this chapter describe their work as an analysis of the political and feminist messages that "challenge hegemonic narratives" with the intention to "spread positivity about feminism." They uniquely explore the music of twelve outstanding U.S. female musicians from the 19*th* to the 21*st* centuries, and conclude that although the selected songs express different messages based on the period in which they were composed and released, they all have the same focus: acknowledging and communicating messages that advance "the role and place of the female gender," and promoting the rights of women in spite of the dominant patriarchal society in which they live and work.

Chapter 6: Broadcasting populism: An examination of Venezuelan Community TV and participatory democracy

Elena M. De Costa

What is the role of the mass media in Latin America? Specifically, what are the expectations of public broadcasting in this region? In answer to these and related questions, the author investigates the concept of community media in a socialist environment in Venezuela under the late President Hugo Chávez. The former Venezuelan leader promoted state-sponsored media in order to counter the monopoly of private media stations in the country, in what was described as giving a voice to people at the grassroots of Venezuelan society, as a form of mass participatory democracy. The setbacks in this approach to media democratization are addressed by the author.

Chapter 7: Music and violence: The complexity and complicity of Pashto "Songs of Terror"

Muhammad Farooq
Syed I. Ashraf

How might cultural songs romanticize militarization, violence and death? The authors untangle this apparent contradiction in their analysis of the Pashto songs among people who live in a cultural setting at the Pashtun Belt region that straddles Pakistan and Afghanistan. They argue that the incessant merchants of death and destruction – Drone strikes invented by modern war technology and the suicide bombings used by the underdogs to fight their vastly armed enemies – have invariably led to the emergence of local songs that have produced a bizarre genre that is called "songs of terror" in a region that has witnessed untold "musicalization of death" and unceasing, systemic violence. Thus, songs as cultural artefacts, have transformed into avenues for political messaging and "celebration" of death in what the authors call a troubled space where organized violence has become the societal norm.

Chapter 8: Political messaging in the Anatolian-Pop: How has this music genre transformed Turkey's socio-political landscape?

Yavuz Yildirim
Mehmet A. Güler

In Turkey, the Anatolian Pop music popped up in the 1960s with political and social messages that transformed the music scene in the country. In this chapter, the authors trace the history of this music genre, examine the top musicians and songs that made waves in Anatolian Pop, provide insights into how the new music brand tells stories about inequalities in the system, and challenge the Western hegemonic concepts and capitalist ideals that had crept into the country and impacted the pristine way of life of the people, all in a situation of censorship of thought and arts in Turkey.

Chapter 9: Praise songs amidst political chaos: Assessing the impact of "Hope Your Justice Will Arrive" on Hong Kong's 2019 Social Movement

Wendy Chan. W. Lam

The 2019 social movement protest in Hong Kong over the controversial extradition bill to China was unique in many ways. One of the ways the protests attracted global attention was when a Christian praise song turned out to be a hit tune and went viral on the Internet, and motivated young audiences to share the song online. The author of this chapter examined the YouTube song, "Hope Your Justice Will Arrive," with specific focus on a textual analysis of the comments left on the Internet by Hong Kong audiences in response to this song.

Chapter 10: From political stump to messaging through music: A study of Madzore's political songs in Zimbabwe

Faith Bahela

It is not often that politicians quit their soapbox and take to music to disseminate their political messages to larger audiences. In Zimbabwe, this was done by Paul Madzore, a former opposition politician who used his voice and music to join the teeming population of citizens the government described as "subversive" elements in the country. Using Foucault's theory of discourse, the author of this chapter explored Madzore's songs, and how they became "a site where political identities are renegotiated and reconstructed as the opposition party is valorized whilst delegitimizing ZANU-PF," the country's ruling party since independence in 1980.

Chapter 11: Political songs, advertising, and development messaging: An assessment of music in promoting socio-economic growth in Tiv society (Nigeria)

Terna P. Agba

This chapter makes the linkage between music and songs, political messaging and socio-economic development in society. Using a purposive sample of songs by four prominent Tiv musicians, the author employed the development communication theory to assess the political content of the musicians, and how the themes in their popular songs were aimed at facilitating the human and socio-economic and political development of their native Tiv land.

References

Baym, G. (2005). The Daily Show: Discursive Integration and the Reinvention of Political Journalism. *Political Communication, 22(3),* 259-276. DOI: 10.1080/10584600591006492

Carpini, M.D.. (2000). In search of the informed citizen: What Americans know about politics and why it matters, *The Communication Review, 4*(1), 129-164. DOI: 10.1080/10714420009359466

Denton, R.E. & Woodward, G.C. (1998). *Political Communication in America.* Praeger.

Garratt, J. (2019). *Music and Politics: A critical introduction.* United Kingdom: Cambridge University Press.

Koivukoski, J. & Ödmark, S. (2020). Producing Journalistic News Satire: How Nordic Satirists Negotiate a Hybrid Genre. *Journalism Studies, 21*(6), 731-747. DOI: 10.1080/1461670X.2020.1720522

Love, N. S. (2006). *Musical Democracy.* Albany, NY: State University of New York Press.

Street, J. (2012). *Music and Politics.* Malden, MA – USA: Polity Press.

Wanta, W. (2019). Foreword. In U. Onyebadi, (2019) (Ed.). *Music and Messaging in the African Political Arena* (pp. xiii-xiv). Hershey PA, USA: IGI Global. DOI: 10.4018/978-1-5225-7295-4

CHAPTER 1

Z/*Sarsuwelas*: Music, theater, and the mediation of political dissent in the Philippines

Rodelio Cruz Manacsa

University of the South (Sewanee), Tennessee, USA

Zeny Sarabia-Panol

Middle Tennessee State University, USA

Abstract

Political messaging through an entertainment medium is usually not done directly; it is a mediated process. An original and innovative theoretical framework was developed for uncovering political messages in cultural texts and entertainment media. The twin focal points of the analysis are the indigenization and contemporizing of the sarsuwela from the Spanish *zarzuela* as a vehicle for political messaging; and the socio-political themes that emerged from the plots, dialogues, characters, and lyrics. The findings indicate that Filipino playwrights and producers generally succeeded in wielding the medium to expose the primary sources of the hardships and social problems of the citizenry. The *sarsuwela* was eventually established as an instrument to resist political overlords, foreign and native, and their local collaborators. It not only created communities of actors, writers, and patrons, it also formed coalitions of conscience as it assumed functions including social protest, sedition breeder, and critique of political structures and socio-economic fissures in the country over the years.

Keywords: *Sarsuwela, Zarzuela, Sarswela,* Philippine Nationalism, Filipino Theater, Philippine Seditious Plays

***

Introduction

> Philippine theater, through three eras of political struggle...
> has never hesitated to go to war.
> - Doreen Fernandez (2001, p. 19)

Filipinos revel in songs, dances, and dramas. Their penchant for these artistic activities has very deep roots. For the country's indigenous communities, songs were the containers of collective stories that they "repeat when they go on sea, sung to the time of their rowing, and in their merry-making, feasts, and funerals" (Colin, 1663, p. 69). And the intensity of their dancing did not escape notice: "they were passionate, but...with steps and measured changes that really enrapture and surprise" (Colin, 1663., pp. 67-68). These songs and dances were usually part of rituals to remember and re-enact significant community events (e.g., bountiful harvest, military victory). For renowned scholar Fernandez (2001), the ceremonies were the earliest forms of Philippine dramatized song-and-dance: "the various imitations of life done in ritual, dance or even play, was community-based drama at its purest" (p. 345).

It is no wonder then that when the Spaniards brought the *zarzuela*, a stylized form of theater-drama with singing, dancing, and dialogue, to the islands, it found resonance in the local communities (Anonuevo & Alcantara, 2008). It became more popular than other colonial entertainment forms probably because the oral nature of the *zarzuela*, with its dialogues and dances, resembles in part the community re-enactments that have been ingrained into the collective psyche of the inhabitants. In addition, the *zarzuela*'s subject matter was people's lives in society rather than those of kings, knights, and dames around whom the Spanish *comedia* revolved. "*Zarzuela* as a dramatic form was valued primarily because of its very nature: a ritual-like community affair" (Mallari, 2011, p. 163).

Filipino artists and composers sought to master the new form's conventions and write and produce *zarzuelas* in the local language, which came to be referred to as *sarsuwelas*.[1] They began to replace the stories of foreign life and themes with those that are more familiar and are readily experienced by their audience. Playwrights began to write about their audience's daily-life problems like the cruel landlord or the usurious and corrupt public official. The Filipinos found a form that was fit for the infusion of their struggles and stories. Their indigenization of the *zarzuela* was similar to the way the Filipinos engaged with

---

[1] *Sarsuwela* or *sarswela* are now generally used to identify musical drama-theater that have been written in Philippine languages (Fernandez, 1996, p. 70; Anonuevo & Alcantara, 2008, p. 221). Other names that have been used are *sarsuela, sarsuyla, dulang inawitan* or *dulang hinohihan* (Tiongson, 2010, p. 149).

Christianity, where their *anitos* (ancient spirits) filled up the "Caucasian-looking statues of Catholic *Santo* and *Santa* (saints)" (Mallari, 2011, p. 164).

The vernacular use of this conventional foreign form permitted cultural encodings to raise important social issues and communicate critiques of the political order. Innovative forms and techniques used made the message of the *sarsuwela* opaque to those in power and yet intelligible and liberating to the locals. Mimicry has, said the critical theorist Homi Bhabha (1994), "an insurgent counter-appeal" (p. 91). The following parts of the chapter will demonstrate how the foreign theater's indigenized version, the *sarsuwela*, was wielded by native writers to resist imperialism and political authoritarianism.

At this point, it is critical to point out that political messaging through an entertainment medium is usually not done directly; it is a *mediated* process. The message to the audience is delivered within the constraints of the artistic genre's form and conventions. Thus, this chapter develops a theoretical framework for uncovering political messages in cultural texts and entertainment media. Then, the authors examine how the *zarzuela* becomes indigenized and contemporized as the *sarsuwela* and how it evolved from being merely an entertainment tool to an instrument of social satire and documentary of Philippine political struggles. Finally, the chapter will interrogate how political dissent was engendered within and through the musical theater form. The twin focal points of the analysis are: (1) the transformation of the *zarzuela* to *sarsuwela* as vehicles for political messaging; and (2) the socio-political themes that emerged from the plots, dialogues, characters, and lyrics.

Interrogating Cultural Texts for Political Messages

The analysis of political messaging, how it is produced, distributed, and received, has gradually moved into the forefront of the political communication field. There are evident differences between *direct* and *mediated* political communication. For example, in political campaigns, the speakers explicitly seek to disseminate a message to influence the political environment (Denton, Trent & Freidenberg, 2019). The goal is to persuade the population, or a segment thereof, towards a particular candidate or policy position. The objective is to communicate a message that is clear and persuasive. However, political messaging is not done directly in entertainment media; it is a *mediated* process. The message to the audience is delivered within the constraints of the artistic genre's form and conventions, whether musical theater, rap music, or interpretative dance.

The foundational perspectives on the analysis of cultural texts were developed by the Frankfurt and Birmingham Schools (Rivera-Perez, 1996; Turner, 1990). The central fissure between the dueling theoretical approaches centered on their views on the autonomy and reception of cultural texts. The Frankfurt School tended to see cultural products as reproductions of the prevailing structures of the political economy. As entertainment mechanisms, cultural forms like theater, music, and television helped consolidate "authoritarianism, conformity, cooptation, and escapism" (Lockard, 1996, p. 151). The dominant ideology provides the framework through which artistic forms are to be understood. Thus, the meaning is primarily determined, "texts always and irresistibly tell us how to understand them" (Turner, 1990, p. 107).

The Birmingham School dissented against viewing the relationship between politics and cultural texts as reflection and determination. Hall (1980) argued that since the recipients would have to use their social contexts to "make sense" of a statement, the audience *necessarily* plays an active role in constructing meaning. He argued that messages' transmission and reception are independent processes. The actual meaning is produced by the recipient and may differ from the intent of the sender. Reception activates the meaning-making process and is "capable of producing various meanings according to the reader's socio-cultural experience" (O'Sullivan et al., 1984, pp. 317-318). The Birmingham theorists expressed belief in an *active* reader. They believe that the socialization process can be "resisted, evaded, or negotiated, in varying degrees, by differently situated readers" (Fiske, 1986, p. 255). In the colorful words of the influential linguist Umberto Eco, the text is "a picnic where the author brings the words, and the readers bring the sense" (1992, p. 24).

Political Messaging as Cultural Decoding:
A Theoretical Framework

The theoretical position being taken in this chapter subsumes both schools' critical insights into a systematic frame to identify and interpret political messages in music and other entertainment media. Unlike Eco (1992), this chapter does not contend that meaning-making is simply a semiotic banquet where the sender brings "the words" and the reader "the sense." It is problematic to view meaning as entirely dependent on reception. In the end, the object, and the message, have a maker. Aesthetic creations are assiduously attached to authors, whose languages and symbolisms are shaped by their historical and socio-economic situations (e.g., gender, class). For Bressler (1994), the fact that the cultural text is somewhat related to the author is undeniable. The creative process serves as the catalyst that "brings together the experiences of the author's personality...into an external object and a new creation" (p. 35).

This chapter accepts that texts can be produced with the intent of diffusing and manufacturing consent to the worldview held by the predominant socio-political forces who allowed such a musical performance to be *produced* and shown to the *public*. Thus, aesthetic creations are "particular ways of seeing the world; and as such, they have a relation to that dominant way of seeing the world which is the social mentality ideology of an age" (Eagleton, 1976, in Keesey, 1987, p. 41).

While this hegemonic positioning can exist at any time, this is particularly acute during periods of colonialism or political authoritarianism. Thus, this chapter asserts that the state remains the ever-present background force "hovering over" message transmission. Elements within the texts where the state seeks to provide "imaginary solutions to unresolvable but real social and political contradictions" are examined (Jameson, 1981, p. 62; Taylor, 1982, p. 69). The most pernicious forms attempt to convince the audience that the cultural presentation is nothing but catharsis through performance: something to enjoy, but illusory, "unable to realize their transformation" (Taylor, 1982, p. 69).

There are times when cultural texts can have direct and intentional political messages that are hegemonic. However, it is contended that the state cannot and will never fully control the process of meaning-making. Texts are "loaded with an excess of meaning leaking through the boundaries of any preferred readings" (Turner, 1990, p. 217). For example, experiencing utopia in theater can lead to the desire for its realization in the present because, in the end, "any symbolic act entertains an active relationship with the Real" (Taylor, 1982, p. 174). Thus, the Birmingham School position is adopted in this regard. The chapter considers the cultural text as a *contested* space for political messaging, a site of struggle where various actors, including the sender and the audience, negotiate meaning (Morley, 1992, p. 21).

This work advances political messaging studies by introducing the concept of *convention encoding*. This concept is especially relevant in contexts characterized by colonialism or political authoritarianism. In the context of musical theater, this alternative, intersubjective layers of meaning are "activated" between the author, text, and audience when recipients "decode" the encodings that are often transmitted through subtle innovations in the entertainment medium's form, language, or performance. For example, Fernandez (1996) stated that the Filipino plays befuddled their American colonizers. However, their political messages were received loud and clear by the audience:

> It took a lot of time before the American authorities noticed that what seemed to be the usual long, 'hopelessly involved and not more than half intelligible' native plays (Riggs, 1951, 204) were making definite statements about the regime which were completely intelligible to their audience (p. 101).

The reading proposed in this chapter involves processing a cultural text into an "interpretive rectangle" to identify and map the dynamics of the political messaging process in musical and entertainment media (See Figure 1.1).

Figure 1.1 Theoretical Framework for Decoding Political Messaging

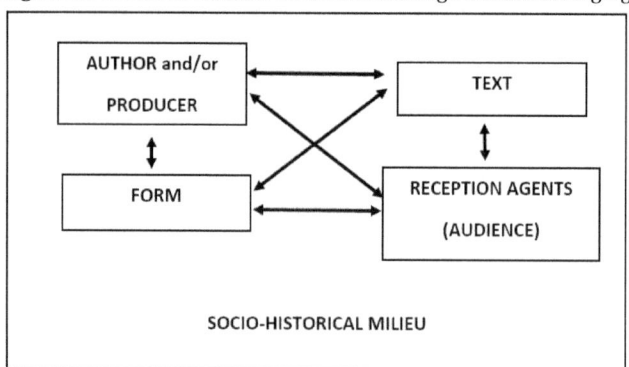

As shown in Figure 1.1, political messaging is essentially a *transactional process* between the Author and/or Producer, text, form, and reception audience, all happening within a specific historical milieu (temporal and societal). Conceptualizing the cultural text as an objective entity divorced from the author unnecessarily undercuts the production process. However, it is crucial to avoid the error of *intentional fallacy*: that the text's public meaning is nothing more than "the expression of the private experiences or intentions of its author" (Bressler, 1994, p. 35). The television program or musical play is a *public* text. Thus, it can possess an identity separate from its author, especially when presented at a different time, another audience, or with innovations in its form.

In this study, *form* refers to the conventions (e.g., manners of acting, ways of speaking, visual representations) through which the message and substantive content are structured and communicated. For example, a play or a television show is usually understood based on the viewer's knowledge and expectations of the genre (e.g., historical drama, comedy). "It is not the mimetic but the conventional elements in art that enable us to understand it" (Keesey, 1987, p. 258). Nonetheless, the meaning of the text can change through innovations in the form. For example, a particular musical presented today can use the text written by an author in 1965. Yet producers can add more layers of meaning through cultural interventions referred to in this chapter as form *innovations*. For example, the exact 1965 text can be presented today onto a stage made out of enormous LED screens that contain projections of images from 9/11/2001. Those *innovations* in the form of presentation will inevitably factor into the extremely fluid process of message-making.

Figure 1.1 also demonstrates that the audience plays an active rather than a passive role. The author *cannot* fully control how the text would be understood when presented in its time or when *re-produced* in the future. A text intentionally produced to serve hegemonic interests can have elements or fissures that can activate an alternative reading, resulting in other, even oppositional, readings. In the end, a cultural text, like a musical theater performance, is a "representation of reality…rather than a mechanical reflection of subjective experience" (Rivera-Perez, 1996, p. 42). Cultural products intended to disseminate the particular worldviews of colonialists, occupiers, or power elites can become localized, dispersed sites for interrupting or resisting domination (Foucault, 1980).

The succeeding sections of this chapter will show how using this theoretical framework can lead to a more comprehensive understanding of political messaging in cultural forms and entertainment media.

Data for this chapter were obtained from 88 *z/sarsuwelas* between 1880-2017 found in the extant popular and scholarly literature. Of the 88 plays, 25 are from the Spanish colonial regime, 44 from the American Occupation, and 19 from the post-colonial period. An exhaustive online search was conducted using keywords (e.g., Philippine *sarsuelas, sarsuwelas, sarswelas, zarsuelas*, Philippine musical theater, and Filipino plays) and a rigorous, comprehensive literature review.

Initially, the authors did a thematic content analysis of the plots, dialogues, and songs. This first-level evaluation was followed by a more detailed discourse analysis of selected illustrative works that were thought to be most informative/helpful in elucidating the theoretical concepts and significant themes that emerged. Primary and secondary source analyses were also employed for the study. Translations were utilized for *z/sarsuwelas* written during the Spanish period and for those made in regional dialects except for productions in Tagalog/Filipino and one other dialect that the authors have sufficient written and oral communication proficiency. For the American and post-colonial periods, primary source analysis was employed.

From *Zarzuela* to *Sarsuwela*: Inception, Institution, and Indigenization

As already noted, political messaging is a *transactional process* between the Author and/or Producer, text, form, and reception audience that transpires within a temporal and societal context. For Knupp (1981), music can be a vehicle for in-group messaging and group solidarity. It is an exceptional medium for expression rather than for instrumental, direct, political use. In addition, music can also be employed to serve as powerful critiques of government actions or policies advanced by dominant groups (Grundligh, 2004; Onyebadi,

2017). Tiatco (2011) discussed the role theater could play in cultural identity formation, especially Asian theater(s). Historically across nations, political messaging in entertainment media is a *mediated* process, and thus a useful starting point is a genealogical analysis of the form.

Inception

The genealogy of this artistic form indicates elitist roots: The Spanish *zarzuela* was engendered to entertain the aristocracy, according to the cultural studies scholar Isagani Cruz (1971), around the 13th century (p. 126). Many of these song-and-dance dramas were staged in Philip IV's (1621-1665) *Palacio de la Zarzuela*, so named because of the prevalence in his domain of a Spanish blackberry bush called *zarza*. The dramas were performed during "*fiestas de la zarzuela*," which were entertainment produced for royalty (Fernandez, 1996, p. 14). Thus, as time passed, the country house's theatrical performances began to be referred to as "*zarzuelas.*"

The status of the *zarzuela* as the pre-eminent dramatic form in Spain would be challenged by the arrival of the Italian opera in the 18th century, which led to a sea-change in taste among the Spanish elites. In 1703, Spanish theater critics described the *zarzuela* as *"un arte vulgar"* (a vulgar art) as the form supposedly lacked the elegance and the "high tone" of its Italian counterpart (Fernandez, 1996, p. 14). However, for the general public, the popularity of the *zarzuela* remained steadfast and intense. The reason may be that the form's plot, themes, and storylines were more familiar to the public. As the *zarzuela* lost favor with the Spanish upper-class, playwrights needed to adapt to their new adherents. The *zarzuela grande*, four to five-act plays with numerous solos, duets, septets, and full choruses, gave way to the short one-acts: the *genero chico*. Initially, these short *zarzuelas* were "inserts" presented in a longer *zarzuela*. Eventually, the *genero chico* supplanted the *zarzuela grande:* "It became the most popular theater form for the next thirty years in Spain" (Cruz, 1971, p. 128).

Institution

The *genero chico*, the "people's choice," peaked in Spain when the *zarzuela* was introduced to Philippine audiences by Diego de Cespedes in 1879. His performers staged *Jugar con Fuego* (Play with Fire), which was very popular in Spain during that time. More *zarzuelistas* from abroad followed them, and they began to perform in regional centers beyond the capital, including Iloilo, Cebu, and Bicol.

The cultural historian Nicanor Tiongson (2010) remarked that "the *zarzuela* form captivated Manila and the provincial capitals, and inspired the formation of local troupes which specialized in the staging of only Spanish *zarzuelas*" (p. 152). Among the notable *zarzuelas* that they staged were *La Marcha de Cadiz* (The March of Cadiz), *El Anillo de Hiero* (Ring of Iron), and *El Rey que Rabio* (The King who went into a Rage). The titles reveal that the themes and characters of the early *zarzuelas* imported to the Philippines involve people instead of saints, gods, and crusaders found in other colonial theater forms.

Indigenization

According to Wenceslao Retana, the *zarzuela* mentioned in historical documents written by a Filipino was by Jose Rizal, the Philippine national hero. His one-act drama, *Junto al Pasig* (By the Pasig River), was performed on December 8, 1880 (Retana, 1907). His *zarzuela* is a significant milestone in Philippine theater's history as a medium for political messaging. There is no doubt that later Filipino playwrights have come across the work and learned from its text, structure, and style. It is averred that three basic messaging features from this work presage how the Philippine *sarsuwela* would develop in the coming years.

Jose Rizal was born in 1861 in Calamba, Laguna. He was born outside the regional centers. However, since his family was middle to upper class, he would later be sent to the capital to study at the Ateneo Municipal de Manila, which was run by the Jesuits. In this university, in 1880, and at the age of 19, he wrote his *zarzuela*. It is important to note that anti-Spanish fervor was already stirring among the Filipinos when Rizal studied at the university. Rizal would stand at the forefront of this struggle to revise the view that the Filipinos had low-level culture before Spanish rule. His first major academic work was a diatribe against Spanish writers who had disparaged Filipino pre-colonial culture, like Antonio Morga's *Los Sucessos de Indios Filipinos*. According to Ocampo (1995):

> Rizal argued that the pre-Hispanic Filipinos had their own culture before 1521, thus they were not saved from barbarism and did not require "civilization" or a new religion from Spain. Rizal insists that the flourishing pre-Hispanic Philippine civilization, obliterated by Spain and the friars, could have developed on its own into something great...Rizal comments that the Philippines of his time was no better than the pre-Hispanic Philippines: *if Spain had not come, or had the left the Philippines to its own devices, everyone would be better off* (pp. 16-17. Emphasis added).

This particular viewpoint was imprinted on Rizal's *zarzuela*. It revolves around the story of a young boy, Leonido[2], and his struggle with Satan. While waiting for the Mother Mary statue in a procession, the main character was confronted by the devil and was told to submit and give up on his plan to give an offering to Our Lady of Antipolo. However, despite his young age and the presence of a powerful adversary, Leonido never gave in. Eventually, Our Lady of Antipolo's angel came into the scene to help Leonido and banish Satan.

This work is essential for several reasons. First, although the *zarzuela* was written in Spanish, Rizal broke from the foreign trope by introducing several *form innovations*. The setting of his play was his homeland, not Madrid or Barcelona, but a provincial town that would have been undoubtedly familiar to his audience. He then populated his story with Filipino characters. His characters were neither royalty nor nobility, which is what the Spanish *zarzuelas* were usually about. Instead, his characters were Filipinos, who, by his choice of names, are "brave" (*Leonido*), "innocent" (*Candido*), and "in need of liberation" (*Pascual*).

Second, Rizal courageously drew from Filipino cultural history. In the framework for this chapter, the authors referred to this as *convention encodings*. In the play, Jesus' mother was not Our Lady of Asturias or Aragon, but the Virgin of *Antipolo*, a famous Philippine icon (Antipolo is a province north of Manila). Satan appeared before Leonido not as a demon but as a "Diwata," a forest spirit in Philippine folklore. In the play, Satan used "Diwata" as a ruse. For a long time, the Spanish colonizers had demonized the local culture as "corrupt" and "low." But there is a false equivalency between the devil and the local spirit of Philippine culture and faith traditions in the play: The pre-colonial beliefs were not demonic. Rizal would develop this viewpoint more fully in his diatribe against the Spanish historian, Antonio Morga.

The third is the creative use of *indirect messaging*. Rizal presented the play at a Spanish university. In this particular setting, it was evident that he could not say things directly. The dramatic form is an excellent way to interrogate or critique the society at large by taking advantage of native symbols and allegories that the author can embed in the play for his audience to *decode* culturally. In the play, Rizal made "Diwata" speak the following lines:

> Los campos rebosaban
> De fragante verdura;
> Sin trabajo brotaban
> De la piadosa tierra,
> Entonces pura…

---

[2] The name could have been probably derived from King Leonidas, the lion-hearted king of ancient Sparta.

Y ahora, sin consuelo,
Triste gime en poder de gente extraña,
Y lentamenta muere
¡En las impías manos de la España!

The fields overflowed
Of fragrant vegetables;
Without work, they sprouted
From the pious land,
So pure...

And now, without consolation,
Sad moans in the power of strange people,
And slowly it dies
In the impious hands of Spain!

Here, "Diwata" is describing the Philippines before Spanish rule. Then, the land was overflowing with food; it bears produce without much human labor and is pure. However, "Impious hands" are now overrunning the land. It is crying for deliverance. In these particular lines, Rizal conveyed a starkly different view of what was happening in his homeland to his audience. The Philippines is *Pascual* (the name of one of the characters), which means "in need of liberation."

These three key features of Rizal's musical theater would figure very prominently in developing the indigenized *zarzuela* as a cultural form and as a vehicle for sending political messages to the public. In 1898, Spain would be fighting a revolution waged against them by the Filipinos and a war with the United States. As these armed conflicts raged, enterprising and bold Filipino playwrights would light the theater stage aflame by writing *zarzuela*s in their vernacular language.

The *sarsuwela* was born.

Sarsuwelas and Anti-Spanish Messaging

At its heart, the *sarsuwela* is a love story that unfolds amidst a myriad of powerful social forces (Tiongson, 1985, p. 13). A one-act piece will have at least four songs, while a three-act will have between 15-18 pieces. Written as an integral part of the script, the songs function "as dialogues, and as asides, comments or soliloquies" (Fernandez, 1993, p. 334). Filipinization of the foreign musical genre created indigenous varieties such as the *kundiman* (Filipino love song), *valse lento* (dance music), and *balitaw* (folk song).

Following Rizal's lead but now written in the local languages, a host of *sarsuwelas* appeared at the cusp of the American Occupation. Several still harbored anti-Spanish, anti-friar sentiments. *Malaya* (The Free One), written in 1898 by Tomas Remigio, is noteworthy because, like Rizal's *zarzuela*, it used *allegory* as a *form innovation*. Given his time's historical and social constraints, Remigio resorted to imaginative ways of communicating political opposition. Born in Sampaloc, Manila, on March 7, 1867, he lived through the repressive Spanish rule, intolerant of any form of dissent as promulgated in the Royal Order of 1856 establishing the Permanent Commission of Censors (Agoncillo, 1974).

Remigio's denunciation against Spain is cleverly wrapped under the guise of a love story with the following allegorical characters: *Malaya* (Free/Independent), daughter of *Katwiran* (Reason), is the object of *Magtanggol's* (Defender) affection and coveted by *Manlupig* (Oppressor/Conqueror). As an allegory, *Malaya* dramatizes the treachery and atrocities committed by Spain represented by *Manlupig* against the Philippines, personified here by *Magtanggol*. *Malaya* rebuffs *Manlupig* in favor of *Magtanggol*, refusing material inducements. *Manlupig's* attempted rape of *Malaya* in Act III is a metaphor of Spain that turned to more violent or brutal methods once bribery failed.

Censorship did not deter other insurgent playwrights from critiquing the Spanish colonial masters. Other *sarsuwelas* derogatory of the Spaniards abound. They include: Gabriel Francisco's *Ang Katipunan* (1889), which called for the end of Spanish rule, Catalino Palisoc's 1897 *Say Liman ng Nagketket Pampinsiwan* (The Hand that Cannot be Cut off Must be Kissed), and Salvador Ciocon's 1899 *Ang Nahigugma sa Iya Duta* (He Who Loves His Country).

The American Period: Colonizing with Incentives and Sanctions

The three centuries of Spanish control were soon followed by five decades of American occupation. While the Americans declared a policy of benevolent assimilation in the Philippines (which contrasted with Spain's use of the sword and the cross), they used incentives and sanctions to maintain their rule. The "carrots" came in the form of universal public education and other policies like the *Pensionado* program that sent Filipinos to the United States. The "sticks" were laws to quell rebellions and censor nationalist sentiments, such as the Sedition Act (1902) and the Flag Law (1907). Aside from defining treason and sedition and the penalties for infractions, the Sedition Act was remarkably insidious to writers because it outlawed speeches, publications, or any writing that would incite "rebellious conspiracies" or advocate for independence. Meanwhile, the Flag Law prohibited displaying the Philippine flag and other symbols of the *Katipunan* (the Assembly), the Filipino revolutionary organization.

The Filipinos courageously fought back with theater. Fernandez (1996) probably said it best: "Seditious, they must have seemed to the colonizer. Still, to the Filipino playwrights...they were quite simply the most effective way of sharing with their countrymen and audiences the insights that the Americans have not come as friends, but as colonial masters" (p. 95). Among these are Severino Reyes' *Walang Sugat* (1902), Juan Abad's *Tanikalang Guinto* (1903), Juan Matapang Cruz's *Hindi Aco Patay* (1903), and Aurelio Tolentino's *Kahapon, Nagayon, Bukas* (1903). The American critic Arthur Riggs commented that the Filipino audience would watch these plays, "on its feet, rabid with fury and frenzy, for *three* hours" (Riggs, 1904, p. 279. Emphasis added).

The *sarsuwelas* were lyrical narratives of love and domestic life, on the surface, but were scathing, encoded indictments of colonialism. Many used alterations to theatrical conventions and utilized sets or props as metaphors of social dissatisfaction and political defiance. Literature professor and writer Amelia Lapena-Bonifacio (1972) referred to these *sarsuwelas* as "chameleon plays." Tiatco and Bonifacio-Remolete (2010) commented that "American viewers would often not recognize that something 'subversive' was being communicated to the audience" (p. 324).

The *Sarsuwela* as Sedition Breeder

Aurelio Tolentino's *Kahapon, Ngayon at Bukas* (Yesterday, Today, and Tomorrow) is most appropriate for close reading with the theoretical framework espoused in this chapter for the following reasons. First, according to Villaraza (2017), "it is one of the most, if not the most, referenced theatrical exemplar of local resistance against imperialism in Philippine history" (p. 95). A riot ensued after the trampling of the American flag at the 1903 performance, which led to one of Tolentino's nine imprisonments by both the Spanish and American governments (Ocampo, 2019). It catapulted Tolentino to eminence and cemented his reputation as a "seditious playwright. Second, *Kahapon* is an appropriate interregnum for this book chapter as the plot straddles between the pre-Spanish period, the Spanish-American period, and the development of the independent Filipino nation. Finally, extensive documentation of its production during Tolentino's lifetime at the Teatro Libertad on May 14, 1903, allows the tracking of real-time meaning-making by an active audience.

Raised in a middle-class family, Tolentino was born in the Philippine province of Pampanga on October 15, 1869. In an unpublished 1908 autobiography, he described his life as "poor and unhappy" (Ocampo, 2019). Aurelio obtained his baccalaureate degree from Colegio de San Juan de Letran in Manila and, in 1891, studied law at the University of Santo Tomas. However, he did not complete his studies due to his father's death as he needed to help the family. His involvement with Jose Rizal's reform-minded society, *Liga Filipina*, the Propaganda Movement, and Andres Bonifacio's *Kataastaasan, Kagalang-galangan ng Katipuna*n (KKK) that riled up the Spanish *conquistadores*, informed his literary works (including *Kahapon*). He also took part in Emilio Aguinaldo's revolt against the American occupation. He penned ten theatrical plays in different languages, eight of which are *sarsuwelas* (*Filipinas at Espana, Sinagtala, Sinukuan, Kahapon, Ngayon at Bukas, Sumpaan, Bagong Kristo, Presidario,* and *Germinal*).

In *Kahapon*, the characters doubled up as personifications of Tolentino's ideas. The protagonist, *Tagailog*, (River Dweller), represented the Filipino, *Dilatnabulag* (Blind with Open Eyes) denoted Spain, and *Bagongsibol* (Newcomer, New Sprout), the United States; *Malaynatin* (Someone We Know or Who Knows), the Colonial Government, and *Inangbayan*, the Philippines. Consistent with his portrayal of Filipinos as friendly people, Tolentino scripted the following dialogue wherein *Inangbayan* rolled out the welcome mat for the Americans:

Inangbayan: Maligayang araw na ngayo'y sumilay,
Hayo't tanglawan mo ang aming tagumpay.

Happy sun that is born today,

light of our triumph.

Bagongsibol: Balang abutan ng aming lawin at lumiligtas sa pagkaalipin,
Balang sikatan ng bituin naming ay lumalaya't di nilalagim.
Alin mang bayan ang sumalilim sa aming bandila'y magluluningning.

Wherever our eagle rules, slavery is banished; wherever our stars shine, liberty and abundance reach. Any people that take refuge under our flag acquires splendor.

By reinforcing the eagle's image with words such as liberty, Tolentino, effectively asserted the eagle's unequivocal symbolism as the embodiment of the American ideals of freedom and independence, whether from political or economic tyranny. In other words, the eagle is America, so to harm this symbol is inflammatory. Attention is drawn to the part when in a dream, *Inangbayan* shoots the eagle. The act of shooting, albeit in a dream, is violent defiance.

Although not unique, Tolentino's use of native character names tended to be more graphic or descriptive of Filipino enemies. Cases in point are *Halimaw* (Monster), the Spanish friar; *Asalhayop* (Beast), the Filipino traitor; and *Dahumpalay* (Venomous Snake), signifying either a foreign oppressor or a traitor. He reserved the fiercest punishment like burning alive for domestic traitors, as shown in this scene. *Tagailog*, in justifying *Asalhayop*'s death by burning when his treachery was discovered, said:

When shall the race of traitors who envenom the people be exterminated from the earth? So *Tagalog* people, do you see how the body of

Asalhayop is consumed by fire? Whoever imitates him, I swear I would also burn him alive...

(Villaraza, 2017, p. 172)

The depth and intensity of *Tagailog*'s disdain of Filipino traitors who spied against their people reflect Tolentino's experiences as a *Katipunero*. Because of this, he saw local traitors as equally repugnant as the foreign colonizers and blasted the excuse that "it is better to be a rich slave than a poor free man." In Act II, scene 4, *Asalhayop* stated:

> Nalugso raw ang aming mga magulang. At ano?
> Kung ipaghiganti ko sila, mabubuhay ba sila muli?
> Babawiin daw ang Kalayaan ng Bayan. At bakit pa?
> Mabuti ang may salaping alipin kaysa mahirap na malaya.
>
> *They say that our forefathers failed, so what?*
> *If I avenge them, would they return to life?*
> *They say they will reconquer the liberty of the people.*
> *To what end?*
> *It is better to be a rich slave than a poor free man.*

Indeed, Philippine history is replete with accounts of Filipino betrayals that led to several failed revolts against Spain, the untimely revelation of the *Katipunan*, and the premature end of the Philippine Revolution. In addition, internal rivalries within the *Katipunan* led to the downfall of Andres Bonifacio, its founder, and Father of the Philippine Revolution.

Tolentino also encoded nationalist messages and symbolisms using materials on stage that most probably would have escaped the Americans' notice. Still, he was confident his audience would be able to decode them. For example, in *Kahapon*, Tolentino alluded to momentous events in Philippine history as they transpired in three important historic places: (1) *Pamitian* Cave: Where Andres Bonifacio declared independence from Spain; (2) *Bagumbayan* (Luneta): Where the three priest heroes (Gomez, Burgos, Zamora, known collectively as "GomBurZa") and Rizal were executed; and (3) *Kawit, Cavite*: Where Philippine Independence was proclaimed in 1898. These events enabled the "growth" of nationalism (symbolized in a searing scene as a plant). It is worth quoting in full:

Inangbayan: Bumagsak ang Pamitian, at ang aming halama'y nagkawalat-walat. Tinangay ng bagyo tanang mga dahon, Dagtang dugong tao ang isinisibol, Saka kinaladkad sa lahat ng ngayon, Sa lahat ng bayan, saan man lumingon, At sa Bagongbayan ay sumasaloysoy, Ang takbo ng dugo...Natapos ang lahat, walang nakapansin, Na bawat alabok ng halaman

	namin, Sa aming kalulua'y matinding tumiin, Nag-ugat na muli at muling nagsupling, At sa bayang Kawit muling tinanim, Tanyag at hindi na binakod ng dilim, Kaya't natanglawan noong maluningning na araw ng bayan at tatlong bituin.
Motherland:	*Pamitian fell, our plant was destroyed, the storm carried away all its leaves, the sap was human blood; dragged through all the barrios, and all the towns, wherever one could look. And in the Bagumbayan, the blood flowed profusely…No one noticed, though, that every particle in our plant fires our souls. It deepens within us and grows. In the town of Kawit, it was publicly planted anew. Hindered by darkness no more, it is furnished with brilliant light by the sun of the people and its three stars.*

In the verses that followed, Tolentino describes the colors of the Philippine flag, with subtlety, using the flowers, but making his meaning unmistakable as they were grown in Malolos, Bulacan, the capital of the First Philippine Republic, which American military power would overthrow later.

	Inangbayan: Saka namulaklak nang lubhang mainam, puti, pula't azul yaong nagging kulay, a bayang Malolos aming pinagyaman. Pinakataluktok, sinuob ng dangal… Oh! Bunso! Himala! Manang isang araw, humaging ang bagio't di naming malaman kung saan at ano ang pinagbuhatan. Nalanta ang bulaklak, saka nalamuray (Villaraza, 2017, p. 395).
Motherland:	*Later, the plant produced beautiful flowers; white, red, and blue were their colors. In the town of Malolos, we enriched the plant. We revered it high and honored. …O, beloved son! A miracle! One day the storm broke, and we could not explain the cause. The flower withered, and their petals fell.*

Disrupting Theatrical Conventions

Tolentino deliberately omitted certain episodic details and incendiary lines in the script, perhaps to elude the censors. He left literal gaps in the manuscript to allow improvisations, a technique many Filipino playwrights used to avoid imprisonment (Villaraza, 2017). In doing this, *Kahapon* provided the opportunity for the layering of meanings by allowing actors to decode the messages he tried to convey. For instance, various newspaper and scholarly accounts indicate that the tearing and trampling of the American flag in Act III by Felisa Roxas, who played *Inangbayan*, was not in the script, nor was the raising of the *Katipunan* flag (Hernandez, 1976). This scene elicited the wrath of the

Americans in the audience and the American authorities and led to Tolentino's and the entire stage crew's incarceration for sedition.

Dizon (1995) claims that like other *sarsuwelas* during the American period, Tolentino's *Kahapon* "came under fire less for actual words than for stagings ..." (p. 667). Both Hernandez (1976) and Villaraza (2017) wrote that the actress playing *Inangbayan* tore the American flag, raised the *Katipunan* flag, and ranted against the Americans. It was also recounted that one of the main actors trampled the American flag. Hernandez (1976) noted that the script specified only the American flag's display, so the shredding of Old Glory, hoisting the *Katipunan* flag, and the tirade against the Americans may have been actor improvisations. However, Riggs (1981) was critical that the actions were "spontaneous" decisions. He stated that:

> (the) costumes of the players were so designed that when at a preconcerted signal they gathered in the apparent confusion in the center of the stage, and as quickly drifted into separate groups, the insurgent or Filipino flag, for an instant was distinctly formed from their dresses, the stripes and triangle being clearly defined (p. 285).

Riggs implies that the staging had directorial control, was intentional, and was not left to the actors.

Overall, *Kahapon*'s original script and the 1903 onstage improvisations created a boiling cauldron that led to a riotous end. One newspaper revealed that Tolentino played *Tagailog* himself as the regular actor fearing retribution declined to perform the role. So Tolentino, who was once a journalist, became the story. He was sentenced to life imprisonment and fined a hefty US$7,000 (Hernandez, 1976). With all its crafty circumvention and clever use of prevailing theatrical conventions to amplify national issues or shrewdly but delicately interrogate colonial oppression, *Kahapon* could very well be the operationalization of Tolentino's concept of independence.

Gendered Constructions and Class Tensions

Both male and female stereotypes that exist in many nationalistic plays are in Tolentino's work. The country is typically played by a nurturing woman like *Kahapon's Inangbayan*. The other female character, *Masunurin* (Obedient), epitomizes the deferential Filipina who can be simultaneously firm but somewhat tentative at times.

Men's roles are predictable as patriots, leaders, and protectors of the Motherland embodied in *Tagailog*. On the other hand, the traitors (*Asalhayop, Dahumpalay*), colonial oppressors, and those committing violence are men. Indeed, priests up to this day are men just like *Kahapon*'s Spanish friar (*Halimaw*) but not hated and cast in such negative light as a monster. In the contemporary

Philippines, Catholic priests, despite the scandals associated with the church's clergy, are generally revered.

Certainly, Tolentino was not alone with the stereotypical depiction of women. Another Kapampangan, Juan Crisostomo Soto, featured a "docile" daughter in *Alang Dios*. Precioso Palma's *Paglipas ng Dilim* revolved around the romance of a demure Estrella and medical doctor, Ricardo. Given the preponderance, Tiongson (1986, p. 261) wrote that many *sarsuwelas* portrayed women in passive roles as "shy, virginal, soft-spoken and addicted to tears" (p. 261).

The pairing of gender and class politics was also evident in *sarsuwelas* during this period. Severino Reyes' *Ang Kalupi*, performed in 1902, portrays the Filipino middle-class family with a domestic maid in addition to its anti-American discourse. Lamenting on his time's social maladies, Pantaleon Lopez in his *Ang Infierno* (1903) implied that the labor class' economic inequities represented by the blacksmith Juan and the wealthy upper-crust represented by Don Ricardo cause marital infidelity, theft, murder, family disintegration, etc. Of course, the standard romantic plots of many *sarsuwelas* involved class tensions, as in Vicente Cristobal's *Nating* (1908), where there is a contest among three suitors: the lawyer Aniceto, the wealthy Enrique, and farmer Jose. In Servando de Los Reyes' *Ang Kiri* (1926), a young woman is sought after by suitors with political power and wealth but falls for the country boy (Fernandez, 1993). As evidenced by these examples, the politicized *sarsuwelas* did entail both cultural and social decoding. As a gendered entertainment platform, the *sarsuwela* was informed by the era's behavioral norms, including gender mores and class expectations that soon changed as the nation cleaved itself from foreign domination.

Post-Colonial Period: Defiance of Despotism and the Consolidation of National Identity

In the first twenty years after independence from American rule, the *sarsuwela* faced stiff challenges from other entertainment forms. With its splashy dances and springy tunes, the American vaudeville was pushing the *sarsuwela* literally off the stage (Fernandez, 1993, p. 336). A new emerging form, the movie film, also emerged as an existential threat to the Filipino *sarsuwela*. The new form was easy to produce and re-produce and paid well for those involved in the production. American and local movie studios (e.g., Sampaguita Pictures, Filippine Films, LVN Pictures) sprouted in the country's major cities. "From then on," said Tiongson (1985), "the actors, directors, and writers of the stage systematically migrated, so to speak, into the new medium of film" (p. 8). The comparative literature scholar Catherine Diamond (1996) concluded that "the *sarsuwela* has been defanged and made into standard melodrama" (p. 143).

The *Sarsuwela* under Military Dictatorship: Indirection and Insurgency

The intensification of the Cold War in the 1960s and the rise of a domestic dictatorial threat led to the re-emergence of the *sarsuwela* as the vehicle of anti-tyrannical and counter-hegemonic dissent. The sixties were a turbulent decade, with the political and ideological conflicts of two superpowers, the United States and the Soviet Union, essentially materializing in several battle zones, including Angola, Cuba, Dominican Republic, and Vietnam.

The Philippines was not spared from this unrelenting combat between communism and liberalism. When a Filipino politician named Ferdinand Marcos was elected in1965, he exclaimed that he was given a "mandate for greatness." However, his administration was made difficult by the rise of two armed challenges to the state's power. In 1968, Jose Maria Sison, together with some student activists, re-established the Communist Party of the Philippines (CPP). At almost the same juncture, an armed Muslim challenge to the government emerged in the southern Philippines (Chalk, 2002). Marcos began to see himself as the "savior" of the country: the person who will go down in history as the one who brought the country back from the brink of disaster. Marcos would interpose himself as the Philippines' savior against communism, backed by the United States (Abinales & Amoroso, 2005, pp. 205-230).

The *Sarsuwela* before the Season of Caesar: Revitalization as Resistance

As the threat of a domestic military dictatorship backed by a foreign power loomed, the *sarsuwela* re-emerged into the scene revitalized and contemporized. It was an effective instrument for protest and counter-despotic purposes because historically, it has been an anti-tyrannical tool. "Since its Filipinization, local playwrights have used this form as a performance of the *bayan* (nation)" (Tiatco & Bonifacio-Remolete, 2010, p. 319). Thus, the *sarsuwela* was the perfect tool to resist a *domestic tyrant* backed by a *foreign force*.

A few years before Martial Law, "seditious *sarsuwelas* during the American period were re-staged. These revivals employed Jose Rizal's indirection strategy much earlier, to attack Spanish imperial rule. Marcos was a foreign-backed despot; thus, musical theater criticizing American power also indicted former President Marcos. However, the producers of the revived *sarsuwelas* did something even more creative and daring: they innovated on the forms to make sure that their political message gets through clearly. Two of the most revived plays were Severino Reyes' *Walang Sugat* (Unwounded) and Aurelio Tolentino's *Kahapon, Ngayon, at Bukas* (Yesterday, Today, and Tomorrow). Both were period plays, set during the transition from Spanish imperial rule to that of the Americans. Tolentino's seditious work was discussed in the previous section, and it was clear why that was revived during Martial Law. The *sarsuwela*'s high point involved *Juan de la Cruz*, the symbolic representation of the Filipino in the collective unconscious, tearing of the American flag on stage and proclaiming *"Mabuhay ang Kalayaan! Mabuhay ang Inang Bayan!"* (Long Live Freedom! Long Live the Motherland!). In the context of dictatorial rule at that time, the message was clear: The fight for freedom from the domestic despot was *inseparable* from the battle for independence from his foreign supporters.

Meanwhile, local producers re-staged Reyes' *opus* in 1970 by keeping the exact text but introduced form innovations to send political messages to audiences. First performed in 1902, Reyes' *sarsuwela*, on the surface, was but a condemnation of oppressive Spanish rule in the Philippines. One of its most dramatic scenes involved the torture of Filipino rebels in colonial prisons, instigated by abusive Castilian friars. It was a very explicit elucidation of the steep price needed to be paid when resisting imperial power. However, the focal point of the *sarsuwela* was the love story between Julia and Tenyong, both Filipinos. When Tenyong's father, Captain Inggo, died due to prison torture, Tenyong decided to join the Filipino rebel group, the *Katipunan* (The Assembly). Julia was then coerced to marry Miguel, an American. The *sarsuwela* ended with Tenyong outwitting the Spaniards to marry Julia, who had rejected Miguel. When presented in 1902, the Americans branded Reyes' work as "seditious" and threw the playwright into prison. The musical theater play was banned from being shown on stage.

In the 1970s, innovative local playwrights unsheathed Reyes' *sarsuwela*, sharpened it, and later wielded it back on stage. First, they reconstructed the music liberally and introduced a new song, "*Bayan Ko*" (My Nation), a patriotic song that would, later on, become the national anthem of the anti-Marcos, anti-American protest movement in the Philippines. Second, the anti-Spanish lines in the play were subtly reworded to imply anti-Marcos sentiments. "The very fact of it having come from the repertory of the past inflamed student enthusiasm" (Fernandez, 1996, p. 90). Finally, the *sarsuwela* concluded with Julia rejecting Miguel, an American who represented the new colonial power. It is fascinating to note that the name "Julia" means youthful, implying that Julia was the young nation Philippines that was just coming out from the horrific imperial rule of the Spaniards and now being coerced into "marrying" a new colonial master, America. Thus, the ending implies another choice: the rejection of the new colonizer and the full embrace of an independent life as a nation. This option is also indicated in the selection of the name "Tenyong" of the lead character, which is a derivative of the Tagalog word *"tayong"* or *"tayo."* Both Tagalog words have the same two possible meanings (based on the intonation used): "We" or "Stand." The political message is that the Philippines would never "grow up" into a nation unless *"we stand up"* to reject the new foreign rulers and their local collaborationists.

New plays before military rule contemporized the *sarsuwela*. First, it dispensed with the lyrical and archaic language and adapted the language of the streets. Second, it introduced new forms of music, including rock and pop, to the musical repertoire. Finally, it updated its form by adapting elements from Bertolt Brecht's plays and the Theater of the Absurd. These attempts at contemporizing can be best discerned in Isagani Cruz's *Halimaw*, first presented in 1971. It was the *sarsuwela* that both critiqued and foreshadowed the coming season of Caesarism in the Philippines.

In 1971, when *Halimaw* was first staged, the Philippines was a powder keg of a nation ready for detonation. Daily protests on the streets criticized the government for the rapidly increasing inequality between the rich and the poor brought by purported corruption and cronyism. Inspired by Maoist ideology, student organizations denounced the evils of feudalism, capitalism, and imperialism. They also prepared for a "people's war" intended to eviscerate the existing political order, to be replaced by proletarian rule. Meanwhile, then-President Ferdinand Marcos convened the Constitutional Convention of 1971 to revise the nation's charter and make it possible for him to prolong his presidency legally.

Isagani Cruz, the playwright, graduated from the University of the Philippines, the focal point of the radical leftist student movement in the Philippines. He later completed a Master's in Literature from the Ateneo de Manila University, a private institution run by the Jesuits, a Catholic order renowned for its commitment to social justice. Thus, Cruz was able to approach the crisis of the 1970s with the eyes of a sharp critic and a perspective deeply informed by his knowledge of the societal solutions advanced by competing groups in the Philippines.

Cruz's *Halimaw* was a fantasy *sarsuwela* with pointed contemporary references. The setting was the Philippines in 1971. However, in the play, the Philippine Constitution had just been revised, and the country was now a monarchy. Cruz drove home the point that the people unto themselves can bring about despotism as a political system. The King was a stereotypical despot: he treats negative information as fake news, beheads critical reporters and opponents, and has multiple spouses. The play effectively foreshadows the Philippine Constitutional Convention's decision to provide Marcos with the legal cover to continue to rule. A dictatorship can indeed be a *self-inflicted* calamity.

The narrative begins with the King's three daughters' abduction, all named *Maria* (a name that traditionally represents the country). At the symbolic level, the Philippines must be saved. The three were abducted by three monsters (*halimaw*). The first is *Binibining Sirena* (Ms. Siren), who represents the sweet song of naïve idealism that dreams of transformation but never commits to action. The second is *Ginang Purista* (Ms. Purist), representing archaic Filipino customs and traditions. Finally, the last monster is *Ginoong Dragon*, a three-headed dragon that represents the foreign ideologies of Capitalism, Bolshevism, and Maoism. The play rejects all three as the answer to the nation's ills.

The protagonist's name is Alberto, supported in his quest to save the *tres Marias* by two people named *Juan*, the typical Filipino person's symbolic name. Alberto would use his innate wit and strength to defeat the three monsters. However, in a plot twist of truly epic proportions, the three Marias, convinced Alberto to become the "new King," an "enlightened monarch" with the proverbial five-year development plan:

> MARIA 1: Tama sila Alberto. Kung ikaw ay hari ay marami kang pera. Lahat ng gusto mong gawin umunlad ang bayan ay kaya mo. Walang makikialam sa mga five year program mo.
> MARIA 1: *They are right Alberto. If you are king, you will have a lot of money. You can do all that you want to do to make our nation prosperous. No one will interfere with your five-year programs.*

Alberto agreed to the proposition and took the three Marias as his wives. When criticized by the ordinary person, Juan, for his decisions, Alberto had him beheaded.

The political message of *Halimaw* pertains to the greatest temptation of all political leaders: the seizure of absolute political power in pursuit of one's vision of the "common" good. Democracy tends to die in the hands of dictators with good intentions. In the final song, the political message is that "everybody is a potential *halimaw*." Thus, the price of freedom and democracy is eternal vigilance:

> Tayong lahat ay halimaw
> Saksakan tayo ng takaw
> Kaya't kailangang magbago
> Huwag padala sa 'ting bisyo
>
> Mabuhay ang kabutihan.
> Nang umunlad ang ating bayan.
> Kaya'y kailangang magbago.
> Huwag tayong mga lilo.
>
> *We are all monsters*
> *We are full of greed*
> *We all need to change*
> *Do not indulge in vices*
>
> *Long live righteousness*
> *So progress can be ours*
> *We all need to change*
> *Let us not be fraudsters.*

Unfortunately, the Filipino was not vigilant enough. Marcos declared Martial Law on September 21, 1972, portraying it as an attempt to save the Philippines from the "rebellion and armed action undertaken by these lawless elements of the communist and other groups organized to overthrow the Republic of the Philippines" (Presidential Decree [P.D.] 1081, cited in Rosenberg 1979, p. 240). The cost of "salvation" was a conjugal dictatorship that brought the Philippines much political, economic, and institutional ruin. It is debatable whether the extent of the danger posed by both the CPP and the Moro National Liberation Front (MNLF) necessitated the extraordinary step of declaring Martial Law (Timberman, 1991, 66-68).

Indirect Interrogations of the Machinery of Military Despotism

Under military rule, the expression of opinions and commentaries was subjected to censorship. The government screened stage plays, and authors of "subversive" writings were arrested and imprisoned. During this dark period, the performance arts remained an effective protest and resistance instrument. Following the tradition that goes back to Jose Rizal, the *sarsuwela* can convey political messages to its audience using form innovations and cultural encodings. The cultural text's ability to interpose critique *indirectly* relies on the shared well of symbolism and archetypes between the playwright and the audience.

In the late 1970s, the revitalization of the *sarsuwelas* presented during the American occupation found some way to continue. As the nation went deeper into authoritarian rule, *Walang Sugat* and *Kahapon, Ngayon, Bukas* were performed in universities and small community platforms, closer to the people, which is just how the *sarsuwela*, the "national theater" that has engendered sedition and insurgency in the past, was meant to be staged.

The new *sarsuwelas* staged during the military rule addressed other pertinent social issues related to Americanization and capitalism. For example, Domingo Landicho's *Sumpang Mahal* (Sacred Vow, 1976) and Isagani Cruz's *Ms. Philippines* (1980) tackled the virulence of colonial mentality to the Filipino psyche; the harmful effects of an ideological lens that looks at anything foreign as "proper" and "good" and one's own as "improper" and *bakya* (low brow). Meanwhile, Amelia Lapena-Bonifacio's *Ang Bundok* (The Mountain, staged in 1977) and Nicanor Tiongson's *Pilipinas Circa 1907* (1982) focused on the increasing role played by Americanization and privatization in the country and their deleterious effects on companies owned by Filipinos, as well as lands owned by indigenous communities in the Philippines.

Amelia Lapena-Bonifacio was trained in the performing arts, with degrees from the University of the Philippines and the University of Wisconsin-

Madison in the U.S. before writing *Ang Bundok*. In 1994, she disclosed that the issue was brought to her attention by a university student where she was teaching. It forced the playwright to look deeper into the issue of ancestral lands both in her family history and in the broader context of Philippine development. In her masterwork, the main protagonist *Umangal* (Objector), was fighting to keep fields that belonged for so many years to his community from foreigners claiming government approval to mine the ancestral lands for 99 years. Violence broke out between the disputants until the multinational corporation sent bulldozers to the disputed lands to destroy the village homes. The community, women, children, warriors, and the old linked their arms to form a human chain to resist the oncoming machines. Their heads, unbowed (until the curtains close), they sang:

> Kung dumating ang panahong dapat kang ipaghanti
> Kapag dumating ang gabing patung-patong na pang-aapi
> Asahan mo, bayan ko, wala kaming pag-aatubili
> Alay-bisig, puso't buhay man sa una mong sabi...
> Tayo na sa ating bukas
> Na tayo ang namumuno
> Ito ang bayan natin!
> Ito ang bayan natin!

> *When the time comes for avenging you*
> *When the night of unrelenting oppression falls*
> *You can rely on us, our homeland, without hesitation*
> *Arms offered, heart, and life at your behest*
> *Onward to a Tomorrow*
> *Where we are in charge*
> *This is our Land!*
> *This is our Land!*

The *sarsuwela* interrogates a national policy that sides with foreigners against their own people. By employing the *sarsuwela* form, Lapena-Bonifacio once again calls on the Filipino national consciousness, one that has been forged through fiery opposition to foreigners, to once again resist the "invaders" and to imagine a future where "we are in charge" in our land, not the empire and their local collaborationists. In the battle between ancestral ownership and capitalist rapaciousness, the Filipino is asked to offer their arms, hearts, and possibly even life to the native cause.

In terms of form, *Ang Bundok* sharply breaks from the usual endings of the traditional *sarsuwela*. Fernandez (1996) commented that the conventional "ending" tended to promote the status quo:

> Most of the *sarsuwela*s have happy endings, perhaps because...Filipino folk writers have wanted plots resolved, knots untied (or tied, as in marriage), order restored, dreams fulfilled, and hope extended. Even more, than it mirrored their actual lives, the *sarsuwela* reflected their aspirations. Since happy endings are less than common in real life, this made for an incomplete realism, but a real one nonetheless, reflective of a period's mores and perceptions (p. 332).

The conclusion of Lapena-Bonifacio's opus did not involve the reconciliation of lovers or the villain's changes of heart. It was also not about the ignition of violent sedition or the protagonist's entry into a revolutionary army. In this one, the people chose to confront their oppressors through determination and collective non-violent resistance. It upends how the *sarsuwela* usually ends, and a new type of "ending" has been heralded. From Marcos onwards, this is precisely how the country would depose its oppressors and tyrants.

The Contemporary *Sarsuwela*:
"People Power" and the Re-shaping of "Happy Endings"

After the 1983 assassination of Marcos' chief political opponent, former Senator Benigno Aquino Jr., the Philippines' political situation instigated massive capital flight (Kline & Worthen, 2006, p. 147). Marcos also had to contend with increasing pressures from the United States and foreign investors, whom Celoza (1997) referred to as the dictatorship's "network of support" (p. 115). As a result, the dictator called for "snap" presidential elections in January 1986, a vote he had no intention to lose. However, Corazon "Cory" Aquino, the widow of the slain Senator, spearheaded a massive civil disobedience campaign against Marcos for cheating in the elections.

With the support of hundreds of thousands of Filipinos, crucial defections in the military, and the withdrawal of American consent and support, Marcos was forced to make a difficult decision between attacking the crowd or, in the words of U.S. Senator Paul Laxalt, "to cut and cut cleanly" (cited in Kline & Worthen 2006, 165). He decided to leave Malacanang palace and went into exile in Hawaii. Passionate, collective non-violent resistance or "People Power" had won. In the spirit of the *sarsuwela*, the Filipinos had sung, danced, and protested their way into history. Post-Martial Law, the *sarsuwela*, will be re-shaped to respond to the needs of contemporary times.

The focus in the years after the dictatorship was the centennial commemoration of the Philippine Revolution of 1896 and the Declaration of Philippine Independence in 1898. Amidst the various globalization challenges, the *sarsuwela* sought to anchor the nation to its long history of bravery amidst all odds and against all political overlords. Two winners of the Centennial Literary Prize for the *Sarsuwela* in 1998, *Paglayang Minahamahal* (Beloved Liberation) by Gregorio de Jesus III and Melba Padilla Maggay's "*Bayan, Isang Paa Na Lamang*" (Motherland, Just One More Foot), were attempts to link the 1896 Philippine Revolution for Independence to the People Power Revolution of 1986.

Maggay's production is a fascinating attempt to bridge the two Revolutions through the use of Filipino folklore. It was based on the legend of Bernardo Carpio, a giant who lives in a cave. The belief is that the giant would come back to life whenever the nation needed his help. One foot is still stuck in a stone bed, but he will answer the call to help a people's uprising for freedom. It has been averred that this folktale inspired the Filipino Revolutionaries against Spanish rule. The literary critic and National Artist F. Sionil Jose commented that "historians tell us that current folk movements that formed the backbone of the *Katipunan* were the expectation that Bernardo Carpio would rise again" (Anonas, 2002).

The Bernardo Carpio legend shared among the Revolutionaries in 1896 was communicated to the Filipino students in the 1986 People Power Revolution by Esperanza (a name that means "Hope"), who lived during the fights against Spain, and who was then protesting against Marcos' rule. The production creatively fuses the two historical events by acting out the scenes from the 1896 Philippine Revolution with projected images from the 1986 People Power Revolution. At the same time, its political message has echoed through the ages: the more insidious enemies of the nation are not the foreign powers, but their native collaborators. In the song "*Sino ang Kaaway?*" (Who is the Enemy), the protagonist Pilo intones:

> Anong klaseng peligro ang darakot sa iyo
> kung balat ng berdugo kakulay mo
> anong uod ang susuot sa kalamnan ninyo
> kung ipagkanulo ang kaluluwa niyo...
> ano ito-ano tayo-ano't ganito ang tao?
>
> *What kind of danger will befall you*
> *if the executioner's skin is the same shade as yours*
> *what worm will tunnel through your sinew*
> *and betray your soul?*
> *what is this-what are we-why are we like this?*

The need to remind the Filipino of the enemy not just from without, but more importantly, from within is probably the reason for the continued popularity of the "seditious plays" of the American period in contemporary times. For example, Reyes' *Walang Sugat* (1902) and Tolentino's *Kahapon, Ngayon, Bukas* (1903) are routinely presented in universities and established theaters. Meanwhile, *sarsuwelas* that expose the harmful effects of colonial mentality, like Precioso Palma's *Paglipas ng Dilim* (Once Darkness Has Passed, 1920), Delos Angeles' *Ang Kiri* (The Flirt, 1926), and Landicho's *Sumpang Mahal* (Sacred Vow, 1976) have also found support. Meanwhile, Bienvenido Lumbera's *Hibik at Himagsik Nina Victoria Laktaw* (Lamentation and Rebellion of Victoria Laktaw, 1998) explores gender justice issues by chronicling the plight of Filipina rebels during the 1899-1902 Philippine-American War.

In 2017, the traditional "happy ending" of the conventional *sarsuwela* would be thoroughly upended by Nicanor Tiongson's "rock *sarsuwela*" *Aurelio Sedisyoso* (Aurelio the Seditionist). The play narrates Aurelio Tolentino's life (of *Kahapon* fame), the premier playwright of the American occupation. It describes the challenges that he faced while writing and staging his anti-colonial plays. The production dispenses with the traditional ballads and employs rock and hip-hop music. It also contemporized the language, jettisoning most of the flowery and archaic wording. However, its most radical contribution to the development of the *sarsuwela* is its innovative use of "reverse staging." To present *Sedisyoso*, producer Toym Imao *inverted* the theater: the audience was made to sit on the stage (on bleachers and mono blocs) while the actors performed where the audience section used to be (Jorge, 2017).

The effect of the reversal on the audience was striking. First, the audience could see the performance from the perspective of the actors who perform on stage. Second, the "third wall" that separates the stage from actuality was effectively gutted. *Who is "acting," and who is being "watched"? Where is the "stage," and where is "real life"?* The message is clear: *What we watch, we can change.* We can fight for our nation, defeat villains, and topple tyrants on stage and in reality. Our life is a performance.

Before the 1970s, the conflicts in the *sarsuwelas* were resolved by a change of heart in the villain, a turn of luck, or an act of God. The post-colonial productions celebrated a history characterized by the people's power to act, as a national community, to depose a despot, whether domestic or foreign. The contemporary *sarsuwela* unfailingly offers its audience not only a diagnosis or hope but also how to act. The political message is that the "happy endings" standard in the *sarsuwela* may genuinely be less common in our real lives, but we often need not wait for fortune or God to make it happen.

The Media's Role: Publicizing the *Sarsuwelas*

Although the analysis of media reports is not strictly within the ambit of this study, it is critical to note that the scholarly literature did mention newspaper stories of the staging of some *sarsuwelas*. During the American colonialization, newspapers like *The Manila Cablenews, Manila Freedom,* and *The Manila*

Times covered culture, entertainment, and the theater. All but the *Times* are defunct. In describing the audience of Tolentino's *Kahapon, The Manila Cablenews*, in its August 2, 1903 edition, wrote, "The audience displayed its greatest pleasure during that part of the play which showed the Filipino people up in arms against the Government" (Hernandez, 1976, p. 131). Typically, the entertainment and lifestyle sections of newspapers are on the inside pages. *The Manila Times*, however, gave front-page coverage of the May 14, 1903 staging of *Kahapon*. Its headline read, "Filipina Tears 'Old Glory' into Shreds" (Villaraza, 2017, p. 211).

During the Marcos dictatorship, *Malaya* had an anti-Marcos, anti-establishment reputation. It reported extensively on the protests in the streets and on the concert and theater stage. By this time, entertainment sections had become regular staples of newspapers. Aside from *Malaya*, other English-language dailies such as the *Manila Bulletin, Philippine Daily Enquirer, The Manila Times*, among others, as well as broadcast media such as the ABS-CBN and GMA likewise devoted print space and broadcast time, respectively, to the simmering discontent of a nation reeling with economic hardships under a despotic regime. By providing media coverage of the *sarsuwelas*, the media created awareness and significantly amplified the messages, thereby achieving a multiplier effect that extended beyond the theater-going crowd, usually middle to the upper crust. The crossing of economic lines is remarkably accurate of radio, which is more widely accessible to the lower class (Fernandez, 1974, 1996).

Because of censorship laws that required the review of scripts, the government authorities regularly kept an eye on the entertainment scene. Thus, in addition to the media publicity, the government authorities, especially the censors, were aware of theatrical productions. Media stories reported the attendance of government representatives at the stagings of *Walang Sugat, Kahapon*, and other "seditious plays" of the American period and during Martial Law (Fernandez 1974; 1996). Currently, the Philippine media is independent and free and regularly reports on cultural events in the nation (See Anonas, 2002; Jorge, 2017; Tiongson, 2010).

Conclusion

In this chapter's analytical strategy, political messaging is a *transactional process* between the Author and/or Producer, text, form, and reception audience that transpires within a temporal and societal context. Political messaging through a cultural form is a mediated rather than a direct and instrumental communicative process. The theoretical framework developed in this chapter can provide powerful analytical leverage in understanding and interpreting other cultural forms, public texts, and entertainment media, both classical and modern (e.g., popular music, social media, podcasts). Using a multidisciplinary and postcolonial lens, this chapter probed the process of political messaging and meaning-making in a mediated entertainment medium as it evolved from its colonial ancestry to its indigenized form.

The authors contend that communicating through the "people's theater" has been effective for three reasons.

First, its forms and conventions speak to ordinary people. Its content always has been about the Filipino's everyday experiences and the challenges they face in their lives. "Staged drama in the Philippines, which had before then been mainly drawn from European metrical romances, had finally found the form in which it was possible to present native day-to-day life on stage" (Fernandez, 1993, p. 328). Because political messaging via the *sarsuwela* is mediated, therefore indirect and layered, it required cultural encoding and decoding for the messages to penetrate and resonate. The genre's conventions are malleable. Thus, in the hands of imaginative playwrights, the *sarsuwela* became potent social documentaries and political conscientization tools.

Second, the *sarsuwela* is nearly always presented in the native language: in Filipino or in one of the many regional dialects. It is a source of national pride, as the theater's content and conventions that have emerged are truly native. In the words of the historian Alfred McCoy (1982), the *sarsuwela* "represents an intellectual and cultural synthesis of the indigenous and foreign for which the most appropriate term would be neither 'Western' nor 'Asian' but 'Filipino'" (pp. 201-203).

Finally, the *sarsuwela* has historically been the communication instrument of choice for resisting political overlords, both foreign and native, and their local collaborators. The theater became an ideological battlefield through which the imperial and the nationalist discourses confronted and interrogated each other. With its anti-tyrannical, counter-hegemonic history, Filipino playwrights used it to expose the political, economic, and gender oppression of all types of usurpers. Indeed repressive regimes produce heroes not only in the traditional battlefields using swords and guns but also in the cultural and literary area using the pen and musical theater.

Filipino playwrights and social groups now know that anytime aspiring political Caesars (foreign or local) emerge as a threat to social order, the Filipino has the *sarsuwela* to sharpen spiritedly and fearlessly wield against them. As public entertainment, the radically-Filipinized sarsuwela not only created communities of actors, writers, and patrons, it formed coalitions of conscience as it assumed functions including social protest, sedition breeder, and criticism of political structures and socio-economic fissures in the country over the years (Trimillos, 1992). The Filipino cultural critic, Doreen Fernandez, probably presented it best: "Philippine theater, through three eras of political struggle, has never hesitated to go to war" (2001, p. 19).

The *sarsuwela* will always resonate with the Filipino because it speaks for a collective unconscious that yearns unceasingly for unity, equality, and, most importantly, freedom.

References

Abinales, P., & Amoroso, D. (2005). *State and society in the Philippines*. Pasig City: Anvil.

Agoncillo, T. (1974). *Filipino nationalism, 1872–1970*. Quezon City: R. P. Garcia Publishing Co.

Anonas, A. (2002, July 14). Bayan, isang paa na lamang. *Philippine Star Online*. https://www.philstar.com/other-sections/starweek-magazine/2002/07/14/168272/bayan-isang-paa-na-lamang.

Anonuevo, R., & Alcantara, R. (2008). Sarsuwela in sarsuwela: enduring story of the people's theater in the Philippines. *Jati, 13*, 221–227.

Bhabha, H. (1994). *The location of culture*. London and New York: Routledge.

Bressler, C. (1994). *Literary criticism: an introduction to theory and practice*. NJ: Prentice Hall.

Celoza, A. (1997). *Ferdinand Marcos and the Philippines: The political economy of authoritarianism*. Connecticut: Praeger.

Chalk, P. (2002). Militant Islamic extremism in the southern Philippines. In J. Isaacson & C. Rubenstein (Eds.), *Islam in Asia* (pp. 187–222). U.S.: Transaction Press.

Colin, F. (1663). Ethnological description of the Filipino native races and their customs. In H. Blair & J. Robertson (Eds.), *The Philippine Island, 1493–1868* (pp. 37–98). Rizal: Cacho Harmanos.

Cruz, I. (Ed.). (1971). *A short history of Philippine theater in the Philippines*. Manila: Cultural Center of the Philippines.

Denton, R., Trent, J., & Freidenberg, R. V. (2019). *Political campaign communication: principles and practices*. Lanham, MD: Rowman & Littlefield.

Diamond, C. (1996). Quest for the elusive self: the role of contemporary Philippine theatre in the formation of cultural identity. *Drama Review, 40*, 141–169.

Dizon, A. (1995). False vision in two plays by Aurelio Tolentino. *Philippine Studies, 43*, 666–680.

Eagleton, T. (1976). Literature and history. In D. Keesey (Ed.), *Contexts for criticism* (pp. 39–46). CA: Mayfield Publishing.

Eco, U. (1992). *Interpretation and overinterpretation*. Cambridge: Cambridge University.

Fernandez, D. (1974). Philippine drama 1972–1984: literature of indirection. *World Literature Today, 58*, 373–376.

Fernandez, D. (1993). Zarzuela to sarswela: indigenization and transformation. *Philippine Studies, 41*, 320–343.

Fernandez, D. (1996). *Palabas: history of Philippine theater*. Quezon City: Ateneo de Manila University Press.

Fernandez, D. (2001). Seditious and subversive: theater of war. *Bulawan: Journal of Arts and Culture*, 6–19.

Fiske, J. (1986). British cultural studies and television. In R. C. Allen (Ed.), *Channels of discourse* (pp. 284–326). Chapel Hill, NC: University of North Carolina Press.

Foucault, M. (1980). *Power/Knowledge: selected interviews and other writings, 1972–1977*. NY: Pantheon Books.

Grundligh, A. (2004). "Rocking the boat" in South Africa? Voëlvry music and Afrikaans anti-apartheid social protest in the 1980s. *The International Journal of African Historical Studies, 37,* 483–514.

Hall, S. (1980). "Encoding/Decoding." In S. Hall, D. Howe, & P. Willis (Eds.), *Culture, media, language* (pp. 128–138). London: Hutchinson.

Hernandez, T. (1976). *The emergence of modern drama in the Philippines (1898–1912)* (Philippine Studies Working Paper No. 1 ed.). Hawaii: Philippine Studies, Asian Studies Program.

Jameson, F. (1981). *Political unconscious: narrative as a socially symbolic act*. Ithaca: Cornell University Press.

Jorge, R. (2017, September 17). *Dangerous theater: tanghalang Pilipino dares audience with "Aurelio Sedisyoso."* https://www.rappler.com/life-and-style/arts-culture/aurelio-sedisyoso-tanghalang-pilipino-review.

Keesey, D. (Ed.). (1987). *Contexts for criticism.* CA: Mayfield Publishing.

Kline, W. & J. Worthen (2006). The Philippines, 1983–86. In E. May, & P. Zelikow (Eds.), *Dealing with dictators: Dilemmas of U.S. diplomacy and intelligence analysis, 1945–1990* (pp. 137–166). Cambridge: MIT Press.

Knupp, R. E. (1981). A time for every purpose under heaven: rhetorical dimensions of protest music. *The Southern Speech Communication Journal, 46,* 377–389.

Lapena-Bonifacio, A. (1972). *The seditious Tagalog playwrights: early American occupation*. Manila: Zarzuela Foundation of the Philippines.

Lockard, C. (1996). Popular music and politics in modern Southeast Asia: A comparative analysis. *Asian Music,* 149–199.

Mallari, J. (2011). Indigenizing the zarzuela: Kapampangan ethnocentric adoption of the foreign genre. *Coolabah, 5,* 161–175.

McCoy, A. (1982). A queen dies slowly: the rise and decline of Iloilo city. In A. McCoy & E. de Jesus (Eds.), *Philippine Social History* (pp. 304–338). Quezon City: Ateneo de Manila University Press.

Morley, D. (1992). *Television, audiences, and cultural studies.* London: Routledge.

Ocampo, A. (1995). Rotten beef and stinking fish: Rizal and the writing of Philippine history. *Archium Ateneo,* 1–38.

Ocampo, A. (2019, September 20). *Aurelio Tolentino's handwritten autobiography.* https://opinion.inquirer.net/124083/aurelio-tolentinos-handwritten-autobiography.

Onyebadi, U. (Ed.). (2017). *Music as a platform for political communication.* Pennsylvania: IGI Global.

O'Sullivan, T., Hartley, J., Saunders, D., Montgomery, M., & Fiske, J. (1984). *Key concepts in communication and cultural studies*. London: Routledge.

Retana, W. (1907). *Vida y escritos de Dr. Jose Rizal*. Madrid: Libreria General de Victoriano Suarez.

Riggs, A. (1904). The drama of the Filipinos. *Journal of American Folklore, 17*, 279–285.

Riggs, A. (1951). Seditious drama in the Philippines. *Current History, 20*, 202–207.

Riggs, A. (1981). *The Filipino drama*. Manila: The Ministry of Human Settlements.

Rivera-Perez, L. (1996). Rethinking ideology: polysemy, pleasure and hegemony in television culture. *Journal of Communication Inquiry, 20*, 37–56.

Rosenberg, D. (1979). *Marcos and martial law in the Philippines*. Ithaca: Cornell University Press.

Taylor, P. (1982). Narrative as a socially liberating act. *Canadian Journal of Political and Social Theory, 6*, 168–175.

Tiatco, A. (2011). Situating Philippine theatricality in Asia: a critique of the Asian-ness/Philippine-ness of Philippine theatre. *Jati, 16*, 131–150.

Tiatco, A., & Bonifacio-Ramolete, A. (2010). Performing the nation on stage: An afterthought on the University of the Philippines sarsuwela festival, 2009. *Asian Theater Journal, 27*, 307–332.

Timberman, D. (1991). *A changeless land*. New York: M.E. Sharpe.

Tiongson, N. (1985). *Pilipinas Circa 1907*. Philippine Educational Theater Association.

Tiongson, N. (1986). *The cultural traditional media of ASEAN*. Manila: ASEAN Committee on Culture and Information.

Tiongson, N. (2010). A short history of the Philippine sarsuwela. *Philippine Humanities Review, 11*, 149–186.

Trimillos, R. (1992). Philippine music as colonial experience and national culture. In B. Aquino & D. Alegado (Eds.), *The age of discovery: Impact on Philippine culture and society* (pp. 17–24). University of Hawaii: Center for Philippine Studies.

Turner, G. (1990). *British cultural studies: an introduction*. Boston: Unwin Hyman.

Villaraza, L. A. (2017). *Yesterday, today, and tomorrow: a study of Aurelio Tolentino's articulation of nationalism and identity through theatre in the Philippines during the American colonial period*. [Unpublished doctoral dissertation]. Northern Illinois University.

CHAPTER 2

Bringing Spirituals onto the Classical Music stage in the service of African American Civil Rights

Julia Schmidt-Pirro

Independent Scholar, Savannah, GA, USA

Abstract

This chapter explores how three path-breaking African American musical artists, Marian Anderson, William Grant Still and Paul Robeson deployed African American folk music, in particular, the spirituals, in classical music settings. In transforming the spirituals for the classical music stage, they promoted the acceptance of African American contributions to American and world music. Each of them took a different path carving out a place in the segregated Western European classical "highbrow" tradition. A dedicated activist for racial and social justice, Robeson put classically arranged spirituals front and center in his concerts. As a classically trained African American singer negotiating the obstacles of racial discrimination, Anderson was drawn into a highly public controversy which led to her "christening" the Lincoln Memorial as a nationally known site of civil rights activism. Considered the "Dean" of African American classical music composers, Still sought artistically to bridge the racial divide within an increasingly anti-Communist liberal framework. By challenging the social and cultural status quo, these three artists created templates for the uses of African American folk music in the civil rights activism of later decades.

Keywords: spirituals, Paul Robeson, Marian Anderson, William Grant Still, Alain Locke, civil rights, classical music

***

Introduction

I, too, sing America.
I am the darker brother.
They send me to eat in the kitchen

When company comes,
But I laugh,
and eat well,
And grow strong.

Tomorrow,
I'll be at the table
When company comes.
Nobody'll dare
Say to me,
"Eat in the kitchen,"
Then,

Besides
They'll see how beautiful I am
And be ashamed—

I, too, am America.

(Hughes, 1925).

During the first half of the twentieth century, three major African American musicians, pursuing careers in the segregated field of classical music, made concert program choices that were politically significant. Incorporating African American folk music, including spirituals, in their concert repertoires, they worked effectively within a classical music scene that was segregated by race and class and achieved public recognition and acclaim. This chapter focuses on aspects of the careers of Marian Anderson (1897–1993), Paul Robeson (1898–1976) and William Grant Still (1895-1978), highlighting those musical performances in which the intended effect on audiences was not only aesthetic but also political. Very much in accord with the ambitions of members of the Harlem Renaissance, the cultural and intellectual movement which gave rise to a new sense of racial pride and acknowledgement of the African roots of American cultural achievement, these artists believed, each in his or her own distinctive way, that the exercise of their artistic vocations would foster recognition of African American cultural contributions and create possibilities for a more inclusive American society. Thus, William Still once declared his goal as composer to be the "elevat(ion of) Negro musical idioms of dignity and effectiveness in the fields of symphonic and operatic music." (cited in Spencer, 1992, pp. 225-226). And Paul Robeson envisioned his art as a means of "bridg(ing) the gulf between the white and black races" (cited in Duberman, 1989, p. 71).

The efforts to employ music to overcome racial and political barriers, by, among other ways, bringing African American folk music into the consciousness of a much broader audience, can arguably be seen as preparing the ground for the politically significant use of African American music during the Civil Rights movement of the 1960s. Highlighting the fusion by these artists of African

American folk sources with classical musical idioms and forms, this chapter especially focuses on the transformation of spirituals into classical concert pieces popularized by singers like Anderson and Robeson. Finally, this chapter notes Still's broaching of the controversial and taboo subject of lynching on the classical music stage.

It is perhaps an obvious point to make at the outset that African American artists who aspired to break into the classical music scene of the Twenties and Thirties, faced major obstacles both general to the larger society and specific to the classical music profession. The decade after the end of the First World War witnessed the resurgence of the Ku Klux Klan in the South and the spread of its membership into other parts of the country. Woodrow Wilson presided over the institution of racial segregation in significant parts of the federal workforce. Law, custom, and economic barriers continued to support residential segregation and employment discrimination by race in communities across the country. The box office successes of *The Birth of a Nation* (1915), celebrating the Klan as a force of American liberation, and the first sound motion picture, *The Jazz Singer* (1927), featuring an acclaimed blackface performer, attested to the pervasive presence of racist tropes in American popular culture. The situation in classical music was no less challenging for African Americans. As a music historian put it:

> Of all the fields of music and art in the early 1900s, none was so thoroughly closed to black Americans as that of classical music. Blacks could succeed in popular music and theater. Comedy was open to them, as was, to a certain extent, poetry and literature. They could sing their spirituals. But the classical concert stage was the exclusive province of America's white elite (Brooks, 2004, p. 436).

Noting the ways in which black musicians continue to be considered exceptions on the classical stage even in the contemporary era, Leon Botstein, music director and principal conductor of the American Symphony Orchestra, explains that this narrow-minded image "reflects decades and generations of discrimination and exclusion, rather than some inherent affinity on the part of members of one so-called race to a certain kind of expressive vocabulary" (Botstein, 2009).

Marian Anderson and Paul Robeson challenged the exclusionary practices and institutions of the classical music profession not only by taking the classical music concert stage as African American artists but also by using this platform to perform concert versions of African American spirituals. This transformation of the spiritual to classically arranged solo voice and piano part, created a performance framework which paralleled that of the Western Classical tradition of Romantic "Lieder." In this regard, Robeson noted that he and his accompanist, Lawrence Brown, who arranged many of the spirituals he performed, "staked our careers-to-be on the concept that the songs of the Negro slaves were concert material, ranking in musical stature with the acknowledged masters" (Olwage, 2015, p. 531). These transgressive moves sparked criticism from many sides, including from those who were protective of the integrity of the folk origins of the spirituals, and – in the case of the backlash against composer William Grant Still – from those who were protective of a certain avant-garde idiom.

For each of these musicians, composing or performing became forms of intentional political activism. They successfully forced the issue of desegregation of "black folk and white classical music" by, as Still called it, "elevating" their craft and African American music (Oja, 2000, p. 345), and entering the space hitherto reserved for "white" and "cultured" elite musicians. In doing this, they claimed for themselves that coveted musical space and challenged audiences' embrace of racial stereotypes, thereby contributing toward the struggle for political, economic and social equality for African Americans. Their efforts contributed substantially not only to opening professional doors for the next generation of African American classical musicians, but also to fostering the reception of African American culture, as the next generation of black activists' used Spiritual songs during the Civil Rights movement.

Growing up in a society characterized by de facto and de jure forms of racial segregation, Robeson, Anderson, and Still faced obstacles in obtaining advanced educations, in finding adequate accommodations while on tour, and in securing certain venues because of their race. They also struggled morally over whether to perform in front of audiences that were racially segregated or that entirely excluded African Americans. Born a generation after the end of the Civil War and the abolition of slavery, they grew up in the presence of people who had direct memories of antebellum oppression and suffering. These personal connections also put them in contact with bearers of the antebellum oral culture of singing and storytelling created by the enslaved people of the United States.

Because of their shared experiences of living and pursuing careers in a racially unjust political, social, and economic order, Anderson, Robeson and Still were aware that their public performances would inevitably be seen as "political." They did, however, differ in the degree to which they welcomed the attribution of political significance to their artistic production. Robeson and Still recognized music's potential as an instrument for influencing social attitudes and hoped that their music might effect change beyond the concert hall. Anderson never saw herself as a public political figure and felt uncomfortable when put under the political spotlight. More than the others, she saw herself as exclusively pursuing a classical music career. Eventually, despite the many social and political obstacles she encountered, she carved out a place for herself in a white-dominated field. Regardless of her focus on music, her career success set a compelling example and challenged public expectations in political ways. Unlike Anderson, Roberson communicated his political beliefs and ambitions directly and outspokenly outside of his musical performance activities. While holding much more conservative political views than Robeson, Still was also outspoken about his intentions to create music that would improve the status of African American artists and African Americans, more generally.

The next sections of this chapter examine these different approaches more closely.

Paul Robeson:
Shepherding the African American Spiritual onto the Classical Music Stage

> Paul Robeson was one of the main cultural links between the last generation of Black slaves and the generation of independent Black leaders who spearheaded the civil rights revolution of the 1960s (Robeson Jr., 1993, p. 86).

Unlike Marian Anderson and W.G. Still, Paul Robeson never deliberately set out to pursue a career in the field of classical music. In 1915, he received a scholarship to study at Rutgers University, which had previously enrolled only two African American students. In the company of only one other African American in this segregated collegiate environment, Robeson faced acts of racism and discrimination but nevertheless managed to graduate as class valedictorian. He went on to attend Columbia Law School, where he met his future wife, Eslanda Goode, who became his close confidante and eventually his artistic manager. His move to Harlem proved vital to his later artistic career as it enabled his networking with artists and intellectuals of the Harlem Renaissance and New York Avant-garde circles, and his developing contacts that would be crucial for his later career as singer and actor.

An unconventional concert at New York's Greenwich Village Theatre on April 19, 1925, set the stage for Robeson's critical acceptance as a singer. The program consisted exclusively of African American spirituals and folk songs, which were to be performed by Robeson and his accompanist, Lawrence Brown, in tuxedos on a classical music stage before an audience dressed in suits, ties and evening gowns. Brown, a skilled arranger of spirituals, recalled that he and Robeson were intimidated by the formal dress of the audience and the fact that the concert was sold out (Boyle & Bunie, 2001, p. 146). For that evening, they had planned a short program lasting less than an hour in order not to strain Robeson's untrained voice. The audience response was positive, with one audience member, wife of the actor Walter Abel, emphasizing Robeson's emotional connection to his audience:

> The tears were running down Paul's face by the time he finished. And I was crying too, and so was half the audience […] Listening to him sing, for the first time in my life, I understood something about the pain of being a child without a mother and I couldn't stop crying (Boyle & Bunie, pp. 147-148).

The lyrics, which evoke the pain of brutal family separations imposed under slavery, include multiple repetitions of the line "sometimes I feel like a motherless child," to powerful emotional effect. Audience members were invited by the lyrics to identify with the suffering of others at the same time that they were consoled by Robeson's emotive singing. The repetition of lyrics and musical phrases in Brown's arrangement could also be seen as recalling older forms of call-and-response performances in which a soloist would engage in a back and forth with a group. Evoking the suffering imposed by the system of American chattel slavery, the spiritual as performed by Robeson communicated a pain whose resonance could be heard and felt by a wider audience than those who sang and heard that spiritual in its original context. Despite the new arrangement, the performance was not strictly executed in a classical manner. Robeson and Brown performed the music partly in folk music style, spontaneously engaging in a call-and-response with each other. Other times, Brown and Robeson harmonized in the interval of thirds (Stewart, 1998, p. 109).

In his review, the critic for the *New York Times* praised Robeson's powerful performance of the spirituals: "Sung by one man, they voiced the sorrow and hope of a people." The critic of *The New Republic* cast Paul Robeson as a symbol "of the increasingly important place of the American Negro on the American concert stage" (cited in Robeson Jr., 1993, pp. 73-74). The review also articulated the hope that artists like Paul Robeson and Lawrence Brown would be able to classicize the tradition of the spirituals and establish a lasting place for it.

Many concerts in this form followed. For the first five years of his singing career, Robeson focused exclusively on performing African American spirituals and folk songs. He lacked classical voice training and this left him unable to project in larger concert halls. While Robeson once described his voice as "embarrassingly delicate," (Dorison & Pencack, 2002, p. 83) his wife emphasized the virtues of his "unspoiled Negro voice...full of over and undertones" with its "peculiar husky coloring," which made him stand out from other classical performers of spirituals (Duberman, 1989, p. 79). The noted cultural figure Carl Sandburg drew a distinction between Robeson's performances of spirituals and those by the classically trained African American tenor, Roland Hayes, to the advantage of the former:

> Hayes imitates music, so when he sings a Negro spiritual the audience remarks, 'What technic (sic); what remarkable music education he must have had!' When Paul Robeson sings spirituals, the remark is 'That is the real thing- he has kept the best of himself and not allowed the schools to take it away from him!' (cited in Duberman, 1989, p. 79).

For his part, Robeson did not consider himself in competition with Hayes but as following in the footsteps of someone who had achieved wide acclaim for his performances of both Western classical music repertoire and spirituals. Hayes taught Robeson that musical performance could, for a time, unify people across racial lines: "I watched the people of both groups sit reverent and enchanted as he sang. Here there was no problem. We were not black or white – but human" (Olwage, 2015, p. 526).

Robeson's sense of his personal connection to the spirituals initially led him to distance himself from the European classical music tradition. "The history [of Frenchmen, Germans, or Italians] has nothing in common with the history of my slave ancestors. So I will not sing their music or the songs of their ancestors." (Dorinson & Pencack, 2002, p, 83). Later in his career, he changed his mind and began adding the folk songs of other peoples, including Russian and Jewish, to his repertoire. He came eventually to consider himself qualified to perform any music expressing the spiritual response of oppressed peoples: "I have sung my songs all over the world...I found that where the forces have been the same, whether people weave, build, pick cotton, or dig in the mines, they understand each other in the common language of work, suffering, and protest" (Dorinson & Pencack, 2002, p. 84).

By the mid-Twenties, it was not unusual to find spirituals in the programs of classical voice recitals. Classically trained African American composers, including Harry Burleigh (1866-1949), R. Nathaniel Dett (1882-1943) and Florence Price (1887-1953) were arranging spirituals for the concert stage. Products of an oral tradition of enslaved New World Africans, spirituals took up the subjects of work, escape, faith, and spiritual redemption through a fusion of Christian hymnal singing and work songs.

Traditionally, they were performed *a capella* by a group of singers. Composers like Burleigh, however, nestled the vocals within challenging and sophisticated piano arrangements.[1] The lyrics were occasionally altered as well. In most cases, dialect was transformed into "proper" English as a way of achieving distance from the degrading tradition of minstrel performance.

Through these efforts, spirituals were transformed from an oral, folk music tradition into a written, European-influenced classical music. In this new setting, the performance of spirituals took on a tone of seriousness and solemnity with audience attention focused on the performance of the singer, standing calmly or "stiffly" by the piano accompanist. One could argue that this setting served to concentrate the audience on singer and pianist and the musical and lyrical content of their performance. The somber stance and manner of performance contrasted starkly with "comical" minstrel performances played in blackface.

---

[1] Burleigh's early publication of "Deep River" (1916/17) is considered the first known arrangement of an African American spiritual for solo voice and piano accompaniment (Boyle & Bunie, 2001, 137).

African American classical singers like Anderson and Hayes as well as Robeson relied on these classical arrangements of the spirituals. White classical singers also made use of these arrangements, sometimes performing one or two of them within the classical art song repertoire or using them as an encore at the end of the program.[2] However, limiting concert programs exclusively to African American spirituals and folk music on classical music stages and heading them as a solo African American singer, as Robeson did, was unprecedented and pioneering. Grant Olwage points out that while the African American tenor Roland Hayes had pioneered recitals of all-Black music before Robeson it was Robeson who became "the driving force in the popularization of the all-spiritual concert in the mid-1920s" because he dedicated his recitals exclusively to arranged black spirituals and secular folk songs (Olwage, 2015, p. 528).

Marian Anderson: An "Accidental" Political Singer with Civil Rights Legacy

> [...] she learned early from the Spirituals and the atmosphere of the spiritual view of life, how to feel with deep simplicity and reverence, how to project with completely impersonal and absorbed power. As I see it, she has just carried this great artistic lesson to the world of sophisticated art-forms [...] (Locke, in Molesworth, 2012, p. 165).

Marian Anderson began her singing career performing at black colleges and churches in the American South, where she was quickly able to establish a name for herself and build a loyal audience. From the start of her career, Anderson, as well as such singers as tenor Roland Hayes, who became an important role model for her, presented programs that mixed European classical music pieces with African American spirituals, folk songs and African American classical compositions.

Anderson usually sang the spirituals at the end of her concerts and this positioning reflected the special significance this genre of music had for her:

> (M)aybe there was something extra in [placing] all the spirituals at the end of the program. I do not know. When I reached them I felt as if I had come home, fully and unreservedly – not only because they were the songs I had sung from childhood but also because the program was almost finished, and I had survived (Anderson, 1967, p. 123).

An early example of Anderson's deployment of spirituals on the concert stage took place at the end of 1917 when the high school age Anderson received an invitation to the Folk Song Festival of the Glee Club of the Georgia State

---

[2] As early as May 1917, the ("white") baritone Oscar Seagle (1877-1945) performed an unprecedented program including a whole set of spirituals in one of his concert recitals (Brooks, 2004, p. 482).

Industrial College, a black college in Savannah (now Savannah State University). The concert, which took place on December 28, 1917, benefited an African American organization supporting "dependent and orphan girls" (Judge, 1917). During the trip to Savannah, Anderson was confronted with her first experience of the humiliation caused by segregation: "I had heard about Jim Crow but meeting it bit deeply into my soul [....] I had looked closely at my people in that train. Some seemed to be embarrassed to the core. Others appeared to accept the situation as if it were beyond repair" (Anderson, 1967, p. 33).

The concert drew a large crowd of 700 people, with approximately 400 white and 300 black people in the audience seated apart from each other. A *Savannah Morning News* article, with the sub-headline, "Prominent White People to Occupy Boxes," noted that the venue's box seats were sold out for the concert and listed the distinguished citizens (all white, of course) occupying each box. In a short paragraph following that list of noteworthies, the article goes on to say that "the most prominent colored citizens of Savannah" (who remained nameless) were "on the first floor in the orchestra" ("Song Festival Tonight," 1917).

Anderson's renditions included Harry Burleigh's arrangements of *Deep River* and *Go Down, Moses*, as well as the Irish ballad *Danny Boy*, and *Island of Gardens* by the Anglo-African composer Coleridge-Taylor and Francesco Tosti's *La serenata*. The city's white newspaper (*Savannah Morning News*) and the *Savannah Tribune*, an African American newspaper, highly praised Anderson's performance and vocal qualities. The *Savannah Tribune*, however, was alone in calling out the segregated seating arrangement, which had been given a pass by the African American organizers:

> What a pity that a large crowd of Negroes could not have heard her exquisite voice but the Jim Crow seating arrangement of the Negroes managing the affair made this impossible for the self-respecting Negroes of the city. ("Protective Ass'n Concert Attracts About 700 Persons," 1918)

While such performances earned Anderson positive publicity, her broader career success depended on building interest in audiences from other parts of the country, especially among classical music critics in the Northeast. Boston, New York and Philadelphia boasted well-established classical music performance traditions and famous concert halls. Breaking into this scene proved to be very difficult for young African American artists.

In 1923, while studying under Guiseppe Boghetti, with the financial support of her church, Anderson became the first African American singer to win the Philadelphia Philharmonic song competition. At the end of the same year, she made her first recordings for Victor Talking Records, singing *Deep River* and *My Way's Cloudy* (issued in 1924) and becoming the first black concert artist to record spirituals for an established American recording company. A reviewer for the magazine *New Masses,* closely tied to the Communist Party, criticized Anderson's performances of the spirituals, in a later recording, as "lacking the requisite rhythmic fire," as "far too polite for comfort," and "castrated replicas of the original" (cited in Smith, 2000, p. 186). This line of criticism was voiced by other reviewers as well. Among the critics was the African American scholar and novelist Zora Neal Hurston, who argued that the performance of spirituals in the European classical tradition with seated audiences and fixed prosceniums was a "disservice to and distortion of the original visceral, communal spirit of the folk from whom the songs had arisen" (Duberman, 1989, p. 82).

Described by her Finnish accompanist Kosti Vehanen as a person who preferred to avoid direct confrontation and sought "to win any victory purely with the implement of her great art" (cited in Dorinson & Pencak, 2002, p. 161), Anderson was drawn into a major political controversy when the Daughters of the American Revolution denied her the use of Constitution Hall for a concert. While the management claimed not to have any dates available for Anderson's performance, this claim turned out to be bogus (Freedman, 2004, p. 57). From the time of its opening in 1929, the Hall had been used by black performers, including Roland Hayes, as a performance venue, but, by 1935, the policy became more racially discriminatory as the DAR, like other conservative-leaning institutions, reacted negatively to the progressive New Deal policies of Roosevelt's administration and the positive reception of these policies by many ordinary Americans (Dorinson & Pencak, 2002, p. 162).

Despite protests, the hall managers did not reverse their decision. As a next step, Howard University, which had sponsored Anderson's concert, turned to the Washington school system, hoping to rent one of the city's largest white auditoriums for the concert. When the School Superintended Frank Balou denied the request, a further series of protests erupted. In February 1939, the First Lady and civil rights supporter Eleanor Roosevelt publicly weighed in on the debate by resigning her DAR membership when she heard of the DAR's refusal of Constitution Hall as a venue.

By the first week of March, 1939, with no other suitable venue becoming available for a concert by Anderson, the possibility of an open-air concert was raised. Howard University's director of music had told the press at some point that, "She'll sing here – even if we have to build a tent for her" (Keiler, 2000, p. 207). Eventually, through the joint efforts of Walter White, executive secretary of the National Association for the Advancement of Colored People, First Lady Eleanor Roosevelt, and Harold L. Ickes, Secretary of the Interior, plans were made to hold the concert at the Lincoln Memorial. On Easter Sunday, April 14, 1939, Anderson gave her concert at the Lincoln Memorial in Washington, D.C. before an integrated audience of 75,000 people.

The program was kept short, to about thirty minutes. Secretary of Interior Ickes gave an introductory speech beforehand, addressing the political significance of the concert:

> In this great auditorium under the sky all of us are free. When God gave us this wonderful outdoors and the sun, the moon, and the stars, He made no distinction of race, or creed, or color[...]Facing us down the Mall beyond the Washington Monument...there is rising a memorial to that other great Democrat in our short history, Thomas Jefferson, who proclaimed that principle of equality of opportunity which Abraham Lincoln believed in so implicitly and took so seriously[...] Genius, like justice, is blind. For genius has touched with the tip of her wing this woman, who, if it had not been for the great heart of Lincoln, would not be able to stand among us a free individual today in a free land (cited in Keiler, 2000, p. 212).

Ickes' indirect reference to the authorship of that famous passage from the Declaration of Independence ("all men are created equal") by Thomas Jefferson, defender of slavery and a slave holder himself, marks the sort of hypocrisy in which even the proponents of racial progress were apt to get entangled. The way in which he frames Anderson's concert as a "tribute" to Lincoln is also problematic. As historian William Pencak observes: "Anderson herself appears here as a passive recipient of a gift of genius that owes thanks to a great nation and its great men" (Dorinson & Pencak, 2002, p. 164). The patronizing treatment of Anderson's racial and gender identities, which this rhetoric manifests, pointed to the distance the country still had to travel in the struggle for equality.

Anderson performed most of the concert with her eyes closed. After the short concert, she briefly addressed the audience: "I am so overwhelmed, I just can't talk. I can't tell you what you have done for me today. I thank you from the bottom of my heart" (Keiler, 2000, p. 213). Walter White's description of the response of a young working-class black woman audience member exemplifies the common view of how important this concert was as a symbol of the American Dream's promise that individual talent could transcend the boundaries of race and class:

> Tears streamed down the girl's dark face. Her hat was askew, but in her eyes flamed hope bordering on ecstasy. Life which had been none too easy for her held out greater hope because one who was colored and who, like herself, had known poverty, privation, and prejudice, had, by her genius, gone a long way toward conquering bigotry. If Marian Anderson could do it, the girl's eyes seemed to say, then I can (cited in Keiler, 2000, p. 214).

At first glance, Marian Anderson's selection of performance pieces at the Lincoln Memorial seems consistent with the pattern of her prior concert programs, in which conventional classical music pieces were paired with classically arranged spirituals. At second glance, however, the choice of songs at the Lincoln Memorial can be seen as having a political logic. The program started with *America: My Country 'Tis of Thee*, a song that had served as a quasi-national anthem in the United States before the official adoption of *The Star-Spangled-Banner*. This choice could be seen to reflect a feeling of pride in American identity felt by an African American, who, despite all of the obstacles thrown up in the highly segregated world of early twentieth-century America, had managed to carve out a place as one of the outstanding female classical singers in the country. At the same time, in singing this song, whose lyrics express a sense of personal ownership - "My country tis of thee, sweet land of liberty, of thee I sing." – Anderson could be seen as staking a claim for the inclusion of herself and other African Americans in the patrimony of the country. In either case, but especially in the latter, Anderson's choice to lead off her concert at the Lincoln Memorial with this song sent a powerful message of equal citizenship and full inclusion of African Americans in U.S. society almost two decades before the Civil Rights Movement. Her program was broadcast (except for the last two songs) nationwide by NBC radio. T.V. stations also broadcast footage of the concert, exposing millions to the event.

Figure 2.1 Marian Anderson at Lincoln Memorial, April 9, 1939. Scurlock Studio Records, Archives Center, National Museum of American History, Smithsonian Institution

Anderson's rendition of *America* was followed by her performance of an aria by Donizetti, Schubert's *Ave Maria*, and, finally, a group of four gospel songs: *Gospel Train, Tramping, My Soul is Anchored in the Lord*, and, as an encore, *Nobody Knows the Trouble I've Seen*. In concluding her program with a rendition of *My Soul is Anchored in the Lord*, Anderson gave special prominence to a piece arranged by an African American woman composer, Florence Price. Choosing *Nobody Knows the Trouble I've Seen* as the encore piece served to end the concert on a powerful emotional note of protest against racial injustice. Its politically resonant use by Anderson foreshadowed its later important role in the civil rights movement.

Besides her politically conscious choice of music, Anderson endowed her concert with political significance in more subtle ways, through musical techniques and choice of words. In performing *America*, she chose to sing the first and fourth verses. Switching out the last line of the fourth verse with a repeat of the last line of the first verse, Anderson ensured that the line "Let Freedom ring" would end each verse. In her first encounter with the word, she stretched "freedom" with a ritardando giving it extra weight. In the following verse, her voice climbs with a crescendo into the high notes, culminating in the word "Let" (freedom ring). In musically underlining the two words, "freedom" and "let" Anderson is indirectly but powerfully making a political statement of hope of, and aspiration for, a different future. The word "I" in the line "of thee I sing" was exchanged with "we" which communicated a message of solidarity and collective effort.

The concert at the Lincoln Memorial, which came about after a series of unforeseen events, served powerfully to politicize Marian Anderson's singing career before a larger American public. However ambivalently, Anderson accepted this new situation as when she responded to Mrs. Roosevelt's resignation from the DAR in the following way:

> I am not surprised at Mrs. Roosevelt's action because she seemed to me to be one who really comprehended the true meaning of democracy. I am shocked beyond words to be barred from the Capital of my own country after having appeared in almost every other capital in the world (cited in Keiler, 2000, p. 203).

Her statement expressed a deeply felt sense of injustice. It does not, however, fully reveal Anderson's great sense of personal unease about the controversy. Anderson later admitted that these events were a heavy burden on her: "It seemed to increase and to follow me wherever I went" (ibid., p. 204). Despite Anderson's personal ambivalence about assuming a public political persona, the concert marked the beginning of her being more deliberately and explicitly political in the choices she made on the concert stage.

The performance at the Lincoln Memorial had raised her cultural profile and endowed her with a political one. It was after the historic performance that Anderson made the conscious decision to stop performing in front of segregated audiences: "I had enough, and I made it a rule not to sing where there was segregation" (Anderson, 1967, p. 178). Her later career path veered more visibly into the political arena. In the 1950s, she became a delegate to the United Nations Human Rights Committee and a Goodwill Ambassador for the United States Department of State. She performed the National Anthem at Eisenhower's second inauguration in 1957 and Kennedy's inauguration in 1961.

Songs of Protest, Inspiration and Aspiration:
The Transformation and Significance of the Concert Spiritual

> It may not be readily conceded now that the song of the Negro is America's folk song; but if the Spirituals are what we think of them to be, a classical folk expression, then this is their ultimate destiny (Locke, in Molesworth, 2012, p. 105).

In the preface to the 1925 collection of spirituals for voice and piano, *Book of American Negro Spirituals*, James Weldon Johnson underlines how Robeson and Anderson contributed to the popularization of concert spirituals and their importation into the canon of classical music: "The superlatively fine rendition of these songs (spirituals) by Roland Hayes, Paul Robeson, Miss Marian Anderson [...] has brought them to the highest point of celebrity and placed the classic stamp upon them" (Johnson & Johnson, 1977, pp. 48-49). Through concerts, recordings, and radio and T.V. broadcasts, Robeson and Anderson were able to expose a large, racially mixed audience, nationwide and worldwide, to the newly transformed "highbrow" versions of the spirituals.

The transformed status of the spirituals blurred the borders between "highbrow" and "lowbrow" music, as well as between different races and cultures. However, even before the deliberate and high-profile efforts of Robeson and Anderson to juxtapose European Western "high art" and African American "low art" as companion repertoires of equal worth, there had been substantial discussion and debate among intellectuals, theorists, and composers about the value of the spirituals and the viability of transforming them for performance on the classical music stage. A brief look at some notable contributions to that discussion and debate will offer insight into how classically performed spirituals could do several kinds of political work, including diffusing the horrors of racist enslavement to new audiences, showcasing the resilience of the African American community, and fostering white audience members' empathetic connection to black experience.

As early as 1845, Frederick Douglass recognized spirituals as an important oral documentation of the pain and suffering caused by slavery. Interpreting the songs as expressing protest against injustice, he understood them as having the politically significant power of conveying the horror of slavery more directly than academic arguments could:

> I have sometimes thought that the mere hearing of those songs would do more to impress some minds with the horrible character of slavery, than the reading of whole volumes of philosophy on the subject could do .... (Douglass, 2019, pp. 31-32).

Along these lines, sociologist and activist W.E.B. DuBois highlighted spirituals as a form of testimony to the pain and sorrow experienced during slavery. He also underlined the hopefulness these songs fostered: "Through all the sorrow of the Sorrow Songs there breathes a hope – a faith in the ultimate justice of things" (Du Bois, 1989, pp. 177, 186). The philosopher Alain Locke argued that the classical "elevation" of spirituals affirmed the worth of African American folk art and fostered an appreciation of that art's power to endow a community with self-validation and resilience. As he points out, the "New Negro" art became the tool by which African Americans could reconcile with, and move forward from a traumatic history to shape for themselves a new identity (cited in Smith, 2000, p. 47).

While there was wide agreement as to the emotional depth and power of the spirituals as folk art and their power of conveying the suffering caused by past enslavement, disagreement arose as to whether their rich musical originality could be retained in a classical music setting within classical musical idioms. Public intellectuals such as Zora Neale Hurston and Carl Sandburg argued for the preservation of the original performance mode of the spirituals, which included improvisation and communal performance. They feared that the classicization of the songs would strip them of their vitality as a mode of expression linking a community to its traumatic past. Hurston argued that the performance of spirituals in the European classical tradition was a "disservice to and distortion of the original visceral, communal spirit of the folk from whom the songs had arisen" (cited in Duberman, 1989, p. 82). She went so far as to claim that as a result of this transformation the spirituals were corrupted from an authentic folk expression into a mere copy of a classical idiom (Carmody, 2014, p. 10). However, in regard to Robeson's performance style of the spirituals she commented that, "Robeson sings Negro songs better than most, because, thank God, he lacks musical education" (cited in Duberman, 1989, p. 595).

In addition to concerns about "elevating" the spirituals, there was unease about exposing intimate emotional responses to white audiences who might respond with ridicule, as had happened in minstrel shows. Robert Moton, an educator and administrator at the Hampton Institute (later Hampton University), recounts how he was taken aback by students publicly performing "Negro spirituals": "I objected to exhibiting the religious and emotional side of our people to white folks" (cited in Moody-Turner, 2013 p. 81).

As early as 1867, Lucy McKim Garrison, who was one of the first collectors of African American spirituals, gave a vivid account of some musical aspects of the original performance of spirituals which, at the same time, explains the difficulty of transcribing the music with classical notation: "The odd turns made in the throat and the curious rhythmic effect produced by single voices chiming in at different irregular intervals seem almost as impossible to place on the score as the singing of birds or the tones of aeolian harp" (Allan et al., reprint from 1996, p. VI). Inevitably, the transcription of the songs turned them into something else, more closely related to the Western European classical tradition.

As with other critics, William Grant Still had concerns about how classical arrangements of spirituals might denature them, rob them of their "folk flavor." His wife Verna Arvey wrote: "No wonder people discover Caucasian influences in them, thought he [Still], when often their whole characters are altered by the foreign quality of their arrangement" (cited in Smith, 2000, p. 330). Still deliberately sought out original spirituals in out-of-the-way places as sources for his musical compositions. Still's wife recalled that her husband actively pursued opportunities to hear spirituals in little known settings:

> He followed a custom ……of going to small Negro churches and revival meetings wherever he found himself, in order to make a mental record of the little-known spirituals and to learn as much as he could about Negro music firsthand as possible (Arvey, 1984, p. 69).

Still considered it imperative that African American composers be free to develop their own creative impulses and not be pigeonholed as mere arrangers of a folk tradition. His wife reports that there was a period of time ("many years") when he "made it a point not to arrange Spirituals" (cited in Smith, 2000, p. 330).

In the reviews of, and reactions to, the concerts given by Robeson and Anderson, one finds near-universal consensus about the deep emotional impact worked on audience members, white as well as black. Part of that impact was generated by the skill of the performances, and part of it was probably generated by the performers' ability to channel their personal experience of living in a racially oppressive society, whose earlier iteration as a slave society had given rise to the spirituals in the first place. During Anderson's 1953 tour in Japan, Peter Grilli, the son of the arts and music critics of the Tokyo newspaper, "Nippon Times," recalls the lasting impression Anderson's performance had made on him as a child:

> Along with (Schubert's) "Erlkönig," the piece that had the strongest impact on me at that concert was "Swing Low Sweet Chariot." At the time, I knew next to nothing about slavery or Negros in American society

...But I'll never forget the intensity of that song. Anderson's power and concentration seemed to be directed inward, and to me that spiritual seemed to flow from her soul directly to the souls of everyone in the audience (cited in Callam et al., 2019, p. 270).

Another audience member described the experience of hearing Anderson's "performance of Negro spirituals" as "religious" (Callam et al., p. 271).

To be sure, white audience members' positive emotional response was not without its contradictions. In regard to these sympathetic audience reactions, folklore scholar Regina Bendix cautions that, "the assumed anonymity and authenticity of the spirituals allowed the white observers to sympathize in a general way with the sufferings of ex-slaves, while not attributing individuality or creativity to the black performers." Bendix's warning reminds us that claims of the universality of emotional appeal of hearing spirituals on the classical music stage can too easily wash out important differences in receptivity (cited in Moody-Turner, 2013, p. 58).

Besides their powerful emotional appeal and their politically relevant role in breaking the European monopoly in classical music concert programs, there is another important effect to consider. Arthur Jones offers the important argument that the transformation of spirituals to concert spirituals helped the genre of the spiritual to survive. During the era of the Great Migration, spirituals were looked down upon because of their association with the slavery. Pastors of African American churches were lobbying for classical music instead of "old-time" performances of spirituals (Jones & Jones, 2001, p. 22). Shirley Moody-Turner explains that in the post-Civil War era there was a movement to turn away from spirituals which were seen as carrying a "badge of slavery" (Moody-Turner, 2013, p. 59). Alain Locke acknowledges the role that the classical arranging of the spirituals played in their cultural survival:

> It was the Negro himself who took them out of their original religious setting, but he only anticipated the inevitable by a generation – for the folk religion that produced them is rapidly vanishing. Noble as the purpose of this transplanting was – the damage was done to the tradition. But we should not be ungrateful for surely, it was by this that they were saved to posterity at all (cited in Molesworth, 2012, p. 107).

In popularizing the spirituals and bringing them into nationwide consciousness Robeson and Anderson contributed to their preservation. It could also be argued that they helped make the spirituals available to the Civil Rights movement of the 1960s, when spirituals or freedom songs made a comeback, but not in classical form. In this new and more political context, they regained their improvisational character and their capacity to foster communal participation.

William Grant Still: Initiating an African American Classical Music Tradition

> Today we are most proud that our contribution has come at last to be regarded as an important part of American music. We are glad that all Americans can listen to the music created by Negros and can say to themselves "This is a part of me" because it has been born in their own land.
>
> (Still, cited in Spencer, 1992, p. 143)

For Robeson and Anderson, classicized spirituals were central to their self-presentation as singers on the classical music stage. As we will see, in his compositional work, William Grant Still ranged more widely across African American folk music genres and popular music forms associated with black Americans. Growing up in musical home and developing an early passion for music, Still received a thorough music education, despite his family's financial challenges. Throughout his early years of study, various teachers recognized his talent and helped him find financial support or offered him free music lessons. In apparent deference to his mother's wish that he put aside his ambition to become a composer, he enrolled in Wilberforce University and worked towards a Bachelor of Science degree. During his studies, Still nevertheless remained very active in the musical life of the university. He left the university without graduating. After receiving a small bequest from his father, he began a program of private study at Oberlin. Impressed by his abilities, his teachers organized a scholarship for him, which enabled him to continue his studies, including, for the first time, in composition.

Between 1915 and 1918, Still traveled with W.C. Handy's band before settling in New York City in 1919, where he continued to work for Handy as a musical arranger and played oboe in the orchestra for Eubie Blake's and Noble Sissle's musical, "Shuffle Along." Still continued to perform while also pursuing a classical music education. Through connections, he became aware of a scholarship, which funded private lessons with the exiled French composer Edgar Varèse. Varèse, an immigrant avant-garde composer, strongly shaped Still's first compositions and facilitated his entry into New York avant-garde music circles. Later, Still would reflect on the important role Varèse played in his musical development: "When I was groping blindly in my efforts to compose, it was Varese [sic] who pointed out to me the way to individual expression and who gave me the opportunity to hear my music played" (cited in Smith, 2000, p. 310).

Testing his talents within the New York music avant-garde, Still found himself competing with members of a group of successful white American composers, who daringly and, at times, controversially married Jazz and other African American musical idioms to classical music (e.g., George Gershwin, Luis

Gruenberg, Aaron Copland and George Antheil). While being a part of this movement, Still distinguished himself from other composers by his ongoing engagements in black entertainment music circles. As the only African American composer in this group of classical avant-garde composers who were appropriating elements of African American music, Still felt a close personal connection to his African American musical heritage: "The music of my people is the music I understand best" (cited in Smith, 2000, p. 51). An early composition from 1921, *Three Negro Songs*, composed for orchestra, already incorporates African American folk melodies. It was during this time that it became trendy for white composers to appropriate Jazz and other black musical idioms. As musicologist Carol Oja points out, this compositional trend helped give impulse to efforts to integrate American concert stages (Oja, 2000, p. 360).

While Still did not entirely fit in with the white avant-garde circle of New York City's composers, his avant-garde bona fides distinguished his work from those of other African American composers of his time. Influenced and shaped by his mentor Edgar Varèse, Still set his work apart from previous, as well as other contemporary, African American composers:

> I don't know of anyone else (in America) who was branching into any decided departure, as far as musical idioms are concerned. My working with Varese had opened this new field (to me, but...) I think that most of the other Negro writers (Nathaniel Dett, Clarence White, Florence Price) were writing just conventional things. (Still, 1990, p. 87).

On February 8, 1925, his first major work, *From the Land of Dreams*, was performed at a concert by Varèse's International Composers' Guild in New York. The score was composed for chamber orchestra and three voices treated instrumentally, without using any lyrics. The ambivalent critical response to his debut illustrates the paradox Still would continually face as an African American composer. While recognizing his compositional talents, prominent critics of the New York music scene, including Paul Rosenfeld and Olin Downes, argued that Still was too reliant on his teacher's style and too neglectful of his African American musical legacy (Downes). Rosenfeld did, however, positively highlight Still's use of jazz motives which he saw as more "genuinely musical" than the use of jazz elements found in the works of such composers as Milhaud and Gershwin (cited in Smith, 2000, p. 223). Downes was more one-sidedly critical, arguing that, "Mr. Varèse, Mr. Still's teacher has driven all that [energy of black folk music] out of him" (cited in Oja, 2000, p. 332).

The conflicting interpretations of Still's music reflect the difficult challenge he faced in developing a distinctive musical voice as an African American composer in the avant-garde. Claiming an equal place among New York's Avant-garde composers, Still encountered a double standard. A kind of ceiling was set on critical expectations about how and what he should compose. As the musicologist Catherine Parsons Smith observes: "his audience was unwilling to recognize anything in his cultural background but the clearest possible references to the spirituals or to the stereotype-laden `revues' he was orchestrating for a living" (Smith, 2008, pp. 33-34). These expectations meant, on the one hand, that he would be seen as outside his lane, so to speak, to the extent that he incorporated avant-garde techniques associated with European influences in his compositions. On the other hand, when he dropped avant-garde gestures and went all-in on incorporating African American folk music, he could be criticized for being too simplistic and naïve.

Perhaps influenced by the hostile critical reception to the avant-garde style of his earlier pieces and seeking to express his African American musical roots more clearly, Still began turning away from modern idioms that embraced dissonance: "Through experimentation, I discovered that Negro music tends to lose its identity when subjected to avant-garde style of treatment. I made this decision of my own free will, knowing very well that pressures would be brought to bear to make me follow the leader, and compose as others do" (Spencer, 1992, p. 226).

The January 24, 1926, performance of Still's composition, *Levee Land*, again by the International Composers' Guild, revealed the new turn in his musical approach. *Levee Land* more directly incorporated Jazz and Blues elements into classical music composition. The "pop" music elements of the composition were emphasized by Still's choice to hire Florence Mills, a successful artist from black musical theater to perform the vocal part.[3] Reviews were positive but mainly focused on "the exotic presence of Florence Hill" (Oja, 2000, p. 334). This reflected the critical establishment's attraction to the importation of African American pop music aspects—in this case, "black" dialect and the use of a popular theater singer--to the classical music stage. A critic from the *New York World* praised Miss Mills's sensuous singing and comic mannerisms (Egan, 2004, p. 145).

A critic from the *Musical Courier* applauded Still for abandoning the "slavish imitation of the noises which Edgar Varèse calls composition" and putting him "on a high plane in the super-jazz field just now in vogue." By contrast, the critic of *Musical America*, judged the production's fusion of jazz and "sophisticated harmony" as faulty. This response echoed another assessment of the piece as "artificial, neither real jazz, nor real modernism, with forced and sentimental affectation" (Olin Downes). In a later self-evaluation, Still saw this work as being a step closer to the "idiom I was seeking" but "still too extreme" (cited in Smith, 2000, pp. 223-224).

---

[3] Mills had performed in *Shuffle Along* (1921) and *Dixie to Broadway* (1924), two plays for which Still had played in the orchestra (Oja, 2000, p. 333).

The 1931 performances of the *Afro-American Symphony* in Rochester and New York marked an important step in the evolution of Still's career. The composition incorporated a "simple little blues theme" into the classical symphonic form (Smith, 2000, p. 231). Criticism was mixed, as exemplified in a review published by *Modern Music*, which faulted the work for its structural failings as a symphony - "it is not cyclical nor symphonic in the accepted sense" - but somewhat patronizingly praised its use of harmony or "color that is essentially racial" (cited in Smith, 1997, p. 382).

In his 1936 review of the symphony after its performance by the New York Philharmonic Orchestra, the composer Marc Blitzstein criticized Still for his inauthentic use of African American forms, which served "to debauch a true folk-lore for high-class concert hall consumption" (Smith, 1997, pp. 382-383). Perhaps, the deepest cut came from Aaron Copland, who essentially took Still to task from the other flank for abandoning avant-garde technique in favor of popular stylizing that "lean(s) toward the sweetly saccharine" (Smith, 1997, p. 383).

Despite the mixed critical reception of Still's work, especially within New York avant-garde circles, his compositions also received wide public recognition. In April 1940, the conductor Artur Rodzinski approached the composer about the possibility of performing one of Still's recent works, a ballad entitled, *And They Lynched Him on a Tree*, which puts to music a political poem by Katherine Garrison Chapin (1890-1977) about the lynching of a convicted murderer. Lynching was a controversial political subject at the time of the piece's performance, with federal efforts to legislate against this racist mob practice continually being blocked by Southern Democratic Senate filibusters. In making lynching the central focus of an artistic piece, Still and Chapin followed in the footsteps of other creative artists. Angelina Weld Grimké's play, *Rachel*, produced in 1916, brought the subject to the theatre stage. During the 1920s, several lynching dramas appeared on Broadway (Stephens, 2011, p. 657). Abel Meeropol's 1937 haunting song, "Strange Fruit," erupted into public consciousness with Billie Holiday's famous 1939 recording. What made Still's artistic treatment of this theme distinctive was that he was the first to introduce it to the classical music stage, a space occupied almost exclusively by middle- and upper-class white audiences.

In his composition, Still chose a complex arrangement, in which he juxtaposed a contralto solo voice, a male narrator, and "black" and "white" choruses (Arvey, 1984, p. 116), the latter of which begins by taking on the role of a lynch mob. Given the politically fraught content of this piece, it is noteworthy that Rodzinski proposed New York's Lewisohn Stadium, a large-scale open-air venue accommodating a big audience (according to a *Time Magazine* article 13,000 people attended the concert – see "I Hear America Singing," 1940). However, upon receiving the music and lyrics, Rodzinski voiced concerns about the concluding line of the composer's piece: "Talk of justice and take your stand / But a long dark shadow will fall across your land." In a letter to Still, Rodizinski expressed a fear that this phrasing "would cause tremendous antagonism" and he expressed his wish to "avoid stirring up new, unnecessary excitements ..... at any price." For this reason, the conductor requested that Still change the ending to "some kind of apotheosis of humanity" (Shirley, 1994, p. 441). Eager for the piece to have a public airing, Still, Chapin, and others involved were sympathetic to Rodzinski's concerns.[4]

Ten days before the concert, Still was made aware that Rodzinksi had commissioned another piece for the program from Roy Harris, a former Composers' Collective member. The piece, *Challenge 1940*, sounded patriotic themes by drawing its text from the Preamble of the Constitution: "We the people of United States, We are the people. In order to form a more perfect Union, we must work together." Its inclusion was a transparent effort by Rodzinski to counterbalance the explicitly controversial subject of Still's piece. The Still family saw this "last minute addition" to the program as an affront and Still interpreted it as an attempt by the Left to plagiarize his work and steal the spotlight:

> Roy Harris read the announcement in the papers early in June and apparently decided that this was something he would like to share. He thereupon wrote a new composition in four days, according to the newspapers: begun on June 10, finished on June 14. It was scored – you guessed it – for Negro chorus, white chorus, and orchestra. He persuaded Rodzinski to open the evening's program with it, so that his use of the two choruses would precede Billy's, and he would appear to be the innovator (Arvey, 1984, p. 116).[5]

The review in the *Time Magazine* of July 8, 1940, noted that the concert was dedicated to "Democracy," with a program that included Paul Robeson's performance of *Ol'Man River*, the *Ballad for Americans*, and a group of spirituals. Still's piece was singled out as the "most ambitious" but also criticized for its too "obvious" attempts at popular accessibility ("I Hear America Singing," 1940). Several of the positive reviews of Still's piece included caveats, many of which centered on his use of an atypical form. Smith relates

---

[4] On May 3 Still argued in a letter to Chapin that there was no time to rewrite the music and Chapin agreed that she would change the text, trying to fit Still's music (Shirley, 1994, p. 441).

[5] As it turned out, Harris did not end up using the black chorus for his piece. According to Chapin, Harris had intended to use both choirs, the "black" and the "white" chorus but she was able to convince the composer not to do so. To Still she wrote: "It seemed to me to be unfair to your composition at its initial performance to use the two choirs before our piece had been given a hearing." (Shirley, 1994, p. 447)

these criticisms to a tendency in which "black and/or female composers were commonly accused of inability to construct large forms, especially when their message, like this one was atypical" (Smith, 2008, p. 64).

Conclusion:
Challenging Racism through three distinct Musical Approaches

Arguably, musicians Still, Robeson and Anderson had path-breaking music careers that saw them pioneering African American entry into the world of classical music in an era when the genre was considered off-limits to musicians of color. All three used spirituals songs to gain deserved recognition and "membership" in the elitist and exclusive world of "white" classical music. This chapter therefore concludes with a brief consideration of the distinctive ways in which the significantly different political motivations of these African American musical artists helped set the groundwork for later challenges to racism in American life.

Robeson used music and his celebrity persona explicitly to propagate leftist, anti-racist values and ideas. Well aware of the "exclusionary" environment of the classical music scene, especially for someone like him - an "untrained singer" with a college football past and aspirations to be an actor - he never sought acceptance from the classical music establishment. Instead, throughout his career, he consciously distanced himself from the classical European tradition by choosing to perform only those classical music pieces composed by members of oppressed "peoples" (e.g., Russian composers) and by highlighting African American folk styles in classical music concert halls. His programming strategy was explicitly shaped by political considerations and driven by his goal of employing music to foster solidarity across racial lines and, in the form of benefit concerts, to support progressive causes.

Marian Anderson, by contrast, was mainly motivated to succeed as a classical music singer. "The essential point about wanting to appear in the hall was that I wanted to do so because I felt I had that right as an artist" (Anderson, 1967, p. 140). While she could not help being aware of the politics of segregation and discrimination, she did not present her music-making as a component of a political persona: "I would be fooling myself to think that I was meant to be a fearless fighter; I was not, just as I was not meant to be a soprano instead of a contralto" (Anderson, 1967, p.137). Despite benefiting from the path-breaking efforts of African American musicians of an earlier generation, she nevertheless had to face endemic racial discrimination. In successfully carving out a musical career, she was bound to become a symbol for both America's continued failings at extending equality to all, on the one hand, and America's promise of social mobility through talent, on the other.

Her Lincoln Memorial concert created a ripple of political effects upon the later struggle for civil rights. As Freedman points out, the concert helped to popularize the NAACP, whose executive secretary had been closely involved in the organization of the concert. Its membership doubled in the year following the concert and it benefited from a wave of new financial support. After the concert, Anderson became a high-profile fundraiser for the NAACP. One of the most important legacies of this concert was its creation of a template for future generations of activists: "it created the format of the modern civil rights demonstrations, and it established the Lincoln Memorial as moral high ground for generations of protestors" (Freedman, 2004, p. 71).

In some ways, William Grant Still walked the most complicated career path of the three. As the first broadly successful African American composer, he faced different and, perhaps, more intractable difficulties. Driven by the search for a new musical language fusing the African American folk and popular music traditions and the European American classical tradition, he expected this fusion of "black folk" and "white classical" genres to foster recognition and acceptance of African American cultural contributions to American and world culture. However, as an African American artist with avant-garde training, Still faced the double bind of being, on the one hand, taken to task for either being too radical and abandoning his black musical roots in favor of avant-garde technique, or, on the other, being accused of currying popular favor in the style of Hollywood or Broadway for his use of folk idioms. He responded by distancing himself both geographically and ideologically from the tight clique of mostly leftwing composers in the Northeast. Moving to the West Coast, he became an outspoken anti-communist. His struggle for classical music success thus took on political overtones, only in this case he combined aspirations to promote black inclusion in the larger culture and society with a fierce rejection of the leftwing politics he associated with the avant-garde circles from which he had earlier felt excluded. In this respect, Still's evolution as a political being mirrored American liberalism's evolution from acceptance of a wartime Popular Front alliance with Communist Party members to a Cold War policy of anti-communist crusading. Still associated himself with the growing conservatism of Cold War liberals. In stark contrast, Robeson remained a leftist who saw the prospects of achieving a just and inclusive social order as tied to a larger push for social justice among various oppressed groups.

Even if Still ended up the most politically conservative of these three African American artists of the twentieth century, we should not underestimate the continuing power of his compositions to unsettle liberal complacency about the state of race relations in America. Against the backdrop of recent Black Lives Matter protests against police violence and "modern day" lynchings, such as the chasing down and killing of Ahmaud Arbery in a Brunswick neighborhood, in Georgia, USA (2020), Still's piece, *And They Lynched Him on a Tree*, retains its relevance. A short glance at the performance history of Still's composition reveals how art works that straightforwardly address racial discrimination and oppression in American life continue to encounter more than the usual difficulties in finding their way to the public stage. *And They Lynched Him on A Tree* has seen few performances since its premiere in 1940. Only two commercial recordings of the piece exist. According to Harlan Zackery Jr. the piece has had "only twenty-eight documented performances" in 75 years, with a majority of these performances taking place in the North (Zackery, 2016, p. 78).

The piece's shocking content and outspokenly critical perspective continue to discomfort performers and audience members. A review of a February 1999 Boston performance appearing in the *Boston Globe* called the piece an "American Stabat Mater touching on such terrible shame and sorrow that the participants….must have lived through some shattering times together just to perform it" (cited in Zackery, 2016, p. 52). A performance production a month earlier, in January 1999, on the campus of Yale University, was staged explicitly for the specific purpose of bringing blacks and whites together. According to Jonathan Berryman, the music director of the Heritage Chorale, which performed as the black choir in the piece, the evening marked one of the few times that African Americans were so strongly present in Yale's concert hall. During the rehearsal process, the musicians voiced their extreme unease with the content. One of the singers performing as a member of the white lynching chorus explained: "Well this was upsetting to me. I then had to take this under my skin and say, 'my people did this' and feel the sadness and feel the disgust." Still, the musicians realized the benefits of performing this radical piece: "It's face to face in an age where we have very little contact with each other … this brings us together in a musical venue which makes it perhaps easier to talk about this" (Blair, E., NPR report, 1999).

It may be an indication of the distance we have to travel in this country that these recent attempts to revive Still's powerful composition on the subject of lynching echo the hopes expressed a half-century earlier by the philosopher and public intellectual, Alain Locke, in his review of the premier of Still's piece: "*And They Lynched Him on a Tree* gives our democracy in crisis just that much-needed heroic challenge and criticism." In so doing, he continues, "(it) universalizes its particular theme and expands a Negro tragedy into a purging and inspiring plea for justice and a fuller democracy." Here, Locke not only points to the effective fusion that can be achieved when music is given political content but also gestures to its lasting aesthetic value: "When on occasion, art rises to this level, it fuses truth with beauty, and in addition to being a sword for the times it is likely to remain a thing of beauty, a joy forever" (Locke, 1940, pp. 228-229).

References

Allen, W. F., Ware, C. P., & McKim-Garrison, L. (Eds.). (1996). *Slave Songs of the United States*. First Published in 1867. Bedford, MA: Applewood Books.

Anderson, M. (1967). *My Lord, What A Morning*. New York: Avon Books.

Arvey, V. (1984). *In One Lifetime. Fayetteville*. Fayetteville: University of Arkansas Press.

Blair, E. (1999, January 29). *National Public Radio report, Play Evokes Strong Emotions*. Retrieved March 15, 2021, from http://www.npr.org/templates/story/story.php?storyId=1050874

Botstein, L. (2009). *Revisiting William Grant Still. American Symphony Orchestra*. Retrieved January 19, 2021, from https://americansymphony.org/concert-notes/revisiting-william-grant-still_2/

Boyle, S. T., & Bunie, A. (2001). *Paul Robeson: The Years of Promise and Achievement*. Amherst: University of Massachusetts Press.

Brooks, S. T. (2004). *Lost Sounds: Blacks and the Birth of the Recording Industry, 1890- 1919*. Urbana and Chicago: University of Illinois Press.

Callam, K. A., Kimoto, M., Ohta, M., & Oja, C. T. (2019). Marian Anderson's 1953 concert tour of Japan. A traditional history. *American Music, 37*(3), 266–329.

Carmody, T. (2014). Missing Paul Robeson in East Berlin: the spirituals and the empty archive. *Cultural Critique, 88*, 1–27.

Dorinson, J., & Pencak, W. (Eds.). (2002). *Paul Robeson. Essays on His Life and Legacy*. Jefferson: McFarland & Company.

Douglass, F. (2019). *Autobiographies: Narrative of the Life of Frederick Douglass, an American Slave / My Bondage and My Freedom / Life and Times of Frederick Douglass*. Varna: Pretorian Book.

du Bois, W. E. B. (1989). *The Souls of Black Folk*. New York: Bantam Books.

Duberman, M. (1989). *Paul Robeson. A Biography*. New York and London: The New Press.

Egan, B. (2004). *Florence Mills: Harlem Jazz Queen*. Lanham: Scarecrow Press.

Freedman, R. (2004). *A Voice That Challenged a Nation: Marian Anderson*. Boston: Houghton Mifflin Harcourt.

Hughes, L. (1925). *I, too*. Retrieved February 1, 2021, from https://www.poetryfoundation.org/poems/47558/i-too

I Hear America Singing. (1940, July 8). *Time Magazine, 36*. http://content.time.com/time/magazine/article/0,9171,795064,00.html

Johnson, J. W., & Johnson, R. J. (1977). *Book of American Spirituals*. New York: Da Capo Press.

Jones, F., & Jones, A. C. (Eds.). (2001). *The Triumph of the Soul. Cultural and Psychological Aspects of African American Music*. Westport, CT, and London: Praeger.

Judge, J. (1917, December 29). Folk Song Festival Rare Musical Treat Pleases Large Audience. Old Negro Melodies Are Beautifully Sung. *Savannah Morning News*.

Keiler, A. (2000). *Marian Anderson. A Singer's Journey*. New York: Scribner.

Locke, A. (1940). Ballad for Democracy. *Opportunity: Journal of Negro Life, 18*(8), 228–229.

Molesworth, C. (Ed.). (2012). *The Works of Alain Locke*. New York: Oxford University Press.

Moody-Turner, S. (2013). *Black Folklore and the Politics of Racial Representation*. Jackson: University Press of Mississippi.

Oja, C. (2000). *Making Music Modern. New York in the 1920s*. New York: Oxford University Press.

Olwage, G. (2015). Listening b(l)ack: Paul Robeson after Hayes. *The Journal of Musicology, 32*(4), 524–557.

Paul Robeson's Chicago History. 1921–1958. (n.d.). http://www.cpsr.cs.uchicago.edu/robeson/links/chicago/chi_tim6.html. Retrieved February 1, 2021, from http://www.cpsr.cs.uchicago.edu/robeson/links/chicago/chi_tim6.html

Pencak, W. (1999). Paul Robeson and classical music. *Pennsylvania History: A Journal of Mid-Atlantic Studies, 66*(1), 83–93.

Protective Ass'n Concert Attracts About 700 Persons. Miss Anderson and Carl Diton Charm Audiences. (1918, January 5). *Savannah Tribune*.

Robeson Jr, P. (1993). *Paul Robeson, Jr. Speaks to America. The Politics of Multiculturalism*. New Brunswick: Rutgers University Press.

Shirley, W. D. (1994). William Grant Still's Choral Ballad And They Lynched Him on a Tree. *American Music, 12*(4), 425–461. https://doi.org/10.2307/3052342

Smith, C. P. (1997). 'Harlem Renaissance Man,' revisited: the politics of race and class in William Grant Still's late career. *American Music*, 381–406.

Smith, C. P. (Ed.). (2000). *William Grant Still. A Study in Contradictions*. Berkeley and Los Angeles: University of California Press. https://doi.org/10.1525/california/9780520215429.001.0001

Smith, C. P. (2008). *William Grant Still*. Urbana and Chicago: University of Illinois Press.

Song Festival To-Night. Prominent White People to Occupy Boxes. (1917, December 28). *Savannah Morning News*.

Spencer, M. (Ed.). (1992). *The William Grant Still Reader. Essays on American Music. A Special Issue of Black Sacred Music: A Journal of Theomusicology* (6th ed., Vol. 6). Duke University Press.

Stephens, J. (2011). Racial violence and representation: performance strategies in lynching dramas of the 1920's. *African American Review, 33*(4), 655–671.

Stewart, J. (Ed.). (1998). *Paul Robeson - Artist and Citizen*. New Brunswick: Rutgers University Press.

Still, J. A. (1990). *William Grant Still. A Voice High-Sounding*. Flagstaff: The Master- Player Library.

Zackery Jr., H. (2016). *A Reception History and Conductor's Guide to William Grant Still's... And They Lynched Him on a Tree*. [Unpublished doctoral dissertation]. University of Southern Mississippi. Retrieved January 26, 2021, from https://aquila.usm.edu/cgi/viewcontent.cgi?article=1332&context=dissertations

CHAPTER 3

"I Am More Than My Body!": Politicizing the *Female Masquerade* performance in the West Indian Carnival

Cherry-Ann M. Smart
Information Smart Consulting, Jamaica, W.I.

Abstract

Carnival masquerades and performances have been unusual but staple forms of political communication since its inception in Trinidad and Tobago circa 1783. Originally, the enslaved and disenfranchised used traditional characters such as the Pissenlit to mock colonial authorities while highlighting social conditions. In the 21st century, contemporary characters consisting of bead-and-bikini masqueraders showcased myriad inequities and stigmas embedded within social and political systems. In response, respective political authorities have attempted to sanction the masquerader, first by "sanitization" which resulted in the banishment of the Pissenlit, and second by the commodification of the female body. These systemic abuses of power have served to silence and/or hinder communication among specific groups, especially women. Through the lens of Merleau-Ponty's Phenomenology of Perception, this chapter explores the female masquerader as a subject/object of perception. Carnival studies have commonly followed the Bakhtinian model characterizing performances as resistance, however, carnival involves a multitude of meanings and is not limited to upheaval as mimicry could also imply communication efforts.

Keywords: Carnival, masqueraders, mimesis, perception, political messaging, Trinidad and Tobago

***

Introduction

The Covid-19 pandemic forced the cancellation of the Trinidad and Tobago 2021 Carnival (Constantin, 2020), for only the third time in its history since

French colonizers started the tradition in 1783. The festivity attracts thousands of visitors annually and generates billions of dollars for service industries in the domestic and international markets. Spin-off carnivals in the Diaspora, with some of the better-known events occurring in Miami, New York, Toronto, and London (Nurse, 1999; Schechner, 2004), entice revelers as well as scholars in areas such as anthropology, culture, music, and politics.

Brief murmurs of protest were reminiscent of early masqueraders to whom Carnival was a time to publicly express displeasure at some public ordinance or government ruling, and communicate through mimetism. Not unexpectedly, a small fraction challenged the government's order by seditiously staging and filming their own "J'ouvert" celebrations. J'ouvert or "start of day" traditionally signaled the beginning of the festivity held on the two days before Ash Wednesday, the beginning of the Christian season of Lent. At around 4:00 a.m. on Monday, a ragtag band of male performers outfitted in brand name street clothes beat steel-pans, blew trombones, knocked enamel chamber pots, and "chipped" (a dance-walk) through the still-dark streets. Their female counterparts, garbed as the traditional character, Dame Lorraine, were masqued in long, vividly colored dresses with overblown appendages attached to breasts and buttocks, "winin'" (a form of dancing which involves rotating the mid-section of the body in a rhythmic pattern) through the streets. Sadly, the controversial "pretty mas" (short for masquerade[r]) with the bikinis and bead-clad women who had become a staple in the contemporary carnival would have to await the passing of the Covid-19 pandemic to express themselves.

Carnival performances often hide multi-layered meanings and political implications (Kohl, 2018; Schechner, 2004). Although most authors see carnival as a medium of resistance and criticism per the Bakhtinian model, not all authors concur. For instance, Kohl (2018) argued the "abnormal behaviour, aberrant costumes, and mummery" (p. 130) in the Guinea-Bissau carnival provided opportunities for communication to the authorities under the guise of anonymity. Similarly, De Jong (2000) identified secret societies, such as the Komo in Mali and the Poro in Liberia who used the masquerade to communicate and connect with politicians.

Alternatively, some authors record different perceptions of the masquerade as licentious, free-form vulgarity and solipsism (Noel, 2009). This perception is often based on the objectification of the masquerader, and then narrowly focused on specific aspects of the character with limited information (Carman, 2008). For Merleau-Ponty, perception is essentially a *bodily* phenomenon; with the body being a person's point of view on their world (Carman, 2008). Even if the body is objectified by others, the individual must not follow, but instead, recognize a deep difference in principle between themselves and their environment (Carman, 2008).

In this chapter, the author attempts to (re)position the discourse on female masquerade performance in the carnival within the realm of political communication inquiry. Political communication (PC) is defined as "an interactive process concerning the transmission of information among politicians, the news media, and the public" (Norris, 2001, p. 11, 631). While not necessarily adversarial, PC is designed to move downwards, horizontally, and upwards. However, it is a form of communication that has been ineffective at best in post-colonial situations and has had limited success with women in the carnival without some form of friction. This breakdown is because authority figures use carnival as another way to appropriate the female body and so no reasonable dialogue can be "expressed within confining patriarchal parameters" (Katrak, 2006, p. xvii).

These boundaries accommodate the sometimes contradictory and unstable depictions about traditional and contemporary masqueraders, whose performances are categorized as either grotesque or exotic based on the viewer's perception. Two masquerades are used as exemplars: the pretty, exotic, and now heavily commodified bikini and bead masquerader, and the obscene, repulsive, and transgendered Pissenlit. Both are considered "jamette" mas, and by their depictions, send strong political messages to the ruling politicos. Their persistence at PC resulted in covert and overt sanctions, i.e., the banishment of the Pissenlit, and the continued commodification of the bikini and bead masquerader. Active patriarchal systems and their derivatives including governments (counting colonial authorities), institutions, the media, and academia purposely ignore the political messages inherent in these performances and instead attempt to (re)appropriate or interrupt these with political messages of their own. The thoughts of Merleau-Ponty is the philosophical lens applied to this study.

The author used an Afro-centric viewpoint to examine the literature to validate the contributions of people of African descent traditionally suppressed by Eurocentric cultural hegemony. The West Indian culture is historically distinct, even during colonialism, from Bakhtin's totalitarian world (Schechner, 2004). Although Carnival originated from medieval European practices, its appropriation by Afro-Trinidadians post-emancipation in 1833 developed into an "Afro-Euro-Caribbean-South-Asian-global" vision that "confounds Bakhtinian theory" (Schechner, 2004, p. 4).

In this study, the author used two primary sources of data: the extant literature and interviews from female masqueraders about their experiences as participants of the carnival. These voices support or counter perceptions and hypotheses found in this and other works. Throughout the study "masque" is sometimes used in place of "mask;" masquerade is sometimes shortened to "mas;" variations in spelling may occur because it is the specific spelling used by a particular author.

The first section of this chapter discusses Merleau-Ponty's phenomenology as it relates to perception and the body. The second section provides a brief history of the carnival and the traditional masques to contextualize the work and lay a foundation for later arguments about happenings in the carnival. This is followed by a presentation of early female representation of the masquerade, exploring some of the traditional characters who participated in the J'ouvert (*Canboulay*) celebrations, in addition to examining the characters portrayed by women, with a specific focus on the Pissenlit, a masquerade that was subsequently banned by the British but which this author contends, was important for its political messages to the ruling colonial government. The Pissenlit was also important to defend the African traditions in the carnival and concretize the use of Merleau-Ponty's philosophical viewpoint in the work. The next section explores the contemporary or pretty masquerade or what spectators commonly refer to as the pretty or "bikini and beads" masquerade.

Phenomenology and Maurice Merleau-Ponty

At the beginning of *The Phenomenology of Perception* (Marshall, 2008), Merleau-Ponty asks the question - *What is Phenomenology?*

French philosopher and intellectual, Maurice Merleau-Ponty (1908-1961), was known for his work on the way individuals perceive the world around them. He maintained that perception was not an isolated event or state within the body, but the organism's entire bodily relation to its surrounding environment (Carman, 2008). In his early years, Merleau-Ponty was associated with existentialism, which included philosophers such as Sartre and de Beauvoir. He was influenced in his thinking by Bergson, Husserl, Heidegger, Scheler, and neurologists such as Kurt Goldstein and others (Toadvine, 2019). In *Perception*, he encouraged a form of reflection that permitted the formation of new meaning and structure to a person's view of the environment and provided a fresh understanding of perception. Phenomenology is a dynamic philosophical movement (Jung & Embree, 2016). Much like the carnival featured here, phenomenology's strength lies in its ability to transform and recreate new ideas and viewpoints using past meanings. Bodily perspectives are also foundational to and inform areas in the humanities and social sciences. Therefore, the paradigm seemed appropriate to understand masqueraders' political communication and their engagement with political figures in this public performance space.

The Carnival

The Carnival in Trinidad and Tobago originated as a celebratory occasion among French settlers in the 18th century (Henry & Plaza, 2019). The French installation into Trinidad became possible under the Spanish *cedula de poblacion* in 1783, as they fled a politically uncertain France to be gifted "nearly 30 acres for themselves, plus half that again for each slave they brought with them" by the Spanish for resettling in the West Indies (Scher, 2007, p. 108). West Indian historians noted a merger of two parallel festivals: one imported from French Creole planters, and the other, an African Creole celebration post-1833-emancipation that culminated in the masque-wearing event enacted two days before Ash Wednesday (Riggio, 2004). While the French occupied the island, their slaves joined in the festivities, extracting joy from the absurd mummery of their masters. The British capture of the island in 1802 failed to stop the celebrations. By then, the slaves had more or less taken over the festivities; the format and presentations evolved and transformed to incorporate more African cultural traditions, customs, and art forms. The injection of these artifacts supported Irobi's (2007) rubbishing of Gilroy's claim in The Black Atlantic that indigenous African performance forms were "irrevocably sundered from their origins" during the middle passage (p. 896). Instead, Irobi successfully argued that during the journey, African artform was "transformed, syncretized, or creolized" (pp. 896-897) in performative practices such as the Carnival masquerade. He also disagreed with scholars who treated the Carnival as a "disjunctive artform," implying that the form of resistance resident in the performances emanated only from slavery conditions. Irobi again challenged this perspective, as he posited that, "the body has a memory and can be a site of resistance through performance" (p.901). If one is to interpret this argument correctly, it suggests that resistance resided within the African's DNA, so no journey across waters could dislodge it.

By the time abolition occurred in 1834, the African components were firmly embedded with the European elements and the event had morphed into celebrations of deliverance (Henry & Plaza, 2019). By then, the festivities looked even less like the Euro-Bakhtin type carnivals, as costumes either showcased or mocked the island's egregious social conditions. Role-reversal performance tradition was not an uncommon occurrence in African societies. Therefore its use by the French to play characters such as the Neg Jadin or "garden slave," where aristocrats pretended to be their servants (Besson, 2011), was not unusual. La Rose (2017) identified African art forms in the Trinidad and Tobago masquerades, which must have been retained during the middle passage. In *The City Could Burn Down, We Jammin' Still!* he described the "Djale mask of Ivory Coast, Gelede masquerade of southern Nigeria, the Owi masquerade of Ikole-Ekiti, Nigeria, and the Moko Jumbie stilt dancers" (p.492). The observation and parallelism supported Irobi's (2007) assertion of the retention of "performative literacies" by Africans exported to the New World, and Smart's (2019) proposition that African's mnemonic retentions were among the first libraries in the West Indies.

Besson (2011) indicated that de-masking was ordered by British Governor Robert W. Keate in 1858, the consequence of some of the many clashes masqueraders would have with the colonial superpower. East Indians arrived as indentured laborers in Trinidad and Tobago from 1845 to 1917 (Sankeralli, 1998). In that same year, spectators could see aspects of East Indian culture incorporated into the celebrations. The newbie East Indians were a conservative group, who confined their celebrations to the villages in central and south Trinidad where they played "music, danced, and performed little skits, leelas" (Sankeralli, 1998, p. 205). Their costumes were a fusion of African, East Indian, and New World culture, as they played characters such as *Red* or *Wild Indian* (Amerindian), *Fancy Indians*, and "coolie devils" masquerade (Hill, 1985). Meanwhile, the more gregarious Afro-Trinidadians continued to have political clashes with British colonial authorities who often resorted to subversive and active attempts to ban or control the festivities (La Rose, 2017). Jamettes played an active part in rebuffing the colonial authority, as they often "routed the colonial police" (La Rose, 2017, p.493) with perhaps loud charivari. Nourbese Philip (1997) drew attention to the term *jamette* and its role in the Trinidad carnival. The word was commonly used to describe prostitutes or loose women who emerged as a natural part of society's social classes and were popular figures when the U.S. soldiers were stationed on the island during World War II. When these working-class Black women self-objectified and protested the commodification of their bodies, the authorities vilified them for their lewd acts.

Ultimately, the masqueraders arrived at a compromise with the British who agreed to make no more attempts to ban the Carnival if the masqueraders would agree to a specific start and stop time. Between 1838 and 1884, the carnival moved from Sunday midnight to 6:00 a.m. Monday, starting with the *canboulay* procession. During slavery, this involved "burning of the sugar cane" and formed part of the festivities when the French occupied the island. Cane burning was abated once the East Indians began to work the sugar cane estates. After Emancipation, J'ouvert remained the ritual opening event of the carnival but featured stick fighters and other performers and performances instead.

Masqueraders were mainly male but consisted of some female parts, although the propensity for cross-dressing did not stifle the creation of female characters. Prominent male costumes were worn by performers such as the Midnight Robber, traditionally a black-clad, austere, and mysterious chap with a broad-brimmed hat, reminiscent of the American Wild West, spouting Shakespearean and biblical speeches called "Robber talk". Another masculine character, the vivid and gregarious, harlequin type, Pierrot Grenade, was considered a "deeply learned scholar," yet characterized as a jester, a clown, as he pranced and twirled his guava or hibiscus whip, delighting the crowd with his elocution and spelling ability. These aspects of the traditional masquerade have since metamorphosed to fit within capitalist models and so the gloomy Robber is now adorned with injections of color. Feminine roles, such as the Baby Doll masquerade involved a cross-dressing male holding the "bastard baby" (Scher, 2007). Jamette bands formed part of the French diameter and, according to Hill (1985), consisted of women who were "matadors" or retired prostitutes who had "gone respectable," and male counterparts who were jamette men or "sweet men".

The few Afro-creole female masqueraders were relegated to non-speaking or support roles. Some of these characters, which were depicted only by women, were Petite Belle Lily, the village sweetheart, who invited suitors while dressed in a queen's costume with ruffled collars; Mme Gros Tete, Mlle Jolle Rouge, Dame Lorraine, and the Pissenlit (Hill, 1985). Non-verbal roles meant the woman had no other choice but to use her body to communicate – her on-the-road theatrical performance was the only weapon she could use to protest, ridicule, engage in satire, or resist an ongoing oppressive system. Social historians placed women's involvement in the masquerade in the late 19th century. By that time, freed slaves were disenfranchised and so carnival became an organized protest against social conditions.

As carnival transitioned, the colonial government's attempts to sanitize the more risqué or vulgar characters depicted in the mas (Smart, 2006), seemed to mainly attack the female masqueraders, including the spectacular "dress up" or so-called jamette women (Franco, 2007). De Freitas (1999) described the jamettes as being exquisitely dressed:

> Beautiful dresses... skirts draped over embroidered, starched petticoats and caught up into their belts. On their heads ...headties over which were placed either hats decorated with flowers and feathers or men's fedoras decorated with croton leaves. Always masked, [their] most shocking behaviour was their habit of opening their bodices to expose their breasts. (p. 15)

Although women's help was eventually accepted to resist the elites, De Freitas (1999) noted their sexual behavior within the society was still suspect. Nevertheless, only one masquerade failed to survive the (R)evolution, the infamous and unsavory Pissenlit (wet-the-bed) or "stinker".

Early Female Representation in Traditional Masquerade

Pissenlit was derived from the French verb *pisser*, meaning to piss or urinate. Variations of the word were *pizali*, *pizane*, and *pisser du sang* which signified menstruation and suggested chief masquers were female. Franco (2000) described the character as jamette masquerade as it symbolized a form of protest by Afro-creole women of their place in society. Besson (2011) reported this J'ouvert mas was not only obscene, but was also smelly, although he maintained it was a role always played by males. However, Irobi (2007) contended that "symbolic gender reversals" (p. 904) were an iconic part of the carnival. According to Scher (2007), jamettes were often prostitutes who were rather aggressive, vocal, and fearless with alleged ties to Port-of-Spain's (the capital city) underworld. It is likely they enjoyed masquerading as Pissenlits, and relished islanders' propensity to use double entendre when speaking; while a translation of Pissenlit meant dandelion, it also meant "soiled flower" or "soiled dove" (Scher, 2007).

The portrayal was an opportunity to further aggravate the Establishment by exhibiting even more of the outrageous behavior that sorely offended the upper ruling classes. Since the female was silenced in the masquerade, any communication would have had to be conveyed in the performance. This perception conflicted with modern scholars who seemed to ascribe rebellious behavior only to contemporary players of pretty masquerade (Noel, 2009), albeit the Pissenlit more likely represented one of the earliest forms of female political messaging through masquerade. Its manifestation seemed similar to a behavior Alexandre (2006) called "body protest," and which she defined as "therapeutic goals of asserting dominance over one's body...expression of womanhood in revolt against a patriarchal society" (p.179). Body protesters used "dance, dressing, performance arts, etc....to highlight the societal restraints imposed on them" (p.179). More importantly, she pinpointed the reluctance of the legal system to protect body protests, thus leaving women at the mercy of stereotypes who deemed many of the liberating functions of the female body as immoral. Here, the term "womanhood" is an inclusive dictionary definition and means "consisting of womanly character or qualities".

However, the carnival is a master of symbolic inversion. Crowley (1997) described the Pissenlit as, "masked men...who unsexed themselves to enjoy the silly novelty of wrapping their big frames in a shapeless bundle of female apparel" (p. 196). Correspondingly, in *The Devil and the Bed-Wetter*, Scher (2007) described the character as one where, "a grown man sporting bed sheets or linens stained red in imitation of bloody menstrual rags or soiled with urine and mock feces, or, in other cases, seems merely to have been a cross-dressing man" (p. 112; see Figure 1). European criticism or fear of these early forms of cross-dressing of heterosexual African men are all the more perplexing given the debaucheries documented in colonial bourgeois society. Contrary to commonly held beliefs, Bullough and Bullough (1993) noted that before the 19th century, cross-dressing was not regarded as a sign that a person was gay or lesbian, but suggested instead it was normal human behavior that permitted persons to experience vicariously how the other gender lived. For some individuals, the act was one of sexual exploration. To support their hypothesis, Bullough and Bullough (1993) examined the act of cross-dressing in several cultures across the globe. Since this research embraced an Afro-centric view, it was interesting to note that among some African tribes, e.g., the Masai, Nandi, and Nuba in East Africa, boy initiates were often dressed as girls (Bullough & Bullough, 1993, p. 17). Crossdressing was also a form of subterfuge. Men of the Bangalan tribe in the Upper Congo who believed themselves troubled by an evil spirit or intent on fooling the devil disguised themselves as women to deceive or escape the malevolent spirit. In these cultures, where women were generally considered as unimportant, dressing up as women guaranteed that the spirits bypassed the men while in drag. The authors also noted that when threats of natural disaster loomed, such as drought, Zulu men dressed in female girdles, as they believed a change in their outward appearance might cause rain. Sometimes, girls and unmarried women dressed in their brothers' clothes and herd cattle for a day to encourage rain. Additionally, when a favorable, speedy outcome for a particular goal was required, men would adorn themselves in women's clothing and pray to the gods. These practices demonstrate the redemptive power of the female body.

The character of the Pissenlit was also interesting because of the interpretation given to the performance – that of resistance, disobedience, incivility, and rage. In the West Indies, the character was an important symbol that can benefit from hindsight, new knowledge, and information since Pissenlit's performance could also be perceived as a complex reaction to a situation that required a more profound attempt at communication.

Murray's (1998) hypothesis seemed an appropriate fit here as he argued that the transgenderfication of Carnival characters, was "dependent on a nexus of particular historical, cultural and gendered forces which do not align to form a singular socio-cultural paradigm but rather exist in a shifting relationship dependent upon speaker and context" (p. 343).

In Baldwin's (2003) introduction of Merleau-Ponty's first book, *The Structure of Behavior* (1942), he explained that human behavior "can be understood only within a distinctive `existential' context that situates the subject...in its world and identifies the structures of its behavior in the light of the subject's `body', its bodily way of making sense of its world" (p. 2). Much of what has been written about the character of the Pissenlit has presumed only a disruptive stance of resistance, given the context of time, place, and space. This interpretation has therefore been concocted and interpreted within the same unwavering patriarchal context. Interestingly, none of the researches on this character has provided an appreciation of the masquerade from an Afro-centric viewpoint. Would Pissenlit still be banned had it been translocated to the African space? What we do know is that the masquerade was eventually banished by a public ordinance in 1895 following a protest by the upper class (Scher, 2007). The disappearance of these and other historical elements was symbolic of the government's sanitation practice of what they deemed undesirable or of little value in the Carnival (Scher, 2007). The unilateral decision taken by a small segment of privileged and powerful people on behalf of the rest of society, is symptomatic of the failure of the political communication process as it relates to the protection of the unprotected, the vulnerable, the marginalized, and Caribbean women. The disappearance of the masquerade was also a potent factor in highlighting the chasm in worldviews between the plantocracy and Afro-creole masqueraders.

Figure 1.1: Trinidad Pissenlit

Photo credit: Kurt Smith

Carman (2008) wrote in Merleau-Ponty's phenomenon of *insight* – the "Aha experience,... (when) seeing is not a product of reflection, but a flash of perceptual recognition; moreover, once you see them, it's virtually impossible not to see them" (p. 113). Given the overall theme of this book, political messaging in music and entertainment, the character of Pissenlit warranted a peripeteia. It is bemusing that a character who materialized for two days out of a 365-day yearly cycle so irked the politico, that it was not only banished, but every image that suggested its existence was erased from the annals. What egregious message was sent via the performance of this character that warranted its annexation from the history books? This is especially in light of the subsequent appearance of more egregious, divisive, and racist masquerades that have offended entire ethnic groups, without receiving such a strong and permanent backlash. In Parks (2019) examination of former President Trump's political communication style, using the Bakhtinian concept, a pattern not unlike the tactics of the Pissenlit emerged. Yet, the behavior culminated in his successful 2016 U.S. presidential election. Correspondingly, the notorious Blackface, which had been a historical staple of White America's performance tradition for centuries has been performed by notable people (actors, politicians, etc.) of both genders. The racist and offensive caricature remained active despite the heavy involvement in the "peaceful" civil rights movement in the USA. Interestingly, in Uruguay, "blackface performers opened the door for the acceptability of *candombe* (style of music and dance that originated in Uruguay among freed slaves) in Carnival" (Sztainbok, 2013, p. 595), and further supports Murray's (1998) premise about socio-cultural context, shifting relationship, and perception.

It is suggested that the perception of the unsavory aspects of the cross-dressing feature of the Pissenlit was too uncomfortable for the ruling class, given the positioning of the Black male in society. Perhaps the masquerade proved too high a risk for the commodification of a stock acquired primarily for reproductive purposes, and so there was a perception of contamination to the gene pool. Stallybrass and White (1986) submitted, the British upper-class banning of the Pissenlit as grotesque suggested that what was "socially peripheral" to that class was in fact "symbolically central" to its formation (p. 5).

Despite the grotesque description of the Pissenlit, it was an important character in the suite of masquerades in the carnival. While there were diverse views about the gender of individuals who masqueraded as Pissenlit, Irobi's (2007) claim about the double-face template of carnival seems legitimate. Merleau-Ponty's teaching on perception also contributed to this view as did the extant literature on cross-dressing and menstruation in global societies.

In a post-Independence study conducted on traditional Ghanaian culture, Oppong (1966) found many restrictions and taboos commonly associated with menstruation. Most of the customs associated with a menstruant woman appeared to follow notions of impurity or uncleanliness as found in the teachings of Leviticus and entailed restriction of social and domestic activities. The supernatural was a key concept for Ghanaians who believed that "water or cloth which has been in contact with menstrual blood can be used to destroy supernatural influences and to cause harm. Simultaneously, the menstruating woman is thought to have special powers so that no ghost, bad medicines or witchcraft can harm her" (Fields, 1948; as cited in Oppong, 1966, p. 36). It was also thought that an unclean woman's proximity to ancestral items could prove harmful to men and so they were best to be avoided (Oppong, 1966). Padmanabhanunni et al.'s (2018) research on the ama-Xhosa cultural group of South Africa confirmed similar findings as Oppong's research conducted more than 40 years earlier. Menstruation was celebrated as a sign of fertility while it also "heightened self-consciousness and shame" (p. 711) when the condition was exposed, although women did their best to hide its occurrence. Kasenko's (2019) study of menstruation in British and American societies found similar reactions as found on the African continent. In addition to its ritualistic uncleanliness, women's monthly bleeding "exhibits the sex divide and conditions women's otherness" (p.147). Menstruation was considered a symptom of female inferiority and defectiveness (p.148). Menstruation was also perceived as a punishment for Eve's sin and treated as a disease, which was also attributed to femininity. Another researcher, Lister (2018), noted that in nineteenth-century Britain, insanity was linked to menstruation and this lack of understanding also positioned women as "the Other" – a marginalized group potentially prone to insanity and instability. This period of Enlightenment, i.e., the early modern period -16th to 19th century - was critical as it not only represented the period under the view of this masquerade but also informed the mindset of colonial controllers. Other researchers suggested that the curse upon women was indispensable as a part of their nature; paradoxically, they represented bodies requiring protection to maintain the power balance. Finally, an early study by Skultans (1970), of low-income women in south Wales found the loss of menstrual blood reaffirmed a woman's acceptance of her social role and also her femininity. Skultans applied a clever intransitive interpretation to women's use of "to lose blood" which resulted in this translation "the importance of coming to terms with their role as `losers' – with little or no control of their body" (p. 640).

Given the perception of menstruation and male in most societies, it would have been interesting to understand why Afro-creole freedmen chose to participate in this particular, minor masquerade. For female masquerades, it was hypothesized, that the depiction could have been communicating their underpowered membership in society; it could have been communicating hopelessness, loss of control over their body – especially as prostitutes – at the mercy of pimps, and police – castoffs. However, if men's participation in this minor role is perceived from the Afro-centric perspective then Pissenlit was an empowering masquerade, communicating a powerful political message to colonial authorities.

The preceding literature makes for an interesting conversation from the perspective that it is perhaps a common interpretation about the Pissenlit masquerade. First, the character was only portrayed by male players and that the depiction was merely a taunt or irritant to colonial powers. Part of this premise was the dichotomy between the African and the European perception of cross-dressing, and the perception of these masqueraders' notion of menstruation in this public space.

Franco (2007) argued that women masqueraders challenged the Black masculinist projection to the nation despite critics' belief that the trend degraded the carnival. The reference was made concerning the nubile, energetic, and independent performers who would appropriate the carnival space as neoliberalism replaced colonialism. This contemporary set of masqueraders would also be referred to as jamettes. Their performance also drew the ire of state officials and respectable society although implicit in these responses would be an element of hypocrisy - their young, scantily dressed bodies drew comments of disapproval "while at the same time satisfied voyeuristic inclinations" (Bentor, 2008, p. 39).

Over the last 50 years or so, the festival has gained widespread recognition due in large part to the masquerades and masqueraders, and images of euphoria on the faces of participants in some incredible postures plastered across social media, billboards, and magazines (Kerrigan, 2018). Feminists and social scientists have gendered the masquerade, highlighting the empowering roles of participants, the exotification, and devilment in the performances. The government has managed to commodify the performances, proclaiming it "The Greatest Show on Earth!" Academics have appropriated aspects of the performance, published and survived, and feminists have thrived on the ability to juxtapose theory with life. In the midst of all this (mis)appropriation, the masqueraders thrive.

The next section looks at the contemporary masquerader – the pretty masquerade.

The Carnival Body – The Masquerader

The body of the Carnival female masquerader is important because the spectators' attention is focused on meanings assigned to physical appearance. Since the Carnival performance is conducted in a public space, the female body is open to valuation, scrutiny, objectification, deification, vilification, and so on. Cremona (2016) noted that Carnival costumes are designed to attract looks either because of their oddity or their beauty. She maintained further, "…the wearer is already in a state of heightened consciousness as to the amount of attention s/he manages to gather through the quality or originality of the costume worn" (pp. 79-80). To achieve this goal, therefore, the masquerader solicits the cooperation of the masquerade maker or designer. In their ethnographic research to understand the contemporary costuming, Copeland and Hodges (2014) learned, costume designers saw their role as simply satisfying customer demands: "For John, Carnival is a business…it is masqueraders who are doing the most to drive changes in masquerade styles…what the masquerader wants to look like ultimately determines what Carnival looks like" (p.193). As a symbol of national identity, it seems unlikely that such a powerful politically charged event will be placed in the hands of masqueraders.

The pretty mas became centripetal to the Trinidad and Tobago carnival from the late 1980s and early 1990s (Kerrigan, 2018). Aching (2010) noted that increased female participation in the carnival was attributed to women's financial independence outside the home. Perkins (2011) concurred, suggesting also growth in social power. Globalization and the growth of diasporic carnival competitions also contributed to this new trend of customer satisfaction. Academics lapped up this new direction appropriating the gender space with conversations about "racial formations, sexuality, the crisis of male identity, and national definitions of morality" (Aching, 2010, p. 420). Female masqueraders reveled in the newfound liberations with various winin' parodies, "misbehaving" and "getting on bad," especially when in the focus of the media lenses. De Freitas (1999) suggested some of this behavior challenged the patriarchal structure. However, winin' was not outlawed as was the ill-fated Pissenlit despite its association with the jamette and other disreputable figures in colonial society (Noel, 2010). Yet, this attention-seeking agenda was not always within the control of the masquerader and required the cooperation of external but connected agencies. Barratt (2017), for example, argued that female masqueraders' representation on social media in the Jamaica carnival was often controlled by photographers, and the press (Kerrigan, 2018). Her curiosity was sparked through observation that many of the Carnival photos posted online would feature mainly women who were "young, light-skinned, with long, curly, or straight hair…slim and outfitted in the skimpier costumes" (p. 186), while "older, dark-skinned, with afro-kinky natural hair or locs were noticeably absent" (p.186). Kerrigan (2018) also commented on the disparity between the lighter hues shown on billboard advertisements about the carnival, and the "phenotypically dark-skinned and black bodies of everyday life" (p. 262).

Power is now exercised through the technologies, such as the various social media platforms, as they supersede the authority of state agencies by (re)appropriating the female masquerader within the neoliberal market. This continuous overt or covert commodification of the Afro-Caribbean female still has its roots shackled in slavery. Despite colonization, decolonization, independence, and for some republicanism, in the 21st century, color bars are often reinforced by institutions, including cultural organizations. Mohammed (2000) blamed male performers of Jamaican popular music, to whom "the browning (light-skinned Afro-Jamaican) still emerges as a prize for the black man" (p. 36).

Of course, some masqueraders defied the obstacle of the color bar and were clever enough to play to racial stereotypes. Former Uruguayan vedette Rosa Luna was one such individual. Sztainbok (2013) wrote this about her, "not a dainty, delicate femininity...potentially threatening and formidable...exaggeration of black feminity" (p. 596). Her unorthodox appearance was contradictory - her sexuality with her maternity. Yet, Sztainbok (2013) referenced Rosa's alluring and powerful performance which was embraced because it disturbed the symbolic order. This power in the performance was a paradox. Cremona (2016) mentioned masqueraders pushing their performance through "hyperbolic action" in the Maltese carnival (p. 80), tangential to what Irobi (2007) referred to as irreverent activities in the African masquerade.

It was this irreverence that sold the carnival. Contemporary masqueraders, proponents of the pretty mas, sanctioned for their lewdness or ability to "get on bad," – expressing self and resisting authority – thus, becoming the new "vagabonds" of carnival not with "dirty mas" of mud and whips but "with glitter, glamour, partial nudity, bikini costumes" (Franco, 2007, p. 44). The female masquerader bought into this commodification, performed for the camera, reveled in the more playful side of the performance, "clowning, ribaldry, irreverent activities, raising the leg... (all things that make)...sexual liberation and catharsis possible" (Irobi, 2007, p. 904). Each complaint resulted in more intensified performances the following year, and each year male participation was "largely erased from media representations by eyes and lens that are focussed on the spectacle of the women performing" (Perkins, 2011, p. 369).

Kerrignan (2016) unapologetically stated, "'Pretty mas' is based upon capitalism – profit, mass production, luxury – and it replaced the high art aesthetic contained in the theatre of the streets Trinidad Carnival was once described to be" (p. 261). Therefore, Scher's (2007) earlier prediction was confirmed. As the carnival expanded as a consequence of commodification of cultural performances, it included the sale of "exotic products," as governments engaged in the commodification of the culture in the neoliberal tourist markets (Green, 2002, 2007).

Aching (2010) exposed the duplicity of politics and social organizations. On one hand, government-funded ministries lectured on diversity, social empowerment, and equality, while another ministry commodified these female revelers, "carefully screening images… to advertise the festival" (Aching, 2010, p.423); commodifying the winin' thus positioning Trinidad and Tobago as a pleasurable tourist destination. Kerringan (2016) too, called out the duplicity in these political messages as the once nationalistic festival segues into a "public performance of social status and wealth" (p. 261).

Yet, the state was not the only appropriator of the carnival masquerader. This public space invited dialogues, conversations, conferences, and scholarly papers from feminists, gender specialists, social researchers, economists, church officials, and so on. Their rhetoric and elocution were reminiscent of the *Midnight Robber* as they analyzed and theorized to rationalize the behavior of the pretty masquerader. In this way, the carnival body became the communal body belonging to the masses and no longer to themselves (Burkitt, 1999). Although masquerade producers boasted sold-out bands, Marshall (2018) cited complaints about "too many bikinis and too much flesh" (p. 16). However, gender specialists such as Hosein (2008) countered as she rebuffed these criticisms arguing women merely sought autonomy and self-determination around their sexuality and bodies. Correspondingly, Perkins (2011) suggested that women were re-evaluating their bodies and so its perceived function as a childbearing machine shifted to realize their concept of femininity, self-fulfilment, and self-actualization.

Bentor (2008) reminded us that each constituency has a different historical memory and lived experience of the carnival. In its current mode, masqueraders in the festival required a delicate balance of the interests of different constituents – traditional mas players, the government, and its agencies such as national security, religious institutions, women's organizations, masquerade bands, ethnic/activist group organizations, businesses, and communities, and academics. Merleau-Ponty would argue that the masquerader had a different memory, the embodiment of her lived experience for which she would require meaning.

Perception in the Carnival Body

Masquerading does not require the possession of any particular skill or talent and is a socially inclusive activity. Playing mas is however a physically taxing activity as it requires long periods of standing, chipping, dancing, even if winin' and gyration are kept at a minimum. Franco (2007) confirmed the preparation leading up to the carnival, with some masqueraders rehearsing dance choreographies to improve their performance. Kerrigan (2018) noted the contemporary carnival body fit easily into the "Western mediascape alongside the MTV booty video aesthetic" (p. 261). This image was in sharp contrast to the "Black female body…the site of violence, ownership, and reproduction"

(Marshall, 2018, p. 17). Alexandre (2006) argued that sexual profiling only served to marginalize women. She defined the activity as "assumptions made regarding women who express themselves through their bodies" (p.178). Her arguments bordered on social stereotypes and stakeholders' perception that neglected to "embrace the female body as a tool for redemption and liberation" (p.178). De Freitas (1999) noted, however, that carnival afforded the woman to be herself, especially as it related to her sexuality and body.

Alexandre (2006) noted a woman's worth and social acceptance were closely annexed to the way she chose to present herself. In the carnival masquerade, body image and costume fit constituted that outer shield and act as façade to a hospitable or unfriendly arena. Franco (1998) pointed out earlier that dressing up was a way for women to be visible "as agents and producers in meaning in their performances" (p. 62), without drama.

Cremona (2016) confirmed the importance of costume selection in Maltese carnival. The right type provided access to potential connections between social stratification based on the quality and subject of the costume itself; "as such, the act of wearing a costume can in itself assume a political or social dimension" (p. 80). Kerrigan (2018) alluded to the all-exclusiveness of the all-inclusive fetes which marginalized a significant number of the population who were unable to pay for access. The choice of bands and sections was also an understandably political, as well as a social move since carnival is itself a highly social affair. The opportunity to be seen, or to connect with, be photographed with, and share a stage with, well-known public figures was a social coupe for many young women. Here is a case in point, in 2015, the incumbent prime minister of Trinidad and Tobago, Keith Rowley then 65, was photographed winin' or wined upon by a 17-year-old masquerader. The photographs created a week-long media frenzy that culminated in multiple comments in traditional and social media surrounding, his fitness for office, election hopes, race (the young lady was Indo-Trinidadian) and ethnicity, sex and marital relations, even the young lady's winin' skills, and so on (Mendes-Franco, 2015). The lack of privacy, despite masking, and the appropriation by spectators and uninterested parties to the carnality of the carnival but who felt obligated to comment, highlighted the thorny terrain of political communication within carnival. This very public space is therefore perceived with some skepticism by masqueraders, especially professional women, and this perception informed their choice of costume and behavior during the carnival.

Using short extracts for an unpublished ethnographic study, I incorporated some responses from participants. Pseudonyms were provided for anonymity and to maintain confidentiality. For Afeisha, a young college-educated professional, the choice of costume entailed finding a design that supported the body and cost. Her choice was also informed by her perception of other masqueraders:

> When choosing a costume I tend to stay away from costumes that look like the masquerader is wearing dental floss. I gravitate towards high-waisted costumes and bras that support heavier chests. Once I have a few options I tend to go to the cheaper option to save some coins. (personal communication, July 29, 2020)

Jennifer, another young, educated, college professional had similar standards although, her perception of the costume was based on her perception of self:

> In terms of costume selection, I am always looking for the design that will support my chest and not make me look 25 years older because I'm a tad more covered up. A lot of costume designers and bands always market towards people with small chests and I honestly hate that. Then they have one section that is "plus-size friendly". What happens to girls who are in the middle? Not skinny but not plus-sized. (personal communication, July 29, 2020)

For Doraine, a young mother of two who was employed in the legal field, the selection was a simple matter:

> I selected my costume based on coverage of body parts, design, and make. (personal communication, July 30, 2020)

In their ethnographic study, Copeland and Hodges (2014) found little connection with modern-day masqueraders and the historical origins of the masquerade. The carnival for most young people was now a rather pricey, exclusive opportunity to socialize in a safe environment, and bond with friends. If feelings of joy were a fair return for the investment, then bandleaders would have satisfied the contract. For Dana, a young New Yorker whose parents were both from the islands:

> Playing mas is a euphoric feeling. No matter how much stress you go through before you touch that road, nothing feels better than chipping with your feathers, make-up, and crew. It almost feels indescribable the amount of joy you feel. The feeling continues to elevate as you hear the songs that you loved for the carnival season. (personal communication, August 4, 2020)

Kerrigan (2018) highlighted the shift in the manufacture of carnival costumes from the domestic market to China. The rationale provided was to reduce cost, increase efficiency, and mass production. Additionally, so many of the accessories, such as beads and colored feathers were already imported from China, so it made good business sense to have everything done in that country. Outsourcing, of course, strengthened the government's relations with China, along with international trade. The downside to this arrangement and one interviewee in Copeland and Hodges (2014) mentioned this, was the loss of local skills in mass production. They also observed the similarity of the costumes to the Brazilian models which seem to be indicative of the neoliberalist opportunities and downsides of globalization.

As Cremona (2016) noted, "Carnival is the situation par excellence of practices placed under the sign of excess" (p. 90). As it related to women in the Trinidad and Tobago carnival, De Freitas (1999) raised the winin' phenomenon and women's tendency to wine on *anything*. This behavior brought women's role in society under question and further questions about what constituted "appropriate female behaviour, the male-female relationship, the construction of womanhood, and ultimately, about women's role in the nation and the representation of the national Self" (p.26). Alexandre (2006) noted some polemical interactions in the engagement between feminists and sex workers. She suggested these women hid their occupation in fear of harsh judgment from feminists. Accordingly, she suggested a re-evaluation of exclusionary categories with clearer instructions that did not marginalize certain categories of women.

As it related to lived experiences of the body and Merleau-Ponty, authors such as Coy (2009) have successfully used phenomenology to explore the concept of how the body was constituted by embodied experiences. In the case of prostitutes, where sexual experiences were negative, it was important to understand how these women viewed their actions as they related to themselves and their choices.

Women in post-colonial countries such as Trinidad and Tobago may collectively relate to a lived embodiment within a patriarchal society. However, for masqueraders, individual experiences may depend on the signals they receive leading up to, during, and after the performance. For instance, how their bodies are appropriated by others, and how they felt during the process. When women became cognizant of the objectification of their bodies, they were forced to see themselves as objects. This (dis)embodiment may be handled in different ways, with either the woman feeling empowered or violated. Alexandre (2006) posited sexual profiling was cogent here as the behavior did put the woman at risk of marginalization. What was particularly profound with her work thus far was an acknowledgment of the need for reform including an increase of women's rights in the judicial system but also for fuller engagement among women's groups.

Political Messaging in the Masquerade

Music is a powerful influencer in the Caribbean psyche, and critical in the development of political and social leaders (Clarke & Charles, 2012). Caribbean music is always associated with liming, a national pastime of powerful social and political networking which some posit was a form of resistance to the Protestant work ethics (Clarke & Charles, 2012). Onyebadi (2018) verified the importance and strength of music in societies, especially when it was used to embed subliminal messages, such as political messages into the lyrics. To this end, Marshall (2018), reminds of the carnival's resistance to political engagement and hierarchical power structures, although race and skin tone continues to be an unshakeable blue devil to Caribbean harmony.

The relationship between the state and Carnival has constantly been shaped by the global economy. First, colonialization provided Afro-Trinidadians with a limited agency to withstand the effects of the colonial ideology. This resulted in repressive rules that impacted the political discourse, couched as it was within local structures of power (Scher, 2011). Later, the discovery of oil and other natural resources propelled the seated political player into greater negotiating powers as more subtle tactics of control and power came in the form of prizes and incentives for reformation (Scher, 2007).

Hinds (2019) categorized Trinidad and Tobago as an intriguing case as it related to its political culture. The key dynamic about the government of this multi-ethnic society was a reluctance to engage with civil society, which ultimately influenced national politics. This unwillingness to engage has led to several insurrections and multiple strikes that have adversely impacted the country's productivity. It is, however, a model of governance, inherited from the British, to which many Caribbean development thinkers accredit the blame (Best, 2001).

Cohen (1974) in Manning (1990) described the carnival as a two-dimensional public drama, a performance in which cultural and political meanings acted upon each other in mutually influential ways. Key changes in the society since its rediscovery by Columbus, appropriation by Spain, France, Britain, and the import of what was still undeniably the biggest illegal trafficking of human beings from the African continent resulted in a festivity that has operated for more than 200 years, and now considered a national cultural event.

Three distinct yet inter-related areas of art expressions connect the carnival – the steelpan, the calypso, and the masquerade. It was the latter performance, specifically the female masquerader that constituted the focus of this study. Of importance were the changes in policies by state officials and other important stakeholders, how these were communicated, and how these women and other stakeholders responded. Ultimately, women's placement in Trinidad and

Tobago's patriarchal-structured society suffered the brunt of any political sanctions. For less-desirable traditional masquerades, the disappearance of the Pissenlit coincided with the 70 years dedicated to Carnival reform starting from circa1880 (Scher, 2007).

While all the works acknowledged African participation, and some mention the geographic origin of some standards and masques used in the masquerade, none seem to spotlight the individual masquerader themselves to ascertain whether the portrayal was more ritualistic than resistant; communicative rather than confrontational; more performative instead of full immersion into the licentious Carnival spirit. In 1 Corinthians 2:11 of the Bible, Paul wrote, *For what man knoweth the things of a man, save the spirit of man which is in him?* While much has been written about traditional masqueraders and the masquerade the empirical evidence is light in support of an individual's choice to play a particular character. Did men make a choice, was it an unconscious selection or was it perhaps with some ritualistic intent so that the witchcraft or voodoo would bring about a change in their circumstances? These questions demonstrate the importance of phenomenological research and consciousness to expand the mind and improve the human condition.

Colonial officers bowed to the pressures of the elite (Besson, 2011), but did not acquiesce to their call to ban the festivities altogether (Alonso, 1990). Similarly, the government has not objected to societal and other special interest groups' authority to impose sanctions and advocate against women's licentious behavior in the contemporary carnival; citing democracy. However, Rohlehr (1999) maintained that morality, respectability, and decency, as defined by an entrenched elite, always sought to banish carnival's laughter.

Additionally, the continued decontextualization and misappropriation of female masqueraders (including as a commercialized cultural product) act as a barrier to the political messages inherent in their performance. The aesthetics of the performance is integral to the message which, if perceived from an Afro-centric viewpoint, incorporates multiple meanings. Women used their body to inform about social and economic conditions. True, some messages were framed in exaggerated and sensationalized performances to infer particular interpretations, but not all messages, like political communication, were truthful. Alas, this framing was often so subtle that politicians remain fairly delphic of the manipulation. After all, there is no carnival without the female body!

Conclusion

In this study, I attempted to (re)position the conversation on female masquerade performance in the carnival within the realm of political communication inquiry. Two key masquerade characters were used to demonstrate how respective government sanctions affected Carnival masqueraders, the Pissenlit and the bikini and bead masqueraders. The concept of masquerade being used as a form of political communication is not novel as Kohl (2018) identified a similar model of masking and discourse among the inhabitants of Guinea-Bissau, West Africa.

Merleau-Ponty's phenomenology was instructive as a perspective to experience and apply a new understanding of the meaning and perception of the body as subject and object. It facilitated the Afro-centric view taken in the research, as carnival performances were situated as multi-dimensional characteristics of rituals and practices that are not wholly European. Accordingly, the expressions and interpretations may not necessarily hold to the predominant Bakhtinian theory of carnival solely as a form of resistance, as found in the literature. The mimetic potential of the masquerade as political communication is a significant premise, especially since this communication continues to be manipulative or sufficiently ambiguous by the state and other agencies of authority

References

Aching, G. (2010). Carnival time versus modern social life: A false distinction. *Social Identities*, *16*(4), 415–425.

Alexandre, M. (2006). Dance halls, masquerades, body protest and the law: The female body as a redemptive tool against Trinidad's gender-biased laws. *Duke J. Gender L. & Pol'y*, *13*, 177–202.

Alonso, A. M. (1990). Men in 'rags' and the devil on the throne: A study of protest and inversion in the carnival of post-emancipation Trinidad. *Plantation Society in the Americas*, *3*(1), 73–120.

Baldwin, T. (Ed.) (2003). *Maurice Merleau-Ponty: Basic writings*. Routledge.

Barratt, K. (2017). Out of many, one people? Representations of female masqueraders in the Jamaica carnival on facebook. *Memorias: Revista Digital de Historia y Arqueología Desde El Caribe*, *32*, 178–199.

Bentor, E. (2008). Masquerade politics in contemporary southeastern Nigeria. *African Arts*, *41*(4), 32–43.

Besson, G. A. (2011, August 22). *The Caribbean history archives*. http://caribbean historyarchives.blogspot.com/2011/08/19th-century-carnival.html

Best, L. (2001, March). *Race, class and ethnicity: A Caribbean interpretation*. Third Annual Jagan Lecture York University, Toronto, Canada. https://cerlac.info.yorku.ca/files/2016/08/Best.pdf

Bullough, V. L., & Bullough, B. L. (1993). *Cross dressing, sex, and gender*. University of Pennsylvania Press.

Burkitt, I. (1999). *Bodies of thought: Embodiment, identity and modernity*. Sage.

Carman, T. (2008). *Merleau-Ponty* (Chapter 3, pp. 76–127). Routledge.

Clarke, R., & Charles, R. N. (2012). Caribbean liming: A metaphor for building social capital. *International Journal of Cross Cultural Management*, *12*(3), 299–313.

Constantin, A. (2020, October 31). *Carnival will not take place next year in Trinidad and Tobago.* https://mylenecolmar.com/carnival-will-not-take-place-next-year-in-trinidad-and-tobago/

Copeland, R., & Hodges, N. (2014). Exploring masquerade dress at Trinidad carnival: Bikinis, beads, and feathers and the emergence of the popular pretty mas. *Clothing and Textiles Research Journal, 32*(3), 186–201.

Coy, M. (2009). This body which is not mine. *Feminist Theory, 10*(1), 61–75. https://doi.org/10.1177/1464700108100392

Cremona, V. A. (2016). Costume in carnival: Social performance, rank and status. *Studies in Costume & Performance, 1*(1), 77–96.

Crowley, J. (1997). *Carnival, canboulay and calypso: Traditions in the making.* Cambridge University Press.

de Freitas, P. A. (1999). Disrupting the nation: Gender transformations in the Trinidad Carnival. *New West Indian Guide/Nieuwe West-Indische Gids, 73*(1–2), 5–34.

de Jong, F. (2000). Secrecy and the state: The Kankurang masquerade in Senegal. *Mande Studies,* 153–173.

Franco, P. R. (1998). Dressing up and looking good: Afro-creole female maskers in Trinidad Carnival. *African Arts, 31,* 62–69.

Franco, P. R. (2000). The 'unruly woman' in nineteenth-century Trinidad carnival. *Small Axe, 7,* 60–76.

Franco, P. R. (2007). The invention of traditional mas and the politics of gender. In G. Green & P. Scher (Eds.), *Trinidad carnival: The cultural politics of a transnational festival* (pp. 25–47). Indiana University Press.

Green, G. L. (2002). Marketing the nation: Carnival and tourism in Trinidad and Tobago. *Critique of Anthropology, 22*(3), 283–304.

Green, G. L. (2007). "Come to life": Authenticity, value, and the carnival as cultural commodity in Trinidad and Tobago. *Identities: Global Studies in Culture and Power, 14*(1–2), 203–224.

Henry, F., & Plaza, D. (Eds.). (2019). *Carnival is woman: Feminism and performance in Caribbean mas.* University Press of Mississippi.

Hill, E. (1985). Traditional figures in carnival: Their preservation, development and interpretation. *Caribbean Quarterly, 31*(2), 14–34.

Hinds, K. (2019). *Civil society organisations, governance and the Caribbean community.* Springer.

Hosein, G. J. (2008). Love for mas: State authority and carnival development in San Fernando, Trinidad. *Journal of Eastern Caribbean Studies, 33*(1), 31–53.

Irobi, E. (2007). What they came with: Carnival and the persistence of African performance aesthetics in the diaspora. *Journal of Black Studies, 37*(6), 896–913.

Jung, H. Y., & Embree, L. (Eds.). (2016). *Political phenomenology: Essays in memory of Petee Jung* (Vol. 84). Springer.

Kasenko, J. (2019). Tracing menstruation in British and American culture: Strategies of invisibilization, stigmatization, and a question of im-purity in historical and cultural context. *New Horizons in English Studies, 4*(1), 144–157.

Katrak, K. H. (2006). *The politics of the female body: Postcolonial women writers.* Rutgers University Press.

Kerrigan, D. (2018). 'Who ent dead, badly wounded': The everyday life of pretty and grotesque bodies in urban Trinidad. *International Journal of Cultural Studies, 21*(3), 257–276. https://doi.org/10.1177/1367877916674740

Kohl, C. (2018). The colonial state and carnival: The complexity and ambiguity of carnival in Guinea-Bissau, West Africa. *Social Analysis,* 126–149. https://doi.org/10.3167/sa.2018.620206

La Rose, M. (2017). The city could burn down, we jammin' still! The history and tradition of cultural resistance in the art, music, masquerade and politics of the Caribbean carnival. *Caribbean Quarterly, 65*(4), 491–512.

Lister, K. (2018). *The Victorian period: When menstruation was a dangerous disease that could lead to madness.* https://inews.co.uk/opinion/columnists/victorian-period-menstruation-nineteenth-century-130987

Manning, F. E. (1990). Overseas Caribbean carnivals: The art and politics of a transnational celebration. *Plantation Society in the Americas,* 47–62.

Marshall, E. J. Z. (2018, October 1). *It's not all sequins and bikinis? Power, performance and play in the Leeds and Trinidad carnival.* https://www.semanticscholar.org/paper/%27It%27s-not-all-Sequins-and-Bikini%27s-Power%2C-and-Play-Marshall/474bf61403f5a94a95dc8ca207914ae07d1be874

Marshall, G. J. (2008). *Guide to Merleau-Ponty's phenomenology of perception.* Marquette University Press.

Mendes-Franco, J. (2015, February 21). *The politics of 'wining' in Trinidad & Tobago.* https://globalvoices.org/2015/02/21/the-politics-of-wining-in-trinidad-tobago/

Mohammed, P. (2000). But most of all mi love me browning: The emergence in the 18th and 19th century Jamaica of the mulatto woman as the desired. *Feminist Review, 65*(1), 22–48.

Murray, D. A. (1998). Defiance or defilement? Undressing cross-dressing in Martinique's carnival. *Sexualities, 1*(3), 343–354.

Noel, S. A. (2010). De jamette in we: Redefining performance in contemporary Trinidad carnival. *Small Axe: A Caribbean Journal of Criticism, 14*(1), 60–78.

Noel, S. (2009). Carnival is woman!: Gender, performance, and visual culture in contemporary Trinidad Carnival (Unpublished doctoral dissertation). Duke University.

Norris, P. (2001). *Political communication.* In *International encyclopedia of the social & behavioral sciences* (2nd ed.). Springer. https://doi.org/10.1016/B0-08-043076-7/04364-3

Nurse, K. (1999). Globalization and Trinidad carnival: Diaspora, hybridity and identity in global culture. *Cultural Studies, 13*(4), 661–690.

Onyebadi, U. (2018). Political messages in African Music: Assessing Fela Anikulapo-Kuti, Lucky Dube and Alpha Blondy. *Humanities, 7*(4), 129–147. https://doi.org/10.3390/h7040129

Oppong, C. (1966). Notes on cultural aspects of menstruation in Ghana. *Institute of African Studies: Research Review, 9*(2), 33–38.

Padmanabhanunni, A., Jaffer, L., & Steenkamp, J. (2018). Menstruation experiences of South African women belonging to the ama-Xhosa ethnic group. *Culture, Health & Sexuality, 20*(6), 704–714. https://doi.org/10.1080/13691058.2017.1371335

Parks, P. (2019). Covering Trump's 'Carnival': A rhetorical alternative to 'objective' reporting. *Journalism Practice, 13*(10), 1164–1184.

Perkins, A. K. (2011). Carne vale (goodbye to flesh?): Caribbean carnival, notions of the flesh and Christian ambivalence about the body. *Sexuality & Culture, 15*(4), 361–374.

Philip, M. N. (1997). *A genealogy of resistance: And other essays.* Mercury Press.

Riggio, M. C. (Ed.). (2004). *Carnival: Culture in action–the Trinidad experience.* Routledge.

Rohlehr, G. (1999). The state of calypso today. In R. R. Premdas (Ed.), *Identity, ethnicity and culture in the Caribbean* (pp. 29–46). University of the West Indies, School of Continuing Studies.

Sankeralli, B. (1998). University of the West Indies, School of Continuing Studies. *TDR/The Drama Review, 42*(3), 203–212.

Schechner, R. (2004). Carnival (theory) after Bakhtin. In *Carnival: Culture in action-the Trinidad experience* (pp. 3–12). Routledge.

Scher, P. W. (2007). The devil and the bed-wetter: Carnival, memory, national culture, and post-colonial consciousness in Trinidad. *Western Folklore, 66*(1/2), 107–126.

Scher, P. W. (2011). Heritage tourism in the Caribbean: The politics of culture after neoliberalism. *Bulletin of Latin American Research, 30*(1), 7–20.

Skultans, V. (1970). The symbolic significance of menstruation and the menopause. *Man, 5*(4), 639–651.

Smart, C. (2006, May). *Piss-en-lit or wine and jam: The dilemma of cultural preservation in the Trinidad and Tobago Carnival.* Paper presented at the 36th Annual Conference of the Association of Caribbean University, Research and Institutional Libraries, Aruba. https://ufdc.ufl.edu/UF00083224/00001

Smart, C. (2019). African oral tradition, cultural retentions and the transmission of knowledge in the West Indies. *IFLA Journal, 45*(1), 16–25.

Stallybrass, P., & White, A. (1986). *The politics and poetics of transgression.* University Press of Cambridge.

Sztainbok, V. (2013). Exposing her body, revealing the nation: The carnival vedette, black femininity and the symbolic order. *Social Identities, 19*(5), 592–606.

Toadvine, T. (2019). Maurice Merleau-Ponty. In E. N. Zalta (Ed.), *The Stanford encyclopedia of philosophy.* Stanford University. https://plato.stanford.edu/archives/spr2019/entries/merleau-ponty/

CHAPTER 4
Military Rhetoric: Making sense of political messaging in Reggae music

Kameika S. Murphy
Stockton University, USA

Abstract

Reggae music carries strong military overtones that shape the identity and political outlook of its performers. By pulling on theories of hidden histories, this chapter explores the groundings and political relevance of military symbolism in reggae music. It discusses various ways in which reggae artistes embody freedom and activism as public figures. While much of this is traditionally attributed to the philosophy of Rastafari, this author contends that a strong religio-martial culture emerged at a critical time in the revolutionary history of reggae music. The chapter draws attention to a proto-army model of resistance that produced the 1831 Baptist War and makes the argument that this political culture remained relevant long after emancipation, through storytelling and music as democratic participatory institutions in its broadest form. It therefore offers insights into the ways in which militarized memory and naming practices in reggae music allow a wide range of performers to negotiate their place in Jamaican society.

Keywords: Reggae, dancehall, Jamaican popular culture, military symbols, rebellion

***

Introduction

Tell dem man a Selassie I federal
Rasta wi a fight war spiritual
Hey, welcome Chronixx, the General…

Full suit a armor, sword inna hand
Ready fi go chant down dutty babylon
Man a warrior woie
Tell dem man a warrior woie
Chronixx real warrior
Selah, real warrior… (Chronixx, 2014).

> [Tell them man is Selassie I's federal
> Rasta we're fighting war spiritually
> Welcome Chronixx, the General...
>
> Full suit of armor, sword in my hand
> Ready to go chant down dirty Babylon
> Man is a warrior woie
> Tell them man is a warrior woie
> Chronixx is a real warrior
> Selah, real warrior...]
>
> (Chronnix, Warrior, 2014)

Amidst rhythmic sounds of a commanding military drumroll in the backdrop, Chronixx's song "Warrior" is an outcry against inequalities facing many marginalized communities in Jamaica and, by extension, across the globe. In the song, Chronixx describes enduring struggles of the urban poor to survive "iniquities" as a war continuously fought by African descendants on a "wild battlefield." In this war, carried out by a metaphorical but spiritually in-tuned army, Chronixx assumes the position of a commanding general. The then 21-year-old dancehall artiste is today one of several young Jamaicans credited for reviving Rasta roots in the musical vibrations of Kingston, Jamaica (Bakare, 2013). This interpretation of Chronixx reflects a tendency to conflate languages of resistance and militancy in reggae with Rastafari. Chronixx does follow in the footsteps of many Jamaican artistes who use military personas to define identity and negotiate their place within the industry. Consequently, a preponderance of military references exists in Jamaican popular music. These cases offer an opportunity to deconstruct militarized overtones in the messaging of a widely globalized performative culture that emerged out of Jamaica's African retentions.

This chapter, therefore, draws attention to a medley of instances where political vocalizations take on particularly militarized inflections. The term military rhetoric, in this sense, is being used to capture ideas about the army in reggae; that is, references to military life, the battlefield, or anything associated with soldiering, however and wherever they are presented. On the surface, there is a philosophical discordance between reggae and formal military institutions, but the music suggests otherwise. Reggae, which is subcategorized into roots reggae (also known as classical reggae) and dancehall, is well recognized for its capacity to contest the state. Conversely, the military is a powerful arm of the state which, beyond its diplomatic and wartime roles, is used to carry out a range of governmental objectives.

Several scholars have argued that the military represents state control, and its purposes include the surveillance of a nation's citizenry (Chretien et al., 2007; Grimes & Pion-Berlin, 2019). Nonetheless, a rich body of literature has already shown that while the army and other types of armed forces are oftentimes thought of in relation to the state, Afro-diasporic peoples retained historically African militaristic formations in resistance to slavery (Gomez, 1998; Heywood, 1999; Kuumba, 2006). African resistance cultures also transcend contemporary reggae music (Ekwueme, 1974; Fergus, 2014; Floyd, 1996; Floyd et al., 2017; Niaah, 2010). Thus, reggae is a post-slavery form that problematizes what the military means in Jamaican society. Yet, there has not really been any study to understand why reggae music makes so much reference to the army, why a lot of actors in the culture associate with soldiers, and what these military metaphors could reveal about how they understand their position within the society. The existing literature readily interpret these military references as a product of the Rastafari movement, which has had significant impact on reggae music (Chevannes, 2015; King and Bays, 2002; Murrell et al., 1998; Waters, 2017). Nonetheless, there are other factors at play.

The ensuing discussion is an attempt to further unpack the historical ethos that produce artistes who self-identify with military ranks and the dynamics that shape when (and how) they employ militaristic language, roles, and other imagery in their work; in this case, music. By doing so, this chapter engages Afro-Jamaicans' perceptions of the army and its morphological bearing on notions of leadership, agency, and change. It argues that while Jamaican popular music is strongly influenced by Rastafari philosophies on oppression and change, militarized messaging is also rooted in a pre-emancipation slave resistance culture that utilized proto-army models to structure agency. Pulling on the framework of cultural theorists and anthropologists as a methodological framework, it uses notions of hidden histories, "unmarked by situated knowledge" (Sheller, 2012), to frame the legitimacy of a much earlier source; that is, the normative value of an 1831 Jamaica revolution (previously referred to as the Christmas Rebellion), which was carried out by Black Baptists. By drawing attention to the parallels between this early nineteenth-century uprising and protest language in contemporary music, the study echoes many scholars of the Caribbean experience who consistently challenge assumptions about what we know, how we know, and who can make such claims about knowing. Pulling on these connections over space and time, it posits the view that military rhetoric in reggae is reflective of a strong religio-martial culture that remained relevant long after emancipation was achieved in 1838. The military undercurrents of reggae music, therefore, offer an alternative perspective on continuities in black agency and presents a new lens for tracing the malleability of slave resistance models. The chapter establishes the relevance militarized music has for addressing questions on what constitutes a leader, who can embody this kind of power, who carries out or define change (or the lack thereof), and where does the military rhetoric sit in this narrative of life in a post-colonial Jamaica. The discussion is especially instructive in speaking to how marginalized communities in Jamaica make confrontations with oppression through the symbolic politicization of the black soldier. Such a study offers an opportunity to understand not just how the oppressed see themselves in the context of constricting systems, but also how they then envision the possibility of change.

Memory and Hidden Histories theoretical framework

Few scholars have looked at how Afro-Jamaicans utilize religious and/or military figures that embody freedom in this context and especially in the pre-independence period (Holt, 1992; Moore et al., 1998; Sheller, 2001; Wilmot, 1997). One explanation for this might be that not many records of pre-emancipation uprisings capture enslaved people's voices and, in so being, they are unable to offer a sense of the internal structure of these movements beyond white interpretations. From a historiographical standpoint, extrapolating connections between reggae and nineteenth-century slave uprisings where there are no physical records of direct connections is problematic. A more interdisciplinary approach is needed, particularly intellectual models and theories that recognize these difficulties in telling the story of Afro peoples in places like the Caribbean. The paucity of records, however, does not mean the connections are not real, even when the details in between are spotty. The history of black people in the diaspora have suffered because Western ideas of knowledge do not lend well to stories of the subaltern (Moore et al., 2003; Morris, 2010; Ogborn, 2019). Proponents of the Caribbean experience - post-colonial poets, novelists, and historians alike - have for years talked about fragmented memories that destabilize Caribbean peoples' sense of self. Fragmented memories, in turn, perpetuate disjointed recollections of cultural heritage (Brathwaite, 2003; de Barros, 2005; Hanna, 2010; Walcott, 1993). There are two notions of memory in this respect. One form is cognizance of the past; awareness usually evoked and nurtured by public discourse, but also illustrated and even celebrated through a wide range of public history projects and the arts. The other, often times less conspicuous form, is grounding; that is, linkages connecting contemporary ethos in politics, language, geography, and identity to its antecedents. This latter form may be considered passive memory and can exist without cognizance.

Recognizing history through fragmented yet enduring memories is relevant to popular culture, even if people on a whole are not aware of, or celebrate, the historical trajectory. The past therefore has resonance regardless of recognition. For this reason, Stuart Hall (1990) offers an alternative understanding of Caribbean culture and argues scholars cannot, "underestimate or neglect the importance of the act of imaginative rediscovery for, 'Hidden histories' have played a critical role in the emergence of many of the most important social movements of our time - feminist, anti-colonial and anti-racist" (Hall, 1990, p. 222). While not denying the impact of forgotten connections, Hall does point to the enduring relevance of hidden histories that, on account of slavery and colonialism, have become inherent to Caribbean realities.

In this, Hall reflects other seminal theorists of the Caribbean experience who talk about fragmented memories, including the Martinican philosopher and post-colonial writer, Édouard Glissant (1999) who perceived a "nontotalized" history of dislocated peoples and their culture. For Glissant, the collective historical consciousness of a people is central to overcoming cognitive ruptures of, and in, the past. According to Glissant, the shocks and dislocations inherent to slavery and colonialism meant the historical consciousness of Caribbean peoples was not continuous. He refers to this disruption to collective consciousness as nonhistory, a legacy of colonial ideologies that obscures the narrative for Afro descendants, and calls for histories of the people that grasp hidden signs and digs deeper into memory.

Increasingly, scholars have responded to Hall and Glissant's argument as a call for works that mend these fragments (de Barros et al., 2005; Hanna, 2010; O'Dell et al., 2020). Derek Walcott (1993) and Kamau Brathwaite (2003) also talk about fragmentation as a culture of dispossession that requires greater attention. Such efforts are, however, not without challenges as they often times run counter to disciplinary conventions that prove inadequate for telling the story of Caribbean subalterns. In addition, scholars who attempt to make sense of these disjointed, latent, and unmarked yet real histories, must also confront tensions and misconceptions about the peoples who form the subject of their work. Such misconceptions served to delegitimize historicity and perpetuate silence (Trouillot, 1995). Sheller, therefore, argues that any attempt to trace "invisible histories" – in this case, subaltern agency - must move beyond conventions of political agency and citizenship to "seek out the unexcavated field of embodied (material and spiritual) practices through which people exercise and envision freedom," (Sheller, 2012, p. 6). Sheller thus offers the notion of erotic agency as an alternative lens. While erotic agency is originally used in relation to the "invisibility of queer subjectivities" (Sheller, 2012, p. 3), it is equally applicable to Caribbean performative culture as a model for its validation of non-traditional methods. One can therefore make the claim that Jamaican popular music is laced with erotic agency. Erotic in the sense of fantasization and storytelling that arouse excitement across audiences, and especially fantasies that are nuanced with military subversion.

Military Reggae

Reggae music emerged in the 1960s out of earlier Jamaica popular music genres, such as *ska* and *rock steady*, all of which took their antecedents from ancestral performative forms such as *mento* (Chang et al., 1998). In these early periods, reggae converged with Rastafari philosophy. Reggae served as a vehicle for Rastafari's heavy political messaging against oppressive neo-colonial structures that could not facilitate the liberative and self-determinative ambitions of Afro-Jamaicans. It became a medium through which marginalized peoples engaged, and rejected, their positions in the society as one of freedoms denied. While Jamaica had gained independence from the British Empire in 1962, the country struggled to find a competitive footing in the global market and, like most of its neighbors across the Caribbean and Latin America, several strategies to capture growth, such as structural adjustment policies, did not translate into more inclusive outcomes for a largely poor Afro-Jamaican labor economy (Gray, 1991; Patterson, 2019; Stone, 1982). Mimi Sheller (2012) argued that across the Americas, as with elsewhere, "Racial, class, and gender boundaries continue[d] to delineate the inequitable distribution of rights, freedom, protection, and justice, both within cities (whether Philadelphia, Port-Au-Prince, Kingston, or London,) and across nations" (p. 2). Rastafari philosophy is grounded in the teachings of Marcus Garvey who advocated for black pride and mobilization to attain self-determination. This provided rich grounds for the music to infuse with what became known as a Rasta cultural revolution (Manuel, 2006).

Many of the early artistes who quickly became the face of reggae music made these declarative connections between the genre and Rastafari. While there were several protest movements at the grassroots, in response to these challenges, Rastafari emerged as a viable form of agency, albeit with significant push-back in its nascent stages from the government. Peter Tosh, for instance, in a 1979 interview for the popular *Sunsplash* stage show, defined reggae music as a transcendent form with a singularly religious purpose. He stated:

> Music is psychology and if the music does not penetrate the heart, soul, and the mind, and the body, then you ain't go[ing to] feel it. Because, reggae music is not something that you hear, it's something you feel. And, if you don't feel it, you can't know it. It is a spiritual music with spiritual ingredients for spiritual purposes...it's a spiritual motivation of inspiration through divine lines of Jah Rastafari (Tosh, 2007).

In a similar fashion, Bob Marley, another major reggae icon, argued that reggae music is a religious yet politically involved consciousness. He argued that reggae "…carries a feel where, if you ask plenty musicians, they know it but they can't do it," and like Tosh, Marley believed, "People [are] still searching for this truth here, which this reggae music bring [a]cross to them and the only purpose it serves is to tell the people about Rastafari" (Mulenga, 2012). Similarly, in his reflection on the messaging about Africa and black power, Marley observed that before reggae:

> People [were] never so conscious about Africa and where their roots come from. Since reggae come now, people get, I mean, not from a point

of music because the music is always conscious, but since the reggae come now, the reggae start talk about Africa, blackness, you know, in a militant way (Canovas, 2015).

Reggae music therefore, from its inception, carried with it significant military connotations, some of which Rastafari invoked. Its earliest performers were conscious of its combative activist value. The significance of Rastafari evangelism to contemporary cultural productions, such as Chronixx's music, is well known. However, it does not adequately explain how and why militarized tones emerge time and again in Jamaican popular music, even when the nature of genre and philosophical compass of the artistes change, as it does with dancehall music.

By the 1980s, dancehall emerged as a new genre of reggae that seemed comparatively less infused with Rastafari. For this reason, dancehall music is often times critiqued as lacking in consciousness. Although there are dancehall artistes who identify as followers of Rastafari - such as Capleton, Queen Ifrica, I-Wayne, Buju Banton, and Sizzla – and whose infusion of Rasta ideologies into dancehall spaces are evidence of continuities between roots reggae and "conscious" dancehall, the two are very different in style and delivery. Dancehall on a whole is recognized for its more heavily sexualized and/or violent language, computerized rhythms, and an ostentatious dress and dance culture that departs significantly from the imagery and messaging of Rastafari-infused reggae music. Yet dancehall remained as complex and combative as its predecessor. In her work, Donna Hope (2006) argued that dancehall emerged as a critical cultural response to the social, political, and economic constraints that defined the 1980s, and while often labeled as vulgar, it uses symbolism and ideologies to legitimize the experiences of the urban poor. Carolyn Cooper (1994) argued that these features should not be overlooked or dismissed for they reflect "a politics of subversion [and] a metaphorical revolt against law and order," (p. 141). While the later iteration served very similar enfranchising purposes in that it offered a platform for the economically and politically marginalized to comment on, and even resist, systemic constrictions, it carried marked differences in production, sound, and meanings. For this reason, when Chronixx made his debut, his music was read as a revival of Rastafari philosophy in Jamaican popular music. As with his predecessors, Chronixx's presentation of self is very militaristic and in this he is not alone.

There are frequent references to the army and militarized conflict in contemporary Jamaican popular music that are consistent with its religious underpinnings, such as Chronixx's. This includes Stephen Marley's collaboration with Buju Banton and Damian Marley called "We Are Soldiers," in which they assert, "We are soldiers in Jah army," (Marley et al., 2011). There is also Jah Cure, "Royal Soldier" from an album with the same title (2019):

I am a king and I will never give up
Step 'pon di battlefield now
Royal soldier
All my loyal soldiers, yeah
I'm right here I'll forever stay up
Soar like a' eagle rise up
Royal soldier
All my loyal soldiers, yeah

Given the strong connections between Rastafari and reggae in these cases, it is very easy to conflate the two. However, there are also several other instances where military references depart from the "Jah army" narrative and, in some cases, these metaphors find strong resonance among people, especially younger generations, who do not identify with the religion. For instance, dancehall artiste Agent Sasco (formerly known as Assassin) opens his song called "Step Pan Dem" on his "Infiltration" album (2005) with a declaration that his audience should "call out the infantry." He also makes rhythmic allusions to the first beat of a military cadence that is usually used to initiate and maintain a regiment's marching parade. The military cadence plays in a loop as the backdrop of the song and Agent Sasco uses it to assert himself as a commanding figure to be respected:

Well I was born brave but I'm bolder now	*Well I was born brave but I'm bolder now*
Was cold from birth but I'm colder now	*Was cold from birth but I'm colder now*
A murder!	*It's murder!*
Them fi know say man a born solja	*They should know that I was born soldier*
Over di years	*Over the years*
I'm still a solja now	*I'm still a soldier now*
So Hut two three four	*So hup two three four*
Betta you stop talk before	*Its better you stop talking before*
Me rise up me guns, bombs, grenades,	*I rise up my guns, bombs, grenades,*
Anthrax, cyanide and c4	*Anthrax, cyanide and c4*
What you wanna war wid me for	*Why do you want to war with me*
You're a punk what you acting like a G for	*You're a punk, why are you acting like a G*
Yo seet, everybody know you a fool	*You see, everybody knows you are a fool*
Run up inna me tool and detour	*Run up into my tool and detour*

In this case, it is Agent Sasco's early upbringing as a "soldier" that makes him a formidable artiste. What his song also speaks to, however, is the fact that in many cases, references to the army in dancehall songs are delivered in context of lyrical warfare with other artistes. Here, Assassin is utilizing military metaphors to contest an unnamed rival. Carolyn Cooper (1994) identifies this style as a "gun tune" or "badmanism" subcategory of dancehall music. Cooper argues the "gun tune" allows the artistes to utilize lyrical and braggadocios badness to not only subvert the political power of oppressive government structures, but also to problematize the socialization of Jamaicans who grow up in the ghetto. So, when Vybz Kartel refashions his relationship with his hometown, Portmore, in the song "4 Star" (2004) he does so in a heroic character:

We ah di general fi di army	*We are the general for the army and the navy*
And di navy	*And the navy*
Dem is bitch, we have bravery	*They are bitches, we have bravery*
We control di air force war	*We control the air force war*
Mi di chief of staff from Portmore star	*I'm the chief of staff from Portmore star*
4 star!	*4 star!*

Much like Agent Sasco, Vybz Kartel frames his identity around armed power and military roles, by portraying himself as the chief of staff for Portmore, as well as a general in the army, navy, and air force. Kartel's example broadens the symbolism to other branches of the forces, but with very similar purposes as Agent Sasco. If reggae culture on a whole is a performative exchange between the artiste and the audience, this type of self-aggrandizement that Kartel uses in the song can be read as attempts to shape the behavior of his audience, whose support is his validation. However, this form of roleplaying also serves to emphasize his own authentication, both as an artiste and a popular public figure who is representing his community.

Other representative examples of how military rhetoric speak to the socialization of Jamaican youth and redefine activism include Demarco's "Fallen Soldiers" (2008). Demarco uses the song as a salute to the many inner-city youth who fell victim to violence that is known to permeate many poor communities across Jamaica. He sings:

Woaah Oh Dis Is For My soldiers	*Woaah Oh This is for my soldiers*
Real real soldiers yeah!	*Real real soldiers yeah!*
Dis is for my fallen soldiers	*Dis is for my fallen soldiers*

We miss you although you gone	*We miss you although you gone*
We with you gone pon di battle field	*We with you gone pon di battle field*
Life is so f***king real	*Life is so f***king real*

Demarco's "Fallen Soldiers" was his debut song. It was an instant hit and remains one of his most popular production. The reference found such resonance among his audience that he followed up with, "Standing Soldier" (2009) and later released both on a 2010 album titled "Standing Soldier". In the song, "Standing Soldier" (2009), Demarco speaks to the hardships and uncertainties faced by young people in Jamaica's poorest communities and clearly lays the blame at the feet of the government:

Yeah Demarco	*Yeah Demarco*
Ghetto youths	*Ghetto youths*
Dem nuh want we reach nuh weh	*They don't want us to reach anywhere*
Dem only wah we listen weh dem teach we seh	*They only want us to listen to what they teach*
Mister MP so you mean to say	*Mister MP so you mean to say*
Ghetto youths nuh fi live no way	*Ghetto youths must not live anywhere*
Dem waan we fi fall	*They want us to fall*
But da nah happen none at all	*But that won't happen at all*
Dem waan we fi fall	*They want us to fall*
Raise up the food and tek di dancehall	*Raise up the food and take the dancehall*
Man a standing soldier	*Man is a standing soldier*
You nah see we bawl	*You won't see us bawl*
Man a real standing soldier	*Man is a real standing soldier*
All when mi back against di wall	*Even when my back is against the wall*
Man a real standing soldier	*Man is a real standing soldier*
We nah bow down and crawl	*We will not bow down and crawl*
Man a real standing soldier	*Man is a real standing soldier*
Jah jah protect us all	*Jah jah protect us all*

In this latter iteration of the military rhetoric, Demarco describes a very complex and difficult life in the ghettos. He is also very vocal on the lack of faith in the established government and members of parliament (MPs) to produce meaningful change. In fact, there is a mistrust of the government, to which the imagery of a "standing soldier" serves in stark contrast. The standing soldier is venerable in a society where young people perceive government as unsympathetic to their plight.

There is also Jahmiel's "Strongest Soldier" which likens the difficulties of life as a young man in Jamaica to the perseverance of a soldier's fight, albeit one marred with obscurities. Jahmiel declares:

Man get whole heap a love	*Man get whole heap of love*
Whole heap a hate	*Whole heap of hate*
Chimney	*Chimney*
More while a the love inna the streets	*Sometimes it is the love in the streets*
Haffi keep me up me G	*Have to keep up my G*
When friends and family fail me (fail me)	*When friends and family fail me (fail me)*
Uh huh	*Uh huh*
And then me step inna me vehic's	*And then I step into my vehic's*
With a piece deh next to me	*With a piece next to me*
Fi enemies weh no stop pree me	*For enemies who don't stop watching me*
Jordan	*Jordan*
Tell dem a the strongest soldiers	*Tell them it's the strongest soldiers*
Get the hardest fight (hardest fight)	*Get the hardest fight (hardest fight)*
And a the realest people	*And it's the realest people*
Live the hardest life (hardest life)	*Live the hardest life (hardest life)*
Sun always shine	*Sun always shine*
Even after the darkest nights (hey)	*Even after the darkest nights (hey)*
So better days are on the way-ay-ay, uh huh	

In this sense, Jahmiel is directly defining the struggles of ghetto youth as one that they can only make sense of through these references to the hardness of a soldier's life. So too does Tommy Lee Sparta who commanded significant attention in the dancehall *lyricscape* as an icon (Campbell, 2015). Tommy Lee Sparta's "Spartan Soldier" (2013) asserts:

> The pain I feel you'll never know (hmm)
> Emotions that I never show
> I'm on a lonely road
> But I walked this lonely road before
> I'm a Spartan soldier
> I was born to conquer

> I was raised and trained for war
> I'm a Spartan soldier
> Till my life is over
> Till my heart can't beat no more (no more)
> Spartans... what is your profession?

The tendency to associate hard life in the ghetto to the rigors of army life did not emerge with the younger generation dancehall producers. A close look at early dancehall and roots reggae shows some precedence. Take, for instance, Welton Irie in a very early dancehall song called "Army Life" where he captures the uneasy misgivings of life in the armed forces. Welton's song states:

> They say that in the army the shoes are very fine
> I asked for number seven they gave me number nine
> They say that in the army the guns are very fine
> Well I asked them for an M-16 they give me an M-9
> So I don't want no more army life
> Skipper I want to go
> Back to my cheerio
> Skipper, I want to go back home
> That a home sweet home

This 1982 song was very popular and made number one of the charts after selling approximately 30, 000 records (Cooke, 2011). What makes it significant here is its use of humor and parody to critique the very tough life that black soldiers would have had in their choice of profession. While his presentation of the army is not a desirable lifestyle, it does point to the resonance of army life among the Jamaican populace and the music suggests this is a profession on the radar for people in search of viability. Therefore, while military symbolism in many of the songs carry a celebratory, if not respectable, tone - in the sense that army roles are interpreted as desirable - this is not always the case.

Consider Bob Marley's song, "Buffalo Soldier" (1983), which is perhaps the most well-known of reggae songs that capture how nuanced military rhetoric is in reggae music. "Buffalo Soldier" illustrates variegated tensions in the history and symbolism of a black soldier's consciousness of self. It describes the arduous life lived by descendants of the enslaved in independent yet socially non-decolonized American societies, and makes the claim that this is best captured by a narrative that conflate Rastafari with the journeys of a soldier:

> Buffalo Soldier, dreadlock Rasta
> There was a Buffalo Soldier
> In the heart of America
> Stolen from Africa, brought to America
> Fighting on arrival, fighting for survival

> I mean it, when I analyze the stench
> To me, it makes a lot of sense
> How the dreadlock Rasta was the Buffalo Soldier
> And he was taken from Africa, brought to America
> Fighting on arrival, fighting for survival
> Said he was a Buffalo Soldier, dreadlock Rasta
> Buffalo Soldier, in the heart of America
>
> If you know your history
> Then you would know where you coming from
> Then you wouldn't have to ask me
> Who the heck do I think I am
> I'm just a Buffalo Soldier

Yet the song is not entirely a narrative of celebrated resilience. While it is significant that the particular soldier reference offers veneration of the remarkable 10th Cavalry Regiment, a black military corps that became the first black regiment allowed into the United States army during peacetime, Marley also draws attention to the almost inescapable trappings of a system that can seemingly liberate and simultaneously oppress. Here, Marley shows the complexities of the army as a model. Although the free blacks gain opportunities by joining the regiment, it also intrinsically, and perhaps cynically, lends support to the same supra-structural oppression that pits black soldiers against Native Americans. It therefore seems that although neo-colonial constrictions on Afro-Jamaicans form consistent parts of the messaging in reggae and dancehall songs, veneration tones are more pronounced in the later types, especially songs of the 1990s and onwards. In these cases, military rhetoric allows the artiste and audience to see virtue in their position as underrepresented but resourceful and tenacious people. In a society where they are unable to perceive meaningful socio-political change, these lyrics become maxims of performance politics joining the artiste and audience.

Perhaps the most striking and enduring of ways in which reggae artistes have adopted military rhetoric is through personification and naming practices. Stage names are part of militarized performance politics in music. For although costumes for stage shows have resonating effects on the reception of the performances and messaging, it is an artiste's stage name that becomes a more enduring abstraction that frames identity and legitimacy. The more popular examples of artistes who took on military titles include General Degrees, General Trees, General B, Major Mackerel, Admiral Bailey, Brigadier Jerry, Lieutenant Stitchie, Major Worries, Captain Barkey, Admiral Tibett, Lone Ranger, General Echo, and Major Lazer. There are also artistes who adopt militarized monikers to promote, and to some extent clarify, their stage name.

For instance, the world-renowned Bounty Killer who then went by the name, "Bounty Killer, the five-star general."

If reggae and dancehall are constituent parts of a larger musical community, there is also relevance in that a wide range of actors in the industry have followed suit (Hope, 2006; Niaah, 2010). Aside from the artistes who have adopted military titles, there are also radio personalities who take on similar designations as a moniker. This includes Captain Collin Hines, who is a Jamaican popular music broadcaster with the local radio station, FAME 95FM. So too are selectors, disc jockeys, and record producers whose skill was mixing, toasting, and clashing with musical rivals using various forms of the sound system. This includes Captain Sinbad in the earlier years and, more recently, people like Rickey Trooper.

Military overtones shape naming practices in other ways. Some performers might not take on an army title, but instead, choose stage names that communicate similar imagery. Artistes likes Shabba Ranks, Cutty Ranks, Delly Ranks, and Ranking Joe, use the symbolism of terms and images in their presentation of self and criticisms of the government. Although their titles are not of a military post, these artistes' use of the term "rank" carries similar meanings. Reggae artistes' interpretation and adoption of military-like sociologies of identity is also reflected in their performance of the music, especially through stage props and costumes that convey the imagery of ranked men at war. This practice of using military symbolism in a variety of ways to reconstruct identity, navigate the entertainment industry, and ultimately negotiate power, further complicates the politics of Jamaican popular music.

On very different terms from the messaging of the "badmanism" that define gun tunes, the ways in which these artistes and their work make references to soldiering suggests there is yet another form of reggae/dancehall; that is, military tunes. Although both oftentimes describe and/or rest heavily on occurrences of violence, military reggae/dancehall is separate and apart from gun tunes. In these instances where there is explicit military roleplay, Jamaican popular music is subverting oppressive structures by lyrically infiltrating government through one of its most robust seats of power; that is, the army. The army allows them to frame that power in such a way that they see themselves as having the ability to attain self-determination – to redefine who they are in relation to their circumstances, community, and the larger society. In essence, they are embracing the power to reconstruct identity and are doing so in a very bold way by taking on the role of a commanding figure. Military reggae, therefore, allows them to find ways to understand and communicate their readings of oppressive legacies that have denied them upward social mobility.

Legacies of the Jamaica revolution

While military rhetoric in music is symbolic, they should not be read exclusively as allegorical interpretations of life among urban poor communities in Jamaica. What emerges in the contemporary music should be understood in relation to much earlier movements for change, especially in actual cases where black Jamaicans had real encounters with spaces and players connected to the Jamaica militia, which later became the Jamaica Defense Force. Some scholars have long pointed out that the antecedents to what we have come to recognize as classical reggae, conscious dancehall, and even the very Rastafari philosophy that has shaped the music to a significant extent, are rooted in the nineteenth-century rebellions (Chevannes, 2015; Price, 2009; Wilmot, 1997). Peter Manuel (2006) found that what made reggae music so powerful across all factions of Jamaican society is its indigenizing elements that prioritized historical roots as its compass, in spite of its ability to also draw on international forces for inspiration. One such historical root to the Rastafari movement, and therefore classical reggae, often cited in the scholarship is the 1865 Morant Bay rebellion. There is, however, an even earlier precursor that carries relevance here; that is, the 1831 Christmas rebellion, also known as the Baptist War or, in more recent histories, the Jamaica revolution.

Much like reggae and the Rastafari movement, the Jamaica revolution used a process of indigenization to reinterpret international forces of revolutionary change to fit local contexts. The uprising was born out of the ideological contributions of late eighteenth-century refugees, known as black loyalists, who brought lessons from the American Revolution with them to Jamaica. Black loyalists were mostly self-freed ex-slaves who gained freedom by fighting for the British in the wars for independence. To consolidate their freedom, black loyalists left with the British. Many of them headed further north into Nova Scotia, but significant numbers went south, into the Caribbean, especially Jamaica and the Bahamas. Wherever they went, black loyalists made cultural deposits in the form of black Christianity. The experiences in Jamaica of these Afro-American refugees and their descendants provide another dimension of a hidden history impacting movements for change beyond the nineteenth century.

These revolutionary refugees arrived in the island mostly between 1782 and 1783. Many settled in urban centers like Kingston and carried out a number of measures to expand freedom over the time they lived there, including registering as free people within small groups, acquiring land and other property, and manumitting other enslaved peoples (sometimes relatives) who arrived with them. Their most enduring impact on the island, however, was the fact that they introduced a Black Baptist movement to Jamaica and, by extension, the Anglophone Caribbean. It is this contribution that forms the basis of a militaristic approach to protest that culminated in the 1831 uprising. Music is also situated in this model they presented. In their mostly auxiliary posts within the militia, black loyalists embodied the sound of the revolutionary armies. They were the trumpeters and drummers. Even the father of the Black Baptist church in Jamaica, loyalist and itinerant preacher, George Liele, played instruments for the militia (Liele et al., 1916). Much of these military roles and the presence of this community continued into the later periods. Traces of this earlier militarized political and religious orientation can be seen in reggae music.

The Jamaica revolution marked a very important junction in Afro-Jamaican history for several reasons. It is widely recognized as the uprising that signaled a death toll to slavery across the British Empire. Scholars who conduct close readings of the rebellion have focused on its transnational connections to this Black Baptist movement. Documents related to the rebellion also provide significant insights into how Black Baptists organized and mobilized across the island, the goals and intentions of the movement, and the outcome for its leaders. In fact, historians agree that the uprising started off as a peaceful protest and interpretations of the records indicate there was no intention among the enslaved, free people, or preachers, to revolt. Samuel Sharpe, a revered itinerant preacher who led the uprising, is remembered as an exponent of the non-violent approach to creating positive change.

However, records left by Europeans who allegedly witnessed the affair, and transcripts from black Baptists who were interrogated, suggest that somewhere in between a non-violent protest and the actual outbreak of war, emerged a proto- army with a clearly delineated chain of command. Records from several accounts indicate the enslaved and free blacks who became Baptists created their own version of a black army, connecting several militarized camps across the island. The Jamaica revolution boasted a military structure that used Baptist meeting grounds as "barracks" and church networks as channels for organizing across several parishes. This Baptist army was the protégé of black loyalists and loyal free blacks in many respects.

The records reveal a very deep sense of military orientation among the men and women who participated in the uprising. Leaders in this Black Baptist army were ranked according to their clout, position and roles in the church. At the helm was Sam Sharpe who was regarded as the General in command. Second to Sharpe was Colonel Gardener and then there was "a negro named 'Dove,' whose rank of lieutenant-colonel, afforded him opportunities to carry into full effect all the craft and subtility [sic] with which he was highly endued," (Senior, 1969, p.185). Bernard Senior (1969), wrote at length about the structure of the uprising's leadership and while he might have been more intent on recording the names of those who rebelled and the roles they played, this record also offers some sense that the perception of an organized black army was not lost on him. As an outsider with little understanding of how these roles were determined, Senior observed that while the self-styled army filled higher ranks,

"The rank of major seems to be somewhat overlooked, as only a few noted ones were distinguished by that appellation," (Senior, 1969, p.185).

Sharpe is fused in Jamaica's national memory as a national hero and the religious elements to the political culture is well preserved, but much of the other members of his army, their philosophy on leadership, militarization, and change, remain hidden. Nonetheless, the contesting spirit of the movement and its leaders remain. Most Jamaicans are familiar with this story and Sharpe's rebellion. His likeness is monumentalized in Montego Bay, Jamaica, and the history is taught at several levels of the education system. Its religious underpinnings to Jamaican political culture are also fairly well preserved, both in its historiography and application. In her track "Times Like These," Queen Ifrica (2011) illustrates the place this uprising still holds in Jamaican political memory:

> They took away the voices that gave the people pride
> Now we're plunging into darkness
> We all have to play our part, make a bold start
> Every disc jock, tell every artist
> Media houses, we notice you love support the slackness
> How so much alcohol in our parties
> While the girls a broke out
> And the something she drink knocked her out
> Now she doesn't care where they prop her up

> It's times like these
> I'm missing our heroes
> Times like these I really wish they were around
> We need you, we need you, we need you
> Sam Sharpe
> We need you, we need you, we need you
> Nanny, yeah

By invoking the memory of Sam Sharpe, the story of his own transformative self-styled identity as a black preacher concerned with the welfare of marginalized Afro-Jamaicans, Queen Ifrica is attempting to shape attitudes about how to reclaim a strong political voice to address contemporary issues. In this, Sharpe's memory reverberates national consciousness to stir the leadership style of historical figures who she identifies as ideal. Along with Sam Sharpe, they are Bob Marley, Marcus Garvey, Miss Lou, and Nanny of the Maroons. Subsequently, an intersection of the military and religious approaches to protest and change has defined Jamaican political culture and it is evident later in the philosophy of Rastafari and again in reggae music, although there has not been a consistent narrative to explain the phenomenon.

Despite the historical fragments, the rebellion provides a remarkable pre-emancipation standard by which marginalized people, free and enslaved, integrate religious and military ideologies to develop a model for leadership roles at the grassroots, in the same way that reggae music utilizes military metaphors. In addition, it is also worth emphasizing here that identity, through self-styled military titles, became a cornerstone of this model and provides reasonable groundings for what remerges later in Jamaican popular music. This is not to say that military understandings of leadership and change began only in the early nineteenth-century period. For it is also well documented that combative performances across the Caribbean are rooted in African legacies, some of which would have predated the arrival of loyalists, but the Jamaica revolution presents a clear outline of an organized army with well-defined creolized ritual through which one can observe what military titles and roles meant in a pre-emancipation context. These occasions give us glimpses into a model that uses the black solider to embody agency and freedom; a practice which is later replicated in reggae music.

Liberating functions of the Army

On the surface, black regiments were an extension of the state, and remained so in relation to its duties to perform directives of the colonial and post-colonial government (Buckley, 1998). Indeed, the army has held an ambiguous place in the Jamaican story. On the other hand, the expansion of black spaces in the nineteenth-century Jamaica militia can be read as an attempt to turn the oppressive nature of the state on its head, in that those who enlisted seized it as opportunities to reshape life. For those who could enlist, the Jamaica militia provided occasions to secure freedom, earn a pension, and develop collaborations with white officers who could vouch for them when needed (Pulis, 1999), in spite of the fact that racial prejudices also prevailed in the army. The same holds true for later iterations of the militia, known as the Jamaica Defense Force (JDF). The JDF was established in 1962 when the country gained independence from Britain. From its inception, the JDF carried a mandate to defend the island from foreign powers, offer emergency aid, and provide other civic services (Muñíz, 1988). It has also played more routine patrolling roles, especially in recent times when the Jamaica Constabulary Force, the police, are overwhelmed with outbreak of violence. Today, the JDF is called upon to help carry out policies to address the country's crime rates. Since 2018, they have been stationed across the island in what are called state of emergency (SOE) checkpoints – known as zones of special operations (ZOSO) - to help stem escalating crime by concentrating their presence in trouble spots. Yet, much like ex-slaves in the Jamaica militia, members of the JDF have many occasions to lay claim on the state. The official black regiments of the Jamaica militia and JDF were, therefore, not entirely different in the microcosm of freedom production than the proto-army of black Baptists. Black spaces in official and non-official formations made the army a complex institution where notions of agency are concerned and this follows through in the music.

One way to make sense of these complexities in the role the army plays in Afro-Jamaican political culture and, in turn, grasp its rhetorical prominence in the cultural landscape of grassroots agency, is to embrace the messy and convoluted but deliberate ways in which subalterns speak (Morris, 2010). The army can be repressive, but it can also serve liberating functions for those who use it, literally and figuratively, to serve such ends. Through Jamaican popular music, military roleplay and naming cultures are informing these understandings of power and agency. Moore et al. (2003) offers a reminder that subaltern voices tend to use cultural practices as a rebuke to totalizing narratives. In this sense, the celebration of resistance symbols (military rhetoric) are deliberate corruptions of dominant discourse (the army).

As the work of performers like Agent Sasco, Jahmiel, and Tommy Lee Sparta show, the lyrics, titles, and other symbols of military reggae are in direct contrast to narratives of an army that exclusively serves a state with which the masses are in a constant struggle. While the army has provided this role historically, contemporary Jamaican popular music offers a new medium through which to maintain a tradition of resistance that appropriate and redefine 'the master's tools.' While military reggae does not fit neatly within narratives of subversion, ideas of the black soldier suggest some retention of revolutionary models. Without question, military reggae offers the musical *lyricscape* as a new form of proto-army by providing a medium for militarized political messaging and ideas of freedom (and struggle), which are embodied in the black soldier. As Michel-Rolph Trouillot (1995) contends, "Human beings participate in history both as actors and narrators." People like Chronixx are narrators in a new plot. In essence, military rhetoric allows performers and their audience to contest, and make claims on, the state. Narratives of the black solider, therefore, provide alternate routes via music.

Yet it also remains overly patriarchal. Although women have held a significant place in the country's armed forces for decades and have also performed visibly active roles as key figures in popular music, they do not engage with these military models. Women in reggae music do not take on military self-styled titles or identify with the army, though they have historically used prefixes such as lady and sister. For instance, women who were instrumental in shaping the industry include Sister Nancy, Lady Ann, Lady Mackerel, Lady Saw, and Lady G. However, they challenge the system in alternative ways. For instance, Queen Ifrica (2009) uses the notions of a lioness with similar purposes in her song, "Lioness on the Rise":

> When the roll is called up
> I'll be standing taller
> To face the darkest and the hardest of times
> We'll be takin care of
> All the children there of
> But if it's required we'll be on the frontline
> You can call me by my name
> I am ready to roll
> Once the rules remain the same
> How the story's been told
> Call me any time
> Never cop out
> Lioness is on the rise
> Don't you ever have doubt
> Never say never we're in this forever to fight and be strong
> Once is for better I'll write every letter in moving right along

Nonetheless, women's presence in the military has not translated into the music in the same way it has for their male counterparts. This is largely because the military is still very masculine in public perception. Women do not feature into these stories of the battlefield and army-inspired subversion through military rhetoric.

Conclusion

While military reggae is, in part, a reflection of the Rastafari movement, it also transcends Rasta roots and is present in other iterations of the music that are less inclined to serve religion as purported by earlier icons like Bob Marley and Peter Tosh. Another historical current shaping political messaging in reggae is the 1831 Jamaica revolution. Recognized as one of the country's most impactful uprisings, the Jamaica revolution produced a proto-army whose use of military structures and self-styled naming formed an enduring legacy. Self-styled military titles were an important element to the planning and execution of resistance during slavery, and this is still visible in contemporary Jamaican popular culture through storytelling and symbolism in the music.

Military metaphors and titles allow musicians to construct and propagate identities that reflect their depth of political awareness, historical consciousness, and competitive prowess. This chapter examined these lyrics and naming practices in both classical reggae and dancehall music and argued that military symbolism allows for these key actors to negotiate self, convey who they are, and communicate what they are about. In turn, this study examined how reggae and dancehall actors are then proliferating these sorts of abstractions about soldiering as a means to access power. By doing so, this chapter demonstrates that military rhetoric is important as a consistent projection in Jamaican popular music, one which provides opportunities for ghetto youth to confront oppression. Overall, this chapter therefore zoomed in on the experiences of young people in particular for whom this rhetoric seems to resonate strongly.

Finally, military rhetoric points to a distinct form of reggae. Although related in their use of figurative violence, military reggae is not the same as gun tunes. When cited, violence in military reggae operates very differently and, for the most part, reflects the masses as victims rather than perpetrators. This discussion situates military reggae as a separate form that shows how Jamaican musicians and other actors make sense of army roles at the grassroots. Its nineteenth-century antecedent finds regeneration through storytelling and offers new channels for reggae music to act as democratic participatory institutions in its broadest form. In post-slavery societies of the Caribbean, therefore, the army cannot be read simply as part and parcel to the policing state. Military rhetoric in reggae suggests it also carries resonance for understanding language and symbolism in relation to leadership and change among marginalized communities.

References

Bakare, L. (2013, October 11). *Chronixx puts Rastafarianism back into Jamaican reggae.* http://www.theguardian.com/music/2013/oct/11/chronixx-roots-reggae

Brathwaite, K. (2003). *Words need love too.* UK: Salt Publishing.

Buckley, R. N. (1998). *The British army in the West Indies: Society and the military in the revolutionary age.* University of Florida Press.

Campbell, W. C. (2015). *Reggae from yaad: Traditional and emerging themes in Jamaican popular music.* Ian Randle Publishers.

Canovas, V. (2015, December 26). *Bob Marley Interview* [Video]. YouTube. https://www.youtube.com/watch?v=E7bSqj_3Q5g

Chang, K. O., & Chen, W. (1998). *Reggae routes: The story of Jamaican music.* Temple University Press.

Chevannes, B. (2015). *Rastafari roots and ideology.* Syracuse University Press.

Chretien, J. P., Blazes, D. L., Coldren, R. L., Lewis, M. D., Gaywee, J., Kana, K., Sirisopana, N., Vallejos, V., Mundaca, C., Montano, S., Martin, G. J., & Gaydos, J. C. (2007). The importance of militaries from developing countries in global infectious disease surveillance. *Bulletin of the World Health Organization, 85*(3), 174–180.

Chronixx. (2014). Warrior. *Zulu warriors FM, Vol. 3.* [Song] ZincFence Records label.

Cooke, M. (2011, July 24). *Story of the song: Welton Irie writes off 'army life.'* http://jamaica-gleaner.com/gleaner/20110724/ent/ent9.html

Cooper, C. (1994). Lyrical gun: Metaphor and role play in Jamaican dancehall culture. *The Massachusetts Review, 35*(3/4), 429–447.

Cure, J. (2019). Royal soldier. *Royal soldier.* [Album]. V and P Records label.

de Barros, J., Diptee, A., & Trotman, D. (Eds.). (2005). *Beyond fragmentation: A pan-Caribbean look at slavery, emancipation, and colonialization.* Markus Wiener Publishers.

Demarco. (2010). Fallen soldiers. *Standin soldier.* [Album]. Star Kutt Records label.

Ekwueme, L. E. N. (1974). African music retentions in the new world. *The Black Perspective in Music, 2*(2), 128–144.

Fergus, C. (2014). From slavery to black power: the enigma of Africa in the Trinidad calypso. *Transactions of the Historical Society of Ghana, 16,* 1–26.

Floyd, S. (1996). *The power of black music: Interpreting its history from Africa to the United States.* Oxford University Press.

Floyd, S., Zeck, M., & Ramsey, G. (2017). *The transformation of black music: The rhythms, the songs, and the ships of the African diaspora.* Oxford University Press.

Glissant, E. (1999). *Caribbean discourse: Selected essays.* University of Virginia Press.

Gomez, M. A. (1998). *Exchanging our country marks: The transformation of African identities in the colonial and antebellum south.* University of North Carolina Press.

Gray, O. (1991). *Radicalism and social change in Jamaica, 1960–1972.* The University of Tennessee Press.

Grimes, C., & Pion-Berlin, D. (2019). Power relations, coalitions, and rent control: Reforming the military's natural resource levies. *Comparative Politics, 51*(4), 625–643.

Hall, S. (1990). Cultural identity and diaspora. In J. Rutherford (Ed.), *Identity: community, culture, difference* (pp. 222–237). London: Lawrence and Wishart.

Hanna, M. (2010). Reassembling the fragments: battling historiographies, Caribbean discourse, and nerd genres in Junot Díaz's the brief wondrous life of Oscar Wao. *Callaloo, 33*(2), 498–520.

Heywood, L. (1999). The African diaspora. *History News, 54*(2), 22–25.

Holt, T. C. (1992). *The problem of freedom: Race, labor, and politics in Jamaica and Britain 1832–1938.* Johns Hopkins University Press.

Hope, D. (2006). *Inna di dancehall.* University of the West Indies Press.

Ifrica, Q. (2009). Lionness on the rise. *Montego bay.* [Album]. V and P Records label.

Ifrica, Q. (2011). Times like these. *City life riddim.* [Album]. 2 Hard Music label.

Jahmiel. (2017). Strongest soldier. *Money house riddim.* [Album]. Chimney Records label.

Kartel, V. (2004). *4 star.* [Album]. Birchill Records label

King, S., & Bays, B. T. (2002). *Reggae, rastafari and the rhetoric of social control.* University Press of Mississippi.

Kuumba, M. B. (2006). African women, resistance cultures and cultural resistances. *Agenda: Empowering Women for Gender Equity, 68,* 112–121.

Liele, G., Cooke, S., Marshall, A., Clarke, J., & Swigle, N. (1916). Letters showing the rise and progress of the early negro churches of Georgia and the West Indies. *The Journal of Negro History, 1*(1), 69–92.

Marley, B. (1983). Buffalo soldier. *Confrontation.* [Album]. Tuff Gong/Island Records label.

Marley, S., Banton, B., & Marley, D. (2011). *Jah army. Revelation Pt. 1 – The root of life*. [Album]. Tuff Gong label.

Manuel, P. (2006). *Caribbean currents: Caribbean music from rumba to reggae.* Temple University Press.

Moore, B., & Wilmot, S. (1998). *Before and after 1865: education, politics and regionalism in the Caribbean: in honor of Sir Roy Augier.* Ian Randle Publishers.

Moore, D. S., Pandian, A. and Kosek, J. (2003). Introduction. The cultural politics of race and nature: Terrains of power and practice. *Race, nature, and the politics of difference* (pp. 1-70). Duke University Press.

More than 600 more JNSC recruits ready for the road. (2021, February 5). *Jamaica Observer*. https://www.jamaicaobserver.com/news/more-than-600-more-jnsc-recruits-ready-for-the-road_214024

Morris, R. (2010). *Can the subaltern speak?: Reflections on the history of an idea.* Columbia University Press.

Mulenga, M. (2012, June 22). *Bob Marley 1979 full HD interview in New Zealand* [Video]. YouTube. https://www.youtube.com/watch?v=xiaZJdOqHw0

Muñíz, H. G. (1988). Defense policy and planning in the Caribbean: An assessment of the case of Jamaica on its 25th independence anniversary. *Caribbean Studies, 21*(1/2), 67–123.

Murrell, N. S. (1998). *Chanting down Babylon: The rastafari reader.* Temple University Press.

Niaah, S. S. (2010). *Dancehall: from slave ship to ghetto.* University of Ottawa Press.

Ogborn, M. (2019). The freedom of speech: Talk and slavery in the anglo-caribbean world. Chicago University Press

Patterson, O. (2019). *The confounding island: Jamaica and the postcolonial predicament.* Harvard University Press.

Price, C. (2009). *Becoming rasta: Origins of rastafari identity in Jamaica.* New York University Press.

Pulis, J. (Ed.). (1999). *Moving on: Black loyalists in the afro-Atlantic world - crosscurrents in African American history.* Routledge Press.

Sasco, A. (2005). Step pan dem. *Infiltration*. [Album]. VP Records label.

Senior, B. (1969). *Jamaica, as it was, as it is, and as it may be.* Greenwood Publishing Group.

Sheller, M. (2001). *Democracy after slavery: Black publics and peasant radicalism in Haiti and Jamaica.* University of Florida Press.

Sheller, M. (2012). *Citizenship from below: Erotic agency and Caribbean freedom.* Duke University Press.

Sparta, T. L. (2013). Spartan soldier. *Spartan soldier*. [Album]. Guzu Musiq label.

Stone, C. (1982). Values, norms and personality development in Jamaica [Paper presentation]. National Consultation on Values and Attitudes, Kingston - Jamaica. https://gtuwi.tripod.com/stonearticle.htm

Tosh, P. (2007, March 1). *Peter Tosh: Interview (during the reggae sunplash)* [Video]. YouTube. https://www.youtube.com/watch?v=jXwOjSVoU3s

Trouillot, M. R. (1995). *Silencing the past: power and the production of history.* Beacon Press.

Walcott, D. (1993). *The Antilles: fragments of epic memory: The Nobel lecture.* Farrar Straus Giroux.

Waters, A. M. (1997). *Rastafari and reggae in Jamaican politics: race, class, and political symbols.* Jamaica Information Service.

CHAPTER 5

Revisiting the role of Popular Culture in supporting the anti-Apartheid Movement (1970s-1980s)

Archie W. Simpson

Centre for Small State Studies, University of Iceland, Iceland

Abstract

This chapter explores how various forms of popular culture including music, sport, and cinema galvanised support for the anti-Apartheid movement, and reviews how these forms of popular culture communicated the anti-apartheid message to a global audience, particularly during the 1970s and 1980s. Global recognition of the anti-Apartheid movement was promulgated by the soft power of popular culture. The message of the anti-Apartheid movement was that apartheid sustained an anti-democratic regime that was racist, unjust and illegitimate. This chapter uses the concept of "soft power" as a conceptual lens to examine how popular culture provided a platform for the anti-Apartheid message and demonstrated support for anti-Apartheid campaigners inside South Africa. From the 1960s onwards, various forms of popular culture responded to apartheid by highlighting its inherent racism and institutional injustices. The chapter outlines what the apartheid system involved before explaining the concepts of "soft power" and "new media spaces." Various examples of the ways in which popular culture conveyed the anti-apartheid message in the 1970s and 1980s will then be outlined including sporting boycotts, films and songs. The example of "Live Aid" will also be discussed as an example of pop music activism in the 1980s. The resulting support for the anti-apartheid movement subsequently translated into political pressure that helped end the apartheid system in the early 1990s.

Keywords: Anti-apartheid, popular culture, soft power, sports, cinema, music

***

Introduction

"She's got a system they call apartheid. It keeps a brother in a subjection. But maybe pressure can make Jo'anna see. How everybody could a live as one."
Lyrics from 'Gimme Hope Jo'anna' (Eddy Grant, 1988)

"Free, free, free, free, free Nelson Mandela."
Lyrics from 'Nelson Mandela' (Special AKA, 1984)

In April 1994, South Africa held its first free and fair elections following 46 years of apartheid. This followed decades of political struggle, economic sanctions and cultural isolation fostered by a global anti-apartheid movement. As a political system, apartheid was based upon the principle of racial segregation in which the majority of the people had no say in government, and economic inequality was promoted to the detriment of most people simply because of the color of their skin. This chapter explores how various forms of popular culture including music, sport, and cinema galvanised support for the anti-apartheid movement in the 1970s and 1980s. Since the focus of this book is on political messaging in music and entertainment spaces, this chapter delves into various forms of popular culture and contextualizes them in the examination of the global anti-apartheid movement of the 1970s and 1980s. Global recognition and support of the anti-apartheid movement was promulgated by the soft power of popular culture. The political message at the heart of the anti-Apartheid movement was that apartheid sustained an anti-democratic regime that was inherently racist, unjust and illegitimate. As a racist form of governance, apartheid was only formally institutionalised by the South African government from 1948 until 1994. Throughout much of its history, but perhaps especially from the 1960s, apartheid received much international criticism from neighbouring states, international organizations and millions of people worldwide. This chapter will begin by setting out some definitions of important concepts before presenting a historical overview of what apartheid was and how it operated. This will establish the inhumanity of the apartheid regime before exploring how forms of popular culture at the global level helped to communicate the anti-apartheid message. Three forms of popular culture will be used here to illustrate how the anti-apartheid message was conveyed to millions of people worldwide, namely: sports, films and music. Examples of popular culture from these three manifestations of soft power will be cited to further demonstrate how the anti-apartheid message became accepted globally. The pressure supported by popular culture both promoted the anti-apartheid movement across the world and sustained those fighting apartheid within South Africa.

Definitions

The term apartheid is an Afrikaans word for "separateness" or "aparthood" and it became a system of government in South Africa throughout much of the Cold War period. As will be shown throughout this chapter, apartheid was a racist system that segregated people according to their color (or ethnicity) and it was brutally enforced by the state. It was, in every sense, an inhumane, unjust and anti-democratic system of government that was established after the Second World War by only one country, South Africa. The aim of apartheid was to ensure that white Afrikaners controlled the governance of South Africa by excluding the participation of blacks and Asians in government and by severely restricting their economic opportunities so that they were essentially second-class citizens. As Sallaz writes, "In their interactions, whites treated blacks with paternalism or scorn" (Sallaz, 2010, p. 297). Apartheid ended in the early 1990s after decades of political and economic pressure from both within South Africa and from the international community.

The concept of culture can be somewhat troublesome to define but there are broadly two general approaches: the first is to attribute culture as, 'to the worlds of creative expression' (Hodkinson, 2017, p.2) involving intellect and artistic activity. Historically this referred to high culture such as literature, art, theatre and music that was deemed for elite members of society. However, since the development of mass communications to cater for bigger populations, larger, more inclusive forms of *popular culture* exist. Forms of popular culture grew exponentially as new technologies such as television, radio, film, mass printings of books and newspapers developed into the 20th century. This, in turn, fermented further growth in forms of popular culture especially involving younger generations; the baby boomer generations following the Second World War began to come of age in the 1960s which saw a seismic explosion in popular culture particularly in the forms of *rock and pop music*, fashion, cinema, television and radio. The ubiquitous nature of popular culture in the post-war period in Western states made it an everyday feature of modern life. The second approach to understanding culture refers to the values, practices, traditions, behaviors and identities that were formed over time, thus creating meanings and norms for society. The daily routines of any society are embedded in such cultural environments and are formed out of a collective way of life by the populace. While each society is both complex and diverse, overlaps of cultural meanings and values occur as a result of social interaction. Over time these interactions result in commonalities in language, political systems, and religions, and which, in turn, generate shared value-systems and points of reference. These two forms of culture are inherently symbiotic. Culture reflects the broader expressions of society by individuals, groups, organisations and by the state itself. Popular culture is a product for, and made by, the mass collective of society. Dolby also writes that, 'popular culture is a place where youth learn about the world' (Dolby, 2003, p. 263).

Soft power is a concept that was originally expounded by Joseph Nye (1990, p. 2004). Power as a political concept has many definitions including, 'A has power over B to the extent that B would not otherwise do' (Dahl, 1957, p. 203) and, 'power is the ability to affect others to obtain the outcome you want' (Nye, 2008, p. 94). In either sense, then, power stems from socio-political relationships and relates to an ability or capacity to achieve certain intended objectives. In the field of international politics, power is often associated with military, diplomatic and economic capabilities, e.g., the bigger the army, the more powerful you are, or perceived to be. In democratic political systems, politicians gain power through electoral politics that allow the population to authorise a transfer of power to politicians who can then form governments.

There are many forms of power including economic power, the power of persuasion, or the power of violence; the context in which power is used therefore becomes important. Hard power refers to military means while soft power is, perhaps, less tangible as it relates to creating an attraction. Soft power, 'rests on the ability to shape the preferences of others' (Nye, 2004, p.5; Nye, 2008, p. 95). This soft power is not simply a form of influence but instead, 'it is also the ability to attract, and attraction often leads to acquiescence' (Nye, 2004, p. 6). Soft power is therefore inherent in democratic political systems. For example, politicians try to gain support and votes by offering attractive policies to the voters (often by using popular culture as a means of delivering their message). Accordingly, there are three sources of soft power involving culture, political values, and foreign policies (Nye, 2004, p.11; Nye, 2008, p. 97). Importantly, according to Nye, popular culture is a resource that produces soft power (2004, p. 12). Forms of popular culture such as music, films, literature and sports help attraction to shape peoples' preferences. For instance, if you are not American but like watching Hollywood movies then you are showing a predilection for American culture and by extension, for America itself. Popular culture can therefore become an instrument of political communication by transmitting, carrying and amplifying a message to a particular audience or to a general audience(s).

A Brief History of Apartheid

In the wake of the end of the Second World War, the idea of European Empires being normal and acceptable also came to an end. In the post-war world, imperialism was viewed by many as being illegitimate, uneconomic, racist and wholly unacceptable especially as the war against the Nazis was largely about fighting a similar racist ideology. As many European states began the process of European integration in the early 1950s as a means to re-build their national economies, the need to hold colonies in Africa diminished. British Prime Minister Harold MacMillan famously asserted, "the wind of change is blowing through the [African] continent" (in Wainhouse, 1964, p. 28). This led to the beginning of the end of European empires around the world. As northerly African states gained sovereign independence and imperialism was beginning to be dismantled, this alarmed the white-dominated governments in southern Africa. The idea of white supremacy was still strong in the region and coupled with the rise in the ideology of white African nationalism also across the region after the war. Chipkin writes, 'Afrikaner nationalism was a classical nationalism. It defined the political community on the basis of race, language and religion, linking full citizenship to whiteness' (Chipkin, 2016, p. 216). This rise in Afrikaner nationalism developed in South Africa, South West Africa, Rhodesia, Angola and Mozambique (Meredith, 2011, p. 116). The notion that black people should have political equality was viewed with many misgivings by white-dominated governments. The victory of the Afrikaner Nationalist Party led by Daniel François Malan in South Africa in the May 1948 election, was largely based on the policy of introducing apartheid. It was also about South African politics in which Prime Minister Jan Smuts' pro-British position during the war had alienated poorer white workers; this cost him the election. While South Africa had plentiful supply of valuable minerals and gems (including gold and diamonds), and there had been economic growth out of this, many non-English speaking [white] Afrikaners did not benefit from this economic boon, and most of them remained in poverty. Malan's electoral win came as a shock as he sought to redress the wrongs of British imperialism and reaffirm white supremacy in the country.

Apartheid was a highly organized and systematic political structure of racial segregation designed to ensure white supremacy in South Africa at the expense of the majority black population. All aspects of society from politics to economics to education and to housing was framed around racial segregation. The white Afrikaner ideology that created apartheid was based upon a narrative that they had been part of a 300-year-old struggle to maintain their culture and Christian heritage against hostile forces, unhospitable terrain and British imperialism. This narrative argued that the British influence in South Africa undermined their Afrikaner language and traditional way of life. Afrikaner nationalism was also born out of a Boer heritage from early Dutch settlers who farmed the land. The Dutch Reformed Church developed an evangelical-communal outlook that sought to defend white Afrikaners and to protect their ethnic identity while advocating their particular brand of civilisation. Meredith writes, 'to ensure that South Africa's whites retained power permanently, white politicians constructed the most elaborate racial edifice the world has ever seen' (2011, p. 117). The population was divided into four ethnic groupings: white (European), black (African), colored (mixed) and Asian (largely Indian), and legislation covered all aspects of life based on these groupings. There had been a level of emigration to South Africa from the Indian sub-continent during the days of Empire, and many Indians had gone into commerce; this was viewed as an economic threat to white Afrikaners. An awareness of racial ethnicity was embedded into the new apartheid system of government by the 1948 election.

The new government established this apartheid approach through changes to the civil service, legislation, and by increasing the numbers of Afrikaners in government positions and in public corporations such as the rail network. Within weeks of the election, 'whites-only' notices were posted in city suburbs, on buses, on beaches, on trains and in smaller towns. In 1950, the Group Areas Act gave the government the power to assign residential and business areas in towns and cities to different ethnic groupings (Dubow, 2014, p. 37). The Population Registration Act of 1950 dictated that every child was assigned a racial category from birth (Sallaz, 2010, p. 296; Dubow, 2014, p. 37). Such laws entwined the bureaucracy of the South African state with racist ethos of apartheid. In addition, there was anti-communist legislation which drove the Communist Party underground; communism was also viewed as a godless threat to the Afrikaner people. Often white Afrikaners who opposed apartheid were called communists. The practical aspect of Apartheid was to ensure a separation of blacks and Indians from whites as much as possible. Wainhouse, writing in 1964, commented that:

> South Africa's policies for the political, economic, and educational development of the territory have been heavily weighted to favor the white residents and to keep the black Africans under strict control (Wainhouse, 1964, p. 49).

The enforcement of this new, radical and racial system of apartheid extended into every aspect of daily life including employment, residences, education, public amenities, transport, and in politics. In essence it was a system of government designed to subjugate black and Asian Africans in South Africa to the advantage of the white Afrikaner people. But there was inevitably opposition to the apartheid system in the country. The African National Congress (ANC) was founded in 1912 (Meredith, 2005, p. 117) but it had proved to be a minor and ineffective political party in its early years. In the 1940s, many black people moved from farming to the cities to escape poverty and hunger to work in the more prosperous wartime industries. However, the housing conditions were squalid, food prices were increasingly expensive and squatter camps began to appear around cities like Johannesburg. Such conditions fostered a militant mood among many workers leading to mineworkers going on strike in 1946. The ANC had called for full citizenship rights in 1943 in accordance with the Atlantic Charter, drawn up by Prime Minister Winston

Churchill and US President Franklin D. Roosevelt (Kissinger, 1994, p. 391: Collins, 2013, p. 25). A wave of younger political activists emerged in the 1940s, including Nelson Mandela, Oliver Tambo and Govan Mbeki; they were part of the youth wing of the ANC. The ANC included liberals, Christians and communists, but this younger generation became increasingly radical as they saw themselves as part of the global anti-colonial movement. With increased urbanisation occurring and the introduction of apartheid, the new leaders of the ANC announced a "programme of action" in 1949 that included strikes, boycotts (of white businesses) and peaceful civil disobedience (Meredith, 2005, p. 119). The government responded by using anti-communist legislation to counter the acts of civil disobedience. For instance, people who were 'named' or labelled as communists by the government could be arrested, their movements restricted and may be banned from any form of public appearance. In 1952, the ANC organised a defiance campaign to highlight the growing injustices of apartheid; this involved a campaign of civil disobedience which was designed to overwhelm the South African court system and prisons. In a five-month period, over 8,000 were imprisoned (Meredith, 2005, p. 119) but the campaign turned the ANC into a mass movement as it showed defiance to apartheid. Mandela was accused of being a communist and was imprisoned. New, tougher laws were introduced in order to combat this wave of popular unrest. The government used mass surveillance, banning orders, harassment of activists and essentially made all protests illegal. In addition, police violence was used extensively followed by mass trials to convict people. The Native Laws Amendment Act of 1952 revised existing legislation, including making it illegal for Africans to visit proclaimed towns and cities for longer than 72 hours, ensuring that carrying identification cards was mandatory, and residency rights could be removed if arrested.

In 1958 Hendrik Verwoerd, a fanatical supporter and proponent of apartheid, became the new prime minister of South Africa. He responded to the growing unrest by introducing a 'divide and conquer' approach to the black majority by sub-dividing the black population into ethnic groups or nations, and then giving them control of their own tribal homelands. The idea was to allow some limited political rights within these homelands but in real terms it meant that the black population was divided in order to contain their ability to act in unison across South Africa. The Department of Native Affairs would indirectly rule over this new arrangement by managing the flow of workers from the homelands to the cities, farms and mines. The territorial separation coupled with apartheid laws on segregation was designed to allow the white population to prosper while ensuring the black majority would remain divided. Verwoerd spoke of a multi-ethnic state with 8 homelands for the black majority (Meredith, 2005, p. 121). Furthermore, in order to control the black population, the Department of Native Affairs built dormitories aside from city centres that were fenced off. It became the law that any black African aged 16 or over had to carry a pass book, or identification card, at all times. The 'pass laws' of 1952 were designed to help monitor the black population and this became a hated symbol of apartheid. However, the 1961 Sharpeville massacre brought the attention of the outside world to the brutality and savagery of the apartheid system.

On 21st March 1961, there was a demonstration against the pass laws in the township of Sharpeville as part of nation-wide protests; Sharpeville itself was a small township. About 5000 demonstrators were involved when the police, without any real warning(s), began to fire shots into the crowd (Dobow, 2014, p. 76). Thörn writes, 'sixty-nine people were killed, and 186 others, including 8 children, were seriously injured. Many of them were shot in the back" (p. 127) as they ran away from the scene of the protests. The police later suggested that shots came from the crowd, but there was no evidence to buttress the police account of the killings, neither were the false claims supported by eyewitnesses. This horrific fracas, depicted in the film *Long Walk to Freedom* (Chadwick, 2013), became symbolic of the violence used by the South African authorities against the black population. Indeed, Sharpeville became, and remains to this day, a by-word for the brutality of the apartheid system. It led to further violence and demonstrations as news about the massacre spread across South Africa. Sharpeville also quickly became a major news story globally and placed apartheid under greater scrutiny as people around the world began to recognise the realities of apartheid. Internationally, the event was condemned and there was a United Nations Security Council resolution blaming the racist policies of South Africa (Meredith, 2005, p. 122) for the Sharpeville massacre. Crucially, Sharpeville became a watershed event in the anti-apartheid movement as its international impact mobilised millions around the world and further galvanised the ANC within South Africa. International support for the anti-apartheid movement grew substantially and the message about the racial discrimination of apartheid was clear. Sharpeville was an important, and tragic event that revealed to an international audience the horrors of apartheid.

The massacre led to further violence, protests, strikes and disorder as people reacted to the news. This, in turn, saw the police shoot more black people in response. Verwoerd stood firm against opposition and introduced emergency powers which his government used to proscribe the ANC. Thousands were arrested and the ANC went underground, supported by a network of allies in South Africa, neighbouring states and further afield. A campaign of mass non-cooperation was orchestrated by Nelson Mandela in the wake of Sharpeville; Mandela was operating surreptitiously from township to township as he evaded capture for several months as an arrest warrant for him had been made by the authorities (Meredith, 2005, p.123). Revolts against the authorities sprang up across South Africa. The government issued new powers for the police and army, and nightly raids were made in townships as the authorities fought to maintain control. A campaign of sabotage against the government began and this lasted for 18 months (Meredith, 2005, p. 125). The campaign involved bombings, attacks on radio masts, attacks on police stations and disrupting electricity pylons. This led to a greater crackdown by the government, more arrests, and more violence by the authorities.

Mandela briefly left South Africa in secret, arrived back and was arrested in August 1962 (Dubow, 2014, p. 94). Along with some others, he was "tried" and convicted on charges sabotage and attempted revolution, and sentenced of life imprisonment; he narrowly escaped the death penalty. Mandela, a lawyer by training, conducted his own defence at the purported trial, and made international news in the process. The crackdown, coupled with the arrests of leading ANC members like Mandela, was a major blow to the struggle against apartheid within South Africa. By the mid-1960s, the South African authorities had seriously and for all practical purposes dismantled opposition to apartheid as most political opponents were either in prison, in exile or dead. The government used the resulting lack of coordinated attacks and opposition against it to unleash violence against black Africans on a daily basis, until such state-sponsored violence became routine and normalized. Many blacks were thus constrained to live in shanty townships in poverty and penury as the apartheid system continued to prosper.

In 1970 the Bantu Homeland Citizenship Act (Sallaz, 2010, p. 297) created a system in which 'homelands' were constructed to relocate the black population. Usually, these homelands were on small, barren patches of land without access to basic utilities and amenities. This further segregated the black population from the white Afrikaners and reinforced the racial inequality of apartheid. Bantu education acts prohibited private schools from allowing blacks and the Native Affairs department centralised education for blacks, only providing basic educational knowledge (Dubow, 2014, p. 119). For a variety of reasons, the economy began to face a downturn by the mid-1970s. The global energy crisis of the 1970s, the falling price of gold, and economic boycotts began to seriously undermine the South African economy. In 1972 there were new laws, 'allowing South African leisure firms to build and operate casino resorts in the homelands' (Sallaz, 2010, p. 297) though the managers of such resorts were white as were the patrons. The idea was to generate new income and ostensibly project an image of racial integration in South Africa to the international audience and community. Places like 'Sun City' were developed (see later) as a means of developing tourism; in some senses this was an attempt at producing soft power to make South Africa more appealing to international tourists. However, the underlying racism of apartheid continued unabated.

On the 16th June 1976 there was a mass demonstration by school children objecting to the new law enacted by the South African government which mandated the use of Afrikaans, the language of the ruling apartheid overlords, as the medium of instruction in local black schools. About 15,000-20,000 (Dubow, 2014, p. 180) children from Soweto, a black township near Johannesburg, marched towards the Orlando Stadium to protest. The police responded by firing tear gas and live bullets into the crowd. Fatality figures vary but it is generally estimated that 176 to 332 people, mainly school children, were killed with about 1,139 others injured (Dubow, 2014, pp. 180-181; Morgan, 2017, pp. 5-6). More people were killed by the South African police and security officials in the course of the following year as the tempo of the protests continued to rise. Thus, Soweto became another watershed moment in South Africa, and again made headline news across the world.

Anti-Apartheid activism through Sports boycotts

The international anti-apartheid movement began in the 1950s as a means of highlighting the inhumanity of the South African regime. The movement sought to put the apartheid regime under as much pressure as possible as a way of ending apartheid (Klee, 2012). As part of this pressure, 'economic, cultural and sports boycotts and sanctions – disinvestment, and divestment – represent[ed] crucial strategies' (Thörn, 2006, p.60) of the movement. Using popular culture as a method of communicating the anti-apartheid message became one element in the soft power of the movement. Sports, and especially rugby union, was a prominent part of life for white South Africans as it gave them a chance to show their prowess. Consequently, sporting boycotts became an obvious and prominent way of protesting and undercutting the apartheid regime internationally. Sporting boycotts became an early, and highly effective, feature of isolating South Africa through popular culture. Maclean writes:

> It was the formation of the Boycott Movement Committee drawing together representatives of anti-apartheid groups from South Africa and the UK in London in December 1959 that marked a significant new level of co-ordination in the campaign coinciding with an emerging activist campaign in New Zealand focussing on the 1960 rugby tour of South Africa under the slogan 'No Maoris, No Tour (Maclean, 2014, p. 1835).

From 1960 onwards, a wide number of sporting boycotts against South Africa led to its exclusion in the sporting world. The legislation that separated blacks, whites and Asians meant that inter-racial sporting events in the country could only occur if a permit was obtained. In 1963 an Indian golfer, Sewsunker Sewgolum, won the Natal Golf Open but the trophy was handed to him through a window and the South African Broadcasting Corporation stopped news reports of the tournament (Maclean, 2014, p. 1836). In 1962 the South African Non-Racial Olympic Committee (SANROC) was established to try to ensure that sports teams were chosen on merit and not on racial grounds. SANROC, alongside similar sporting bodies inside South Africa, 'were created with the aim to not only isolate South Africa from international sport but also to help destroy the policy of apartheid' (Klee, 2012, p. 159). South Africa was not invited to the 1964 Tokyo Olympics as it was alleged by SANROC that the South African Olympic Committee was practicing racial discrimination. Leaders of SANROC were arrested, put under house arrest, went in exile or went underground (Nixon, 1992, p. 77). The racist attitude of the South African government in the 1960s became increasingly evident as they asked the New Zealand All-Blacks Rugby Union team not to pick any Maori players in their squad (Dubow, 2014, p. 151) in the 1967 tour and called the English cricket team not to pick Basil D'Oliveira (Thörn, 2006, p.142; Klee, 2012, p. 161) for their 1968 tour of South Africa due to his color. D'Oliveria was born in Cape Town, South Africa and was the only non-white in the English cricket team at that time. Initially, he was not chosen for the tour until another player got injured, and he was chosen as a replacement, although there had been widespread protests about his exclusion. When he was chosen to be part of the tour, the South African authorities cancelled the English team's visit. The D'Oliveria case became a catalyst for anti-apartheid activists when the South African Springbok[1] tour of Britain in 1969-70 led to protests, pitch invasions and public debates. Indeed, sporting boycotts became a highly effective means of isolating South Africa culturally. Nixon writes,

> In countries where the premier sports overlapped with those of South Africa – Britain, most of Africa, India, New Zealand, Pakistan, the Anglosphere Caribbean, France, Ireland, Australia, Sri Lanka, Italy and Argentina – outrage over competition against white South Africa teams gave vital impetus to local anti-apartheid movements (Nixon1992, p.70).

The D'Oliveria case became an important incident in isolating South Africa from the rest of the sporting world as it opened up a public debate about apartheid, it motivated anti-apartheid activists, and it (again) highlighted the racism of the apartheid regime. Crucially though, it also pushed the anti-apartheid movement from symbolic protests and demonstrations to direct action. The Springbok tour of 1970 became highly political as anti-apartheid activists carried out a range of direct actions against the tour including demonstrators running onto pitches during games, throwing orange smoke pellets at players, protests at games, activists chaining themselves to the tour

---

[1] The term Springbok is used as a name for the South African rugby union team.

bus as well as other violent clashes involving protesters and the police (Thörn, 2006, p.150). Such direct action dominated news headlines and consequently brought the anti-apartheid message to millions of people around the globe. In parallel with direct action, the anti-apartheid movement published and posted thousands of leaflets to ensure that the message was communicated as widely as possible inside South Africa and beyond.

The anti-apartheid message using sports as soft power had a clear success when South Africa was suspended from the 1968 Mexico Olympics. SANROC which had collapsed in 1964 as its leaders were detained or were in hiding from the authorities but was reformed in 1966. It began a campaign of lobbying and was able to convince 32 African states and 8 others to threaten a boycott of the Olympics if South Africa participated (Nixon, 1992, p. 78). In fact, 50 nations threatened to boycott the games in Mexico and, in addition, African-American athletes in the US Olympic team also threatened non-participation in Mexico if South Africa was permitted to compete. Following from this pressure, changes to the International Olympic Committee in 1970 meant that South Africa was expelled from the Olympic movement. The anti-apartheid movement, through SANROC, had succeeded in isolating South Africa from the Olympic Games. Such success led to a chain of events in which teams or nations refused to participate in sporting events with South Africa. Boycotts and protests extended towards any other nation or organization that maintained sporting ties to South Africa. This meant that New Zealand came under pressure from the anti-apartheid movement. Indeed the 1976 Montreal Commonwealth Games[2] were subject to a mass boycott by African states following a New Zealand rugby tour of South Africa (Nixon, 1992, p. 78). The sporting boycotts of South Africa continued until the end of apartheid. This soft power of sport as a form of popular culture conveyed a powerful message. While there were a few rogue tours, usually involving cricket, the sporting boycott of South Africa held firm. South African teams could not go abroad, they could not tour other countries, and were quarantined from the sporting world.

Boycotts involving rugby union were particularly arduous on South Africa as this was seen as its [main] national sport. For the most part this boycott involved British and Irish national teams (England, Scotland, Wales, and Ireland), New Zealand, Argentina, and Australia. By the mid-1970s South Africa was in sporting isolation aside from its involvement in the Davis Cup tennis tournaments. Tennis was, possibly, the only major sport that had not yet boycotted South Africa and in 1978, South Africa was still able to compete in

---

[2] The Commonwealth Games are an international multi-sporting event held every four years. Competing nations are former members of the British Empire; this includes England, Scotland, Northern Ireland and Wales.

the Davis Cup. The Davis Cup began in 1900 as a competition between the USA and Britain but expanded allowing for other national tennis teams to compete (Daviscup.com, n.d.). By the 1970s, it was the prominent national tennis competition involving some 50 states. In 1974, South Africa won the Davis Cup (Daviscup.com, n.d.). South Africa was briefly banned from the Davis Cup after refusing a visa to African-American Arthur Ashe in 1970 from competing in tennis tournaments (Morgan, 2017, p. 4); however, the government later granted Ashe permission entry to the country.

According to Morgan, 'in 1976, the American Coordinating Committee for Equality in Sport and Society (ACCESS) served as a coalition of over a dozen organizations and advocated for an international sport boycott' (Morgan, 2017, p. 4). ACCESS lobbied sporting organizations in the US to support the boycott of South Africa. Tennis became a focal point for ACCESS as there were few sports in which South Africa competed with the US especially after the other sporting boycotts. President Carter, a strong advocate of human rights, had been elected as US President and he sought better relations with African states. It is also important to recall that the civil rights movement in the US throughout the 1960s had a particular focus on the rights of African-Americans. ACCESS lobbied the American government and the American tennis authorities to support a ban on South Africa. A debate about a potential ban of South African participation in the David Cup began with arguments on both sides; on the one hand allowing South Africa to compete was seen as supporting apartheid but the counter-argument was that sport should not mix with politics. The Davis Cup round involving the US and South Africa went ahead with heavy security. Following the example of anti-apartheid activists in Britain, there were protests, demonstrators that disrupted matches, and motor oil was poured onto a court (Morgan, 2017, p. 9). Many more protests took place and events like the Soweto uprising in 1976 and the death of Stephen Biko inspired the demonstrations (see later). At the least, the arguments about apartheid were being seriously debated in the US. Ray Moore, a South Africa's most prominent tennis player said he would not compete in the 1978 round of the Davis Cup as it was becoming political (Morgan, 2017, pp. 11-12). Attendance levels at matches were affected, security costs were increasing and protests continued. The controversy over South African participation in the Davis Cup and, in particular, playing in the US-led to two years of protests. Eventually, the International Tennis Federation expelled South Africa from both the Davis Cup and the Federation Cup. In 1979 the South African government was asked to form a non-racial tennis organization. The government refused to comply, so South Africa's expulsion followed. (Morgan, 2017, pp. 12-13). The tennis boycott lasted until 1992, when the reforms to end apartheid commenced.

The sporting boycott meant that by the late 1970s South Africa had its membership either cancelled or suspended from a wide range of international sporting organizations (MacLean, 2014; Morgan, 2017, p. 2). Consequently, South African sports was severely curtailed in cricket, netball, football/soccer, basketball, swimming, cycling, tennis, and in the Olympics. At the international level, the anti-apartheid message was supported by many sub-Saharan African states, many of which had achieved independence from former colonial powers. The Soviet bloc, including much of East-Central Europe was also firmly supportive of the anti-apartheid message. Importantly, the sporting boycotts achieved many objectives in terms of conveying the anti-apartheid message. First, as a form of popular culture sports was important to the white Afrikaner people. It aligned favorably with their self-perception as strong, robust and 'civilised' people. Sports was also a means to maintain contact with 'white' European and Commonwealth nations, especially in rugby union. In some respects, sport was of some importance psychologically to the white Afrikaners as a collective as it bonded them together. Second, the boycotts were supported by the ANC and other anti-apartheid activists from *within* South Africa. The boycotts were viewed as important ways of showing solidarity with the black majority population and as a means of pressurising the South African government. Third, the boycotts clearly brought apartheid to the attention of millions worldwide. The various controversies involving sports including the exclusion of blacks in South African teams as well as pressure by the South Africans to exclude black players in other national teams made headline news around the world. The boycotts both highlighted the problems of apartheid and were part of a wider anti-apartheid agenda. Sporting boycotts were also practical ways for athletes and the general public to show their dislike of apartheid. Shocking events like Sharpeville horrified millions worldwide and thus boycotts of South African products and sports became a way to show distaste for apartheid. By isolating South Africa in sporting terms, the soft power of popular culture became a tangible and effective means of coercing the regime to jettison its obnoxious policy of racial segregation.

The Anti-Apartheid message in Films

Since the end of apartheid in 1994, there have been a myriad of films about South Africa relating to the apartheid era. Films like "Cry: The Beloved Country" (1995), "Skin" (2008), "Invictus" (2009), and "Long Walk to Freedom" (2013), have all been set (or partially set) during the apartheid period. The "Long Walk to Freedom" (2013) is the biopic of Nelson Mandela based upon his autobiography. These films, importantly, conveyed a narrative about life during the apartheid era. Issues of racial segregation, violence against blacks, racial prejudice, education under apartheid, and the politics of apartheid are communicated through these films. The central theme throughout sets out a highly real but negative view of apartheid albeit from a retrospective viewpoint. In many respects, they conform to the mainstream anti-apartheid message that developed since the 1950s. But there were also films made during the apartheid period that also showcased the cruelty and violence of South Africa. Films like "Cry Freedom" (1987) and "A Dry White Season" (1990) portrayed the horrors of apartheid while "Lethal Weapon 2" (1989) chose South African characters as the baddies. The soft power of films as a source of information and as an audio-visual representation of apartheid fed into the anti-apartheid message. The verisimilitude of such films acted as an effective means of communicating the anti-apartheid message to millions of people worldwide by fostering a greater awareness about the situation. According to Ansell, films about Africa in general terms, fulfil a number of objectives such as providing an image(s) of Africa, allowing African voices to be heard, explaining the relations of Africa with Western states, and helps viewers to see a relationship between their own lives and those of people in Africa (Ansell, 2002, p. 4). Films released during the apartheid era, such as "Cry Freedom" (1987) contained powerful narratives about life under apartheid that were largely critical of the South African authorities.

The film "Cry Freedom" (1987) starred Denzel Washington as Steven Biko and Kevin Kline as Donald Woods, and tells the story of Biko. Steven Biko was a black journalist and activist in South Africa in the 1970s who became involved in helping anti-apartheid activists in the mid-1970s. He formed a friendship with white journalist Donald Woods and the film is partly about their relationship but largely about Biko's activism which led to his death in the hands of South African police. The film depicts many aspects of the daily realities of apartheid including the shanty townships, the poverty, the daily violence by the police towards blacks, and the killing of Biko by the South African police. It also presents an account of the Soweto uprising. The visceral depiction of the horrors of apartheid are evident throughout and the anti-apartheid message communicated by the film is clear. The [suspicious] death of Biko became a *cause célèbre* and part of the anti-apartheid narrative as illustrated by this film and by the song "Biko" (1980) by Peter Gabriel. As a form of popular culture, this film was able to portray apartheid as a brutal, racist and unjust form of governance to a mass audience. Moreover, the film was based on actual events and was not a wholly fictional account of apartheid. And much of the international audience would have been unfamiliar with the kind of reality faced by black South Africans at that time. The film was directed by Richard Attenborough who had also directed the biopic "Gandhi" (1982) which also included some depictions of South Africa under apartheid.

The film "A Dry White Season" (1990) was released at the end of the Cold War starred Marlon Brando and Donald Sutherland. This film is set in 1976, the year of the Soweto uprising, and it focuses on a white teacher called Ben Du Toit, played by Sutherland, who ignores the politics of South Africa. The film is fictional but inspired by the context of politics in South Africa. When the son of his black gardener is arrested by the police for being part of a demonstration, Du Toit agrees to investigate the matter. The film highlights the racism and police brutality inherent in the white Afrikaner community. In the course of the film, Du Toit's gardener is tortured and killed by the police. Concerned over the death of his gardener, Du Toit tries to use the justice system to find some justice but he loses his case. He then becomes embroiled in the politics of the anti-apartheid movement. Unfortunately for him, in the course of the film, his family becomes disenchanted with his activities and his daughter betrays him. In essence, the film communicates the everyday racism of the apartheid society, the violence used routinely by the police, and how the politics of apartheid divided people in South Africa. Like "Cry Freedom" (1987), some liberal white people in Afrikaner society are depicted as perhaps suggesting that reforming the system of apartheid was possible.

While both "Cry Freedom" (1987) and "A Dry White Season" (1990) could be said to be politically-literate films that clearly conveyed the anti-apartheid message, "Lethal Weapon 2" (1989) was a blockbuster film. As part of the "Lethal Weapon" franchise, its target audience mainly consisted of younger people on a mass scale; the main purpose of this film was to entertain. The main characters in the films are played by Mel Gibson (Riggs) and Danny Glover (Murtaugh) as detective/cops in Los Angeles. The storyline revolves around them protecting a police informant, played by Joe Pesci, while investigating a shipment of gold Krugerrands (South African currency). In their investigation, they link the Krugerrands to drug smuggling and to the involvement of South African diplomats. In one scene, Riggs and Murtaugh go to a South African consulate in which Murtaugh (an African-American) pretends to want to emigrate to South Africa. The scene is comically ironic but serves to communicate the anti-apartheid message. To those with some knowledge of apartheid, the scene is ironic; to those without knowledge, it raises an awareness about the nature of apartheid. The symbolism of the "Lethal Weapon 2" (1989) is twofold: the anti-apartheid message had become mainstream in Hollywood by the late 1980s, and that the message was now through popular culture the dominant narrative about South Africa. In a real sense, portraying South African Afrikaners in popular culture as the baddies was now commonplace.

Films released in the post-apartheid period also dealt with apartheid such as the film "Skin" (2008) that tells the true story of Sandra Laing who was born to white parents but she had a mixed-race appearance. She is sent to a boarding school but her appearance leads to complaints from other pupils and she is registered as being 'coloured' by the authorities. Following an international outrage, she is re-classified as white. However, the day-to-day racism and problems caused by her appearance leads her to live her life as a black woman in South Africa. The film highlights the institutional racism of apartheid as it relates to the experiences of one woman. The true-life nature of the film makes it a powerful statement about life in apartheid South Africa.

Both "Invictus" (2009) and "Long Walk to Freedom" (2013) focus on Nelson Mandela who was imprisoned for 27 years by the apartheid regime. Mandela became a talisman for the anti-apartheid movement and a central political figure in transforming South Africa from apartheid to democratic rule. Indeed, he became President of a multi-racial, multi-ethnic South Africa in 1994 as the first free-and-fair elections took place in the country. The film "Long Walk to Freedom" (2013) is the biopic of Mandela as it details his life in South Africa and explains how he got involved in the struggle against apartheid. The Sharpeville massacre is part of the narrative and Mandela's trial is portrayed as he is sentenced to life in prison. "Invictus" (2009) includes imagery from Mandela's early life but focuses on how he used the Rugby Union World Cup in 1995 as a way of unifying South Africa as a multi-ethnic, multi-racial society. Both films feed into the mythology of Mandela as a great political leader.

The role of film as a source of soft power in communicating the anti-apartheid message is interesting. Many of the films mentioned in this chapter were inspired by actual events and the imagery of townships, racism, police violence, and how the politics of South Africa affected the daily lives of people are both powerful and compelling. Depictions and references to real events like the Sharpeville massacre, the Soweto uprising and the death of Steve Biko explain why the dissensus of the anti-apartheid movement was morally necessary. Indeed, the depiction of actual historical events serve as a means to remember such incidents and to re-affirm the moral integrity of the anti-apartheid movement. While some distasteful aspects of the movement are perhaps ignored or overlooked in these films, the core message about the racist and immoral nature of apartheid as a political system are clear. As forms of popular culture, the imagery, narratives and artistry of films act as a form of soft power that informs the political perceptions of viewers. In conjunction with the political machinations of the anti-apartheid movement both within and outside South Africa, films gained a greater resonance with the message. Films about apartheid were (and are) able to simplify complex political and historical issues into narratives about how the black majority were treated during the apartheid era. They also increase awareness about the issues raised by apartheid and illustrate through imagery and sound and thereby become forms of information.

Rock and Pop music and the Anti-Apartheid message

Rock and pop music became a more prominent stimulus in carrying the anti-apartheid message in the 1980s. As a significant form of popular culture, music has always been able to communicate messages and commentaries about society. Indeed, national anthems are used to project patriotic messages about the states they represent. Street writes, 'there is...a familiar and long tradition of songs which...have become associated with social movements' (2003, p. 122). Popular music, arguably, underwent a revolution in the 1960s as the baby boom generation came of age. This revolution was central in establishing a youth culture that celebrated freedom, diversity and a better future despite the context of the Cold War. An explosion of many forms of rock and pop music occurred spurred on by innovative groups like the Beatles, the Rolling Stones, Led Zeppelin, and many others. A song like *The Times They are A-Changin'* by Bob Dylan (1964) was quasi-political but it reflected wider generational changes in most Western societies. The civil rights movement in the US coupled with the politics of the Vietnam War throughout the 1960s fed into popular culture in many ways but particularly through pop music. This youth culture largely encouraged by music, films, television and radio became a ubiquitous feature of contemporary society. Pop culture and youth culture became integral parts of popular culture in Western states and, perhaps especially, in the USA.

By the early 1980s, a number of important developments occurred that promoted pop culture further. Firstly, technology was improving in terms of the delivery of pop culture. This included the development of the Walkman: a small, portable tape-playing device that could be carried by the individual who could listen to music through headphones; the development of the CD (Compact Disc) player that become the dominant way to play music in a high fidelity and digital format; and the development of satellites that fostered many new television channels. In the USA, this meant an expansion of Cable TV channels, including the Cable News Network (CNN) and, importantly, the music television channel, MTV. This increase in television channels was duplicated across Western Europe; American channels could now be accessed in Europe as well. The launch of MTV in 1981 in the USA was very important for youth culture and popular culture. The synergy of popular culture, new technologies and consumerism reached a zenith in the 1980s. Sociologists may argue that such developments contributed towards the idea of the 'global village' that characterizes globalization. Secondly, by the 1980s pop music culture had matured since the 1960s. The 1970s had seen a rebellious form of music through punk rock that morphed into post-punk by 1980. Rock and pop music created many international stars like Mick Jagger, Paul McCartney, Michael Jackson, Madonna and Bruce Springsteen. Consequently, several forms of rock and pop music developed. New forms and styles of music like rap, hip-hop, new wave and electronica emerged as new technologies changed how music was made. The development of the "pop video" was also important as singers promoted their newest songs to international audiences; MTV proved to be particularly important in this cultural shift.

In Britain, Prime Minister Margaret Thatcher and her conservative domestic policies were controversial; they led to industrial strife with a year-long miners' strike. Higher levels of unemployment followed as she implemented her conservative economic reforms. In the US President Ronald Reagan also followed a conservative agenda that caused some levels of economic turmoil. The despondency created by social and economic changes were reflected through rock and pop music both in the United States and Britain. As Street (2003) acknowledges, "Music has long been a site of resistance" (p. 120), so some British pop groups became politically militant in their songs. For example, in 1981, *The Specials* released the song "Ghost Town" (The Specials, 1981) that was a lamentation of the changing industrial landscape in Britain as it affected young people. This turn in using music to communicate political messages was *not* a new phenomenon as such, but it was reaching a new audience in the 1980s.

Such developments were instrumental in [some] rock and pop music becoming political. There were, of course, many songs by anti-apartheid artists in South Africa itself. The anti-apartheid message became a part of rock and pop through a number of important songs. Songs like "Biko" (1980) by Peter Gabriel and the anthemic "Free Nelson Mandela" (1984) by the Special AKA became well known (and are still well known today) and created a greater awareness of the apartheid problem to a younger generation (Martini, 2014, 84). Indeed, both these songs highlighted key figures in the struggle against apartheid and they reflected the antagonism towards South Africa. *The Specials*, who had produced "Ghost Town" (The Specials, 1981) collaborated with others to become '*the Special AKA*'. These songs had powerful political messages that reached out to international audiences and serve as examples of soft power. Other similar songs like "Gimme Hope Jo'Anna" by Eddy Grant (1988)[3] and "Something Inside So Strong" (1987) by Labi Siffre were political calls for change and solidarity in South Africa. Importantly these popular songs became part of the anti-apartheid message in the 1980s and they fed into the pop culture of the 1980s; these songs also had accompanying videos and were played (and still are) at concerts. With new media channels like MTV showing the videos and CNN reporting news stories about state violence against blacks

---

[3] The 'Jo'Anna' in the Eddy Grant song is shorthand for Johannesburg.

in South Africa, the synergy of anti-apartheid images and sounds carried a powerful anti-apartheid message globally.

In the late autumn of 1984, there was a BBC news report about one of the most terrible famines of the 20th century that was taking place in Ethiopia (Dercon and Porter, 2012; Davis, 2010). Scenes of thousands of skeletal people walking across hard deserts to find food and water were shocking. Indeed, the scale of the famine was of biblical proportions. Davis writes that the news reports, 'graphically portrayed the horrors of mass starvation' (2010, p. 91). Dercon and Porter write, 'up to a million people may have died, and many more were left destitute, making it one of the worst famines in recent history, and on par with the Chinese famine of 1959–1961' (2012, p. 928). Bob Geldof, the Irish lead singer of the rock group The Boomtown Rats saw the news and felt that something had to be done to help the Ethiopian people. In simple terms, the politics of the Cold War meant that Western intervention was impossible as Ethiopia was a communist state aligned to the Soviet Union. Geldof called his friend Midge Ure, a Scottish pop star and they wrote a song. The song was "Do They Know its Christmas Time" (1984) and the idea was to record and release the song as a means of raising funds for Ethiopia (Davis, 2010, p. 92). They called upon many other rock and pop stars to help record the song and it was released before Christmas 1984. The famine in Ethiopia dominated news headlines in Britain and quickly became a major international story. 1 million records were sold in its first week and it became the number one single in Britain for 5 weeks becoming the fastest single of all time (*The Guardian*, 2016). It led to calls for a major concert to raise more funds and maintain the awareness of the problem. The concert was called Live Aid and it took place on 13th July 1985 (Davis, 2010, p. 95). The concert began at Wembley stadium in London but additional concert sites around the world included Philadelphia and Tokyo; the concert was broadcast over 16 hours around the world. The soft power of pop music (or pop activism) was making a difference. In the US, it spurred the song "We Are the World" by USA for Africa (1985) (Davis, 2010, p. 92) that illustrated the global concern for Ethiopia. These songs had accompanying videos, concerts, and symbolised a humanitarian spirit that echoed the anti-apartheid movement. Both songs also raised millions in cash to alleviate the situation in Ethiopia as much as possible. Live Aid was a historic event in many respects as it fully utilised new visual and telecommunications technologies to raise approximately $70 million (Davis, 2010, p. 95).

One of the resorts developed by South Africa to encourage tourism was called "Sun City". It was a large luxury hotel and casino resort that opened in 1979 offering gambling that was illegal in South Africa. Sun City was located inside a 'homeland' and so it was technically deemed to be outside South Africa. It was obvious that this was only a ruse. Many singers were invited to perform there including the Beach Boys, Status Quo, Rod Stewart and Queen. This caused controversy because of the cultural boycott of South Africa. In 1985, a member of the E Street Band, Steven van Zandt, used Sun City as the subject of a song with others including Bruce Springsteen. 49 singers were involved in recording 'Sun City' (1985) with the lyrics, "I ain't gonna play Sun City" as part of the chorus. The recording was credited to *Artists United Against Apartheid,* and it was a clear political statement about the apartheid regime. The song, with accompanying video, became part of the global anti-apartheid message. Like Live Aid, it communicated an overtly political message to millions of people. Pop activism as a means of soft power was partly about raising awareness, changing perceptions, showing solidarity with those suffering, and using new technologies to disseminate popular culture. In conjunction with other forms of popular culture like film and sports boycotts, pop activism increased the cultural isolation of South Africa further.

Cultural isolation by the soft power of popular culture

The anti-apartheid movement involved a wide range of protests, symbols, boycotts, lobbying and political persuasion. Activities like encouraging economic boycotts, holding mass demonstrations, starting petitions, highlighting examples of injustice through traditional media, offering evidence at parliamentary inquiries, and publishing magazines and leaflets were all carried out globally. In Glasgow, Scotland's biggest city, a street was named Nelson Mandela Place in 1986, where the South African consulate was located. This was a deliberate way of embarrassing South Africa (The Glasgow story website, 2004). The ANC encouraged the cultural boycott through newsletters, speeches by activists, posters and lobbying. As events like the Sharpeville massacre, the imprisonment of Mandela, the Soweto uprising and the death of Biko kept South Africa in the news headlines around the world, the inherent racism of apartheid was evident to all. Such events both highlighted the need for an anti-apartheid movement and galvanised political, economic and moral support for the movement. The use of popular culture in conveying the anti-apartheid message was a logical, organic and spontaneous process that mirrored wider developments in Western societies. It also illustrated the soft power of popular culture. Dolby writes, 'popular culture is not simply fluff that can be dismissed as irrelevant and insignificant; on the contrary, it has the capacity to intervene in the most critical civic issues and to shape public opinion (Dolby, 2003, p. 259). It is certainly true that the power of popular culture over a sustained period of time to undermine apartheid in South Africa shaped the perception of millions worldwide. On June 11, 1988, a tribute concert in honor of Nelson Mandela for his 70th birthday was held in London. It attracted tens of thousands of his and anti-apartheid supporters and sympathizers inside the Wembley Stadium, venue of the event, and was broadcast to an audience of 600 million in 67 countries (Martini, 2014, p. 82).

The various forms of popular culture reviewed in this chapter that contributed towards the anti-apartheid movement helped end apartheid. While economic boycotts, political isolation, internal dissent and international condemnation of apartheid pressurised the South African regime over several decades, cultural boycotts and artistic criticism of apartheid communicated the anti-apartheid message. When the apartheid bubble began to burst with the release of Nelson Mandela from imprisonment in February 1990, South Africa was rewarded by the cultural and sporting community. In April 1990, there was a charity concert for South Africa and Mandela appeared, a few months after his release from prison (Gibson, 2013). The concert was partly a celebration of Mandela's release but it was also the beginning of the end of the cultural boycott of South Africa. Following the 1994 elections, South Africa became host nation to the Rugby Union World Cup in 1995 and they won the tournament. This was a hugely important event for the rugby-loving country as it signalled that South Africa was now an accepted member of the international community. In 1996, South Africa was given the go-ahead to host the African Cup of Nations by the Confederation of African Football (CAF). This was after Kenya, the original host, sent a last-minute notification to CAF that it could no longer host the football tournament. The football fiesta was watched all over the African continent and beyond.

Conclusion

The anti-apartheid movement in the 1970s and 1980s reflects a number of important lessons. For Thörn (2006) the anti-apartheid movement constituted part of the evolution of a global civil society alongside other social movements like the environmental (or green/ecology) movement, the gender equality movement and the peace movement. In the context of a global civil society, it also reflects the changing developments in media technology and its role in changing perceptions. However, the use of popular culture in various forms (sports, film and popular music) highlights ways in which soft power has the ability to raise awareness and change perceptions. The cultural isolation of South Africa during the apartheid era gradually evolved over several decades partly in response to tragic events, partly in response to encouragement from anti-apartheid forces within and outside the country but largely because of the inhumane, unjust and anti-democratic nature of apartheid.

In some ways, the response to apartheid followed a pattern of behaviour. As the mechanics of apartheid were developed by the South African government through many pieces of legislation and maintained by violence by the security services, internal opposition grew. Dubow writes, 'the policy of apartheid was born in fear, nurtured in hubris, and sustained through obfuscation' (2014, p.276). As the policies of apartheid took hold in South Africa, the consequences for many of its people were devastating. Imposing racial segregation, building townships, denying civil liberties on the basis of skin color, restricting educational opportunities, limiting economic rights, and corrupting the judicial system to enforce white supremacy were counter to Western and indeed human values. In the context of post-war decolonization in which many states gained sovereign independence, South Africa was an archaic rogue state. The crackdown on internal dissent, shown graphically by the Sharpeville massacre of 1961, illustrated the extent to which the South African authorities would go in order to maintain apartheid. In responding to apartheid, the international sporting community reacted appropriately. By refusing to play against South Africa and carrying out boycotts, international sports were able to begin isolating South Africa in a cultural sense. To some extent, it could be argued that at the time (in the early 1960s-1970s) this was a logical and practical response to show contempt for apartheid. With events like Mandela's trial, the death of Biko and the Soweto uprising, films emerged as a way of exposing the racist idiosyncrasies of apartheid. Films like *A Dry White Season* (1990) showcased how apartheid divided South African society and implemented a racist form of governance. Such films fed into the perception of apartheid and became part of the narrative that undercut the South African regime. Alongside pop activism and the many anti-apartheid songs that emerged in the 1980s, apartheid was viewed by millions worldwide as an illegitimate form of government.

The cultural isolation of apartheid South Africa demonstrates that popular culture can be a source of soft power. Popular culture through forms like film, music videos and songs can carry overtly political messaging that changes or informs perceptions about politics. In the case of South Africa, the anti-apartheid message became hegemonic in most Western states, in African states, in India and China, and in the Soviet bloc states during the Cold War. This cultural quarantine of South Africa was a vital part of the overall anti-apartheid campaign. It fulfilled a number of roles including increasing the awareness about apartheid, highlighting the injustices and inequalities of apartheid, and exposing the consequences of apartheid. Of course, the cultural boycott of South Africa was carried out in conjunction with other forms of political and economic pressure but the cultural dynamic perhaps symbolised an intellectual counter to the idea of apartheid. The soft power of popular culture, as shown by the case of South Africa, certainly indicates it has a potent ability to transform political systems.

References

Ansell, N. (2002). Using Films in Teaching about Africa. *Journal of Geography in Higher Education, 26*(3), 355–368.
Artists United Against Apartheid (1985). *Sun City*, EMI.
Attenborough, R. (Director). (1982). *Gandhi* [Film]. Columbia Pictures.
Attenborough, R. (Director). (1987). *Cry Freedom*. [Film]. Universal.
Band Aid (1984). *Do They Know it's Christmas Time?* [Song]. Phonogram (UK), Columbia (US).
BBC. (1988, June 11). *Nelson Mandela Birthday Concert* [Video]. YouTube. https://www.youtube.com/watch?v=QOWW5udtVcg
Booth, D. (2003). Hitting Apartheid for Six? The Politics of the South African Sports Boycott. *Journal of Contemporary History, 38*(3), 477–493.
Chadwick, J. (Director). (2013). *Long Walk to Freedom*. [Film]. 20th Century Fox/Pathe/Distant Horizon.
Chipkin, I. (2016). The Decline of African Nationalism and the State of South Africa. *Journal of Southern African Studies, 42*(1), 215–227.
Collins, M. (2013). Decolonization and the "Federal Moment." *Diplomacy and Statecraft, 24*(1), 21–40.
Dahl, R. A. (1957). The Concept of Power. *Behavioral Science, 2*(3), 201–215.
Davis Cup.Com. (2021, February 26). *David Cup History*. https://www.daviscup.com/en/organisation/davis-cup-history.aspx
Davis, H. L. (2010). Feeding the World a Line?: Celebrity Activism and Ethical consumer Practices from Live Aid to Product Red. *Nordic Journal of English Studies, 9*(3), 89–118.
Dercon, S., & Porter, C. (2014). Live Aid Revisited: Long term Impacts of the 1984 Ethiopian Famine on Children. *Journal of the European Economic Association, 12*(4), 927–948.
Dolby, N. (2003). Popular Culture and Democratic Practice. *Harvard Educational Review, 73*(3), 258–284.
Donner, R. (Director). (1989). *Lethal Weapon 2*. [Film]. Warner Bros.
Dubow, S. (2014). *Apartheid 1948–1994*. Oxford: Oxford University Press.
Dylan, B. (1964). *The Times They are A-Changin'*. [Album]. Columbia Records.
Eastwood, C. (Director). (2009). *Invictus*. [Film]. Warner Bros/Spyglass.
Fabien, A. (Director). (2008). *Skin*. [Film]. Jour de Fete Films/BBC Films.
Gabriel, P. (1980). *Biko*. [Song]. Charisma Records.
Gibson, M. (2013, December 6). Highlights from Nelson Mandela's 1990 Appearance at London Wembley's Charity Concert. *Time*. https://entertainment.time.com/2013/12/06/highlights-from-nelson-mandelas-1990-appearance-at-london-wembleys-charity-concert/
Glasgow Story. (2021, February 26). *Nelson Mandela*. https://www.theglasgowstory.com/image/?inum=TGSA00948
Grant, E. (1988). *Gimme Hope Jo'anna*. [Song]. Parlophone EMI.
Hodkinson, P. (2011). *Media, Culture and Society*. London and Thousand Oaks: Sage.
Kissinger, H. (1994). *Diplomacy*. New York and London: Simon and Schuster.

Klee, J. (2012). Multinational sport participation replaces apartheid sport in South Africa – 1967–1978": The role of BJ Vorster and PGJ Koornhof. *New Countree, 64*, 155–170.

MacLean, M. (2014). Revisiting (and Revising) Sports Boycotts: From Rugby against South Africa to Soccer in Israel. *The International Journal of the History of Sport, 31*(15), 1832–1851.

Martini, S. (2014). *Nelson Mandela's 'Ordinary Love' Addressed in Pop-rock Music: a Long Song of Freedom.* Retrieved February 18, 2021, from https://riviste.unimi.it/index.php/AMonline/article/view/4471

Meredith, M. (2005). *The State of Africa.* London and New York: Simon & Schuster.

Morgan, E. J. (2017). Don't Play Ball with South Africa: the United States, the Anti-Apartheid Movement, and the David Cup Protests. *International Journal of the History of Sport, 34*(3–4), 1–17.

Nixon, R. (1992). Apartheid on the Run: The South African Sports Boycott. *Transition, 58*, 68–88.

Nye, J. (1990). Soft Power. *Foreign Policy, 80*, 153–171.

Nye, J. (2004). *Soft Power.* New York: Public Affairs.

Nye, J. (2008). 'Public Diplomacy and Soft Power.' *Annals American Academy of Political and Social Sciences, 616*, 94–109.

Palcy, E. (Director). (1990). *A Dry White Season.* [Film]. Metro Goldwyn Mayer.

Roodt, D.J. (Director). (1995). *Cry: The Beloved Country.* [Film]. Miramax Films/Distant Horizon.

Sallaz, J. J. (2010). Talking Race, Marketing Culture: The Racial Habitus In and Out of Apartheid. *Social Problems, 57*(2), 294–314.

Siffree, L. (1987). *Something Inside So Strong.* [Song]. China Records.

Special AKA (1984). *Free Nelson Mandela.* [Song]. 2-tone Records.

Street, J. (2003). Fight the Power': The Politics of Music and the Music of Politics. *Government and Opposition, 38*(1), 113–130.

The Guardian. (2016). *UK's million-selling singles: the full list.* Retrieved February 26, 2021, from https://www.theguardian.com/news/datablog/2012/nov/04/uk-million-selling-singles-full-list

The Specials (1981). *Ghost Town.* [Song]. 2-tone Records.

Thörn, H. (2006). *Anti-Apartheid and the Emergence of a Global Civil Society.* Basingstoke and New York: Palgrave Macmillan.

Thörn, H. (2007). Social Movements, the Media, and the Emergence of a Global Public Sphere: From Anti-apartheid to Global Justice. *Current Sociology, 55*(6), 896–918.

USA for Africa (1985). *We Are the World.* [Song]. Columbia Records: CBS.

Wainhouse, D. W. (1964). *Remnants of Empire. New York and Evanston.* Council on Foreign Relations: Harper and Row Publishers.

CHAPTER 6

Political music in Brazil: An examination of *Punk Rock* in Brasília, 1979-1985[1]

Silvio César Tamaso D'Onofrio
Universidade de São Paulo, Brazil

Marta Fernanada Tamaso D'Onofrio
Universidade de São Paulo, Brazil

Henrique César Tamaso D'Onofrio
Fundação Armando Álvares Penteado, Brazil

Abstract

This chapter examined the Brazilian political, cultural and social context in which the music movement known as Rock of Brasília emerged in the late 1970s and early 1980s. It traced the history of Brazilian music through the political content of its compositions, and specifically analyzed the lyrics of the songs released by two of the first, and to this day largely unknown, *Punk Rock* bands that appeared on the music and entertainment scene in the capital city, Brasília: the *Escola de Escândalo* and *Anti-tédio* (literally meaning *School of Scandal* and *Anti-boredom* respectively). This chapter also examined the expedients used by the bands to further explore and continue with their art and political ideology in the face of unrestricted fight against the "system" and the "state of things" in the country, while managing to escape the overarching and ubiquitous censorship imposed by the ruling dictatorship in Brazil.

Keywords: Politics, dictatorship, Brasília, *Punk Rock*, Escola de Escândalo, Anti-tédio

***

---

[1] Note: The authors did all translations used in this chapter.

Introduction

Historically, Brazil is said to have been "discovered" by Portuguese explorers in the 15th century. However, it is arguable that it was only at the beginning of the 20th century that the country truly became aware of its culture that lay at the crossroads of the following ethnic groups: Black Africans, indigenous natives and white Europeans (Ribeiro, 1995, p. 19). This awareness was only possible because, with an increasingly agglomerated population in urban centers, access to educational and other resources became easier. And, slowly but noticeably, the mixed population and culture of people in these urban centers began to develop. In addition, there was the emergence of an aesthetic movement known as Brazilian Modernism after World War 1 which, prompted by multiple motivations, sought to promote authentic Brazilian art and culture that was then heavily influenced by imported culture, especially from Europe. Evidence of this "imported culture" was prevalent in the nation's concert halls and other forms of artistic work, such as literature and fine arts.

Some critics consider Brazilian Modernism to be no more than a collection of influences from the European artistic avant-garde of the time, albeit with local themes. Nonetheless, the movement that had as its inaugural symbolic launch at the "Semana de Arte Moderna" (Modern Art Week) in São Paulo (1922), emphasized and championed the originality of Brazilian art. Critics Candido and Castello (1968, p. 9) say this about the literature of this aesthetic context: "No other (genre) reflects the movements of the national soul with such fidelity, and at the same time with so much creative freedom."

The innovations in the Brazilian music scene of the 20th century, especially in the 1950s culminated in the creation of Bossa Nova and, later, Tropicália (Dunn, 2001, p. 13). These were entirely Brazilian musical typologies that, among their derivatives, promoted the integration of the local music with global musical movements such as Rock (Dapieve, 1995, p. 11). By the late 1970s, Brazilian music had in particular embraced one genre of Rock, the so-called Punk Rock. More anarchic and rebellious, this type of Rock music arrived in the city of Brasília almost at the same time its first chords were strung in places like United States of America and the United Kingdom.

For the filmmaker Vladimir Carvalho, the construction of Brasília in the middle of the Brazil, in a place that a few years earlier was a virgin land, was an epic undertaking. According to him, "Another epic, this one of another extraction, took place in the noisy lira of the Brasília's rockers of first-line, born and raised rebels without cause, in friction with the environment and the establishment" (Carvalho, 2009, p. 133). This absence of a cause for rebellion seems to point to some elitism in the genesis of the punk movement in the federal capital. Yet, also according to Carvalho (2009, pp. 134-135), the Rock of Brasília is "the most authentic product of local culture" in spite of being spearheaded by the "children of diplomats and university professors," and Brazilians who had returned from their places of residence outside the country.

As the political and administrative capital of Brazil, Brasília hosted a number of diplomats and tourists from all over the world. Musicians were no exception. Some of their music also arrived in the country in real time, such as the first albums of bands like *Sex Pistols* and *The Clash* in 1977. It was quite common to see young people on the streets of Brasília dressed up like these foreign musicians, as they wore army boots, torn pants and shirts, pins, chains and buttons, and with their hair spiked by a fixing gel. Local bands that were influenced by this style of dressing, and music, also appeared almost every day, with some of them becoming famous in the federal capital city, as in the case of Aborto Elétrico (*Electrical Abortion*), which gave rise to the Legião Urbana (*Urban Legion*). This band, together with Plebe Rude (*Rude People*) and Capital Inicial (*Initial Capital*), collectively became known as the "Rock of Brasília" (Alexandre, 2013, p. 166) and the three main trailblazers of the Brazilian cultural movement of the second half of the 20th century.

Thus, Brasília is considered one of the cradles of Brazilian Punk Rock, a music style which, like its manifestations in other countries, was marked by a discourse with high political content, and also by an anarchist and even nihilistic ideology. With lyrics that praised the independence of "do it yourself," Punk Rock in Brasília fearlessly fought the military dictatorship still in full force and in power at that time. This challenge to the military government helped to make Punk Rock quite unique in the country.

This chapter therefore makes a retrospective analysis of the political content in the lyrics of the songs of two of the first "Rock de Brasília" bands, Escola de Escândalo (*School of Scandal*) and Anti-tédio (*Anti-boredom*) that rocked Brazil's capital city, Brasília, with protest music in the early 1980s. The choice of Escola de Escândalo and Anti-tédio bands is justified by the political content of their music, and also by the need to tell their story because, despite these bands being part of the first wave of punk rock bands that emerged not only in Brasília but in Brazil as a nation, their music and history are practically unknown even in modern times. Overall, this chapter is also an attempt to shed light on these pioneer Punk Rock bands as well as on the rather obscure history of this form of music artistry.

Antecedents: Politics in Brazilian music

Political messages in Brazilian music, or political attitudes involving musicality, are as old as the country's history. The historian and researcher of Brazilian ancestry, Fernão Cardim, recorded the musical custom among indigenous natives in the first decades of Brazil's existence after its "discovery" in 1500. Cardim noted that the people valued their musical culture even in situations of adversity. According to the historian, if the indigenous Indians happened to take a rival male "good singer and inventor of troves" in the trap, they spared him because, in addition to being friends of music and dancing, the natives "were great composers of improvisational songs" (Cardim, 1939, p. 155). Several years later in the 18th century, two musical styles emerged in Brazil. One was called the Modinha (*Little Fashion*), which was of Portuguese origin. Its lyrics essentially dealt with melancholic love themes, in a slow rhythm, referring to calm and tranquillity. The other was Lundu (this word has no specific meaning), which was of African origin. It was marked by danceable rhythmic beats and was more sensual in character. These two rhythms continued to exist into the 19th century, but now alongside other styles that appeared along the way. One of the novel styles was called Choro (Cry), or Chorinho (Little Cry), which was a mixture of Lundu and Modinha, and European ballroom dancing.

The birth of Choro or Chorinho paved way to a great deal of European musical influence on the Brazilian music scene and lyrics. Soon, Polka, also of European origin, was introduced in Brazil and also left its imprint on the country's music. According to Mário de Andrade:

> Polka was danced, on the occasion of the carnival, by actress Clara del Mastro, two years after being launched in Paris. The repercussion, turned into an authentic fever, left a trace in the name of an epidemic illness, a kind of influenza that spread in 1847 nicknamed "Polka" (Andrade 1989, p. 37).

With the growing migration to the urban areas, Polka soon became the dominant dance form and mass music in Brazil. According to José Miguel Wisnik:

> Someone has already said, with a certain hyperbolic property, that, from *Ragtime* to *Rock-'n'-Roll*, everything is Polka. In fact, Polka starts the dance music market, accompanied by the frisson that corresponds to it and all the implications that this will have on musical life as a whole, when urban popular music spreads through the means of mass reproduction, acting and narrowing the respectable space that concert music and opera came to have in Europe throughout the 19th century (Wisnik, 2003, p. 36-37).

It is clear, therefore, that the music practiced and heard in Brazil at the time had its origins in, or was highly influenced by, music made overseas. It was an imported custom, usually in an anachronistic way, arriving in Brazil months or years after their introduction in their countries of origin.

In political terms, it can be said that the main feature of these musical formats is the popularity or non-exclusivity of their performance; they were not limited to a select or affluent audience or public, neither were they only performed in very exclusive and exquisite environments and ballrooms. On the contrary, they were rhythms also found on the "rodas" (wheels), as people met on the streets and public squares or during popular events, to play, sing and dance freely. It is also noteworthy that the Brazil of that era had a political monarchy, which also represented the religious power of a Catholic majority in the country. Like monarchies in other countries, the rulers in Brazil were generally intolerant of any form of threat to their power and authority. Thus, the simple act of people gathering in public places and open arena to sing and dance was considered subversive. For instance, Capoeira, a martial art dance style mainly of Brazilian origin, was prohibited and classified as a crime, according to Article 402 of the Brazilian Criminal Code promulgated in 1890 (Decree 847).[2] Although slavery was abolished in Brazil in 1888 and the country became a republic the following year, Capoeira was only decriminalized in 1937.

At the beginning of the 20th century, the foundations of what would be the musical rhythm that became known as Samba, the first more legitimately Brazilian musical genre, contemporarily speaking, began to emerge. Samba is a word without any particular meaning; it was not just merely a word because it was also a musical genre that appears to have originated from "semba" in the Quimbundo language, originally from Africa. Semba means "batida de umbigos" or "umbigada" (*belly buttons beat* or *clash of belly buttons*), in the tradition of some African dances, with dancers projecting their bodies towards each other, so that their bellies touch. Umbigada takes place inside a circle called "batuque de umbigada" (*drumming of beating belly buttons*), where one or two characters dance more intensely in the centre, while they are surrounded by the other participants who dance more sparingly. Whenever a dancer at the centre of the circle gets tired due to the intensity of his or her gyrations, and wants to leave to rest, that person would approach someone in the circle, give him or her a belly button beat that signals that they should trade places, and both immediately swap positions.

Like most musical genres, Samba originated from a dance, initially from the hills and peripheries of the urban areas of Rio de Janeiro and Recife, and displayed as a mixture of the batuques (*drumming*) and the capoeira circles, with beats in homage to mystical entities, coupled with songs and ritual practices. Its evolution as the symbol of Brazil's music, however, cannot be attributed to a particular "birthplace" or ethnicity. As Hermano Vianna contends:

---

[2] Decree 847, Oct. 11, 1890 – Brazilian Criminal Code. See: https://www2.camara.leg.br/legin/fed/decret/1824-1899/decreto-847-11-outubro-1890-503086-publicacaooriginal-1-pe.html

> Many groups and individuals (blacks, gypsies, people from Bahia, people from Rio de Janeiro, intellectuals, politicians, folklorists, classical composers, French, millionaires, poets – and even an American ambassador) participated, with greater or lesser tenacity, in this "fixation" as a musical genre and its nationalization. [...] There was never a ready, "authentic" Samba, later transformed into national music. Samba, as a musical style (was) created concurrently with its nationalization (Vianna, 1995, p. 151).

"Pelo telephone" (*Over the phone*) was the first music style classified as Samba to attain huge success in Brazil. It was recorded and released in 1916 and quickly became a popular, polemical and controversial composition because of the political content of its lyrics. Songwriters, Donga and Mauro de Almeida are officially considered the composers of "Pelo telephone." Interestingly, almost everything about this song generated some controversy: its authorship, the claim that it was the first recorded Samba music, the reason for the lyrics, and even its categorization as Samba. All of these issues became embedded in the history of Samba, and made the style so unique.

Structurally, "Pelo telefone" sounds a bit naive and disorderly. Its instrumental introduction is intermittently repeated, a device often used at the time, and each of them had different melodies and choruses, giving the impression that the composition was being made in bits, with the combination of melodies chosen at random or collected from folk songs.

For instance, its lyrics say as follows:

> The police chief
> Over the phone
> Send me a note
> That in the Carioca
> There is a roulette
> To play with

This is the best known version of the composition, said to be a parody which, ironically, achieved more success than the original song that only referred to the celebration of the carnival itself. In the original version, the opening passage went as follows:

> The revelry chief
> Over the phone
> Send me a note
> May it be joyful
> Don't question yourself
> To play

The "Carioca," the word referred to in the most popular version, is the place called "Largo da Carioca," a public square in the historic centre of the capital, Rio de Janeiro. This parody version would have been made by the journalists of the newspaper *A Noite*, since their own reporters had placed a roulette wheel, prohibited at the time – as it is also currently - in the square to demonstrate how the police allowed the roulette game to go on. The political tonality of the composition is clear: denouncing the corruption that existed in the Rio de Janeiro society of the early 20th century.

Over the decades, Samba took on different characteristics, each with a specific nuance in terms of rhythm, lyrics, orchestration and spaces of performance. The common thread that brings together all of these genres is the musicality that refers to legitimate Brazilian customs and culture. The lyrics of the songs commonly deal with political issues as well, requiring the authorities, for example, to solve problems, denouncing or satirizing public officials, laws, customs and habits. There is room for exaltation also, the celebration of ephemeris or the applause to a life trajectory or even a city, among other themes.

With the growth and popularity of the radio in the 1930s and 1940s, Brazilian popular music became richer, more complex and diverse. The following singers and composers were outstanding in this period: Ary Barroso, Lamartine Babo (creator of the great success "O teu cabelo não nega" or *Your hair doesn't deny* composition that is today re-evaluated for its racial content), Dorival Caymmi and Noel Rosa. There were also the great interpreters of Brazilian popular music then and after, such as Carmen Miranda, Mário Reis and Francisco Alves. With their composed or interpreted lyrics, each of these musicians incorporated political themes in their work, be it the samba known as "Gasparino" by Ary Barroso which got its name and main theme from the political decision in the country that was made in 1878; or Caymmi, who composed nothing less than the "Anthem of the Prestes Campaign," when Luiz Carlos Prestes was running for the Federal Senate in 1945 as the candidate for the Brazilian Communist Party. Noel Rosa was another musician who infused political themes in his sambas. An example comes from one of his best-known songs, "Com que roupa" (*With what clothes*), with the refrain, "With what clothes do I go with, to the samba you invited me?" This is an enigmatic verse whose author had cause to explain and define on a number of occasions. However, the lyrics point to the difficult economic situation in the country in the late 1920s, and the dire political conditions immediately before the coup d'état that brought Getúlio Vargas to power in 1930, the same year the composition was recorded.

In the middle of the 1940s, Luiz Gonzaga, the *King of Baião*, stood out in the Brazilian music scene. Baião was then a completely new musical style, the most prestigious in Brazil before Bossa Nova (Ribeiro, 1985, 1134), indigenously

Brazilian, with lyrics invariably dealing with the cultural context of the north-eastern region of the country. This region was associated with arid climate, with little rain and high temperatures, and so unique in its customs and language. Luiz Gonzaga became a national success with songs such as "Asa branca" (*White wing*). He sang so much about the charms of the north-eastern hinterland, and also about politics in the themes of some of his special compositions, such as the one he composed for the meeting he had in July 1981 with Brazil's President João Baptista de Oliveira Figueiredo. Gonzaga used the occasion to present a request in the form of a Baião, a demand for the solution to a family conflict, which was in fact political, as it involved political leaders from his hometown. An excerpt from the song goes as follows: "Taking this opportunity, I want to ask from my heart, take a look around our land, I count on you, Mr. President" (Lima 2020, p. 142).

While Baião and Forró, a related style from Baião that was explored with great ease by Luiz Gonzaga continued to be successful, new music successes released and played by Jackson do Pandeiro and Alvarenga and Ranchinho introduced new songs/styles in the country. Thus, the songs became the Música Sertaneja (*Backlands Music*) and also Samba-canção (Samba-song). With a calmer and more orchestrated rhythm, the lyrics of the Samba-canção spoke mainly of love or, as some prefer, the "pain-in-the-elbow," that is, the desires, especially those unrequited, or the pain-in-love, as some people also say. Along with the lyrics came the popular expression that without a little drama, disappointment, or a broken heart, then there is no Samba-canção. The giants of this musical genre include: Dolores Duran, Marlene, Emilinha Borba, Dalva de Oliveira, Ângela Maria and Cauby Peixoto. The political content of their music lay in the attitude of the composer or singer. In the lyrics of the songs, the singer, for instance, would pose as the victim of love in order to attract attention, even some sympathy from the person he or she loves.

At the end of the 1950s, the *Bossa Nova* emerged. This is a sophisticated and smooth style of samba music whose main proponent were Elizeth Cardoso, Tom Jobim and João Gilberto. Bossa Nova accompanied Brazilian beauties abroad, making it a huge success, especially in the United States.

Several musicians became successful in various parts of the country in the 1970s. Nara Leão, for instance, recorded songs by Cartola and Nelson do Cavaquinho, important names from the middle of the 20th century, and in a way still largely unknown in the country. Coming from Bahia, Gal Costa and Maria Bethânia were successful in large cities in the south and south-east regions of the country. Equally successful were Djavan (from Alagoas), Fafá de Belém (from Pará), Clara Nunes (from Minas Gerais), Belchior and Fagner (both from Ceará), Alceu Valença (from Pernambuco) and Elba Ramalho (from Paraíba). In the more traditional Funk music scene, and flirting with Soul music and Swing, artists such as Tim Maia and Jorge Ben Jor also became some of the best-known names in this genre.

These were the immediate antecedents to the Brazilian musical panorama in the late 1970s and early 1980s. They were to pave the way for the emergence of the Punk Rock of Brasília.

Brazilian political context (1960-1985)

The inauguration of Brasília as capital city took place in the midst of the democratic climate that had been developing in Brazil since 1945, when the authoritarian leadership of President Getúlio Vargas, the so-called Estado Novo, ended. In 1960, a national election took place upon the end of the tenure of President Juscelino Kubitschek who was elected to office in 1955. The result of the 1960 election was that Jânio Quadros became the new Brazilian president, with João Goulart, simply known as Jango, as his vice-president. However, President Quadros surprised his compatriots with his resignation after only seven months in office. The crisis precipitated by his sudden resignation was further aggravated by the fact that the military establishment did not want the vice-president to assume the presidency as laid down in the constitution. The issue was resolved with a constitutional change from the presidential to parliamentary democracy. Thus, on September 7, 1961, João Goulart assumed the presidency, but with diminished authority as he now shared power with a prime minister.

President Goulart's tenure saw a further deepening of the political crisis in the country, especially between the far left and far-right politically ideological factions. All sorts of factors further complicated the crisis, and on April 1, 1964, President Goulart was ousted in a military *coup d'état*. The government installed by the military junta was very authoritarian and politically aligned to the U.S.A. As expected, the government suspended the legislative and judicial powers enshrined in the Brazilian constitution, and concentrated all governmental powers in its hands. To showcase itself as being legally in power, the military enacted the Institutional Act (1) to legitimize itself in office. Their leader, General Humberto de Alencar Castello Branco, was then sworn in as president.

Brazil was to witness a succession of Institutional Acts that kept the military generals in power, with each administration moving farther away from democracy and being more repressive than its predecessor. So, in 1967, the second general, Costa e Silva became president. He was known a hardliner like General Branco. In December 1968, Institutional Act (5) was promulgated, expanding the presidential powers of repression and state-sponsored violence. In Brazil, the period between 1968 and 1974 was marked by the greatest military excesses, abuse of power, political disappearance of opponents of government, allegations of torture of political agitators, and disrespect for human and civil rights. Those years have gone down in Brazil's history as the "years of lead" of military dictatorship.

In 1969 General Emílio Médici became Brazil's third military dictator-president. He was succeeded in 1974 by another army general, Ernesto Geisel, who ruled the country until 1979. It was at the end of General Ernesto Geisel's term that the first echoes of *punk rock* music were heard in the federal capital, Brasília, and possibly all over Brazil.

General Geisel had assumed the presidency, promising a "slow, gradual and secure" return to politics and democracy in the country. The combination of both internal and external factors and pressures forced the hands of the military government to ease the instruments of dictatorship in Brazil, culminating in General Geisel abolishing the Institutional Act (5). The last military president in Brazil was João Batista Figueiredo (1979-1985). He continued to ease restrictions that were started by his predecessors, and finally signed the law that gave amnesty to people formerly persecuted by previous military governments, and allowed the first direct elections since 1964 to take place in 1982. However, the elections were restricted to the principals of state governments. It is noteworthy that after the 1964 take-over of government, the military unilaterally appointed governors, mayors and even senators in the country, and charged them with limited authority. None of them was elected, resulting in people pejoratively calling them "bionic" officials.

Such was the political environment in which punk rock was born in Brazil. However, quite notably, while the military rulers engaged in political repression and hounded people who opposed them into detention, Brazil gained a bit of modernization and urbanization (Ridenti, 2005, p. 102). Nevertheless, the economy remained a problem. In spite of the growth in the number of people employed in various government sectors of the economy, poverty and inequalities loomed large in the country, thus leading to the emergence of musical bands such as Escola de Escândalo and Anti-tédio that sang against the bleak economic situation in the country. Discussing the economy, Ribeiro (1985, 2417) noted as follows:

> The majority of the workforce in the primary sector is made up of marginals to the current economy, because they cannot earn a minimum wage per month, during the entire year [...] The increase in the tertiary sector, in services, is mainly increased by workers subordinates such as washerwomen, maids, odd jobs and beggars. Only in the secondary sector does the working class grow numerically, encompassing regular workers. Most of these, however, are tied to small companies, which pay

lower wages and transmit their insecurity to everyone, in the permanent fear of unemployment.

Brasília and the Music scene

During Brazil's 1955 presidential election campaign, candidate Juscelino Kubitschek made a promise to the electorate: to build a new capital city in the central region of the country, and move the capital out of its then location in the coastal city of Rio de Janeiro since 1763. Kubitschek based his decision and campaign promise on the fact that the country's first constitution promulgated in 1823 had a provision for building a new capital city in central Brazil (Ribeiro, 1985, 1614). His argument was that a capital city that was equidistant from the other areas of the country was necessary for the effective governance of the territorially extensive nation that shared borders with several countries, including Argentina, Uruguay, Paraguay, Bolivia, Peru, Colombia and Venezuela.

Once elected president in 1955, Kubitschek began the task of building a new capital city, and completed the job in 3 years and 10 months. The new capital, Brasília, was inaugurated on April 21, 1960, with 300,000 inhabitants, 1,000 kilometres (about 621 miles) away from the sea "where Brazil has been loitering since 1500," according to sociologist Darcy Ribeiro (1985, 1616). There were reports that at the beginning of the construction, a house made of wood was erected for the president to stay and monitor the work going on. Other reports had it that the house also served as where the president's daughter, who always accompanied him on official trips, could have her guitar lessons with her tutor who was one of Brazil's famous guitarists, Dilermando Reis. That house, or the Catetinho as it was known, turned out to be the cradle for music production in Brasília. According to Fábio Zanon: "In 1960 Dilermando Reis even released a Long Play called *Melodias da Alvorada* (*Dawn Melodies*) [....] which contains works that have become true unofficial anthems of the city, such as the samba "Exaltação à Brasília" (*Exaltation to Brasília*), which were the first musical works composed in and for the new capital" (Zanon, 2007, time: 05m23s).

After the military junta ousted the elected government in 1964, the deposed president of Brazil, João Goulart and many authorities, among whom was the ex-president Juscelino Kubitschek, fled into exile. Dilermando composed a waltz song entitled, "Nuvens que passam" (*Clouds that pass*), and dedicated it to Juscelino with these words: "None of this matters. Everything will come to an end. What is there is just like the clouds that pass and make the sun shine again" (Zanon, 2007, time: 05m56s). The figurative language leaves no doubt about the "clouds" reference to the political context of that time, that is, the military's coup d'état. It is therefore plausible to say that from the time of its construction, Brasília hosted a complex relationship between politics and music.

Although not based in Brasília in the 1960s, the composer and performer Raul Seixas, was a prominent figure during the nascent Brazilian rock scene. According to Arthur Dapieve, "Raul would become a point of reference, both for those who insisted on making Rock'n'Roll in Brazil and for those who insisted on listening to the trumpets of the local musical apocalypse." (Dapieve, 1995, p. 19). Dapieve says "apocalypse" because in the late 1960s and until the final years of the 1970s, Brazilian rock almost got lost, many times, by the psychedelia of the so-called progressive rock. In this context, Raul Seixas established himself as a true bastion of salvation for those who still believed in the rawest rock, which contemplated space for both rebellion and humor and irony – without getting lost in endless keyboard solos and lazy lysergic atmospheres.

The definite impulse to establish a new and rebel kind of rock music in Brazil, as it had occurred overseas, came from the political and economic sphere, with the end of Juscelino Kubitschek's "golden years," a moment when there seemed to be certainty that Brazil would be the country of the future, a nation on its way to glory. According to Marsiglia (1990):

> "The economic miracle" was over and, in the late 1970s, Brazil was watching inflation soar and unemployment soar. And for poor young people, without work, without fun, marginality began to gallop. In the musical field, MPB's (Brazilian Popular Music, *note from the authors*) expensive productions mythologized the artistic process and Brazilian rock lived on the fringes. The music coming from outside didn't help either. Disco and progressive rock refused to get in touch with the real world of that generation. In a nihilistic way, it would be necessary to start from scratch (p. 17).

So, from the end of the 1970s, new rock styles began to emerge in Brazil and became very successful, with strong influences from abroad. The show "Rock in Rio," from the early 1980s, served to boost rock music nationwide. With a strong urban theme and dealing with social, youth and love themes, a number of new musical groups also came on to the scene, almost using the punk style. The bands that emerged in this period include, Paralamas do Sucesso, Titãs, Ultraje a Rigor and Ira! From Brasília, bands such as Legião Urbana, Plebe Rude and Capital Inicial also emerged, and recorded huge successes with rapid, speedy music that were not long in duration, and with repeated basic chords and rebel lyrics.

In 1978 Aborto Elétrico, the first Punk Rock of Brasília, which later became Legião Urbana, made the audience to *pogo* (punk dance style where people basically jumped around without rhyme or rhythm) in shows in Brasília's underground scene with "Que país é este?" (*What country is this?*), a song selected as one of the 100 best Brazilian compositions of all time by *Rolling*

Stones Brazil magazine (1987). Chosen as producing the most outstanding protest music in Brazil (*Último Segundo*, 2013), Legião Urbana's first album recorded in 1985, had political lyrics that resonated with the audience when it was released, as much as it is still valid in modern times. Its lyrics say:

> *In the favelas, in the senate*
> *Dirt everywhere*
> *No one respects the Constitution*
> *But everyone believes in the future of the nation*
> *What country is this? (3x)*
> *In Amazonas, in Araguaia*
> *In the Rio de Janeiro lowland*
> *Mato Grosso, Minas Gerais (Brazilian states – note from the authors)*
> *And in the northeast all in peace*
> *In death I rest*
> *But the blood is running loose*
> *Staining the papers*
> *Faithful documents*
> *To the rest of the boss*
> *What country is this? (4x)*
> *Third world if it is*
> *Joke abroad*
> *But Brazil will get rich*
> *Let's make a million*
> *When we sell*
> *All our Indians' souls at auction*
> *What country is this? (4x)*

Formed in 1981, Plebe Rude was another of the first rock bands that emerged in Brasília. It had a hit song, "Proteção" (*Protection*), from its first album, "O concreto já rachou" (*Concrete already cracked*). In "Proteção," released during a repressive military dictatorship, Plebe Rude was quite critical about what was going on in Brazil. The band sang as follows:

> *Is it true, isn't it?*
> *Nothing I can talk*
> *And all this for your protection*
> *Nothing I can talk*
> *Police on the street, the National Guard*
> *Our fear your weapon, seem all ok*
> *The institution is there for our protection*
> *For your protection*
> *Tanks out there, army on duty*
> *Pointed here inland*

And all this for your protection
So the government can impose itself
Police on the street, our fear of living
The consolation is that they will protect me
The only question is: protect me from what?
I'm a minority but at least I say what I want despite the repression
...It's for your protection...
...It's for your protection...
Shock troops, armed policemen
Keep the people in their place
But he was soon arrested, marked ideology
If anyone wants to rebel
Repressed opposition, radicals silenced
All the anguish of the people is blocked
Everything to maintain the good image of the State!
I'm a minority but at least I say what I want despite the repression
...It's for your protection...
...It's for your protection...
Polished weapons, and pipes heat up
Waiting for your role
Angry army and the government laments
That the people learned to say "NO"
Until when will Brazil be able to support it?
Penal code doesn't let the people rebel
Municipality is based on guns – you can't!
And this is all for your safety
For your safety

Brasília Punk-Rock:
"Escola de Escândalo" and "Anti-tédio" against the dictatorship

The punk rock bands, Aborto Elétrico/Legião Urbana and Plebe Rude, to mention a few of them, exhibited a great deal of courage in singing songs and performing in public spaces against Brazil's military dictatorships. The bands continued to use their platforms for political messaging, undeterred by the military's use of violence and repression to counter whatever they saw as "subversive" act, and in an environment of active censorship and multiple state-sponsored informants spying on people who opposed the government.

So, why devote this section to "Escola de Escândalo" and "Anti-tédio?" The rationale is that very little have been documented and written about them. The focus in the literature has mostly been on Aborto Elétrico, Legião Urbana and Plebe Rude, regarding their activities, successes and awards, records, lyrics, grants and the fact their songs still command some airtime on radio, and are quite popular with the audience. On the contrary, although both "Escola de Escândalo" and "Anti-tédio" were there at the birth of punk rock in Brazil, very little have been written about them. Yet, their contributions to the growth of punk rock and political messaging through music cannot be minimized.

Going back to history, it is fairly incontrovertible that the punk rock bands that emerged in Brasília throughout the 1970s were influenced by the hippie and progressive rock movements in the country and abroad. At the end of that decade, and by the mid-1980s, the first bands of the new musical style that was then identified as Punk Rock began to appear in Brasília, almost at the same time as their counterparts in England and the United States of America, the countries that are considered to be the birthplaces of Punk Rock.

O diário da turma 1976-1986. A história do rock de Brasília (The Guys' Diary 1976-1986. Brasília's rock history), by Paulo Marchetti, is a seminal book on the chronology of events in the history punk rock in Brasília. The book is based on interviews with 61 people (Marchetti 2001, p. 198-199), all of whom were directly involved with the first bands that appeared at the dawn of punk rock in Brasília. The book is a fairly comprehensive record of testimonials of people who were active in the punk rock movement of that era. Marchetti's work narrates the first movements that gave rise to the emergence of Aborto Elétrico, considered as the first punk rock band in the federal capital. The band appeared on the scene in 1978.

A total of 18 bands were formed in Brasília from the time Aborto Elétrico appeared in 1978 to 1983 when another band, Anti-tédio, came on to the scene. By the following year, 1984, five new bands were born, among them, *Escola de Escândalo* that is highlighted in this section. Marchetti's study shows that from the genesis of the "brasiliense" punk rock (punk rock from Brasília) in 1978 to 1984, 24 musical groups of this genre were formed, but 11 had ceased to exist by 1984. Marchetti attributed this relatively high rate of band dissolution either due to simple discontinuity, or because the bands had metamorphosed into other groups with other names. Also, according to journalist, Hermano Júnior, some of these groups "lasted a few months, (while) others only managed to survive in the midst of an endless exchange of musicians" (Hermano Júnior, 1983, p. 38). By all accounts, it would appear that Anti-tédio and Escola de Escândalo were the fifth and sixth bands respectively to emerge in this period, and both had a measure of durability. Despite being part of the core of the first bands in this genre, both can also be considered as derivative bands, as some of their members belonged to previous punk rock bands, dating back to a few years before their formation. In the case of Anti-tédio, for instance, its origin is linked to the band called 3rd *Polo*, which briefly appeared and then disappeared in 1982. Their guitarist, Danilo, later moved over to Anti-tédio.

The origin of the Escola de Escândalo is more complex and distant. Its bassist, Geraldo "Geruza" Ribeiro, came from Blitz 64 (renamed Blitx 64 after a year), the second punk rock band formed in Brasília whose initial formation dates back to 1980. In 1981, two other bands emerged, with their members later becoming members in Escola de Escândalo: from Vigaristas de Istambul came vocalist Bernardo Muller, and guitarist Luiz "Fejão" Eduardo came from Nirvana. Even before Escola de Escândalo, these two, Fejão and Bernardo, had already joined Geraldo Ribeiro, and Blitx 64 had already been discontinued, only to re-emerge in 1983 as the band known as XXX. In 1984, XXX ceased to exist, and then reappeared as the Escola de Escândalo. XXX's drummer was the only person who did not join the new band.

These early bands generally disappeared as fast as they were formed. Marchetti opined that "they (some bands) lasted about six months, they did just one show and, sometimes, not even that." Nonetheless, Marchetti (2001, pp. 86-87) noted that some form of stability had become noticeable among the bands, such that by 1983 bands such as "Legião Urbana, Plebe Rude, Capital Inicial, Escola de Escândalo and Elite Sophisticada were ready for the market." They were, on average, well supplied in terms of professional talents – instrumentalists and vocalists, and equipment, with two or three songs in their vault. The bands in Brasília only acquired a status of "stable" condition at this time, between 1983 and 1985, according to Carlos Marcelo, journalist and biographer (Marcelo, 2011, time 47:55). Of the five top bands listed by Marcelo, Escola de Escândalo was the only one that seemed to have the lyrics of its songs more professionally composed and laid out.

It is important to contextualize and provide a glimpse into the music environment in which Escola de Escândalo functioned and played concerts in Brasília and Brazil. According to a media report entitled "Sinal dos Tempos," (*Sign of times*) detailing an episode in one of Escola de Escândalo's shows:

> The rock show that groups Ira! and Escola de Escândalo gave in Brasília caused a rather unusual atmosphere in the comfortable headquarters of Army Club.
>
> When Bernardo, lead singer of Escola de Escândalo, began to sing "Just one more song about soldiers and wars," the officers – who with their families occupied the boxes – heard chilling lines like "The army turns boys into men and men into corpses." None of the group was arrested. Unthinkable situation a few years ago.
>
> (Sinal dos tempos) [Newspaper clipping], n.d.)[3]

---

[3] Sinal dos tempos is a newspaper clipping. The authors searched but could not determine its date of publication.

Although not dated, the newspaper's report was most likely published around 1985, the year of Brazil's re-democratization and the end of the military dictatorship that had been at the helm of national politics and leadership since 1964.

At its formation, Escola de Escândalo was made up of the following: Bernardo Muller (vocals), Geraldo "Geruza" Ribeiro (bass), Luiz Eduardo (guitar), and Manuel "Totoni" Guimarães Fragoso (drums). The band's vocalist, Bernardo Mueller, was considered a good lyricist at the time (Marchetti, 2001, p. 139). The first level of the themes in his lyrics explored conflicts in the life of the youths, more like some form of psychological analysis. The second level was more about political issues camouflaged as issues arising out of youthful exuberance and subjectivity. Given the history of Escola de Escândalo's formation, the impression was created that some of their songs and themes predated the band itself since its members came from pre-existing bands. However, Geraldo Ribeiro noted that songs in Escola's repertoire were composed by the band. One of Escola de Escândalo's most successful songs is "Complexos" (*Complexes*) whose lyrics challenged the establishment and explored some socio-political issues of the day. It was composed by Bernardo Muller, and the lyrics are as follows:[4]

> "Complexos"
> Passo horas seguidas olhando a imagem no espelho
> Vejo o defeito como seria bom não tê-lo
> Mudo de ângulo, tento esconder
> Tento disfarçar
> Mas esse problema nem um milhão de anos irão apagar
>
> Ninguém é perfeito
> (Obstáculos que não me deixam passar)
> Mas isso não é consolo
> (Tentáculos que querem me segurar)
> Ninguém é perfeito
> (Corrente contra a qual é inútil nadar)
> Mas isso não é consolo
> (Âncora que não me deixa avançar)
> Complexos, complexos, complexos, complexos
>
> Qualquer desvio do normal é visto como uma fraqueza,
> Mas quem foi que instituiu esses padrões de beleza?

---

[4] The official video clip, made about 30 years after the song was originally composed, is available on Youtube (https://youtu.be/_6pEDLy1mBI). Also the first recording with the legendary guitarist, Fejão, can be heard at: (https://youtu.be/fa2cvcdLouA)

Imagine um mundo onde não houvesse comparação
Quem nos salvaria da monotonia da perfeição?

Ninguém é perfeito...

"Complexes"
I spend hours straight looking at the image in the mirror
I see the defect as it would be nice not to have it
I change the angle, I try to hide
I try to disguise
But this problem, not a million years will erase
Nobody is perfect

(Obstacles that won't let me through)
But this is no consolation
(Tentacles that want to hold me)
Nobody is perfect
(Flowing against which it is useless to swim)
But this is no consolation
(Anchor that won't let me go)
Complexes, complexes, complexes, complexes

Any deviation from normal is seen as a weakness,
But who instituted these standards of beauty?
Imagine a world where there was no comparison
Who would save us from the monotony of perfection?
Nobody is perfect... (CHORUS)

Based on the context in which this music was released, when the economy was experiencing a monthly 2-digit inflation rate, and 70 percent of young people living in urban regions, with 10% of the population unemployed or underemployed (Alexandre 2013, p. 57), it becomes clear why this voice in the song, the narrator (maybe a young person?), with access to information, but unable to have fun or take care of himself, rebels against the system. Whether the rebels liked rock music or not, most young people in such an environment could already be described as "punk," a word commonly used to describe a jobless person and vagrant.

Deconstructing the song, "Complexes," one can identify the subject's political posture and his predilection for democracy, given that Brazil was under a military dictatorship in 1983-1984 when the song was released. By noting that, "But this problem not a million years will erase," the subject is dispirited that the problem his country was facing might persist and be impossible to be overcome. Again, this young voice laments the "Obstacles that don't let me through." These obstacles were many and herculean. They include: the heavy traffic that slows down everyday life; the gates at the entrance to public buildings where people require proper identification to be let through; and the censorship that impeded free circulation of ideas, etc. The daily life in the Brazil of that time appeared to be made up of obstacles, at least for part of the population – the underprivileged.

The verse that reads, "Tentacles that want to hold me" uses the old figurative association of animals, even monsters, with Brazil's notorious bureaucracy that was always oversized, expensive and largely inefficient, to showcase how people are disadvantaged in the system, including those who think differently, including the young, nonconformists, democrats and everyone who was an antipode of tradition. The lamentation goes on because the young voice says, "I try to hide, I try to disguise" but it doesn't work, hence the feeling of helplessness. The lyrics sum up the hapless fate of the youth with the following imagery: "Flowing against which it is useless to swim," and "Anchor that won't let me go." In other words, everything is difficult, complicated, and complex, as the title suggests.

Along with some of the first punk bands that emerged in Brasília at the same time, groups that had national recognition, such as Legião Urbana, Plebe Rude and Capital Inicial, the Escola de Escândalo apparently had similar record of sound quality, impactful lyrics and playing in the same circuit of shows, especially in the Rio de Janeiro-São Paulo axis. However, in the middle of the 1980s, and unlike the other bands, Escola de Escândalo did not record a solo album. Two of their songs in the collection *Rumores (Rumors)*,[5] from 1985, were recorded in collaboration with the bands Detrito Federal (*Federal Detritus*, a splinter group from of Anti-tédio), Elite Sophisticada and Finis Africae, all based in Brasília. *Rumores* was the first collective album recorded with the Rock of Brasília. It is noteworthy, though, that *Rumores* was the first punk album from Brasília and third punk album recorded in Brazil: there were two albums already published with punk bands from São Paulo, *Grito suburbano* (*Suburban scream*) in 1982, and *Começo do fim do mundo* (*The beginning of the end of the world*) in 1983. The two songs recorded by Escola de Escândalo in *Rumours* were "Complexos" and "Luzes" (*Lights*), both by Bernardo Muller. To produce this record, the band had a new line-up: Geraldo "Geruza" Ribeiro (bass), Luiz Eduardo (guitar), Eduardo Espinoza "Balé" (drums), Mariele Loiola (vocals) and Bernardo Muller (vocals). The band Legião Urbana also recorded its first album in 1985, the first album by a single Rock band from Brasília, and this was under the famous recording studio EMI.

---

[5] Rumores. (1985). Sebo do Disco. Brasília. https://www.youtube.com/watch?v=nFuQGWgQmZI

To conclude the reflections about Escola de Escândalo and one of its most important songs, it may be appropriate to think about it having what Antonio Bivar, scholar of the punk movement, said about the political engagement of the early punk rock in Europe:

> If the politics in the adult world is confused, greater political coherence of the punk movement should not be charged.... because it is a movement of teenage revolt (that)..... has only an average age around 18. A generation that, dissatisfied with everything, has just invoked the spirit of change (Bivar, 1982, p. 47).

Johnny Rotten, the leader of the English punk rock band Sex Pistols that was formed in London in 1975, appeared to have affirmed Bivar's contention that the music was rooted in anarchy. Bivar noted that Johnny Rotten said this about the driving force behind punk rock: "We are not interested in music. We are interested in CHAOS." (Bivar, 1982, p. 47).

Bivar went on to assert that Punk was more of a revolution than political; more of a feeling than consciousness. When the press began to use rhetoric to explain what punk rock meant, calling it a political movement, Johnny Rotten retorted: "The press does not know what it says. How can I be a political if I do not even know the name of the prime minister!" (Bivar, 1982, p. 50).

Another important figure at the beginning of the punk movement in Brazil, Kid Vinil, attended a concert by The Clash band in England in 1978, returned with many of the band's records to Brazil, formed his own punk band, had radio shows, wrote about the music genre in the newspapers and today he is part of the history of Brazilian punk. On the subject of ideas or political postures, and the demands of Brazilian punks at the initial stage of the music in the country, Kid Vinil made this statement that is similar to that of Johnny Rotten:

> We didn't care. You know, punk has these things about contesting, shooting and not knowing where the target is. At the time, punk was that. Nonsense, you know? What in England they called a Blank Generation: an empty generation, with nothing to offer. There was no need to offer anything (...) I identified with punk culture because I really ended up being a supporter that nothing else existed. It was a self-destruction thing, because at the time everything was so chaotic (Vinil, 1984, p. 47)

If the political message is not very clearly enunciated in the lyrics of "Complexos" by Escola de Escândalo, the same cannot be said about the next song by Anti-tédio. Formed in Brasília in 1983, one the group's most prominent songs was "Revolta" (*Revolt*), which has a direct call for a revolution in the country. The lyrics say as follows:

"Revolta"
Pé na estrada
vou andando
Sem olhar para trás
Mundo sendo destruído
Incapaz de falar

Mas é hora de revolta
Vamos todos rebelar
Seja punk ou playboy
Vamos todos gritar
Revolta – Oi oi!
Revolta – Oi oi!

"Revolt"
Foot on the road
I'm walking
Without looking back
World being destroyed
Unable to speak
But it's time for revolt
Let's all rebel
Be punk or playboy
Let's all scream
Revolt – Oi oi!
Revolt – Oi oi!

The first observation about this song is its use of the expression, "oi oi." Ordinarily, it is an exclamation attributed to the more radical side of punk rock and its artists. It is symbolic of their rejection of the commercialization of punk rock for monetary gain, as they consider such money-making acts antithetical to, and a betrayal of, the ideals of the music genre. Its use in this song by Anti-tédio is surprising as the group is normally not regarded as belonging to the radical wing of the punk rock movement. Therefore the inclusion of the expression in "Revolta" might well be indicative of Anti-tédio's disgust with politics and governance in Brazil, and the need for the people to rise and revolt against the system.

"Revolta" consists of two main stanzas. In the first, the narrator, "I," appears to be on the move, probably because he or she (it is not explicit) does wish to look back, figuratively, at past occurrences in the country. So, he moves along, although he is attentive to the present, and perceives the "world being destroyed." Seeing the destruction, he is "unable to speak," and maybe shocked. An unknown force appears to compel him to continue walking along, "without looking back." In the first three verses, the narrator talked about a "road" he was walking on, possibly in the expectation of reaching a goal, and in full knowledge of the pressure of time to realize that goal. Perhaps, the perception of the inexorable passage of time and the necessity for change, were what forced the narrator not to look back, despite finding so much destruction that left him speechless.

The second stanza is more political and powerful. The narrator is no longer contented with a walking past the debilitating past, but is concerned with some action to change the present and herald a new future. In it, the movement seems to cease, because "it's time for revolt; let's all rebel." That is, behind an apparently very simple composition, there is an elaborate mechanism that indicates that, in order to prevent the Brazilian world from being destroyed, it was necessary to act. And this benevolent, saving action depends not on the movement (walking along), but paradoxically on its interruption. In the final analysis, what the narrator seems to want to do, is to awaken people's conscience. He appears to question people who, in their everyday rush of life, cannot look back and say or do something in the face of the destruction of the world. "Oi oi!" is a wake-up call to action.

"Oi" represents an invitation to reflective awakening, to become rebellious. In this context, the person who busily undertakes the journey, without spending some time to look back and reflect, can be interpreted as a symbolic representation of some working-class people who, upon investing all their energies and time in jobs that were not very rewarding, often did not have the time or consciousness or radicalism to look back and critically evaluate their plight, thus becoming tacitly enslaved. Even though they perceive things (destruction) happening around them, they cannot rebel against the system that oppresses them, but rewards it with more and more work. In this sense, *Revolta*, aligns with the poem "Canção amiga" (*Friendly song*) by Carlos Drummond de Andrade, a famous Brazilian poet. The last verse of the poem states the following: "I prepare a song/ that makes wake up men / and fall asleep children." (Andrade 1948, p. 59).

The style and strategy of writing lyrics with double meaning is found in musical compositions by Escola de Escândalo and Anti-tédio. However, they were not the first or the only bands to make use of the ruse. One of the best-known cases in the use of this strategy involved Chico Buarque and Gilberto Gil, both famous composers and interpreters of the so-called Popular Brazilian Music. In 1973, they jointly composed the song entitled "Cálice," with lyrics full of double meanings. In this song, they disguised their criticism of the military regime with apparent religious evocations (*cálice* means *chalice* in English). At the same time, in Portuguese, the word "cálice" has almost the same sound as the expression "cale-se" which means "shut up" – the symbolic expression of the political repression and censorship prevalent in the country. In doing this, they not only dodged the censorship of that era, but had their song played on radio stations throughout the country, and people could sing loud and clear: "Father, take away from me this ---- shut up! (a voice adds)"

Conclusion

Given the evidence provided in this chapter, it is plausible to posit that punk rock was a protest musical genre that communicated and denounced the ills in the Brazilian society. At times, punk rock musicians simply saw themselves as anarchists who only believed in the destruction of the system, without necessarily providing alternative views on governance. In other cases, they used their platforms to urge people to revolt against the oppressive system in which they lived. Overall, the common feature among all punk rock groups examined in this chapter is their staunch refusal to capitulate amidst the repression and censorship unleashed by various military governments in Brazil to silence them. They stood firm in their beliefs and continued to use their music to challenge the authorities.

The historical approach adopted in this chapter in examining the punk rock phenomenon in Brazil shows that this musical genre appeared to have hit its peak as a commanding form of artistic expression in the 1980s. Apparently, punk rock began to slide into decline in the 1990s to the point where today, there are genuine doubts about its popularity, even existence, in the country, at least in terms of audience pull and financial successes the music and its artists recorded in the 1980s. Furthermore, it might be quite herculean to pinpoint the extent to which the punk rock bands or in fact their music contributed to eclipsing the Brazilian dictatorships from the time of their inception in 1964 to when the last military authoritarian government quit the political scene in the country in 1985. No doubt, the case can be made that the punk rock musicians sensitized and influenced Brazilians in their quest to oust the military dictatorship and reintroduce democratic governance in the country. However, assessing the extent of their contribution is beyond the scope of this chapter, although we can also say that there were other local and external factors that coalesced to force the military out of power. It was not only the work of the punk rock bands, their musicians and the political messaging contained in the lyrics of their songs, that ended Brazil's authoritarian regimes.

When evaluated organically, and looking at the trajectory of their music and performance, the Brasília punk rock bands, from Escola de Escândalo and Antitédio, to Legião Urbana and Plebe Rude and others, appear to align with what sociologist Raymond Williams, described as the structure of feelings, that is, something not so immediately perceived by the actors of the moment. Williams opined that "when this structure of feeling has been absorbed, it is the connections, correspondences, and even epochal resemblances that stand out most. What was then a lived structure is now a recorded structure that can be examined, identified and even generalized" (Williams, 1987, pp. 18-19). So, when seen retroactively and holistically, the bands basically resembled one another because their motivations and lived experiences were about the same. Moreover, the bands fitted into what Ridenti (2005) noted was a pre-existing structure of non-conformism, followed by their resolve to disrupt governance and social life as they existed.

No doubt, the Brasília punk rock bands left their indelible footprints in the history of Brazil, especially as it relates to music, with their focused and relentless political messaging that challenged the status quo in the country, in spite of the overwhelming censorship and intimidation they faced. It is therefore important to understand their place in history vis-à-vis the political and socio-cultural milieu in which they operated.

References

Alexandre, R. (2013). *Dias de luta: O rock e o Brasil dos anos 80 (Struggle days: Rock and Brazil in the 80's)*. Porto Alegre: Arquipélago.
Andrade, C. D. de. (1948). *Novos Poemas*. Rio de Janeiro: Livraria José Olympio Editora.
Andrade, M. de. (1989). *Dicionário Musical Brasileiro (Brazilian Musical Dictionary)*. Belo Horizonte: Itatiaia/Brasília: Ministério da Cultura/São Paulo: IEB.
Bivar, A. (1982). *O que é punk (What is punk)*. São Paulo: Brasiliense.
Candido, A. & Castello, J. A. (1968). *Presença da Literatura Brasileira – III Modernismo (Presence of Brazilian Literature – III Modernism)*. São Paulo: Difel.
Cardim, F. (1939) (2nd Ed.) *Tratados da terra e gente do Brasil (Treaties of the land and people of Brazil)* São Paulo: Companhia Editora Nacional.
Carvalho, V. (2009). Ruínas do future (Ruins of the future). *Revista da Biblioteca Mário de Andrade (Magazine of the Mário de Andrade Library)*, 65, 124-138.
Dapieve, A. (1995). *BRock: O Rock brasileiro dos anos 80 (BRock: Brazilian Rock in the 80's)*. São Paulo: Editora 34.
Dunn, C. (2001). *Brutality garden: Tropicália and the emergence of a Brazilian counterculture*. USA: University of North Carolina Press.
Hermano Júnior. (1983). Ai de ti, Brasília (Woe betide you, Brasília). *Mixtura moderna (Modern Mixture)*. Rio de Janeiro.
Lima, J. C. (2020). *O retorno do rei: As representações política e cultural de Luiz Gonzaga, traços de uma trajetória (The return of the king: Luiz Gonzaga's political and cultural representations, traces of a trajectory)*. [Unpublished Master's Thesis.] Universidade Federal da Paraíba (Federal University of Paraíba, Brazil). https://repositorio.ufpb.br/jspui/bitstream/123456789/20300/1/Jos%C3%A9CunhaLima_Dissert.pdf
Marcelo, C. (2011). Interview. In V. Carvalho *Rock Brasília – Era de ouro (Brasília Rock – Golden Era*. [Documentary]. https://www.youtube.com/watch?v=Lgdj3giiwfM

Marchetti, P. (2001). *O diário da turma 1976-1986. A história do rock de Brasília (The Guy's' Diary 1976-1986. Brasilia's rock history)*. São Paulo: Conrad.

Marsiglia, L. (1990). *História do rock brasileiro (Vol. 3) (History of Brazilian Rock, Vol. 3)*. São Paulo: Abril.

Ridenti, M. (2005) Artistas e intelectuais no Brasil pós-1960 (Artists and intellectuals in post-1960 Brazil). *Tempo Social: Revista de Sociologia da USP (Social Time: Journal of Sociology at the University of São Paulo)*, *17*(1), 81-110. https://www.scielo.br/j/ts/a/f4Ztm8ZzQsWhgywLyjWNWJq/?lang=pt&format=pdf

Ribeiro, D. (1985). *Aos trancos e barrancos: Como o Brasil deu no que deu (By leaps and bounds: How Brazil turned out)*. Rio de Janeiro: Guanabara Dois.

Ribeiro, D. (1995). *O povo brasileiro: A formação e o sentido do Brasil (The Brazilian people: The formation and meaning of Brazil)*. São Paulo: Companhia das Letras.

Último Segundo (Last Second). (2013, June 21). *"'Que País É Este?' é escolhida a música de protesto mais marcante do Brasil" ("What country is this' is chosen as the most outstanding protest song in Brazil")*. iG. https://ultimosegundo.ig.com.br/cultura/musica/2013-06-21/que-pais-e-este-e-escolhida-a-musica-de-protesto-mais-marcante-do-brasil.html

Vianna, H. (1995). *O mistério do samba (Samba's mistery)*. Rio de Janeiro: Jorge Zahar.

Vinil, K. (1984, January 4). *Revista IstoÉ (IstoÉ Magazine)*, São Paulo, Brazil.

Williams, R. (1987). *Drama from Ibsen to Brecht*. London: The Hogart Press.

Wisnik, J. M. (2003). Machado maxixe: o caso Pestana (Machado maxixe: the Pestana case). *Teresa: Revista de Literatura Brasileira (Teresa: Journal of Brazilian Literature)*, 4-5, 13-79. https://www.revistas.usp.br/teresa/article/view/116360

Zanon, F. (2007 August 1). O violão em Brasília [Audio Podcast]. https://vcfz.blogspot.com/2007/08/83-violo-em-braslia.html

CHAPTER 7

Political Messaging in Indian Cinema: Core or Periphery?

N. Usha Rani
University of Mysore, India

Abstract

In this chapter, the author examines the evolution of political cinema in India, based on the premise that film producers in states in the country where communist political parties are in power, tend to produce politically engaging films with aesthetics, style and extraordinary content that are more regional in focus, than those that have a more national appeal. Specifically, this chapter focuses on films produced in the eastern state of West Bengal and the southwestern, coastal state of Kerala, both states being where the Marxist ideology largely shapes political and cultural awakening among the people. Using the descriptive analysis as methodology, this author traces the complexities and nuances of regional language in political cinema in West Bengal and Kerala, and attempts to provide a response to the query about the present-day status of political cinema in these two politically conscious states of India. Furthermore, this chapter provides insights into the cinematic experience of Indian filmmakers whose works use the cinema as a medium to confront political issues in the country, in a way that creates an informed audience and challenges the notion of films being solely made for the purpose of entertainment.

Keywords: Political cinema, parallel cinema, India, Marxism, leftists, right-wing party, Neorealism, *New Wave*

***

Introduction: What constitutes a Political Film?

The cinema is a far-reaching art that largely offers an intangible experience. It is a visual and transcultural aesthetic experience that transcends the boundaries of language, race, culture and religion. In pre-industrialized societies, the cinema was the single most potent factor that proved resourceful in educating and entertaining the masses that had migrated from traditionally protected communities to newly formed urban societies. The cinema changed the social order, and influenced culture and value system, prompting media critics to advocate the mass society theory that blames the cinema, especially Hollywood cinema, for the social evils in modern American society.

Today, movie making is an established mass entertainment showbiz industry that produces different genres of films. Nevertheless, historically, there is sufficient evidence to support the extensive use of the mass media such as the cinema, as tools of political propaganda by governments across the world. The premise that cinema can connect with masses led to the belief that as a medium, it needed to be controlled directly or indirectly by every government in power, or by people who intend to capture power, for the purpose of spreading their propaganda. From 1927 to 1945, the German cinema was derailed by Adolf Hitler's obsession with cinema, leading to his stringent control and regulation of the medium. So-called nationalist films were made during this period by Hitler, his Nazi government and allies, with propaganda-centric themes that were designed to influence the masses.

Mainstream cinema has attempted to integrate art and politics through realism or imaginative narrative. Political content is the fatal attraction of cinema. In this regard, Phillip Gianos says that "Politics and movies inform each other ... Both tell about the society from which they come" (Gianos, 1995, as cited in Christensen & Haas, 2005, p.20). Political films tend to have an ensuring power and presence, just like politics and politicians. Over the years, parallel cinema or *New Wave* cinema or alternative cinema, have heavily explored and propelled the ideology of Marxism onto the center stage of the cinema, thus enabling audiences to differentiate between such serious films and cinema relating to issues of democracy. On the other hand, the film industry in some countries has been criticized for its politically conservative attitude and behavior towards political issues.

There is also evidence that interest in understanding political debates captured in films is on the rise. This is the result of the sea change in the global political climate and increased interest of audiences in political institutions across nations. This therefore raises the question: Does political content on reel affect the real world? Although this question is somewhat difficult to answer, one can assert that in the context of Hollywood, "films like Fahrenheit 9/11 have demonstrated that worlds of film and politics are increasingly intertwined and interdependent" (Christensen &Haas, 2005, p. ix).

A political film is invariably described as one with political content. Some scholars, such as Christensen and Haas (2005), also believe that every film has political content, significance and meaning (p.4). Louis D. Giannetti contends that, explicit ideological messages may be present in films entirely devoid of explicit political referents; however, many of the political messages sent by movies are not the result of conscious planning by filmmakers (Giannetti, 1996, as cited in Christensen & Haas, 2005,p.6). However, political films are not generally considered a specific genre unlike horror, war, science, comedy, romance or others, because political perspectives and elements may run in the thread of different genres. Sklar (1982) noted:

> Such films take political situations or issues - suspicious doings within a large organization, a politician's struggle for power, a community's effort to come to terms with some collective issue - as their primary, foreground subject and often use their story in order to make a point about the inadequacies or the nobility of political institutions and assumptions (Section 2, p.1).

Indian Cinema and Socialism

Indian cinema is 100 years old, with credible cinematic credentials that have transformed the industry into a formidable soft power that spans across nations and continents, regardless of language, religion or culture. According to the Indian Central Board of Film Certification (CBFC), the industry has an annual turnover of US$ 4 billion and is considered as the largest industry in the world, producing over 1,000 films in a year in 27 languages in 2019 (CBFC, 2021). From the film, *Raja Harishchandra*, the first-ever silent film of Indian cinema produced in 1913, the industry has metamorphosed into a cinematic phenomenon that has created an Indian identity in global cinema.

The initial days were characterized by its engagement with historical and mythological themes to reinforce the relationship between people and mass culture. This mythological focus dominated the Bollywood and regional cinema for over two decades during 1940s. The mythological emphasis in the films made the Indian Gods more real, not less (Mukhopadhyay, 2006, pp. 279-292), and illustrates the power of mass media in reinforcing culture, beliefs and values. Nevertheless, the postcolonial mapping of films also reveals that Bollywood explored political themes portraying Indian vision of socialism and the rise of modernism. Filmmakers Guru Dutt, V. Shantharam, and Raj Kapur, made films like *Mother India, Do Bigha Zameen, Naya Daur,* and *Duniya Na Mane*, advocating Indian socialism intended to give a realistic experience of class struggle and poverty in the post-colonial period. According to Paunksnis (Paunksnis, 2015, p.45), the "Politically engaged cinema and social reality until very recently existed in a two-dimensional relationship. The so-called New Wave cinema was often very critical and skeptical about the promises of development and emancipation that the state and its ideologies had to offer."

Bollywood, the international identity of Indian cinema produced some of the finest films immediately after the end of colonial rule, making the category of films on nationalism and the political philosophy of socialism more visible in the country. In its early days, the cinema in India was impacted by Marxism, but local electoral politics was the main influence in the post-independence period. In this period, the left-wing socialists managed to influence a number of cultural institutions like the theatre and cinema, especially the Indian People's Theatre Association (IPTA). The cultural wing of the Communist Party of India- IPTA was also instrumental in evolving progressive perspectives to protect cultural institutions in the country, as well as preserve local folk traditions (Pradhan, 1979).

Entertaining and Sensitizing Value of Political Cinema in India

Overall, films contain political messages that are critical of the political system, although the extent and intensity of such messages vary. The filmmaker's intent determines whether the film is political or apolitical. In general, various categories of films entertain their audiences, but not all members of such audiences agree with the messages being canvassed by the filmmaker. However, there is a category of films that is structured on political institutions with recognizable political leaders, the purpose of which is to reach out to a receptive audience with hard-hitting political messages. This specific type of films invokes aesthetics and creativity in the treatment of political content. As Christensen and Haas (2005, p.11) noted, "despite the benign intentions of their creators, both the socially reflective and politically reflective types of film are frequently pregnant with political meaning."

The political modernist Indian film, *Lage Raho Munna Bhai*, (produced in 2006, a Hindi language film directed by Rajkumar Hirani), is a mainstream political satire on Gandhism. The film treated Mahatma Gandhi's ideology with reverence and advocated Gandhism for the country. It won the hearts of a variety of Indian audiences, despite the fact that the main protagonist in the film was a small-time local gangster in the garb of a social worker. In India, it is unusual for a political film to rely on Gandhi's ideals to address India's problems of corrupt politicians and tons of other problems. However, *Lage Raho Munna Bhai*, is a new age political film that entertained audiences to the core, using an authentic formula of *Dadagiri* (gangster) vs *Gandhigiri* (professing Gandhi's ideals). This particular film made audiences to revisit the philosophy of Gandhi's *Satyagraha* and *Ahimsa* –truth and non-violent resistance – which was an unusual plot for a Bollywood film. The message that three bullets could kill Gandhi but not his philosophy and ideology, worked like magic and created a new genre in Indian films, that is, a political film that has the elements of aesthetics, entertainment, and ideology. This film grossed huge revenue, of US$ 18 million in India alone and was the first Hindi film to be screened at the United Nations on 10 November 2006.

The much-acclaimed 2006 film *Rang De Basanti* (directed by Rakesh Omprakash Mehra) a cinematic portrayal of political radicalism, illustrates that political films connect with audiences when storytelling is innovative and unique. Mainstream films with political messages do not distort reality and people love that their opinions about politics are reinforced by these films. The climax in *Rang De Basanthi* film had a tragic ending and was criticized for advocating fascism. However, the audience, though jolted by violent ending, loved the film for its sheer rationale and felt sad at the deterioration of political system. The film gave an inimitable experience to the audience and connected with the masses.

It is noteworthy that a critically acclaimed film such a *Rang De Basanti* (produced in 2006) was a huge commercial success, resonated with the audience with its fresh political thoughts, and created history in the annals of India's political cinema. Such success challenged the misconception that films about freedom struggle or patriotism or nationalism no longer appealed to audiences. *Rang De Basanti* proved the critics wrong. It is the story of a middle-class youth who gets frustrated with the political system, revolts against the government, takes over a radio station and fatally shoots politicians.

Nonetheless, films are just one of the major sources that influence public perception of politicians. As noted by Christensen and Haas (2005, p.14), "Political movies give messages and they are part of a larger political socialization where (the) audience learns about political systems and other social institutions." That said, it is rather challenging to conclusively demonstrate that political messages bring about behavioral changes in audiences, and persuade people to believe in a given political ideology. However, researchers Elliott and Hamlin (1979), in one of the earliest studies on the Hollywood chart-buster, *All the President's Men (1976)*, noted as follows:

> Exposure to a well-constructed message, such as this film, can have at least a short term influence on a particular political attitude but this influence does not generalize across political attitudes....We are not arguing that a single film, even one as well done as *All the President's Men*, will have significant impact on the political and social order. Yet, the repeatedly negative portrayals of politicians in entertainment media may be more alienating than their treatment in news (pp.552-553).

This assertion is supported by Leab (1994, p.49) who claimed that "the power of any single movie to influence one's viewpoint is limited, but obviously repetition has its effect." Political movies are also a reflection of the functioning of a political system, especially in determining whether the system addresses the problems encountered by the people. The audiences are generally well aware of how the political system works and films are a means of reinforcing their commonly held beliefs. Unfortunately, although the audiences might wish the system to change or become more amenable to solving their real-life problems, they seldom expect movies to change the system.

Some scholars, such as Kazmi (1999) consider the entire gamut of Indian cinema as political cinema, as they largely discuss and articulate ideological positions. Kazmi (1999, p.215) argues that Indian conventional (or mainstream) cinema is, "a political cinema and is ideologically loaded. Its raw material is always social reality." This argument appears vindicated, especially when one evaluates films like *Lage Raho Munna Bai, Lagan* (produced in 2006), *1942: A Love Story* (produced in *1994*), *A Wednesday (*produced in *2008)*, and *Jaane Bhi Do Yaaro* (produced in 1983). These films are a critical political satire on Indian politics. They resonate with audiences of different generations in contemporary India.

Political Cinema in India's West Bengal and Kerala

West Bengal State: The trilogy of "*New Wave*" filmmakers

This chapter is premised on the correlation between a political system and the type of cinema produced in it. In this regard, the Communist Party ruled states of West Bengal and Kerala are at the forefront producing highly acclaimed political films than other states in India with non-Communist Party governments in power.

Although cinema is an art, it is also a part of the political process as the political system impacts the content of cinema. Quality and meaningful cinema emerged from the creative castles of Satyajit Ray, Mrinal Sen and Ritwik Ghatak, all from West Bengal where, unlike the Indian federal government, the state was under the regime of the Communists who influenced both theatre and cinema. Bengal cinema exposed India to the Neorealism school of filmmaking that gave the audience a new experience of art, aesthetics and political consciousness in cinema.

Hindi cinema or Bollywood is generally considered the face of Indian cinema. However, as Kumar (2011, p.1) observed, this conceptualization overlooks a wide range of films that can be considered as multilinguistic and multicultural but were made at the regions. India is a multi-lingual and multi-religious country that has strong regional language cinema industry that is neither controlled nor financed by the government. In this regard, there cannot be an objective and realistic analysis of Indian cinema without reference to ace film director, Satyajit Ray from West Bengal.

Satyajit Ray

Ray is respected for his vision of cinema. He made a remarkable entry into global cinema at a time when the cinema revolution gave birth to Italian Neorealism, French Nouvelle Vague, Soviet films, and British cinema, coupled with post-war films from Europe. In his reflection of Ray's film, *Pather Panchali*, fellow filmmaker, Shyam Benegal in the foreword said:

> Satyajit Ray had shattered the mold that had bound filmmakers in India to a form of filmmaking that had remained unchanged since the introduction of sound.... (he is a) first-time Indian filmmaker in a film language and idiom that was both modern and entirely his own. The locations and the people in the film were believable and culture specific. It was beyond anything that I had imagined films of being capable of achieving; a true watershed in Indian cinema (Benegal wrote in foreword in Ray, 2011, pp. x-xi).

Bengali films in the pre-independence days in the 1930s and 1940s were held in high esteem as most of the films were based on literary works of classic writers such as Sarat Chandra Chatterjee. Ray followed the path of adaptation of literary works for his films. He worked on all genres of films and demonstrated his mastery of the film art, producing notable films such as *Pather Panchali* (1955), *Aparajito* (1956), *Parash Pathar* (1958), *Apur Sansar* (1959), *Devi* (1960), *Goopy Gyne Bagha Byne* (1968), *Pratidwandi* (1970), *Seemabaddha*(1971), *Hirak Rajar Deshe* (1980), *Ghare Baire* (1984), *Ganasatru* (1989), *Shakha Proshakha* (1990), and *Agantuk* (1991).

Ray deservedly gets the credit for breaking stereotypes in Indian filmmaking and providing a new perspective in films to his audience. He introduced the Indian audience to a new language of films which was different from films of the previous age and era. His transition was the defining moment in the history of Indian cinema that shaped the country's national identity.

Mrinal Sen

Mrinal Sen is a sensitive filmmaker renowned for making some of the forceful and finest socio-political films in India. His classic works include *Akash Kusum* (1965), *Matira Manisha* (1966), *Bhuvan Shome* (1969), *Interview* (1970), *Calcutta 71* (1972), *Padatik* (1973), *Mrigayaa* (1976), *Oka Oori Katha* (1977), *Ek Din Pratidin* (1979), *Akaler Sandhaney* (meaning in search of Famine) made in 1980, and *Khandahar* (1984).

Sen belonged to the Bengali left-wing theatre group, and was an ardent follower of Brecht's theory of realism in filmmaking. He experimented with the application of this theory in his radical, left-wing political films. Sen, who is credited with establishing Brecht's cinema in India, is an authority on political cinema. He introduced the left-wing political ideology in his films. Ganguly (2000) says this about him:

> Sen single-handedly invented not only Brechtian cinema in India but the radical left-wing political cinema as well, thereby posing the first serious challenge to the realist, liberal-humanist aesthetic inaugurated by Satyajit Ray in 1955 with *Pather Panchali/ Song of the Little Road* (Ganguly, 2000, p.55)

Sen's *Akaler Sandhaney* film made in 1980 is about famine of 1943 in Bengal province during World War II and in British colonial rule in India. Over three million people died in that famine which, according to a *The Guardian* newspaper report (Safi M, 2019, para 4), was alleged to have been man-made as a result of policy failure by the British colonial administration. Sen's film explored the famine through radical, left-wing lenses, placing the famine on the door-step of the colonial regime.

Ritwik Ghatak

Ritwik Ghatak, the legendary filmmaker of the realism school and a hard-core leftist intellectual contributed some of the finest films to political cinema in India. His repertoire consisted of the refugee trilogy –*Meghe Dhake Tara* (The Cloud–Capped Star, 1960), *Komal Gandhar* (E- Flat, 1961), and *Subanarekha* (Golden Lining, 1962). These post partition films focused on trials and tribulations of refugees and the political divide that aggravated the sufferings of ordinary people.

Ghatak is known for cinematic narratives that deconstruct the socio-political realities of a nation entangled in huge refugee problems after partition of India. The partition of both Punjab and Bengal provinces created the worst sorrows and sufferings for people in these regions whose identity suddenly changed from citizens to refugees. Ghatak was born in Dhaka in 1925, and witnessed the Bengal famine in 1943, as well as the partition of Bengal in 1947 and the creation of Bangladesh in 1971. A revolutionary filmmaker, Ghatak was instrumental in raising the bar for creating a cinematic experience that dealt with people's sufferings and sorrow arising from famine and other forms of national tragedies. Regarding his motivation to make this form of films, Ghatak noted that (Roy, 2016, para 5):

> Cinema, to me, is a means of expressing my anger at the sorrows and sufferings of my people. Being a Bengali from East Bengal, I have seen untold miseries inflicted on my people in the name of independence – which is fake and a sham. I have reacted violently to this – and I have tried to portray different aspects of this in my films.

A powerful storyteller, some of Ghatak's celebrated films include, *Ajantrik (1958), Titash Ekti Nadir Naam, Jukti Takko ArGappo, and Bari Theke Paliye.* In his last film, *Jukti Takko Aar Gappo* (Reason, Debate and A Tale, 1977), he played the role of a protagonist - an alcoholic intellectual - who basically critiqued of partition and the rise of Naxalite movement in Bengal. Ghatak distinguished himself as a truth seeker and anti-establishment celluloid rebel who adopted cinema as a means of political discourse.

Political Cinema in post *Left-Front* rule

Most of the films made by Ray, Sen and Ghatak were produced during the period of political transition when the state of West Bengal witnessed tremendous human sufferings and poverty. The Communist Party had won elections and governed the state for over three decades, from 1977-2011. Unfortunately for the left-leaning political activists and the Communist Party that controlled the government, the vicissitudes of politics resulted in them gradually losing ground in Bengal, thus replicating the global trend where Communists lost relevance in many countries and could not connect with the masses. The people or masses whom the communists had claimed to represent, wanted change, rejected the leftist political party in West Bengal in 2011, and embraced liberal thoughts. This shift was also reflected in the films. Bose and Chakravarty (2012) noted that:

> In cinema, a continuity may be traced between the later films of Satyajit Ray and Mrinal Sen, which begin to look at subjectivities and the 'inner turmoil' of their middle-class protagonists, and the films that emerged as middle-brow art at the turn of the present century. There is a marked shift from ideological moorings of the Left – let us say from stark documentation to conversational personalized exchanges, from the mutinous to more negotiational, even reconciliatory, modes of filmmaking (p.131).

The shift from the left-oriented films to liberal films is attributed to changes in the aspirations of middle class who wanted to experience the socio-economic changes and technological advances that were invading the nation. Calling oneself as non-Leftist became a fashion statement among the middle class who rejected the Marxist ideology and embraced liberalism. Young people wanted a different kind of cinema as they were disillusioned with the leftist ideology and thoughts. Young middle class and urban educated people observed the change in the loyalties of writers and intellectuals like Mahasweta Devi, a writer and a core leftist who became sympathetic to non-leftist political ideologies.

The hybrid nature of Bengal cinema pushed the industry through that difficult phase in the 1990s. However, despite making a few good films breaking fresh ground, Bengali cinema could not recreate the art cinema of world acclaim in the post- Satyajit Ray era, but his legacy was revived by a new breed of talented filmmakers who were more liberal and radical in their films in the early part of 21st century. Filmmakers such as Goutam Ghose, Aparna Sen, Srijit Mukherjee, Moinak Biswas, Arjun Gourisaria, Suman Mukhopadyay and Buddhadeb Dasgupta made attempts to stabilize the legacy of intellectual cinema and did help in creating space for a new genre. Films like *Sthaniya Sambaad* (Spring in the Colony, 2009), *Mahanagar@Kolkata* (2010), and *Autograph* (2010), indicated the emergence of new stories that were forceful commentaries on the political parties. This cinema genre provided space for criticizing the left's lofty ideology that saw regular violence and unrest that characterized life in urban Bengal. These political films were made when the left-leaning government was losing its battle to retain political power, and faced with highly disillusioned voters. Bengal cinema captured this political transformation from Ray's Nayak (Hero, 1966) to *Mahanagar@Kolkata*(2010).

Nonetheless, what followed was that the television appeared to have captured the Bengal audience more than the cinema, as most people were unable to connect with the hybrid films that were churned out by the industry in this period. However, the industry appeared to rebound later. This is mainly attributed to Rituparno Ghosh who is generally credited with reviving the Bengal film industry and engaging the middle-class audience in a dialogue at the dawn of political liberalization era, without sacrificing Ray's intellectualism. His unique art of storytelling established him as a game changer by treading the middle path that could neither be called art nor commercialism. Consequently, the middle-class, urban audience was enthralled by Ghosh's films with his considerable reference to sexuality and his uninhibited performance of the same in public, something that was a novelty in the history of Bengali cinema.

Indeed, the LBGT movement was Ghosh's forte as he explored neo-liberal sexual identity politics in his films (Datta et al., 2015). This became a trendsetter in Indian cinema. Ghosh's radicalism in cinema ruled the industry from 1997 to 2013. As Bose and Chakravarty (2012) noted:

> Mainstream communist, nationalist and other modes of asceticism are being challenged by these (Ghosh's) films even though these are still relatively circumscribed and genteel forms of experimental cinema. However, even within circumscribed parameters, they have begun to bring uncomfortable questions of adventurous, transgressive, mutinous behavior (sexual or otherwise) to an audience hitherto largely unexposed to any such explorations on the screen without a moral framework of guilt, punishment or penance being attached to them (p.132).

And, following Ghosh's footsteps was another filmmaker, Srijit Mukherji, who connected with the educated urban audience and helped to some extent save Bengali films from becoming a relic of history.

Political Messaging in Cinema, Rock Music &Over-the-Top (OTT)

At the turn of 21st century, anti-left political atmosphere began to influence the entertainment industry in general, and the music industry in particular, in Bengal. This saw the emergence of the Bangla rock band whose music was loud, but the lyrics were far from the aesthetics of Bangla literature in the land of Sarat Chandra Chatterjee and Rabindra Sangeet. The lyrics reflected new political ethos, urban dreams, and the aspirations of urban middle class critical of society and the political system. The musical revolution through Bangla rock band in the *City of Joy* challenged the left's monopoly on intellectualism. It created a rock culture and lead singers like Moheener Ghoraguli, credited with forming India's first rock band from Kolkata, and Rupam Islam of *Fossils*, roused Bengali consciousness by producing music on social issues that won the hearts of youth. According to Dhar (2020, December 20), "their songs aspired to be anthems of resistance and alluded to conflicts raging across the world — from Vietnam to Bengal." Other rock bands like *Bhoomi, Underground Authority, Prithibi, Cactus,* and *Lakkhichhara* also captured the young Bangla minds with their progressive hard rock compositions and performances. The rock music reflected political statements on anti-capitalism and social protests. They provided a spectacle of musical culture of dissent, characterized by unorthodox and non-conformist counter culture. Rock music, a new means of expression bonding with the youth, thus began to define the entertainment industry in Bengal. Interestingly, the creative outcomes of political themes in the cinema and Rock music have migrated to the social media in modern Bengal.

The emergence of Over-the-Top (OTT) platforms in Bengal in regional language of Bengali has the potential to entertain and mainstream political stories. OTT media and communications services are internet-connected, subscription-based streaming platforms for media content. OTT services are presumed to be changing consumers' internet consumption behavior. According to the *Financial Express*, India witnessed a rise in subscription to 29 million as of July 2020 (Biswas, January 18, 2021, para 3).

Launched in 2017, the OTT platforms like *Hoichoi*, meaning excitement, optimized the Covid-19pandemic period to garner more subscribers. *Hoichoi* Bengali OTT has also gone global, garnering 40% of its direct revenue from international subscriptions from clients spread in over 100 countries. The OTT platforms have again reached the Bengal urban middle class and are providing entertainment to the core with web shows, and independent films made for video streaming. The OTT has brought fresh talent and new stories of different genres, entertaining over 13 million audience in general and the Bengali Diaspora in particular, with new cinematic experience. The Bengali feature films are released in digital platforms that connect Eastern India with the rest of the world. The most prominent genres in these films and web shows are thrillers and detective stories that are far from the intellectual base of the cinema of the past.

The Bengali entertainment industry has a vast market of 230 million native speakers, located all over the world, with digital space founders like *Hoichoi*, *Addatimes* which began operations on June 15, 2016, and KLiKK which was launched in November, 2020. The platforms have revolutionized the formats and devices of storytelling, bringing original and classic Bengali films under one roof, and bridging the rural urban divide in the entertainment experience.

Political Cinema: Core or Periphery in Bengal

The trio of filmmakers introduced an era of realism, humanism and liberalism in Indian cinema in general and Bengal cinema in particular for over five decades from 1950s to 1980s. There is no doubt that filmmakers who leaned heavily on the leftist political ideology contributed considerably to the growth of political cinema in Bengal. Nevertheless, the filmmakers never hesitated to self-critique their work, and at the same time exposing and attacking their communist comrades in their films, thereby lending credibility to their messages.

The urban audience has always patronized literature, theatre and cinema in Bengal. By contrast, rural Bengal has taken to commercial movies and has become disconnected with the cinema of the urban middle class.

The cinema in Bengal has undergone a transformation, so also the politics in the state, from left to right-wing ideologies. In the present circumstance of high level of political intolerance in Bengal, one cannot expect such narratives in films that criticize political violence, casteism, capitalism and signs of authoritarianism in democracy. Political cinema did justice to the cause of political problems in Bengal from the 1950s to 2013, producing politically important films that still generate discourses in academic and intellectual circles.

In 2020, the right-wing political party, the *Bharatiya Janata Party* (BJP), began making inroads to win elections in West Bengal, using Hindus for its political advantage. However, the possible impact which the BJP's presence in West Bengal will have on cinema, literature and theatre is worth pondering. BJP is a technology and media-driven political party which has a huge army of followers in social media to counter any campaigns and propaganda against the party. The pertinent issue is the future of political cinema in Bengal, and who will wear the mantle of continuing the tradition of making intellectual films that will integrate rapidly changing politics with the Bengal culture. Ray, Sen and Ghatak films explored the power of cinema in dissecting the Indian society from a political perspective, whether it was about poverty, refugee crisis or the Naxalite movement between 1950s - 1990s. Wedded to Marxism, the intellectual trio made films that were overtly political in a land of extreme political consciousness.

In the post liberalization period, filmmakers like Rituparno Ghosh explored liberal thoughts and brought about the transition from realism to humanism in films, and also explored issues of sexuality, gender, diversity, equity, social justice and caste in their work. To an extent, this new approach to filmmaking embarrassed the left-wing intellectuals.

The political debates on inclusiveness and social change have found its way into subaltern narratives in theatre, literature and cinema in the post leftist rule in West Bengal (2011-2021). There is now a marked awareness of the rights and means to resist state policies and programs even among the subaltern class. Furthermore, the middle class appears to totally disregard the intellectualism of the past films, and shows an indifference to politics in the state. Overall, the transition from humanism to subaltern cinema has not enriched political cinema in West Bengal, as the change is more in the periphery than in the core.

Kerala State: Excellence in Political and Social Cinema

During the period when film goers' attention was pre-occupied with *Bengali* films, it was cinema from Kerala, in south-western India, and another Communist-ruled state that was known for high education attainment, that successfully gained prominence by producing some of the brilliant filmmakers who excelled in social and political cinema. The golden era of Kerala cinema began in 1970s and was supported by the conducive environment created by folk culture, classical arts, literature and theatre.

Perhaps for the first time in the history of independent India, the Communist Party of India came to power and formed a government in Kerala as early as 1957. The party's electoral victory is attributed to its manifesto which spoke about providing land reforms, guaranteeing social justice for lower castes, promoting equality for women, and a promise of nationalization of privately-owned organizations. The CPI formed the first-ever non-Congress Party government in India in the state of Kerala, under Chief Minister E.M.S. Namboodiripad.

Neorealism Movement in Kerala

Filmmakers in Kerala state were influenced by Italian Neorealism film movement. This influence enabled them to experiment with their political ideology and theory of cinema, both of which culminated in a realistic portrayal of the struggles of the masses. The same influence aroused the consciousness of filmmakers to use the medium to encourage political participation among the masses. The rise of political films in Kerala is also attributed to the influence of the French New Wave film movement. The Kerala filmmakers did not want to identify with propagandist films but sought to view political ideology from the perspective of the masses, thereby providing a unique cinematic experience to the audience.

Kerala experienced a new political consciousness after the declaration of the state-of-emergency in 1975, when civil liberties were suspended and censorship was imposed on the media. The infamous episode of the death of an engineering student, P. Rajan in police custody during emergency shook the entire country, and especially Kerala. Shocked by the brutality of police force during emergency, Rajan's gruesome story was made into a film, *Piravi* by Shaji Karun in 1989. The film won both national and international awards, including one at the Cannes film festival. This story caught national attention and for the first time in the history of independent India, the Chief Minister of Kerala, K. Karunakaran, was forced to resign. The death also triggered a movement of political awakening in the state and country. For instance, Shaji who made a strong political statement through his first film, continued the tradition with his other films, including his second film, *Swaham* (My Own) in 1994. His films documented the brutality of the police force in suppressing the people's voices for political gain.

It is quite plausible to conclude that political films of Kerala evoked anger, frustration, and skepticism against the political system.

New Wave Movement

The works of the French *New Wave* film movement demonstrate that films could be made in different formats other than the conventional mainstream filmmaking, and tell political stories with greater sensitivity. The French movement gave Indian filmmakers an insight into radical experiments that liberated films from the propagandist mold. Not only were the Indian filmmakers radical in their content, they were also very cinematic in the form they presented to audiences. The *New Wave* films adopted the new style and unconventional narrative which required audiences to walk an extra mile to really understand and interpret images and content. The filmmakers in Kerala followed the national movement and produced some of the best political films of India; films that reflected indigenous talent on par with world cinema in the categories of Neorealism and *New Wave* movements.

Furthermore, the emergence of *Third World Cinema* was also another factor that influenced political filmmaking in the state of Kerala. India joined other

Third World countries to be identified as the makers of cinema that shook the conscience of filmmakers against the cultural onslaught of Hollywood cinema on the Indian film industry. The establishment of Film Societies in Kerala and the leftist ideology paved the way for the emergence of political films in the state.

Initially, Kerala filmmakers were ardent followers of the Marxist ideology and aspired to bring a cultural revolution through cinema. *Kabini Nadi Chuvannapol*, a film made in 1975, is a classic example of the work of the New Wave Malayalam young filmmakers that reflect the Maoist ideology. The film, directed by P. A. Backer and Pavithran, assumes importance for being made during political turbulence and Emergency. The government did not like the film, nonetheless it marked the beginning of the era of *New Wave* political films in Kerala. Incidentally, the production of these films was not demanding, as filmmakers managed to produce them with low budgets, using simple film equipment. However, they appealed to the audience of likeminded people who were willing to watch the films either in theatres or film societies.

It is noteworthy that the political cinema created a film culture that aroused political awareness among the youth in Kerala state who were interested in bringing radical reforms through cinema, as the revolution promised by the politicians during the campaigns that brought them to power did not materialize. The people believed that political films would have desirable impact on society.

There is something in common between the filmmakers of the French New Wave and the Kerala film group. Both believed in the left-wing political ideology. As expected, Kerala became the home of the *New Wave* film movement in India. The new political awakening led to the making of new films which integrated Kerala's rich regional culture with modern political thoughts. Kerala, a state that professed Marxism encouraged making serious films with radical thoughts. Some of the big names that emerged from the state include, Adoor Gopalakrishnan, John Abraham, G. Aravindan, M. P. Sukumaran Nair, and Shaji Karun. These distinguished directors influenced filmmaking in Kerala and drew national and international attention to the state and their work. Several film critics wanted the *New Wave* cinema to stay, and came to its defense against negative media reports about them. The political cinema in Kerala survived as their work consisted of the political element as well as their entertainment content. Above all, the filmmakers wanted to show their sensitivity to political issues in a state that had recognized and appreciated *New Wave* films.

Political Messaging in Kerala Cinema: Core of Periphery?

Malayalam political cinema appears to have lost its glee and glamor. Political messages which once occupied the prime and core space on the canvas have drifted to the periphery. Politically motivated cinema that was proactive in illustrating realism appears to have suffered immense fragmentation and disintegration, just like the political systems in which they were produced.

Since 2011, Malayalam cinema has transformed from *New Wave* to *New Generation* cinema. The cinema, like any other in the Indian film industry, is now engaged more with box office revenue than with art or narratives. This has inspired young filmmakers to make off-beat films. The films appeal more to a younger audience, and serve as a viable alternative to Bollywood. They are different from the *New Wave* films, but are equally innovative, artistic, authentic, and realistic. They can be called neorealist films in that they have a mass base, evoking favorable attitude from the audience. They almost effortlessly build empathy with the audience as they deal with a wide range of themes, from social to political issues.

Storytelling is also different in the New Generation cinema, as they tend to dwell more on very local content than the star value of their actors or on the intellectualism of the early films in West Bengal. An example of such local content is the increasing issue of interfaith marriages between Hindu girls and Muslim boys. Another issue that has caught the attention of the new filmmakers is beef eating. Kerala is a multi-religious state where political ideology is linked to the choice of food. Today, food is classified as conservative right-wing or liberal left-wing, with beef-eating becoming the bone of contention in food politics. It is a sociological discourse in a country where cows are worshipped by the majority population of Hindus. Interestingly beef has been secularized through the New Generation films and has been widely acclaimed by the audience. The films have dealt with people's right to a choice of food, compelling even the right-wing political party in the state to take a stance in opposing the ban on beef consumption in Kerala where Muslims and Christians constitute over 40 percent of the population. Beef eating has become the radical agenda of recent politics and also of the political films.

Political filmmaking has arrived in Kerala in a new avatar that is aimed to entertain, illustrating the premise that movies after all are meant to reflect real world for audiences find them entertaining. The cinema has changed the perception of entertainment. The old premise that people go to movies to escape from the drudgery of life is now an illusion because filmmakers always make films that deal with issues of the time, while entertaining and informing the audience. Today people want to see films that stimulate them into thinking about political issues as every aspect of people's life undergoes a political process.

The Kerala films have overcome that critical question of advocating a communist propaganda as the filmmakers making this New Generation political films are not identified with any political ideology, but focus more on modern political thoughts and social values. Politics of Kerala, the land of communists, continues to retain its influence on filmmakers.

Filmmakers cannot stay away from political themes in the political heartland of India. Politics has always fascinated filmmakers of Kerala who engage with audiences in entertaining and creating political awakening. The Core refers to the sensitivity of filmmakers to articulate political messages that bring intense dialogue, unconsciously affecting political views of the audience. Such films happened in Kerala where people may not have agreed with political messages, but they were motivated to recognize the problems. Kerala has the presence of intellectual filmmakers who envisioned regional cinema through the lens of masters of world cinema like Sergei Eisenstein, and made it the creative hub of Indian cinema. Filmmakers like G. Aravindan whose films made us understand the aim of cinema to create a compassionate and strong humanity in an interview with Chandrahasan (1989) noted that, "no work of art directly or indirectly changes society or human beings. However, cinema has the power to influence the human mind." Some of the G.Aravindan's films like *Esthappan* were acclaimed to have something in common with classic *Rashamon*, the film by Akira Kurasawa. The cinematic perspective of the new game of politicizing religion and other issues have destabilized the secular identity of Kerala State, thus compelling filmmakers to reflect on new political thoughts.

Conclusion

Indian cinema's tryst with realism cinema dates back to 1940s and continued till 1969, demonstrating the extraordinary brilliance of Indian filmmakers in enriching cinema. *Do Bigha Zamin* (directed by Bimal Roy in 1953), *Pather Panchali* (directed by Ray in 1955) and Mrinal Sen's films, adopted the realistic expression of political content preoccupied with realism. The birth of Parallel Cinema in India was a defining moment in 1969 that gained momentum until 1975. Breaking away from realism was its major attribute as seen in films like *Bhuvan Shome, Uski Roti* and *Sara Akash*. The new style of filmmaking challenged the school of realism. Shyam Benegal's middle-of-the-road cinema later came up, and merged the attributes of neorealism and parallel cinema. His films such as *Ankur* (1974), *Nishant* (1975) and *Manthan* made in 1976, were forceful political statements of a disillusioned nation. "They refined the style as well as the content of cinema, representing the subaltern, and articulating dissatisfaction with social and political conditions of the masses." (Paunksnis, 2015, p.45).

All the three schools of Indian cinema changed the notion of entertainment. Shyam Benegal reportedly asserted in an interview with Rajya Sabha TV channel in the year 2014 that, "to me the definition of entertainment is very broad. It includes anything that engages me and is able to bring new insights into my own way of thinking." (Shyam Benegal cited in Pathak, 2020, May 30). In India, the political climate curtailed the free expression of political thoughts by filmmakers in many instances. For instance, Shyam Benegal's *Nishant* was banned for being anti-establishment and its fierce critique of feudalism.

Unfortunately, the political ecosystem in India has not changed much. This is a sad commentary on the notorious and stranglehold of politics on freedom of expression and artistic freedom in cinema. Filmmakers are critics of events in society, and the making of cinema is seen as a political move to reflect on events that disrupt the well-being of people in the society. Political cinema has a mission to fulfill, that is, to arouse the political consciousness of people at a time of social media platforms undermining the power of cinema. "Films should pluck people out from their private worlds and establish a missing consciousness. It's very important that people become aware of their own conditions and exploitations instead of blindly following what political parties are telling them," according to Benegal (Shyam Benegal cited in Pathak, 2020, May 30).

Political cinema in India has drifted from its core to the periphery, thus shattering the illusion of identifying a truly political film.

References

Biswas, S. V. (2021, January 18). *2020: Rise of paid subscribers. The Financial Express.* https://www.financialexpress.com/brandwagon/2020-rise-of-paid-subscribers/2172942/

Bose, B., & Chakravarty, P. (2012). Kolkata Turning: Contemporary urban Bengali cinema, popular cultures and the politics of change. *Thesis Eleven, 113*(1), 129–140. https://doi.org/10.1177/0725513612457234.

CBFC (2021, July). Central Board of Film Certification. https://www.cbfcindia.gov.in/main/

Chandrahasan. (1989, July). *Filmmaker as an intuitive artist: the cinema of G. Aravindan.* https://lokadharmi.org/chandradasan/

Christensen, T., & Haas, P. J. (2005). *Projecting politics: Political messages in American films.* Sharpe.

Datta, S., Bakshi, K., &Dasgupta, R. K. (2015). The world of Rituparno Ghosh: texts, contexts and transgressions. *South Asian History and Culture, 6*(2), 223–237. https://doi.org/10.1080/19472498.2014.999441

Dhar, A. (2020, December 20). *Moheener Ghoraguli, India's first rock band from Kolkata whose legacy thrives in resistance.* https://www.firstpost.com/longreads/remembering-moheener-ghoraguli-indias-firs

Elliott, W. R., &Schenck-Hamlin, W. J. (1979). Film, Politics and the Press: The Influence of 'All the President's Men. *Journalism Quarterly, 56*(3), 546–553. https://doi.org/10.1177/107769907905600312

Ganguly, S. (2000). A Cinema on Red Alert: Mrinal Sen's Interview and In Search of Famine. *The Journal of Commonwealth Literature, 35*(1), 55–70. https://doi.org/10.1177/002198940003500105.

Giannetti, L. (1996). *Understanding Movies*, Prentice Hall.

Gianos, L. (1995). *Politics and Politicians in American Film*, Westport, CT: Praeger.

Kazmi, F. (1999). *The politics of India's conventional cinema: imaging a universe, subverting a multiverse.* Sage.

Kumar, K. J. (2011). India's Many Popular Cinemas. *Journal of Creative Communications*, 1–14. https://doi.org/10.1177/0973258613499095

Leab, D. (1994). Blacks in American cinema. In G. Crowdus (Ed.), *The political companion to American film* (pp. 41–50). Lakeview press.

Mukhopadhyay, B. (2006). Cultural Studies and Politics in India Today. *Theory, Culture & Society, 23*(7–8), 279–292. https://doi.org/10.1177/0263276406073230

Pathak, A. (2020, May 30). *As a filmmaker, I'm a critic of the present: Shyam Benegal reflects on his best films. Huffpost.* https://www.huffpost.com/archive/in/entry/shyam-benegal-interview-ankur-nishant-bhumika-manthan_in_5ed0f459c5b692b68e06746

Paunksnis, Š. (2015). Postmodern Experience in India: Imaginary Subaltern Space and Cinema. *History and Sociology of South Asia, 9*(1), 36–52. https://doi.org/10.1177/2230807514546799

Pradhan, S. (Ed.). (1979). *Marxist Cultural Movement in India: Chronicles and Documents 1936–1947.* India: Distributors, National Book Agency.

Ray, S. (Ed.). (2011). *Satyajit Ray on Cinema.* Columbia University Press.

Roy, R. (2016, August 15). *All these years later, nobody has chronicled the Partition like Ritwik Ghatak. The Scroll.in.*http://www.scroll.in/reel/813977/all-these-years-later-nobody-has-chronicled

Safi, M. (2019, March 29). *Churchill's policies contributed to 1943 Bengal famine- study. The Guardian.*https://www.theguardian.com/world/2019/mar/29/winston-churchill-policies-contributed-to-1943-bengal-famine-study

Sklar, R. (1982, July 18). Politics in film: how moviemakers handle hot issues. *The New York Times.* https://www.nytimes.com/1982/07/18/movies/politics-in-film-how-moviemakers-handle-hot-issues.html

CHAPTER 8
Musicians and Political songs in the struggle for freedom in Zimbabwe

Bhekinkosi Jakobe Ncube
University of Johannesburg, South Africa

Abstract

This chapter discusses political messaging, songs and the power of musicians in the struggle for various freedoms in post-colonial Zimbabwe. Most studies on the relationship between music and politics in Africa in general and Zimbabwe in particular have tended to focus on the role of political music in the struggle for independence from colonialism. Other studies that have discussed political messaging in music in post-colonial African countries lean more on subtly anti-establishment protest themes by musicians. This chapter takes a detour and focuses on protest political music that acts as a vehicle for social change in post-colonial Zimbabwe through discussing music that overtly acts as political agency. Using Zimbabwean musician, Desire Moyo's music as a case study, the chapter concludes that music can be considered the weapon of the oppressed and marginalised in the struggle for freedom in post-colonial Zimbabwe.

Keywords: Political messaging, resistance, music, freedom, Zimbabwe, Moyoxide

***

Introduction

This chapter examines music and its relationship to protest and politics in post-colonial Zimbabwe. Specifically, the aim is to explore the intersection of protest music as an explicit and overt commentary on political power in the country. As a case study, the focus is on Zimbabwean musician, Desire Moyo whose stage name is Moyoxide. Moyo describes himself as a freedom poet in the mould of South African anti-apartheid musician-poet, Mzwakhe Mbuli. His political poems-songs can be considered as part of the struggle for freedom for the oppressed and marginalised in Zimbabwe, Africa and the world at large.

The choice of Moyoxide for this study was influenced by motley of factors, including the political content of his music, its topical nature and the fact it comes after the fall of long-time Zimbabwean leader, Robert Mugabe. Mugabe ruled Zimbabwe from 1980 when the country gained its independence from Britain until his ouster in a military coup in November 2017. Therefore, it is apposite to discuss political music's fight for freedom in what is termed the "second republic" in Zimbabwe. The broad aim is to interrogate the interlocking ways in which Moyoxide's popular music is steeped in Zimbabwe's contemporary politics.

It is also opportune to study music and political messaging in Africa, to engage debates on the role and significance of music in the continent as far as political messaging is concerned. Scholars such as Allen (2004) have argued that "music functions as a trenchant political site in Africa primarily because it is the most widely appreciated art form on the continent" (p. 1). Barber (1987, p. 10) also views music as the most fecund of all African art forms. It is therefore important to discuss political messaging and the power of musicians in Zimbabwe against such assertions with a view of locating the artist under study within protest music in Africa.

Background and Context

Contemporary Zimbabwe is on the brink of being labelled authoritarian as far as freedom of expression and information is concerned (Ncube, 2017). While its constitution guarantees freedom of expression, Zimbabweans of all walks of life, from ordinary citizens to politicians and journalists, are harassed and arrested for exercising that freedom (Mpofu, 2016). These arrests usually take place when people say anything members of the ruling elite consider an anathema and threatening to their power base. Even the social media, which cultural theorists (Curran et al., 2016) had predicted would open up the public sphere and offer ordinary citizens a space to coalesce on issues affecting them, has turned out to be a constrained space in the country. Zimbabwean journalists, such as Hopewell Chin'ono, are routinely charged to court, accused of publishing what the authorities determine to be false news on the social media platform, Twitter.

The Zimbabwean government's tight grip on the media, especially broadcasting media, has left Zimbabweans with limited avenues to voice their grievances (Dube & Ncube, 2019). Only recently, in 2020, did the ruling Zimbabwe African Nation Union - Patriotic Front (ZANU-PF) - government grant a few private television broadcasting station licences. The first private radio stations, ZiFM and Star FM were licensed in 2012. Nevertheless, almost all of those granted licences have connections to the government (Ndlovu, 2021).

Many Zimbabweans had hoped that after the toppling of late President Robert Mugabe in a military coup d'état in November 2017, the repressive media laws such as the Access to Information and Protection of Privacy Act (AIPPA) and the Broadcasting Services Act (2001) would be repealed. The hope was that the obnoxious laws were going to be replaced with those allowing for freedom of speech and expression. However, the post-Mugabe Zimbabwean government came up with the Zimbabwe Media Commission (ZMC) Bill, and the Cyber Security and Data Protection Bill to replace AIPPA. The two bills were criticised by the Voluntary Media Council of Zimbabwe (VMCZ) that described them as undemocratic. They make it possible for ordinary members of society to be arrested for social media dissent. In such a milieu, music and songs began to be appropriated as platforms for contestation and agitation by the masses (Dube & Ncube 2019, p. 150). It was against this environment that Moyoxide music sprouted.

The Musician: Desire Moyo (Moyoxide)

Desire Moyo (Moyoxide) is a trained teacher by profession. He is also the director of Victory Siyanqoba Trust, a non-governmental organization whose mission is the liberalisation of the arts through its flagship programme, Eziko Theatre Laboratory. Moyoxide has written several controversial plays on human rights issues and democracy. Moyoxide has won several local arts awards, including the Outstanding Spoken Award at the nation's RoilBulawayo Arts Awards in 2019.

Moyoxide has performed before regional audiences such as at the United Nations Women summit in Ethiopia in 2014 and the Global Power Women's Network forums in several countries. South Africa's anti-apartheid musician-poet, Mzwakhe Mbuli invited Moyoxide to perform at his 60th birthday celebrations. His songs are distributed on compact discs (CDs). He also shares his music on various platforms such as WhatsApp, Soundcloud and YouTube.

In 2014, Moyoxide ventured into poetry and released two albums titled *Never Again* and *Here Comes Trouble*. Both albums boarded on protest music. Speaking to newspapers then, Moyoxide said:

> Of late, I have been addressing a myriad of social and political issues through theatre, but now I want to establish myself as a poet – a freedom poet. Freedom poet, aka Moyoxide, is a practical idea of voicing issues. It is a poetic journey whose destination is freedom of expression (Sibindi, 2014).

By declaring that his poem-music is "poetic journey whose destination is freedom of expression," Moyoxide locates the role of music and that of the musician within the realm of politics. This implies an intrinsic relationship between politics and music. Politics impacts music. In turn, musicians and their songs participate in the politics of a country. This leads to political messaging through music.

This chapter therefore discusses how music contributes to the articulation of political ideas, the organization of political action for social change, and its role in political messaging in the struggle for freedom in post-colonial Zimbabwe. Using Moyoxide's music as a case study, the author argues that music is not just mere sound track but is the substance of politics.

Political Music and the role of Musician in Society

To explore the relationship between music and political messaging in Africa in general and in Zimbabwe in particular, there is a need for an overview of political music and the role of the musician in society.

Music and politics have always been intertwined. Since time immemorial, music has always been a powerful medium for mobilization purposes in many societies (Street et al., 2008). Writing about music and social movements in America, Eyerman and Jamison (1998, p. 59) trace the relationship between music and politics, and music as an agent of social change in America, to three movements in late nineteenth and early twentieth century. The argument is that in America, music began to be appropriated as an agent of social change during the American Populism in the late nineteenth century, the Industrial Workers of the World at the turn of the century and the Communist Party of the United States of America (CPUSA) during the Great Depression.

Eyerman and Jamison (1998, p. 60) further argue that since then, protest songs have been one of the tools to generate a mass movement and as such unlike a political pamphlet, speech, or political manifesto, music can be memorised, repeated and disseminated. Nketia (1986) and Thorsen (2004) also posit that music has also played and continues to play an integral part in the political and social development of societies. The implication here is that music plays a crucial role especially in political messaging. This is precisely because music as the first form of popular culture, especially in Africa, highlights the socio-political struggles faced by the majority in societies.

Yyairo and Ogude (2005, p. 226) argue that popular music in most cases shape a country's politics. The authors give an example of Kenya where Gigi Gigi Maji Maji's song *Unbwogable* played a crucial role in the election campaign of the opposition in the country's 2002 elections. Englert (2008, p. 9) argued that as part of political discourse, popular songs' themes are usually on political situations in the artist's country of origin. Similarly, there are also songs which praise political leaders. In most Africa countries, songs that praise political leadership receive more airplay in state-controlled radio and television stations.

Scholars such as Street (2003; 2012) have also noted that music does not exist autonomously of other social, economic and political institutions, but has a symbiotic relation with politics. Street (2012) called attention to some confusion in previous studies about the relationship between music and politics. The confusion stemmed from some assertions that music and politics must not be treated as "two discrete realms of human existence and endeavour," (p. 2) but as extensions of each other. Street (2012) debunked this contention. DeNora (2000, p. 163) had also supported the close relationship between music and politics, arguing that both intervene and interact with each other. Also asserting that there is an illusionary boundary separating music and politics, Street (2012) stated that "music embodies political values and experiences, and organises our response to society as political thought and action (and) music does not just provide a vehicle for political expression, it is that expression" (p. 2). In other words, music and politics coexist and inform each other. It is therefore plausible to argue that when musicians perform their songs, they are also performing and participating in politics.

To buttress this relationship, and to stress the point that music and its political messages play a key role in society, Street (2012, p. 4) provides the example of the trial of Rwandan musician, Simon Bikindi at the UN International Criminal Tribunal for Rwanda. Bikindi was charged with "direct and public incitement to commit genocide" (Street, 2012, p. 4) during the 1994 Rwandan Genocide that saw between 800,000 and one million Tutsis and moderate Hutus killed by Hutu extremists (Mamdani, 2020).

Bikindi's songs were alleged to have contributed to the slaughter of Tutsis. Despite contentious questions regarding the influence of Bikindi's songs, and how many times they were played, the fact that he was arraigned before the tribunal and accused of having contributed to the genocide through his songs makes it clear that music and political messaging are intrinsically related. This also brings to the fore the power of musicians in society.

Politicians have also used songs for propaganda purposes. As Street (2003, p. 115) observed, the Nazi in Germany used popular music for propagandist purposes. The Horst-Wessel Song for example was made compulsory in schools and at Nazi youth training (Street, 2003, pp. 116-117).

Similarly, in Africa, nationalist movements fighting colonialism exploited the power of music in their crusade. And in post-colonial African, some of the newly elected leaders, or those who assumed power through ousting elected governments, also used music to consolidate their regimes. A classic example is President Mobuto Sese Seko of Zaire (now Democratic Republic of Congo) who belongs to the latter group. He made extensive use of music bands such as OK Jazz to sing his praises in the 1960s right through the 1970s (Street 2003, pp. 115-116), after shooting his way to power in the country.

Liberation war armies in Africa also used music as counter-propaganda to the colonizers' political messages. Pongweni (1982) observed that liberation movements in Zimbabwe for example, used music for counter-propaganda purposes during the war to arouse the people's nationalist feelings and exploit their grievances. Pongweni (1982)'s argument is that as counter propaganda, the liberation choirs composed songs for winning over to their side those who sympathised with the colonial government. As Pongweni (1982) also opined, "songs that won the liberation war articulated the pressing issues of the day more eloquently than any political speech or historical treatise" (p. 2). This is evident of the role of political music as an agent of social change and the power of musicians in society.

Vambe (2000) asserted that just like Mobutu Sese Seko of Zaire, Zimbabwe's former president, Robert Mugabe, attempted to use music for nation-building projects. However, Mugabe's initiatives were not in tandem with some artists' intentions. In 2018, the ruling ZANU-PF party in Zimbabwe appropriated musician Jah Prayzah's song *Kutonga Kwaro* as its campaign song. The song had previously been banned from being played at ZANU-PF rallies by the former first lady, Grace Mugabe, on allegations that it was propping up the then vice president, Emmerson Mnangagwa, instead of Mugabe.

In South Africa, members of the ruling African National Congress (ANC) in 2017 and 2018 sang and danced a rendition of Lusanda Spriritual Group's *Zizojika izinto* (Things will finally change) song in praise of Cyril Ramaphosa, during the country's elections. Eventually, the song became the theme song for the ANC's election campaigns.

These examples highlight "the continued attempt by parties, politicians and states to harness music's perceived power for propaganda purposes" (Street 2003, p. 116). This therefore reveals that music has been regarded as a source of power and political songs play a critical role in societies.

Writing about the role of political songs during the 2011 Arab Spring revolution and protests at Tahrir Square in Egypt, Wahdan (2014) opined that music "incited and sustained the state of unity, political sensibility and readiness" (p. 53). This is in line with the Frankfurt school's position that popular music can be used both as a source of power and as a source of fear. In this regard, the protesters at Tahrir Square sang songs to create unity among them and to instil fear in the government.

According to Sheba (2009, p. 54), the power of music and its close relationship with the people has at times irked oppressive regimes. Such regimes have arrested, imprisoned and at times forced musicians into exile. Despite the risks, Sheba (2009, p. 54) contends that musicians have dared to challenge the abuses of the state and social injustice.

The power of musicians and the importance of music and its political messages can upset the status quo in society. This is evident when states censor music and musicians. DeNora (2000, p. 16) argued that the "urge to censor music for fear of its effects is as old as music itself." For instance, when it became obvious to Mobutu Sese Seko and Robert Mugabe in Zaire and Zimbabwe respectively, that some musicians were using their songs to protest the injustices in their societies and targeting their governments, both dictators wasted no time clamping such musicians into jail and banning their songs being played on national radio. Human history is full of such incidents where musicians faced the ire of dictators.

Dictatorial leaders are not the only ones afraid of musicians and making concerted efforts at running them out of towns and cities. Street (2012) cited a 2010 example of Islamic hardliners in Somalia's capital, Mogadishu. Afraid of music and its power, the hard-line Al-Shabaab militias forced DJs in all radio stations in Mogadishu to drop "evil songs" (p. 9). All the 14 radio stations complied with the ultimatum. According to Street (2012, p. 9).), these "evil songs" were replaced with meaningless "poems and jingles with random animal or vehicle noises" That those in power can perceive certain type of music as "evil" and ban it underscores the power of music and musicians in society.

The Taliban also banned music when they took over power in Afghanistan. Although the Taliban's ban of music was also for religious and theocratic reasons, Street (2003) observed that it affected weddings and other celebrations such as "the art of production of musical instruments and the life of the musicians and the cultural heritage" (p. 119). The argument here is that music sustains ways of life and identities, and the Taliban's ban on music was slowly eroding the cultural heritage of the Afghan people. Little wonder therefore that Afghans celebrated the overthrow of the Taliban by the US army in 2002 by hoisting their radios and playing loud music (Street 2007, p. 322) in the streets of Kabul and other cities in the country. It is telling that although music was not the only thing the Taliban had banned (possession of homing pigeons, chess and marble were also banned), celebrating the fall of the Taliban using music shows that music has a particular significance among Afghans.

Musicians as Artists in African Societies

Musicians in African societies are artists and their roles include extolling the values and morals in their communities, and singing against the decadence in them. African musicians, like their counterparts elsewhere, are associated with, and sing about, the political, social and cultural institutions within their nations and specific communities. Consequently, the musician reinforces the ideas and ideals that sustain their communities (p'Bitek, 1986, p. 13). The musician does this by using "indirect language...metaphor and symbol" (p'Bitek, 1986, p. 39) and through creating images in the minds of the people using oral narratives, music, songs and dance. p'Bitek (1986) submitted that the musician as an artist in Africa "carves his moral standards on wood and stone, and paints his colourful 'dos and don'ts' on walls and canvas... the artist expresses the joys and sorrows of the people" (p. 40).

Allen (2004) agreed with this description of a musician as an artist in Africa and further stated that musicians are "continually expected to use their privileged access to a platform to engage socio-economic issues and even to reveal wrong doing if necessary" (p. 2). In this context, musicians are expected to use their poetic licence to expose the ills in society.

Sheba (2009, p. 55) also contended that musicians as artists provide the necessary checks and balances to authority. Thus, according to Sheba (2009), the artist becomes the "oral centre of morality and purpose, guidance and direction for the community's aspirations, hopes, dreams and development" (p. 56). It is through the musician as an artist that a society expresses its hopes, aspirations and fears.

The late Nigerian musician, Fela Anikulapo-Kuti, exemplified the typical role of musicians as artists in African societies, and their relationship with those in authority. According to Osuagwu (2019), black American Jazz and politics inspired Fela and he pioneered modern protest music in Nigeria. His clever and sarcastic humour, rebellion against authority and political consciousness, were evident in his music. Fela used protest music specifically to criticize a succession of military regimes in Nigeria. Consequently, Fela worked under incredibly traumatic conditions that include constant state harassment, intimidation, imprisonment, and physical violence on his person (Olaniyan, 2004, p. 57). The Nigerian singer sang about a vast array of subjects, "from the quotidian to the arcane" (Olaniyan, 2004, p. 57). All his music was about the people of Nigeria, Africa, and the African world and their relations among themselves as well as with the rest of the world.

Fela's music was so politically incisive that the then Nigerian military ruler, Olusegun Obasanjo, during his first session as dictatorial head of state accused him of "destroying the lives of Nigerian youth" (Olaniyan, 2004, p. 84). What Obasanjo actually conceded was that Fela, through his music, ideas, and even his lifestyle, was successfully broadcasting to young people new, rebellious, and impatient desires that completely challenged people in power and authority. Fela responded through music and insisted that it was Obasanjo as head of state that had "destroyed the lives of an entire nation" (Olaniyan, 2004, p. 84). That a musician could have such an exchange with a military head of state signifies the power and influence of a musician as an artist. In such a situation, the artist becomes the ruler (p'Bitek, 1986).

Against this scenario, Ngugi (1998, p. 12) is of the view that the power struggle between the artist, in this case, the musician, and the state, is for the control of the performance space; and that space from which both derive their power is the audience or the community. The state tries to control this space through censorship so that musicians do not have influence over the community. According to Street et al. (2008, p. 273) censoring of music is an attempt to muzzle free speech. By linking music censorship to the issue of free speech, Street et al. (2008, p. 273) rightly moves music outside its framing of being merely for entertainment purposes, towards the realm of politics. Thus, censoring music puts it at the heart of political life and as such music negotiates both time and space (Street, 2003, p. 22).

Musicians, on the other hand, have found ways to escape censorship. Englert (2008, p. 11) observes that one strategy used by artists to escape forms of repression such as censorship is to frame their criticism in more subtle ways. They use attributes of language such as metaphors, slang and irony to send their messages to audiences. This is what makes the choice of Moyoxide exciting in that the musician departs from the norm and overtly expresses the community's grievances in Zimbabwe. Moyoxide's music therefore qualifies to be called protest music. Protest music here refers to music which carries a political message that is associated with a particular political protest or social movement; that is, deliberate political communication expressed through music. Such music, according to Hall (1997), is a site of resistance. Hall (1997) further states that when popular cultural forms such as music become sites of resistance, this helps in freeing art and culture from pre-existing forms of power. In this process, a critical public is produced. That is, music engages people's moral and political sympathies.

The production of a critical public through protest music means that music can be used as "weapons of the weak" (Scott, 1985). In that case, music and musicians become instrumental in giving expression to resistance. Scott's argument is that when used as a weapon of the weak, music provides the means by which the weak and the marginalised could express political resistance and organize opposition.

Nonetheless, Sheba (2009, p. 29) warned against romanticising the weapons of the weak concept. This is precisely because the weapons of the weak are unlikely to do more than marginally affect the various forms of exploitation that the marginalised peasants face. It is in the tenacity seen in ridicule, complaints and in this case lambasting authorities that one can celebrate music as weapons of the weak and political participation.

Regarding participation necessitated by political music, Street et al. (2008) are of the view that music can be used as a way of seeing the inner life of participation. That is, music "is an unexpectedly powerful force for social and political change" (p. 273). Such music becomes part of the counter public sphere as seen by Fraser (1992, p. 123). The public sphere according to Habermas (1992, p. 27) represents that space in which the private people come together as a public and as such, challenge the general rules governing relations in the privatized but publicly relevant sphere of commodity exchange and social labor. Fraser's own account of the public sphere diverges from Habermas' in that it introduces the idea of subaltern counter publics. The argument here is that the public sphere cannot only be constituted by debate and deliberation about politics, as it also includes art, music and literature.

Methodology

A purposive sample of Moyoxide's songs (eight in all) were selected and analysed in this chapter. They are: *Dear RG, Dear Africa Kayise, Bhalagwe Dreams, Moyoxide 2, Dear Order, I will not reconcile, Dear Big Guns, Dear Pilate.*

Battaglia (2008) describes the purposive sampling method as that in which a choice is made by an expert in a logical manner, and opines that the sample represents the entire population of data for an inquiry. This sample is based on the specific purpose of the research, hence its description as *purposive*.

The bulk of the analysis comes from his songs, *Dear RG* and *Dear Africa Kayise*, because they encapsulate the problems that bedevil Zimbabwe as a country. The role of political music and the power of musicians in the fight for various freedoms in Zimbabwe can be seen in the lyrics of these songs.

The discourse analysis approach was adopted by the author in the examination of these songs. This approach considers the content, form, and context of the songs as inextricably linked. The idea is to take Moyoxide's songs as communicative texts, as discourse analysis helps to "gain a deeper understanding and appreciation of texts" (Chimombo & Roseberry 1998, p. ix).

Fairclough (1989) observed that using this approach encapsulates the entire productive process, context, interpretation, the social conditions from which it stems, and the nonverbal aspects of performance. In this chapter, the lyrics of the songs were analysed together with the social conditions under which the text was produced. This involves describing how language is used in the songs to construct meaning. It is important to analyse Moyoxide's music using this approach because Zimbabwe's political, social and economic landscape contains numerous symbolisms, political signposts and era-specific situations that are critical to the appreciation of his music.

Fairclough further states that in a social struggle the relationship among power, language, and social structures becomes more important because discourse itself "has effects upon social structures and contributes to the achievement of social continuity or social change," (1989, p. 37).

Moyoxide has three albums, in which *Bhalagwe My Son* has seven songs, *Mene Mene Terkel Parsin* has 19 and *Coro-Shit* has 25 songs. Dear RG is his trademark song. This is because it covers all the economic and political challenges the country is facing. The songs selected have direct messages on politics, and are thematically grouped for analysis in the discussion section.

Discussion

I grew up listening to the works of the people's poet (Mzwakhe Mbuli). His creative wisdom, him being a social commentator, fearlessly tackling undemocratic and repressive elements by the apartheid regime, ignited the Moyoxide in me (Moyoxide, 2018).

A nuanced reading of Moyoxide's songs indicate that his music belongs to the confrontational form of community action. His songs are replete with lyrics that speak to, and dramatize his community's shared experiences. Street (1997, p. 34) argued that such music brings people together and evokes for them a collective emotional experience to which common meanings are assigned. This is because a text like music is decidedly a site for politics since it is a source of varying and sometimes conflicting interpretations. Street (1997, p. 34) avers that:

> Even where the artist is explicit about his or her purpose, and where everything seems to confirm a single reading, no text escapes counter or multiple other readings . . . it is the struggle over rival interpretations that is most revealing of the politics of the text.

It is against this background that Moyoxide's music is analyzed in relation to political messaging and the power of musicians in the struggle for various freedoms in post-colonial Zimbabwe. The underlying conviction is that his music is a product of Zimbabwe's politics, and politics is at the root of his music. As already indicated, his songs are about social change, politics and explicit commentary on power, all couched in the aesthetics of protest. Consequently, the following is a thematic analysis and discussion of his songs.

Defiance and Singing the Protest in Zimbabwe

Political music such as Moyoxide's, has a historical and social context. Looking at his songs, they are a form of direct political education. The songs are associated with political and social causes, thus making his music a platform for the marginalised to exercise agency. The overarching theme of his music is defiance and a call for the country's leaders to stop looting the country's resources.

Moyoxide's music can be described as performance poetry. Just like South African musician, Mzwakhe Mbuli, Moyoxide's music is an infusion of poetry and Zimbabwe's Ndebele traditional music forms.

Evidently, the song that captures the "Moyoxide in me" is *Dear RG*. Released after the overthrow of Robert Gabriel Mugabe by the military in 2017, the lyrics of the eight-minute song are a direct address to Mugabe. The song begins by reminding Mugabe of his Gukurahundi crimes and lambasts him for refusing to apologise for the genocide that saw 20,000 innocent civilians mostly of Ndebele-speaking ethnic group being killed by the Mugabe-led government soldiers. The poet says to Mugabe:

> Dear RG
> The unapologetic self-proclaimed Gukurahundi maniac
> The dictator of our time

The lyrics narrate the physical, mental and emotional suffering by Zimbabweans at the hands of Mugabe and his successors. The background of the song is that when Mugabe was toppled in November 2017, millions of Zimbabweans danced and ululated in celebration. The hope was that the years of tyranny, arrest of opposition party members, and suppression of general freedoms like freedom of expression were over. However, the musician reminds his audience that:

> Once again Zimbabwe is suffering from a martyr syndrome, the messiah complex. Those who think they are more Zimbabwean than others, those who think they died for us more than Christ himself. Why don't you people with hands red with our blood change once and for all?

The lyrics touch a state of mind and emotional disposition shared among the poor people of Zimbabwe. The song chronicles Mugabe's demeanors. First,

Moyoxide compares Mugabe to the likes of Bokassa, a military dictator who ruled Central African Republic and called himself the Emperor of Central Africa, former dictators Mobuto Sese Seko of DRC and Mengistu of Ethiopia. He sings:

> Former CAR president Jean-Bedel Bokassa was a syndrome Mobutu Sese Seko Kuku Ngbendu Wa Za Banga of Zaire became a pandemic. General Idi Dada Amini was a plague to Uganda. Mengistu Haile Mariam of Ethiopia became a thorn in the African throne.

By likening Mugabe to former dictators of African countries, Moyoxide artistically reveals that Mugabe's rule was dysfunctional and bad. So bad was his rule that he equated it to pandemics and plagues. The insinuation here is that Mugabe's rule was so dreadful that he did not deserve sympathy for being overthrown.

Although Mugabe deserved to leave office, Moyoxide laments that those who took over from him have not fared any better. Reminding Mugabe of how terrible the Zimbabwean economic and political situation he helped to create and perpetrate is, Moyoxide sings about those who took over from him:

> Dear RG. Once again, the Zimbabwean alternative to your regime has become a disease. We are once again no longer at ease. *Indwangu zakho azilahlanga iziphongo* (your lookalikes are doing the same as you). The billion-dollar deals have remained a myth. The country's economy is in the rectums of economic logic. We joined them in looting and we got ourselves looted into the concrete walls of correctional services and became prisoners of note.

The defiance in Moyoxide is very clear when he sings that just like Mugabe, those who took over power from him have continued to plunder the economy and it is now "in the rectums of economic logic." They have continued to promise billion-dollar deals but these deals "have remained a myth." In addition, those who have decided to join the politicians in the pilfering of the country's national resources have found themselves in jail as "prisoners of note."

The musician reminds Zimbabwe's political leaders that "we are tired of smelling the political stink that make the skunk flee in freezing spring." Such overt and crude political messaging sets Moyoxide apart from other musician in Zimbabwe in that his message is caustic, direct and defiant. Such defiance can be equated to that of the late Nigeria's Fela Anikulapo-Kuti.

Moyoxide warns that he fears for the descendants of Matabeleland (mainly people of Ndebele ethnic origin) as the "situation in the country has reached another level." This is a play on words because the late Major-General Sibusiso

Moyo uttered these words, "the situation has reached another level," while announcing the military coup d'état that toppled former President Mugabe. Moyoxide sarcastically juxtaposes Mugabe's rule with that of the current President Mnangagwa and says both are killers and looters. "We have seen road accidents not by any accidents but by some sacred designs we have never seen during your disaster years." Moyoxide protests, "Since you left RG we have seen sin, we have seen it all."

Reminiscing about the August 1, 2018, shooting of demonstrators in central Harare and the police brutality on shop looters during anti-fuel price hike strike in January the following year, Moyoxide laments that "people are being shot during demonstrations, people are being shambocked (beaten) during looting times."

The musician complains that Cyclone Idai which hit Zimbabwe in 2019 killed hundreds but the country's leaders are downplaying the numbers.

> The people are getting washed way in hundreds by Cyclone Idai – yes and they continue to tell us only 89 are dead. Even mere mathematics counting of numbers they cannot comprehend. Everything is against the ED republic of martyrs.

ED are the initials of current President Emmerson Dambudzo Mnangagwa. Here, the musician is playing the role of the voice of the voiceless, protesting against the official downplaying of the death figures caused by the cyclone in Manicaland province of the country.

Defiance, Humor and Ridicule

Quite notably, Mugabe was revered in Zimbabwe and all over Africa for taking the anti-colonial fight to the former colonizers. Nevertheless, Moyoxide is not oblivious of the former president's poor human rights record in Zimbabwe and for the economic collapse that reached its peak in 2008. Moyoxide mocks Mugabe. He reminds him of all the evil he unleashed in the country with his wife, Grace, while he was in power. As if talking to Mugabe face-to-face, Moyoxide defiantly reminds Mugabe of his wife's now-infamous statement at rallies by singing "I remember RG, not once but thrice madpower Madam Stop it."

In a mocking tone, he sings (in the song Dear RG):

> When you chose Swahili Asante Sana instead of, Thank you, on that anxiety ridden evening, I knew it was the beginning of an era, an era of trust. When you retired from the zenith of the corridors of power..... I was shell shocked, tongue-tied. ... When you were overthrown under the

throne in a horrendous horrific stance typical of holocaust behind the scenes by your own brewed, bred semi aquatic reptiles called crocodiles from your dearest zoo, the Gushongu farm, I knew you were gone.

Moyoxide explicitly mocks Mugabe for being betrayed by his own lieutenants, the "semi aquatic reptiles called crocodiles from your dearest zoo." He mocks Mugabe for getting the test of his own medicine (the irony of being overthrown by his former right-hand man, now President Mnangagwa, the man that is popularly known as the crocodile). Moyoxide mocks and chides the former leader and at the same time reminding him of the lavish life he lived, ignoring the squalid conditions under which the majority lived. He sings of Mugabe's 25-bedroomed mansion built on 44 acres. Through this, Moyoxide shows the extravagance that characterised Mugabe's rule. This is against the widespread view of Mugabe as a pan-Africanist par excellence, in several African countries.

Singing about the folly that characterized the support given to Mugabe's successor, Emmerson Mnangagwa, Moyoxide regrets being engulfed in euphoria and getting "drunk in the political quagmires of Edpfeeism (Mnangagwa's supporters use the slogan, ED Pfee to announce his takeover of the reigns) despite the heavy fear of uncertainty." Moyoxide comforts Mugabe that he was not the first African leader to be overthrown in a coup d'état for "Keita in Mali was consumed, Nnamdi Azikiwe of Nigeria was consumed, Nkrumah was consumed, Amílcar Cabral in Guinea Bissau was consumed, and Patrice Lumumba was never spared when the coup d'états in Africa became as frequent as breakfast." The musician shows that he is not only singing a protest song about Zimbabwe but about Africa as a whole. Here he laments the coup d'états in Africa.

Moyoxide does not close the door on Mugabe. He thinks he can reform himself and sings that, "just like other biblical personnel did change their names, you can be reformed to some other sober name and come to Matabeleland and say sorry, it wasn't a moment of madness but a clandestine collaborative devilish mission with some of the second republic coup elements." In 1999, during the funeral of former Vice-President Joshua Nkomo who was once the leader of the opposition party for which thousands of Gukurahundi genocide victims were killed, Mugabe had described the genocide as a *moment of madness*. Moyoxide then urges Mugabe to apologise for his role in the genocide together with some of those now in power "maybe only then shall nature stop being so angry against Zimbabwe."

Moyoxide links the supernatural world to the events that are happening in Zimbabwe. Through this, the musician reveals the link between musical taste and political values. This shows that music is key in understanding social order (DeNora 2004, p. 163). One can therefore argue that Moyoxide is engaged in explicit political protest. His songs emerged as sites of protest and revolution in that the lyrics seek to break away from the consumer-driven music industry and, more importantly, reflect the spirit of defiance, the spirit of challenging autocrats in power.

Vuka Africa: A Call for Remedial Action

When Moyoxide links Mugabe's rule to the current leaders, and asks rhetorical questions like "Kanti thina eZimbabwe saloywa yini" (Who has bewitched us in Zimbabwe that we allow such oppression), his songs become transformative and revolutionary in the messages they carry and the meanings they seek to convey (Wahdan, 2014, p. 56). Both messages and meanings are not only associated with emerging events such as the coup d'état, the August 2018 shooting of civilians, but are also reflective of deeper understandings of the power relations that are inherent in Zimbabwe. It is little wonder that Moyoxide says the crocodiles that Mugabe "brewed and bred" betrayed him.

In *Bhalagwe Dreams*, Moyoxide yearns for a new Zimbabwe where there is rule of law. He dreams of:

> A new Zimbabwe where politics is for the politicians only. A new Zimbabwe where prison is for the ruthless only. A new Zimbabwe where money is banked and earns profit. A new Zimbabwe where tribal politics belong to the dustbins of history, where popular poems like this one are pieces of joy –
> I feel now is the time for a new Zimbabwe.

One can read Moyoxide's music as political antagonism. In *Dear Africa Kayise*, and *Dear Big Guns*, the musician appeals to the collective. He chides African citizens in general and Zimbabweans in particular for being docile at the hands of the oppressors. He urges the ordinary members of society to be proactive. He sings:

> Just because your founding fathers have gone, do not pretend you are sickly toddler waiting to be bottle-fed like a young monkey in a white man's zoo. Get up your feet and face the fight.

Against such lyrics, one sees a musician calling for unity against societal injustices. Moyoxide is calling for sacrifice and he sings that he himself is an "institution that man cannot control." Such lyrics, Wahdan (2014, pp. 53-54) observes, emerged as the loci of the seemingly paradoxical phenomena of unity against societal divisions, selfless sensibility against religious divides and sacrifice of life for dignity.

In the song *Africa Kayise*, Moyoxide makes a clarion call to all Africans, "Vuka Africa, Vuka" (wake up Africa, wake up). He sings that Africans must wake up and challenge, "Cockroaches of democracy who continue to feed on the pieces of cake, denying the rest of their democratic shares." Here Moyoxide criticises and shames the political elite for their selfishness in looting the coffers of their countries dry, leaving the downtrodden in the pale and wallowing in poverty. In such songs, Moyoxide fulfils the role of a musician in society, that of condemning the socially repugnant behavior in society.

Moyoxide continues to appeal to the consciousness of ordinary Zimbabweans and leads in the critique of unprincipled political leadership. He sings in *Africa Kayise* that he is an "enemy of chameleon leadership, those whose principles are unstable like popcorn." He further sings that it is such leadership "whose promises dance zig-zag turnarounds and inconstancy bum jives." Drawing imagery from the Bible, Moyoxide sings, "I neither condone such Iscariotic diplomacy nor condemn repentance." In blatantly criticising the country's leadership for "Iscariotic diplomacy," Moyoxide feels the leaders have betrayed the trust of the country's ordinary citizens. As DeNora (2004, p. 16) contends, it is such music that forges a relationship between the polis, the citizen and the configuration of consciousness. This means that "music is much more than a decorative art ... it is a powerful medium of social order," (DeNora, 2004, p. 16).

Moyoxide's music sends clear political messages. He is part of the singers who are against "the excision of force against general citizens" (DeNora, 2004, p.16). In this light, one can compare Moyoxide's music to that of Fela, the Nigerian musician who "was particularly adept at popularising the most abstract topics of transnational processes and relations into bits that were digestible by the bulk of his proletariat and lumpen-proletariat audience," (Olaniyan, 2004, p. 57).

Just like Fela, Moyoxide's music lampoons the class snobbishness and lack of imagination of the Zimbabwean middle class. These include such *Big Guns* like other musicians, soccer players, churches and teachers. He feels the middle class has let down the ordinary citizens through their "divisive patriotism" and they must join him as he runs "berserk against dogma politics" and "amok in defence of my rights."

Moyoxide's protest music can also be equated to other protest music witnessed in the continent such as the Tahrir Square during the Egyptian protest which, according to Swedenburg (2012), was not a soundtrack, not a reflection, not a commentary or a report on events, but something integrally tied to and embedded within the social movement. Similarly, Moyoxide's songs are not mere reports of events but a call for remedial action. This is against the belief that at the level of daily life, music has power and it is implicated in every dimension of social agency (DeNora, 2004, p. 16).

One can infer a major reason for Moyoxide's venomous opposition to ZANU-PF rule. It is his solidarity with the oppressed lower classes, irrespective of ethnicity, that can be described as socialist. A former schoolteacher who lives in the midst of the poor, Moyoxide feels he is the community messenger. In *Big Guns*, he sings "receive me now dear community and give me your ears." Consequently, he is trumpeting the sounds of the community to national attention. He is also experiencing the community's brutalization at the hands of official lawlessness. Moreover, in the same song he sings, "the poor nation of us cannot fight two evils – Covid-19 and police brutality, it must be the police maintaining order not the order called upon to maintain the police."

Through concerns in the songs referenced above, one hears of issues and events that constitute Zimbabwean people's experiences. In other words, Moyoxide's music as an example of popular music documents a people's history, a people not well served by their rulers. To this end, Nyairo and Ogude (2005, p. 226) assert that such popular music "gets woven into the soundtrack of events, moments and experiences; it is mnemonic and therefore certain songs carry the capacity to make one recall a particular place or specific events." Moyoxide therefore uses his songs to recount the painful history of his community.

Moyoxide's protest songs can therefore be seen as political messaging, as part of political communication. The songs are the immediate, intentional and articulate expressions of the thoughts, meanings and ideas that emerged as a result of years of living under oppression and violence, while simultaneously rejecting both. His protest songs bring out the political agency, that is, the relationship between music and politics, which is defined by politics of resistance; and music expressing anti-establishment protest in Zimbabwe.

Dreams and Hope

In *Bhalagwe Dreams* Moyoxide sings that, "In the new Zimbabwe, I see schools becoming learned institutes, parastatals recovering from this paralysis, graduates with an array of job choices, making a decent living from decent employment." This song represents an art form that attempts to reclaim specific historical experiences that were lost or suppressed during the period of exploitation and repression. He dreams that they can be reclaimed.

Moyoxide invokes the spirit of renowned African protest poets and musicians, such as Mzwakhe Mbuli, Augusto Neto, Don Mattera, and Oswald Mtshali. These great poets- musicians had some of the strongest impacts on the struggle against apartheid (Sheba 2009, p. 26). When Moyoxide sings in *Bhalagwe Dreams* that he is a revolutionary, "a viper whose venom vigorously vexes the vast visionless," and that he "stands for vocal cords that were sabotaged by the corrupt governance system and personnel," he attempts to elevate himself to the level of these renowned poets. His music then captures the emotions and contributes to the collective consciousness of people marginalised and denied their freedom to express themselves. Consequently, Moyoxide manages to speak, march and provide expression to people's emotions.

By invoking the other poets, musicians' spirit and mentioning them in his songs, Moyoxide seeks to ignite the spirit of antagonism, a spirit of defiance in these great artists (Randal 2005). In this way, Moyoxide performs his role of an artist. For an artist, according to Okot p'Bitek (1986, p. 40) "carves his moral standards on wood and stone, and points his colourful dos and don'ts on walls and canvas." Okot p'Bitek also contended that an artist is the ruler, "guiding the people in morality simultaneous to the leadership of the king or ruler of the nation" (Okot p'Bitek, 1986, p. 40).

Political Music and the Aesthetics of Protest

According to Jenzen et al. (2020, p. 212) music conveys sentiments and ideas through an aesthetics of protest that is layered, semantically unfixed, and playful rather than insistent. In this regard, songs "cannot simply be read as documents of political aspiration or resentment or compliance, they have to be seen first and foremost, as sources of aesthetic pleasure" (Street, 2003, p. 128).

Singing about the disease, dysentery, which affected Zimbabwe's second-largest city, Bulawayo residents due to dirty water supplied by municipalities, in 2018, Moyoxide says: "Dear RG. We have seen diarrhoea we didn't see during years of diarrhoea." Here, the singer makes the audience laugh at Mugabe's "years of diarrhoea" by comparing the disease levels of Mugabe's time to the current situation. This reveals the link between pleasure and politics.

Vulgarity and aesthetics are the soundtrack of protests in most instances. Werbner et al. (2014) opine that:

> The building materials for an aesthetics of protest and revolt are mined from social, political and national histories, and assembled to subvert the aesthetically embodied, materially constructed edifices of tyrannical, authoritarian or neoliberal regimes. (p. 1)

This observation makes sense when one listens to Moyoxide sing "*Zawukhotha umtshaza kaHobo onkukhundini zingazi akusinyama neze*" (how a chicken was deceived by the red color of the squirrel's rectum), in reference to people who celebrated and welcomed the coup d'état that ousted former President Mugabe, oblivious of the suffering that was to follow.

Moyoxide also sings that the country's economy is "in the rectum of economic logic." Such crude imagery that borders on vulgarity is a weapon of the weak, a way for the marginalised members of the society to hit back at the elite. Instead of violent protest such as stone throwing, the weak "deploy humour, satire, parody and caricature to debase autocratic leaders," (Werbner et al., 2014, p. 5).

Thus, humour, satire, parody and caricature have been the hallmark of protest movements in many parts of the world. Werbner (2014, p. 235) states that in Botswana, protesting workers constructed the president as an autocrat by singing songs of rebellion that mocked and satirized him and members of his cabinet. In those protests, several songs mocked the so-called "bootlickers" or those members who did not join the strike but wasted their time trying to negotiate with the government officials and ministers (Werbner, 2014, p. 236). Similarly, Moyoxide also mocks some musicians like Thomas Mapfumo, "who just came for selfies or national tours and could not listen to Majaivana who never got deceived by the chameleon leadership."

Continuing his theme of mockery, Moyoxide further sings that:

> Oh, dear *Africa Kayise*. There comes a time when even words go out *dressed* naked without the undergarments of euphemism and proverbial petticoats of censorship to free the world from human mess.

Thus, drawing on jokes, puns, images and a shared history, Moyoxide manages to aesthetically protest and enact a universal morality that transcends the local. His songs therefore represent an aesthetic of protest and in the process become pivotal part of political communication across many political spheres, including but not limited to street protests.

Music for Mobilization and Creation of Public Spaces

Music is an art form used to mobilize and create new public spaces. Moyoxide sings in *Moyoxide 2*:

> I represent over a million Moyoxide clan,
> The real rebels mumble with razzmatazz,
> Uncontainable soldiers of fortune
> Those whose democratic reserves accumulate rather than diminish.

Moyoxide sings that he is not alone, there are many like him "whose democratic reserves" do not diminish. When he sings, "freedom of expression is not guaranteed, if it is, then it is freedom after expression that is not guaranteed," he is calling for the political leaders to allow people to engage and debate issues. Such music provides a third space, a counter-public sphere where the marginalized people can coalesce on issues of their nationhood.

Moyoxide's music-poetry is political and although it is rooted in the present and the daily hardships of life, the lyrics create an alternative voice and space. Cajoling his colleagues in the entertainment industry, he sings:

> Dear Big Guns. People are not at peace. Government is using guns to silence citizens. But Big Guns are quiet; we have gone on mute. It is time to consider people's plight. Let us cry out loud on behalf of our people. We are the artists.

These lyrics emotionalize the relationship between the artists, in this case, musicians and ordinary Zimbabweans. Moyoxide wants the ordinary citizens to be protected from the excesses of the government.

Conclusion

The chapter discussed political messaging and the power of musicians in the struggle for various freedoms in post-colonial Zimbabwe. The conclusion is that the relationship between politics and music is revealing. Music can be socially disruptive and can also provoke political response. When a political response is provoked, it shows that music and musicians are powerful and they can be a voice for the voiceless.

Politics inform and shape Moyoxide's music. His songs are articulate, specific in their lyrics and sharp in tone. It is such articulateness and specificity that makes them historical and relevant as far as political messaging and the power of musicians in the struggle for various freedoms in post-colonial Zimbabwe is concerned.

Moyoxide's songs allow for the creation of a third space, away from the mainstream media. He personifies strident criticisms against the rottenness in society; and against the powerful and privileged – the *Big Guns* - who sustain such malfeasance. In Dear RG, he sarcastically points to the ephemeralness of power, exemplifying the fate that befell former president Robert Mugabe, and even warns the current president, Emmerson Mnangagwa, nicknamed the *crocodile*, to be wary of the "crocodiles" around him who will eventually tear him apart. And, like other forerunner African poets and musicians before him, Moyoxide uses his music to urge the oppressed people of Zimbabwe not to sit down and do nothing about their oppression.

Nonetheless, Moyoxide's songs are not all about gloom and doom; rather, they offer hope for Zimbabwe that one day, in the not too distant future, "Zimbabwe will be a free nation." He articulates this hope in his song, *Bhalagwe Dreams*.

References

Allen, L. (2004). Music and Politics in Africa. *Social Dynamics*, *30*(2), 1–19.
Barber, K. (1987). Popular Arts in Africa. *African Studies Review*, *30*(3), 1–78. https://doi.org/10.2307/524538
Battaglia, M. P. (2008). Purposive Sample. In P. Lavrakas (Ed.), *Encyclopedia of Survey Research Methods* (pp. 645–647). Thousand Oaks, California: Sage Publications, Inc. https://doi.org/10.4135/9781412963947
Biddle, I. & Vanessa, K. (2006). Introduction. In I. Biddle, & K. Vanessa (Eds.), *Music, national identity and the politics of location: Between the global and the local* (pp. 1–18). London & New York: Ashgate Publishing Limited.
Chimombo, M. & Roseberry, R. L. (1998). *The power of discourse: An introduction to discourse analysis*. New York: Lawrence Erlbaum Associates Publishers.
Chitando, E. (2002). *Music in Zimbabwe*. Harare: University of Zimbabwe Publishing Press.
Curran, J., Fenton, N., & Freedman, D. (2016). *Misunderstanding the internet*. London; Routledge.
Dalia, W. (2014). Singing the Revolt in Tahrir Square: Euphoria, Utopia and Revolution. In P. Werbner, M. Webb, & K. Spellman-Poots (Eds.), *The Political Aesthetics of Global Protest: The Arab Spring and Beyond* (pp. 52–66). Edinburgh: Edinburgh University Press Ltd.
DeNora, T. (2000). *Music in Everyday Life*. London: Cambridge University Press.
Dube, V. & Ncube, B. J. (2019). Majaivana and Protest Music in Zimbabwe: A Challenge to Political Hegemony and Marginalization. In U. Onyebadi (Eds.), *Music and Messaging in the African Political Arena* (pp. 149–165). Hershey, PA: IGI Global.
Englert, B. (2008). Popular music and politics in Africa: Some introductory reflections. *Wiener Zeitschrift Für Kritische Afrikastudien*, *18*(8), 1–15.
Eyerman, R. & Jamison, A. (1998). Making an alternative popular culture: From populism to the popular front. In R. Eyerman, & A. Jamison (Eds.), *Music and Social Movements: Mobilizing Traditions in the Twentieth Century* (pp. 48–73). London: Cambridge University Press.
Fairclough, N. (1989) *Language and power*. London: Longman Inc.
Fight the Power: The politics of music and the music of politics. (2003). *Government and Opposition*, *38*(1), 113–130. https://doi.org/10.1111/1477-7053.00007
Fraser, N. (1992). Rethinking the public sphere: A contribution to the critique of actually existing democracy. In C. Calhoun (Ed.), *Habermas and the Public Sphere* (pp. 109–142). Massachusetts and London: MIT Press.
Habermas, J. (1992). Further Reflections on the Public Sphere. In *Habermas and the Public Sphere* (pp. 421–461). Massachusetts and London: MIT Press.
Hall, S. (1997). Introduction. In S. Hall (Ed.), *Cultural Representation and Signifying Practices* (pp. 1–12). Newbury Park, California: Sage.
Jenzen, O., Erhart, I., Eslen-Ziya, H., Güçdemir, D., Korkut, U., & McGarry, A. (2019). Music videos as protest communication: The Gezi Park protest on YouTube. In Jenzen, O., Erhart, I., Eslen-Ziya, H., Güçdemir, D., Korkut, U., &

McGarry, A. (Eds.). *The Aesthetics of Global Protest: Visual culture and communication* (pp. 211-232). Amsterdam: Amsterdam University Press.

Mamdani, M. (2020). *When victims become killers: Colonialism, nativism, and the genocide in Rwanda*. Princeton, New Jersey: Princeton University Press.

Mpofu, S. (2016). Zimbabwe's state-controlled public media and the mediation of the 1980s genocide 30 years on. *Journal of African Media Studies, 8*(2), 145–165.

Ncube, B. J. (2017). Diasporic online radio and the mediation of Zimbabwean conflict/crisis. In O. Ogunyeni (Ed.), *Media, Diaspora and Conflict* (pp. 89–103). London: Palgrave Macmillan.

Ndlovu, M. (2021). "Walking through history" together: Gukurahundi, memory and the role of digital media in shaping "post-conflict" Zimbabwe. In J. Maweu & A. Mare (Eds.), *Media, Conflict and Peacebuilding in Africa* (pp. 210–223). London & New York: Routledge.

Nketia, K. (1986). *The music of Africa*. New York: Victor Gollanez.

Olaniyan, T. (2004). *Arrest the music!: Fela and his rebel art and politics*. Bloomington: Indiana University Press.

Osuagwu, T. R. (2019). Protest music and political consciousness among Nigerian youths. In U. Onyebadi (Ed.), *Music and Messaging in the African Political Arena* (pp. 241–260). Hershey, PA: IGI Global.

p'Bitek, O. (1986). *Artist, the Ruler: Essays on Art, Culture, and Values, Including Extracts from Song of Soldier and White Teeth Make People Laugh on Earth*. Nairobi: East African Publishers.

Pongweni, A. J. C. (1982). *Songs that won the liberation war*. Harare, Zimbabwe: Gweru, College Press.

Randal, A. J. (Ed.). (2005). *Music, Power, and Politics*. New York & London: Routledge.

Scott, J. C. (1985). *Weapons of the weak: Everyday forms of peasant resistance*. London: Yale University Press.

Sheba, K. Lo. (2009). People's poet: Mzwakhe Mbuli and the power of the poet in the liberation struggle and in the "new" South Africa. [Unpublished doctoral dissertation]. Howard University, Washington DC.

Sibanda, S. (2004). You don't get to sing a song when you have nothing to say: Oliver Mtukudzi's music as a vehicle for socio-political commentary. *Social Dynamics, 30*(2), 36–63.

Sibindi, S. (2014, April 25). Victory Siyanqoba boss goes poetic. *Southern Eye*. https://www.southerneye.co.zw/2014/04/25/victory-siyanqoba-boss-goes-poetic/

Street, J. (1997). *Politics and Popular Culture*. Philadelphia, Pennsylvania: Temple University Press.

Street, J. (2003). Fight the power: The politics of music and the music of politics. *Government and Opposition, 38*(1), 113-130.

Street, J. (2007). Breaking the silence: Music's role in political thought and action. *Critical Review of International Social and Political Philosophy, 10*(3), 321–337.

Street, J., Hague, S., & Savigny, H. (2008). Playing to the Crowd: The role of music and musicians in political participation. *BJPIR, 10*, 269–285.

Street, J. (2012). Music and Politics. Cambridge: Polity Press.

Swedenburg, T. (2012). Egypt's music of protest from Sayyid Darwish to DJ Haha. *Middle East Research and Information Project (MERIP)*, 265(1). https://www.merip.org/mer/mer265/egypts-music-protest

Thorsén, S. (2004). Sounds of change: Social and political features of music in Africa. *Swedish International Development Cooperation Agency.* https://www.africabib.org/htp.php?RID=325701482

Tom, P. (2015). Towards a new public space: performance culture in 1980s South Africa. *Journal of African Cultural Studies*, 27(3), 311–325.

Vambe, M. (2000). Popular songs and social realities in post-independence Zimbabwe. *African Studies Review*, 43(2), 73–86.

Vershbow, M. E. (2010). The Sounds of Resistance: The Role of Music in South Africa's Anti-Apartheid Movement. *Inquiries Journal/Student Pulse*, 2(6), 1–4.

Wahdan, D. (2014). Singing the revolt in Tahrir square: Euphoria, Utopia and revolution. In K. Spellman-Poots, P. Werbner, M. Webb. (Eds.). *The Political Aesthetics of Global Protest: The Arab Spring and Beyond* (pp. 53-66). Edinburgh: Edinburgh University Press Ltd.

Wa Thiong'o, N. (1998). Decolonising the mind. *Diogenes*, 46(184), 101-104.

Werbner, P., Webb, M., & Spellman-Poots, K. (2014). Introduction. In K. Spellman-Poots, P. Werbner, M. Webb. (Eds.). *The Political Aesthetics of Global Protest: The Arab Spring and Beyond* (pp. 1–30). Edinburgh: Edinburgh University Press Ltd.

Yyairo, J., & Ogude, J. (2005). Popular music, popular politics: Unbwogable and the idioms of freedom in Kenyan popular music. *African Affairs*, 104(415), 225–249.

CHAPTER 9

Stylistic vernacular jingles in political messaging: An analysis of Igbo language jingles in Nigeria's General Elections (2019)

Cecilia A. Eme
Nnamdi Azikiwe University, Nigeria

Benjamin I. Mmadike
Nnamdi Azikiwe University, Nigeria

Abstract

In the course of the political campaigns for the February-March 2019 general elections held in Nigeria, the competing political parties "advertised" and "sold" their candidates to the electorate by means of propaganda, especially the use of jingles in the broadcast media. This study examines the political jingles rendered in the Igbo language in order to analyze their stylistic features. The jingles were categorized according to the three major political parties that contested the elections – the All Progressives Congress (APC), All Progressives Grand Alliance (APGA) and the People's Democratic Party (PDP). The jingles were analyzed descriptively, and results show that they used such stylistic devices as repetition, parallelism, epithet, hyperbole and the imperative-hortative expressions in their political messaging. In using these styles in the radio jingles, each political party aimed to persuade the electorate to cast their votes for its candidates.

Keywords: Jingles, propaganda, campaign, politics, electorate, persuasion, slogan, political messaging

***

Introduction

During the Nigerian general elections held in February and March, 2019, the contestants and their sponsoring political parties used all forms of political advertising to persuade and win the votes of Nigeria's burgeoning electorate. In their bid to win as many votes as possible, the political parties, especially the three most prominent in the country – the All Progressives Congress (APC), All Progressives Grand Alliance (APGA) and the People's Democratic Party (PDP) – used multiple campaign strategies to persuade voters to support them. Such strategies included the traditional modes of political campaigns, such as the use of very large billboards, banners, posters and handbills, and print and electronic media platforms.

In this chapter, the authors focused attention on the use of radio jingles, presented in vernacular language to drive home the political messages designed by the political parties under whose aegis the candidates contested the elections. More precisely, the authors analyzed the radio jingles released by the political parties in Anambra State, in the eastern part of Nigeria, using the Igbo language, the main vernacular language of communication in that state.

Political campaigns involve the use of propaganda, musical performance, rhetorical devices and other types of persuasive techniques to convince, lure and persuade the electorate to cast their votes for a particular candidate. What is central and common in these strategies is the use of language to package the political campaign messages. Aduradola and Ojukwu (2013, p. 106) conceptualized such messages as follows:

> A campaign message is an important and potent tool that politicians use to express their views and feelings to the public with the intention of reshaping and redirecting the electorate's opinions to align with theirs... The campaign message ought to contain the salient ingredients that the candidate wishes to share with voters and these must be repeated often in order to create a lasting impression on the voters.

Such impression becomes immensely stronger when the political message is couched in the language best understood by, and indigenous to, the target audience, as in the case of this study where the radio jingles being analyzed were made in the Igbo language of the people of Anambra State, Nigeria.

The use of radio jingles during political electioneering campaign periods is quite popular in the Nigerian political environment. Because of the ubiquitous presence and reach of the radio in the country, aspirants for political office in Nigeria quite often use radio campaign jingles to reach their supporters and the wider electorate in soliciting votes. Jingles constitute a major aspect of election propaganda. According to Nnadi (2010, p. 342), propaganda involves:

> The systematic effort to manipulate people's beliefs, attitudes, or actions by means of words, gestures, banners, monuments, music, clothing, insignia, hairstyles, designs on coins and postage stamps, etc. The propagandist has a specified goal or set of goals, primarily to change the

cognitive narrative of the people (that is, to alter a people's perception of the true situation). To achieve this goal, the propagandist deliberately selects facts, arguments, and displays of symbols and presents them in ways he thinks will have the most effect.

The nature of radio jingles effectively positions them as effective tools for political campaigns, especially in societies where music and dance are integral components of the people's culture. A typical jingle is usually a short, catchy tune that is quite easy to commit to memory. Ashipu (2015, p. 6) identifies a jingle as a short song or tune that usually contains slogans. The author sees a slogan as a "memorable phrase used on a clan in political, commercial, religious and other contexts as a repetitive expression of an idea or purpose, with the goal of persuading members of the public or a more defined target group." With specific reference to politics, Aduradola and Ojukwu (2013, p. 6) assert that: "A campaign slogan is a simple catchy phrase...that encapsulates the aim and objective of the political party or candidate for a position." Jingles help politicians in consolidating their parties' slogans and etching them in the psyche of the electorate.

In spite of the primacy of slogans in political campaign messaging, it is also important to have those slogans appropriately embedded in jingles that resonate with the electorate, especially in the language they best understand. What might otherwise be a good and potent slogan might lose its forte and effectiveness if buried in a jingle that is not catchy and, therefore, is incapable of arousing the consciousness and interest of the listening electorate. The authors of this chapter therefore contend that the stylistic features weaved into the jingles equally become imperative, in addition to the tunes created for the jingle. This chapter was therefore conceptualized with the overarching research question that sought to identify and evaluate the stylistic features of the Igbo language radio jingles used by the three major political parties in Nigeria's Anambra State during the 2019 general election in the country.

Literature Review

With specific reference to Nigeria, Ojekwe (2016) reported that voters in the country were getting more exposed to political advertising and becoming more knowledgeable on issues that feature on campaign manifestos. One way that candidates for political office and their supporting political parties articulate and disseminate their political messages in the country is through the use of radio jingles. The radio platform is particularly important in Nigeria where, like several African countries, the radio is still a powerful medium to reach the populace, especially people who reside in remote areas or people who dwell in cities but cannot afford the television or subscribe to other channels of communication.

A jingle is a short musical piece specifically composed to send a direct message in product advertising, public service announcements or for political and other purposes. Apart from the use of jingles in product and other forms of advertising, they also feature in political campaigns. Thus, a political campaign jingle is a brand of advertisement that is used to "market" a politician to the electorate. According to Abellanosa et al. (2012, p.4), campaign jingles are "songs being composed and featured in a political advertisement to add impact that will influence the electorate to vote a particular politician." Furthermore, the authors noted that, "politicians as well as advertisers must take into account the situation of the people and what they need in order to please them and win their support" (p.18).

Political campaign jingles are usually characterized by a skillful manipulation of language, generally known as propaganda. According to Aduradola and Ojukwu (2013, p. 107), propaganda refers to "the expression or actions carried out deliberately by individuals or groups for predetermined ends through psychological manifestations." Propaganda is a deliberate systematic attempt to share perceptions, manipulate cognitions and direct behaviors to achieve a response that furthers the desired intent of the propagandist. Thus, political propaganda is laden with elements of manipulation aimed at influencing the electorate into participating in elections and voting for the propagandist's preferred candidate. Akomolede-Onafuwa (2017) found that major political parties and their supporters in Nigeria use propaganda to communicate their agenda and influence the electorate.

One of the ways to make political propaganda most effective is through the use of slogans. These are usually short, memorable and seductive phrases or expressions that identify and define a politician who is seeking an elective position. According to Saduov (2018, p.10), "A slogan summarizes the programs of a politician in one catchy word or phrase and effectively communicates it to the general public." Like jingles, slogans have transcended the domain of product advertisement into the realm of political campaign. Thus, a slogan "has become all the more central to political communication, as marketing techniques have become more commonly used in the field of political propaganda" (Hare, 1993, p.1). Hare's study concludes that the analysis of campaign slogans "can be a useful teaching strategy in sensitizing students to a communicative approach to language" (p. 14).

Jingles and full-blown musical compositions are alike in some ways. Both are rendered as song. Like jingles, music has also become widespread in its use for political electioneering campaigns. It bears a peculiar role in inspiring, motivating and energizing political campaigns. According to Nketia (1974), (cited in Titus & Bello, 2012, p.168), music performance is "the act of playing musical instrument, singing with the voice, dancing with the body, or acting in a music drama." Consequently, Titus and Bello (2012) opine that the use of music for mass mobilization during political electioneering campaigns is simply about creating awareness about candidates, political parties, and the issues on their political manifesto. The adoption of music in the mass media, especially radio and television, for political campaign purposes is therefore meant to reach the electorate who would want to hear or listen to politicians and their messages, possibly in their local language. Nigerian politicians have come to appreciate the impact of radio jingles in electioneering campaigns, and have come to exploit them to their advantage in their quest to win elections. An example of the power of jingles/songs for political campaigns in Nigeria was offered by Ojekwe (2016). The author observed that Akinwunmi Ambode, the candidate who eventually won the 2015 Lagos State governorship election, extensively relied on jingles and songs during his gubernatorial campaign and successfully mobilized the electorate in his favor. Ojekwe (2016) thus concluded that "the use of theme songs in political ad campaigns is effective in seizing the electorates' attention, which could in turn mean a change of choice of candidate" (p. 26).

Methodology and Data Presentation

Three main political parties, the All Progressives Congress (APC), All Progressives Grand Alliance (APGA) and People's Democratic Party (PDP), contested the 2019 general election in Nigeria's Anambra State, the focus of this study. All three political parties used a variety of jingles to market themselves and their candidates to the electorate. These political parties were chosen because of their prominence and spread in practically all electoral constituencies in the state. They too were the main contestants in the elections nationwide. In other words, other less prominent political parties with limited presence in the state were excluded from analysis in this chapter.

The jingles analyzed in this study were exclusive to the political parties. All jingles were aired on radio stations in the state. Although the political parties commissioned and used multiple jingles in their electioneering campaigns, the authors of this study decided to use a purposive sample of three jingles from each of the political parties for analysis. Overall, the selected jingles not only represent the core of the political parties' campaign programs, they also deal with the character of the candidates representing the political parties.

Data collection was manually done by the authors through recording the jingles on tape as they were being played on any of the radio stations in Anambra State, including Purity FM and Radio Nigeria (Awka). The authors played the jingles over and over during the transcription process to in order to assure a good rendition of the jingles and their content. Upon completion of the transcription of all selected jingles, the authors analyzed the data, using the descriptive approach. This approach facilitated the determination of the various stylistic devices in the jingles, and what specific function(s) each identified device performed in the jingles. Each stylistic device was deliberately used by the political parties in an effort to persuade the electorate to cast their votes for them and their candidates.

Upon close examination of the selected jingles, the authors, both of whom are linguistic experts with combined specialization in phonetics, phonology, syntax and semantics, determined that the total of 43 jingles used in this study had the following devices: Repetition, Parallelism, Epithet, Slogan, Hyperbole, Metaphor, Allusion, Presupposition, Inclusive pronoun, Rule of three (Three-part list), Voice modulation, Syllable structure repair, Ululation and fixed refrain, English expressions within Igbo jingles, Dialectal, Interrogative, Imperative, and Hortative words.

For clarity in data presentation, the authors serially numbered the political parties as alphabetically arranged: 1, for APC; 2, for APGA, and 3, for PDP. For proper identification and cross-referencing in the findings and analysis, the lines of jingles are also numbered, using the numerals 1, 2, 3 etc., in their original Igbo language and the corresponding English language translation. Equally important is the authors' reference to originality in the Igbo data, that is, they are tone marked, using Green and Igwe (1963) tone marking convention, where the High tone is left unmarked, and the Low tone is marked with grave accent [`], and Down step tone marked with macron [̄]. The song parts of the jingles are in italics. Also, the English language words or expressions within the jingles are retained as shown in the tables.

Findings and Analysis

Essentially, this chapter deals with Igbo language radio jingles used by the three major political parties in Anambra State, Nigeria, during the country's 2019 general election campaign period. The jingles were examined for their use of stylistic devices to send strong messages to the electorate. The analysis of the data presented in the earlier section shows that no less than 18 stylistic devices were used in 43 jingles examined in this chapter. The distribution of the jingles selected for analysis are as follows, based on their political party origination: 14 jingles for the All Progressives Congress (APC); 23 jingles for the All Progressives Grand Alliance (APGA); and 16 jingles for the People's Democratic Party (PDP).

Following our analysis of the jingles, we found the following stylistic devices used by the three political parties in their radio campaign jingles, as expressed in the tables below. The jingles are presented and associated with the political party that created and aired them.

Stylistic vernacular jingles in political messaging 213

Table 1.1: All Progressives Congress (APC) Jingles

	Igbo Jingle	English Translation
1	Ìgbà 2019, anyị zùrù kà e mee	Igba 2019, we are equal to the task
2	Ìgbà 2019, anyị zùrù kà e mee	Igba 2019, we are equal to the task
3	Njìkọ̀kà, Dunùkọfīā nà Ànàọcha	Njikoka, Dunukofia and Anaocha
4	Maka onye a na-ekwu, nwelù ife ọ na-eme	He who is praised earns the praise
5	Ụmụ̀nnē m̄ ndịNjìkọ̀kà, nà Dunùkọfīā nà Ànàọcha	My brothers and sisters from ...
6	Ndị ife ọma nà-àdị mmā, ndị nā-ākwàdo ife ọma	Lovers and supporters of good
7	Bikōnù kà ànyị pùtanù n'ìgwè	Please let us come out enmasse
8	Kà ànyị kwàdo onye ǹke ānyī, nnwa afọ̄ ānyī, onye anyị jì èmè ọnū, Ambassador Elijah Ònyeāgbā, Ìgba kā ̀ịgbà, màkà ndị na-abịa n'iru	Let us support our own, our son, our pride, excellence/superstar, Ambassador... for the upcoming generation'
9	Onye ga-enyelụ ānyī aka n'irū àlà nkwà	He who will help us reach the land of promise
10	Onye gā-ākwàdo ọlụ ngō dị ichè ichè	He who will support all contracts
11	Ụmù akwụkwọ ānyị gà-èje akwụkwọ	Our students will go to school
12	Ọkụ latrììk na-enwu ēnwū, okporo ụzọ̄ dị lầrỉ̀ị, ọnọ̀dụ̀ mmùta bụ ̀ịgbà	Effective electricity supply, smooth roads, good education
13	Kà ànyị bìnye akā ebe e sèlù ùkwù azīzà	Let us vote for the broom logo
14	APC, Change! APC, Change! Change! Change for the people!	APC, Change! APC, Change! Change! Change for the people!

Table 1.2: All Progressives Grand Alliance (APGA) Jingles

	Igbo Jingle	English Translation
1	APụGĀ nà-àkpọnụ̄ anyịooo Zomanzo	APGA is calling on us
2	Ikembà Ojukwū nà-àkpọnụ̄ anyī ōōō (Zomanzo)	Ikemba Ojukwu is calling on us
3	Willie Obiānọ nà-àkpọnụ̄ anyịeeeee (Zomanzo)	Willie Obianọis calling on us
4	Akpọkùedikē nà-àkpọnụ̄ ānyī ēēē (Zomanzo)	Akpokuedike is calling on us
5	Ife ọ nā-ēkwu Zomanzo	What he is saying
6	Ọ nọ̄ n'ụnọ̀ (Zomanzo), ì nọ̀ n'ezi? (Zomanzo), ì jèlù ọlụ? (Zomanzo), ì nà-èje akwụkwọ? (Zomanzo), gị nàtaba (Zomanzo)	Those at home, are you abroad? Are you out on assignment? Are you a student? you, return
7	Ka anyị jee bìnye akā, ebe e sèlù ọ̀kụ̀kọ màkà ndozi òbòdo ānyī Zomanzo	Let us go and cast our votes where fowl is the logo; for the development of our community
8	Òjukwū, Ezēl̀gbò, gwàlù ànyị nà ǹke à bụ̀ ǹke ānyị	Ojukwu, the Igbo leader told us that this is our own
9	APụGÀ bụ̀ ǹke ānyị	APGA is our own
10	Onye ọ̄bụ̄nà tụ̀nye akwụkwọ yā ebe e sèlù ọ̀kụkọ̀ màkà ndozi òbòdo ānyị	Let all cast his/her vote where fowl is the logo for the development of our community
11	Ụmụ̀nnē m̄, kà ànyị tụnyelụnụ̀ ndị niīne na-azọ ọ̄chịchị n'òtù APụGÀ	My brothers/sisters, let us cast our votes for all APGAcandidates

12	Màkà ndị nā-ejelu ānyị House of Assembly, nà ndị nā-ejelu ānyị Federal House of Representative nà Presidential candidate of our great Party, Senate nàkwà Governorship	For those contesting for House of Assembly, and Federal House of Representatives, and Presidential candidate of our great Party, Senate, and also Governorship
13	APụGÀ gà-ewètelu ānyị mmepe dị ichè n'òbòdo ānyị	APGA will bring multifarious development to our community
14	A gà-àlụlụ ānyị okpolo ụzọ malụ mmā, street light gà-àdị ebe niīnē	Good roads will be built for us, there will be street lights everywhere
15	A gà-ènye ndị ntolobịà anyị ọlụ	Our youths will gain employment
16	Ụmụ ānyị gà-àgụkwa akwụkwọ n'efù	Our children will enjoy free education
17	Nni gà-àdị nyàfụ̀ nyàfụ̀	Food will be plentiful
18	A gà na-àkwụ ndị ọlụ oyìbo ụgwọ	Civil servants will be paid their salary regularly
19	Ndị pensioners gà na-èli ūgwọ fā	Pensioners will receive their pension regularly
20	Anyị gà-ènwe ezigbo nchekwa ndụ̀ nà àkụ nà ụ̀ba, nà ife ndị ọzọ dị ichè ichè	We will have security of life and property, and other good benefits
21	Ụmụ̀nnē m̀, ndị ihe ọma nà-àdị mmā, ya bụ̀, jèe bìnye akā ebe e sèlụ̀ ọ̀kụkọ̀ màkà ezi ọlū	My brothers/sisters, lovers of good, go and cast your votes where fowl is the logo, for quality service
22	Kà ànyị jee bìnye akā ebe e sèlụ̀ ọ̀kụkọ̀ màkà ndozi òbòdo ānyị	Let us go and cast our votes where fowl is the logo; for the development of our community
23	Kòkòroǹkòooò Ònye aghànà nwannē yā	Cock-a-doodle-doo Be your brother's keeper

Table 1.3: Peoples Democratic Party (PDP) Jingles

	Igbo Jingle	English Translation
1	Anambra Central gā-ēso yā	Anambra Central will follow her
2	Anambra Central ga-esō ya	Anambra Central will follow her
3	Nwaanyị dị mma na-ēme mmā	A good woman that does good
4	Uche Ekwūnīfe kā ānyị chọ̀lụ̀'	Uche Ekwunife is our choice
5	Ya kà ànyị jì wèe nā-èkwu màkà Dr. Mrs. Uchè Ekwūnife, Iyòm	That is why we are talking about Dr. Mrs. ...., Iyom- holder of a revered title
6	Ọ nà-apụ̀ta dịkà Senator ndị Anambra Central Senatorial Zone	She is contesting for Anambra Central Senatorial Zone
7	Ọ gāgoro ānyị House of Rep ùgbòrò àbụọ mà mee ọ̄fụma	She had represented us twice at the House of Rep and did well
8	Jee Senate, ebe ọ bụ̀ nwaànyị ìzìzì nà kwà onye South East ìzìzì nwetara ọkwa dị kà Chairman, Senate Committee on Petroleum Downstream Sector	Went to Senate, where she was the first woman to become the Chairman, Senate Committee on Petroleum Downstream Sector
9	O nyèrè scholarship, lụọ ụnọ̀ akwụkwọ dị ichè iche	She awarded scholarships, and built many schools
10	Ọ lụ̀rụ̀ borehole, nye ọlū, kwụrụ chìm̀ inyērē ndị ǹtorobịà nà ụmụ̀ nwaànyị̀ aka	She constructed borehole, provided employment, and stands firm to help the youth and women
11	Ọ nà-ènyekwara ụmụ̀ nwaànyị̀ di hā nwụ̀gòrò aka, na-ènye nneta āhụ ikē n'efù	She also helps the widows and provides free medical care

12	Ụzọ̀ ọ rụ̀ụ̀rụ̀ ànyị kàrị̀rị̀ àkarị	The number of roads she built is numerous
13	Ndị o nyèrè ọlụ bụ̀ atụrụ̄ tàba	Those she provided employment for are too many
14	Ụlọ̀ akwụkwọ ọ rụ̀rụ̀ àrụ, gbànyụụ	The schools she built, very many
15	Tụ̀nyerenụ̀ Dr. Mrs. Uchè Ekwūnife, Ịyọ̀m, dị kà Senator na-anọ̀chite anya Anambra Central n'ọ̀kpurù PDP, Party e jì umbrella mara, dị kà akàrà ha	Cast your votes for Dr. Mrs. Uchè Ekwūnife, Iyọ̀m, as Senator under PDP, a party whose logo is umbrella
16	PDP, Power! Power, To the people!	PDP, Power! Power, To the people!

Devices and Analysis

Repetition

Repetition is an effective stylistic feature in political jingles and propaganda. It involves the reiteration of words or group of words. By so doing, the attention of the listener is captured and the message contained in the message becomes activated in the minds of the electorate, making the jingles to be more memorable. It is also used for emphasis. The three political parties extensively used repetition in their jingles. As shown on Table 1, the APC reiterated the idea that "We are equal to the task" to assure the electorate that the party is capable of solving the problems faced by the people. On its part, the APGA opted to use the call-and-response approach by reminding the electorate that some well-known names such as "Ikemba Ojukwu" and "Willie Obiano" are "calling on us" to join the party, and urging the people to cast their votes "Where fowl is the logo (APGA's) for the development of our community" (Table1. 2). The PDP chose to endear itself to the electorate. In its jingles, the party played on the notion of brotherhood, by calling potential voters "My brothers and sisters" and extolled them as "lovers of good things" (Table1. 2). Examples of repetitions are provided below.

Table 1.1: 1-2. 1. Ìgbà 2019, anyị zùrù kà e mee (*Igba 2019, we are equal to the task*).

2. Ìgbà 2019, anyị zùrù kà e mee (*igba 2019, we are equal to the task*).

Table 1. 2: 1-4. 1. APụGĀ) nà-àkpọnụ̄ anyịoooZomanzo (*APGA) is calling on us*).

2. (Ikembà Ojukwū) nà-àkpọnụ̄ anyị̄ ōōō (Zomanzo) (*Ikemba Ojukwu) is calling on us*).

3. (Willie Obiānọ nà-àkpọnụ̄) anyịeeeeee (Zomanzo) (*Willie Obiànọ) is calling on us*).

4. (Akpọkùedikē) nà-àkpọnụ̄ ānyị̄ ēēē (Zomanzo)(*Akpokuedike) is calling on us*).

7. ...ebe e sèlù ọ̀kụkọ̀ màkà ndozi òbòdoānyị̄ (Zomanzo). (*Where fowl is the logo; for the development of our community*).

10. ...ebe e sèlù ọ̀kụkọ̀ màkà ndozi òbòdoānyị̄. (*Where fowl is the logo; for the development of our community*).

Table 1.3: 8. ...Ìzìzì'first' ìzìzi *(first)*. This is an emphasis on the fact of the politician being the "first" in these commendable areas- the first female as well as the first Southeast Senator to be the Chairman, Senate Committee on Petroleum Downstream Sector. (The tonal difference on the last syllable is because of the sentence structures where the two words appear- the former in the main clause and the latter in a subordinate clause). We even see that an expression could be repeated by two or more political parties. For example, political parties I and II share the following expressions:

Table 1.1: 5-6. Ụmụ̀nnē m̄ ... (*My brothers and sisters ...*). Ndị ifeọma nà-àdị mmā... (*Lovers of good things*).

Table 1. 2: 21. Ụmụ̀nnē m̄, ndị ihe ọma nà-àdị mmā (*My brothers and sisters, lovers of good things*).

In these examples, the politicians exploited their knowledge of the Igbo culture where brotherhood and sisterhood are great bonds. By repeatedly referring to the electorate as Ụmụ̀nnē m̄, ndị ihe ọma nà-àdị mmā (*My brothers and sisters, lovers of good things*). They not only endear themselves to the electorate but also make the voters have a sense of revered self-worth, since they are viewed as "lovers of good things."

Parallelism

In parallelism, ideas are emphasized in a way to show they are of equal weight and importance, and presented in the form that makes the ideas memorable. Politicians use the device to make the electorate remember the ideas they project so that they will get massive votes from them. See the following examples:

Table 1.3: 9. O nyèrè scholarship, lụọ ụnọ̀ akwụkwọ dị ichè iche (*She awarded scholarships, and built many schools*).

10. Ọ lụ̀rụ̀ borehole, nye ọlụ̄, kwụrụ chịm̄ inyērē ndịñtorobịà nà ụmụ̀ nwaànyị̀ aka (*She constructed borehole, provided employment, and stands firm to help the youth and women*).

Epithet

An epithet is a word or a comparison that describes a person, or something which strengthens emotional expression and gives information about the person or thing to which it is attached by emphasizing its emotive meaning (Staugaite, 2014). Epithets in the jingles include:

Table 1.1: 8. nnwaafọ ānyī (*the son of our womb; our son*). Here, the person being referred to is projected as a son or daughter; not a slave, a foreigner or an outcast. This attribute gives him/her the impetus to contest for the leadership position he / she wants to occupy. Also included is the expression, onyeanyịjìèmeọnụ (*the person we boast about; our pride*). A person which this epithet qualifies must be somebody cherished by the people (voters) because of his or her enviable attributes, and for contributions to society.

Table 1.2: 8. Ezêİgbò (*the Igbo leader*). The use of this epithet is reserved for great people who have led the Igbo as a people. Òjukwū is the one the epithet fits. The idea in bringing him into the jingle is to let the Igbo electorate know that their leader (Chukwuemeka Odumegwu Ojukwu, though late) had an interest in the party which they, as a people, should protect by casting their votes in favor of the candidate being campaigned for.

Table 1.3: 13. mmepe dị ichè (*development that is exceptional or unprecedented development*). The kind of development so qualified must be such that everyone yearns for. The electorate will stop at nothing to ensure that the candidate in question is a person that will provide such a development.

Table 1.3: 3, for instance, extols *Nwaanyịdịmmana-ēmemmā* (A good woman that does good). The implication is that if the candidate is good and does good, the electorate cannot have a better choice than her.

5. *Iyọ̀m* refers to the female holder of a revered title. This is not a title that is bestowed on ordinary people, but only to high achievers. It is such a revered cultural title for responsible, wealthy, intelligent and influential Igbo women, such that any woman that bears it is seen as a worthy representative of her people.

Slogan

Slogan, with specific reference to politics, is a very simple catchphrase that compels the attention of the listener. It captures the candidate's or party's objective in a way to convince the electorate to vote for the candidate or party. Here are examples:

Table 1.1: 14: APC, Change! APC, Change! Change! Change for the people*!*

Table 1.2: 8. ǹke à bụ̀ ǹkeānyī (*this is our own*).

9. APụGÀbụ̀ ǹkeānyī (*APGA is our own*).

23. Kòkòroǹkòooò Ònyeaghànà nwanne yā (*Cock-a-doodle-doo. Be your brother's keeper*).

Table 1.3: 4. Uche Ekwunīfe kā ānyichọ̀lụ̀ *(Uche Ekwunife is our choice).*

17. "PDP, Power! Power, To the people!"

Hyperbole:

According to Staugaite (2014, p.28), hyperbole is "a figure of speech when the speaker exaggerates and overemphasizes some words or phrases in order to produce more noticeable effect or to stress a specific point of the speech." In most cases, it is the ordinary understanding of the politician's hyperbolic expression that contributes to his/her being accused of not fulfilling campaign promises. Although the authors have provided the appropriate English language expressions of Igbo hyperboles in the jungles, some of the renditions tend to blur their seriousness as Igbo language statements. Here are examples:

Table 1.2: 14. Street light gà-àdị ebe niinē (*There will be street lights everywhere*). This is a hyperbolic statement for the simple reason that it is impossible for street lights to be erected "everywhere" as expressed in the jingle.

16. Ụmụ ānyị gà-àgụkwaakwụkwọ n'efù (*Our children will enjoy free education*). The truth about this statement is that parents/guardians must definitely contribute much to the education of their children/wards.

17. Nnigà-àdịnyàfù nyàfù (*Food will be plentiful*).

Table 3, 12. Na-ènyennetaāhụ ikē n'efù (*Provides free medical care*).

13. Ụzọ ọ rụ̀ụ̀rụ̀ ànyị kàrịrị̀ àkarị (*The number of roads she built is numerous*).

14. Ndị o nyèrè ọlụ bụ̀ atụrụ tàba (*Those she provided employment for are too many*).

15. Ụlọ̀ akwụkwọ ọ rụ̀rụ̀ àrụ, gbànyụụ (*The schools she built, very many*).

Metaphor

Metaphor is based on conceptual association. In cognitive linguistics, it "is understood as a mapping between two conceptual domains, where properties from one domain (the source) are transferred onto another domain: the target" (Caballero & Ibarretxe-Antunano, 2012, p. 268). Metaphor becomes a stylistic device when two different things are compared in a way that one is said to be the other. The following examples illustrate this point:

Table 1.1: 8. Ìgba kā ìgbà (*a drum greater than other drums*) stands for excellence/superstar. In this case, the politician is likened not just to any drum, but that which produces the best sound compared to others, thus portraying him as the best the electorate can ever have. This candidate is thus associated with the resounding sound of the African drum. This metaphorical expression is intended to portray the candidate as excellence personified, and the electorate is being convinced to vote for the best.

Table 1.1: 9. irū àlà nkwà (*to reach the land of promise*) stands as a metaphor for what is commonly referred to in the local parlance as "deriving the dividends of democracy."

Allusion

Allusion is a reference to a historical or prominent figure, event, or object. Politicians often use this device as a way of pushing forward their rightful claim to the political office. Our data show instances of the use of allusions.

Table 1.2: 2. Ikembà Ojukwū nà-àkpọnụ anyị (*Ikemba Ojukwu is calling on us*). The late Ikembà Ojukwū is a revered figure among the Igbo because of his efforts and leadership role in safeguarding the Igbo nation. If he personally supports the candidate by calling on all to vote for him, the likelihood is that the electorate will be influenced in that direction.

3. Willie Obiānọ nà-àkpọnụanyị (*Willie Obianois calling on us*). Willie Obiano, the Anambra State Governor, won in all the 21 Local Government Areas of the state in the election under APGA. Having served as governor and won reelection, he is regarded as a huge political force in the state's political arena. It was therefore reasonable and pragmatic to use his name in the jingle to beef up the credibility of the party and its candidates.

8. Òjukwū, Ezē Ìgbò, gwàlụ̀ ànyị nà ǹke à bụ̀ ǹke ānyị̄ (*Ojukwu, the Igbo leader, told us that this is our own*). The politicians want the electorate to think and act right; that if actually the Igbo leader told the Igbo people that APGA is "our own," the electorate must decide not to have anything to do with the other parties and their candidates. With this allusion, the politicians hope to achieve their political ambition since the decision of the electorate would propel APGA to victory.

Presupposition

In presupposition, a background assumption is tactfully weaved into an expression. Thus, there is usually some piece of information which the speaker believes the hearer already knows. Here are some examples in the jingles.

Table 1.1: 9. Onye ga-enyelụ ānyị̄ aka n'irū àlà nkwà (*He who will help us reach the land of promise*) presupposes that they are yet to reach the "promised land".

12. Ọkụ latriìk na-enwu ēnwū̄, okporouzọ̄ d larịị̀, ọnọ̀dụ̀ mmụta bụ ịgbà (*Effective electricity supply, smooth roads, good and quality education*) is an indication that their electricity is not functioning; the roads are not smooth, and education is sub-standard.

Table 1.2: 14-17. 14. A gà-àlụlụ ānyị okpolouzọ̄ malụ mmā, street light gà-àdị ebe niīnē (*Good roads will be built for us, there will be street lights everywhere*) is a presupposition that the roads are dilapidated and there are few or no street lights.

15. A gà-ènye ndị ntolobịà anyị ọlụ (*Our youths will gain employment*), shows that the youth are not employed.

16. Ụmụ ānyī gà-àgụkwa akwụkwọ n'efù (*Our children will enjoy free education*) presupposes that students pay school fees.

17. Nni gà-àdị nyàfụ̀ nyàfụ̀ (*Food will be plentiful*) underscores food scarcity in society.

18. A gà na-àkwụ ndị ọlụ oyìbo ụgwọ (*Civil servants will be paid their salary regularly*) is based on the reality that the state's civil servants do not receive their salaries on a regular basis.

19. Ndị pensioners gà na-èli ūgwọ fā (*Pensioners will receive their pension regularly*) is a clear indication that pensioners are hardly paid their pension.

20. Anyị gà-ènwe ezigbo nchekwa ndụ̀ nà àkụ̀ nà ụ̀ba, nà ife ndị ọ̀zọ dị ichè ichè (*We will have security of life and property, and other good benefits*) assumes the lack of security of life and property, and other life-enhancing benefits.

Inclusive pronoun:

Politicians often use the inclusive pronoun "ànyị" (*we*) as an affective expression to firmly associate themselves with the electorate and impress them to the extent that the voters would feel and act the way the politicians want them to. This makes the electorate see the politician as truly one of them and makes them disposed to agree to cast their votes for him/her. Some examples are as follows:

Table 1.1: 7. Bikōnụ̀ kà ànyị pụ̀tanụ̀ n'ìgwè (*Please let us come out en-masse*) to vote.

8. Kà ànyị kwàdo onyeǹke ānyị̄, nnwaafọ̄ ānyī, onyeanyịjìèmeọnụ̄, Ambassador Elijah Ònyeāgbā, Ịgba kāịgbà, màkà ndịna-abịan'iru (*Let us support our own, our son, our pride, excellence/superstar, Ambassador Elijah Ònyeāgba for the upcoming generation*).

9. Onyega-enyelụ ānyī aka n'irū àlà nkwà (*He who will help us reach the land of promise*).

Rule of three (Three-part list)

This is a popular structural device employed in the language of politics. According to Beard (2000, p. 39), "The effect of these lists does not rest solely in the repetition: they are spoken aloud; so prosodic features, such as pitch, tempo and rhythm, also play a major part in their effect." For some reasons, people generally find things grouped in threes particularly pleasing. In other words, while talking about a person (politician in this case), there is the tendency to garnish your speech with a minimum of three tangible examples of his or her achievements to really catch people's attention. We illustrate with the following examples in our data:

Table 3, 10. Ọ lụ̀rụ̀ borehole, nyeọlụ̄, kwụrụ chị̀m̀ inyērē ndị̄ntorobị̀à nà ụmụ̀ nwaànyị̀ aka (*She constructed borehole, provided employment, and stands firm to help the youth and women*).

Table 1.3: 12-14:

12. Ụzọ̀ ọ rụ̀ụ̀rụ̀ ànyị kàrị̀rị̀ àkarị (*The number of roads she built is numerous*).

13. Ndị o nyèrè ọlụ bụ̀ atụrụ̄ tàba (*Those she provided employment for are too many*).

14. Ụlọ̀ akwụkwọ ọ rụ̀rụ̀ àrụ, gbànyụụ (*The schools she built, very many*).

Voice modulation

Voice modulation is used in the jingle to "catch" the attention of the electorate. We see it in Table 1.2: 16, with the slogan "Change" said with such modulated voice and tonation that the word draws attention to itself in order to "capture" the voters. Voice modulation is also used for emphasis.

Syllable structure repair

The syllable structure in the Igbo language does not permit the cluster of consonants, especially in political advertising jingles. When a word has a structure with a consonant cluster, it is repaired through, especially, vowel insertion. This type of syllable structure repair is seen in Table 2, with the Igbo pronunciation of the name of the party, APGA, transformed as APụGA by the insertion of "ụ". This makes the syllable structure of the word to be a VCVCV pattern in linguistics, where a letter is inserted to convert a word into a two-syllable word. The structure arising from the repair is also in conformity with the open syllable structure of Igbo, as Igbo is a NO CODA language (lacks consonant clusters). We see that after the repair by vowel insertion, none of the three syllables has a consonant cluster or is realized as a closed syllable.

Ululation and fixed refrain

Ululation device and refrain contribute greatly in making a jingle melodious. In ululation, a vowel is inserted and pronounced with such an elongation that it draws attention to itself. In our data, ululation is often directly followed by a refrain which is fixed, as it does not change its structure. "Zomanzo" is the fixed refrain. See the following examples from Table 1.2:

1. APụGĀnà-àkpọnụ anyịooo Zomanzo (*APGA is calling on us*).
2. Ikembà Ojukwū nà-àkpọnụ anyị̄ ōōō (Zomanzo) *(Ikemba Ojukwu is calling on us)*.
3. Willie Obiānọ nà-àkpọnụ anyịeeeeee (Zomanzo) *(Willie Obianọis calling on us)*.
4. Akpọkùedikē nà-àkpọnụ ānyị̄ ēēē (Zomanzo) *(Akpokuedike is calling on us)*.

In 1 and 2, the vowel "o" is inserted and ululated, yielding "ooo". For 3 and 4, the inserted and ululated vowel becomes "e" and results in "*eeeeee*".

English expressions within Igbo jingles

Switching or mixing English expressions in Igbo speech is almost becoming a norm among most Igbo-English bilinguals. Here are instances of Igbo language campaign jingles that are juxtaposed with English expressions:

Table 1.1: 14. *APC, Change! APC, Change! Change! Change for the people!*

Table 1.2: 12. Presidential candidate of our great party

Table 1.3:10. Borehole. 15. Party umbrella. 16. PDP, Power! Power, To the people!

Dialectal words

Igbo speakers usually bring in their dialectal words (or expressions) in speech. This could be inadvertent or deliberate, depending on the intention of the speaker. For example, if the politician wants to be recognized to have come from a particular part of the state which he feels will place him at an advantage over his/her opponents, dialectal words or expressions are brought in to assert this identity. Examples in our data are:

Table 1.1: 4. nwèlụ̀ (*has/have*) or nwere; 4 and 6 where Ife (*something*) is also ihe.

Table 1.2: 5, 20. Ife (*something*) or ihe.

5. Jee (*go*) or gaa.
6. Gwàlụ̀ (*told*) or gwara.
7. Obụnà (*every*) or ọbụlà; sèlụ̀ (*drew*) or sere.
8. Tụnyelụnụ̀ (*cast for*) or tụnyerenụ̀; niīne (*all*) or niile.
9. Gà-àlụlụ (*will build for*) or gà-àrụrụ; okpolo ụzọ̄ malụ mmā (*good roads*) or okporo ụzọ̄ mara mmā).

10. Ntolobìà (*youth*) or ntorobìà; ọlụ (*work/job*) or ọrụ.
11. Nni (food) or nri.

All the dialectal words come from the area where the precinct or district where election is being contested. By bringing in these dialectal words, the contestant not only identifies himself/herself as coming from the dialect area, but attempts to prove to be "at home" with the peculiar variety spoken by the people he/she intends to represent.

Interrogative

Interrogative expressions are meant to bring out the realities in the district in the form of questions. Examples from Table 1. 2, line 6, show the following: ì nọ̀ n'ezi? (*are you abroad?*); ì jèlù ọlụ? (*are you out on assignment?*); ì nà-èje akwụkwọ? (*are you a student?*). In the contest of the jingles, these interrogative statements show that whoever you are or whatever you do, the candidate being presented is your best choice.

Imperative

Imperatives in the jingles are designed to "persuade" the electorate to vote wisely. These are examples from Table1. 2, line 21says: ...jèe bìnye akā ebe e sèlù ọ̀kụkọ̀ màkà ezi ọlụ̄ (*go and cast your votes where fowl is the logo, for quality service*). Table 1.3, line 15 says: Tụ̀nyerenụ̀ Dr. Mrs..., Ịyọ̀m, dị kà...n'òkpurù PDP, Party e jì umbrella mara, dị kà akàrà ha (*Cast your votes for...as ... under PDP, a party whose logo is umbrella*).

Hortative

The Hortative device helps to make a strong plea to the electorate. These are some examples: Table 1.1: line 7: kà ànyị pụ̀tanụ̀ n'ìgwè (*let us come out en masse*).

8. Kà ànyị ịkwàdo onyeǹkeānyị̄, nnwaafọ̄ ānyị̄... (*Let us support our own, our son...*)

13. Kà ànyịbìnye akā ebe e sèlù ùkwù azị̄zà (*Let us vote for the broom logo*).

Table1. 2, line 7 says: Ka anyị jee bìnye akā, ebe e sèlù ọ̀kụkọ̀; màkà ndozi òbòdo ānyị̄ (*Let us go and cast our votes where fowl is the logo; for the development of our community*).

11. Kà ànyị tụnyelunụ̀ ndị niīne na-azọ ọchịchịn'òtù APụGÀ (*let us cast our votes for all APGA candidates*).

22. Kà ànyị jee bìnye akā ebe e sèlụ̀ ọ̀kụkọ̀; màkà ndozi òbòdoānyī (*Let us go and cast our votes where fowl is the logo; for the development of our community*).

Conclusion

In this chapter, the authors analyzed 43 radio jingles used by the three major political parties in Nigeria's Anambra State during the country's 2019 electioneering campaigns. The authors conducted the analysis against the framework of 18 linguistic/stylistic features in the jingles, as used by the political parties to present their candidates and enhance their favorability among the electorate.

As the data show, every stylistic device employed was intended to perform some specific functions such as the imperative of persuading voters to wisely cast their ballots, using the inclusive pronoun "ànyị" (*we*) to demonstrate some form of affinity and association with voters, and the interrogative device which was intended to show that no matter who you were or what you did for a living, the candidate being showcased was your best choice for the election.

In terms of their overall significance, these devices function as tools for implanting specific political messages in the minds of the electorate. Thus, apart from capturing the attention of the listener as well as for emphasis, repetition was designed to make the jingles more memorable; epithet was used to address a renowned person in the society as a way of convincing the electorate that members of the political party were responsible people in the society; and voice modulation had both attention capturing and emphasis functions, while ululation and refrain made the jingles melodious and entertaining.

Although a total of 18 stylistic devices were used in this chapter, they cannot be classified as forming an exhaustive list of possible devises for the analysis of political campaign messages. In addition, this study only examined radio jingles produced in the local Igbo language of the people, and only focused on three major political parties that contested the elections. While these constituent parts of this study provide important insights into the political messages used in the 2019 election in Anambra State, we suggest that feature studies extend the use of language to include the English language, as well as the inclusion of other political parties that also contested the elections for a more robust understanding of the role played by jingles used in the election.

Finally, this is a largely descriptive study of the radio jingles used in the 2019 general elections in the state. It will also be useful and instructive for future studies to measure the impact of the jingles, and attempt to determine which of the stylistic devices resonated with, and impacted the voters in that election.

References

Abellanosa, H. J., Abao, K. H. N., Luis, N. I., Obsioma, J. I., Paderanga IV, & Tañedo, A. C. (2012). Effects of political ads on television on the choice of presidential candidates among first-time voters of Liceo De Cagayan University. *Advancing Literature and Communication Research, 1*(1), 1–20. https://doi.org/10.7828/alcr.v1i1.171

Aduradola, R. R., & Ojukwu, C. C. (2013). Language of political campaigns and politics in Nigeria. *Canadian Social Science, 9*(3), 104–116.

Akomolede-Onafuwa, O. E. (2017). *Propaganda or persuasion? A review of the Nigeria 2015 presidential election campaign process via social media (Part One).* https://papers.ssrn.com/sol3/papers.cfm?abstract_id=3080836

Ashipu, K. B. C. (2015). An analysis of phonostylistic devices in some selected Itiang (proverbs) Bette. *Journal of Literature, Language and Linguistics, 11*, 1–6.

Beard, A. (2000). *The language of politics.* London & New York: Routledge.

Caballero, R., & Ibarretxe-Antuñano, I. (2012). Ways of perceiving, moving, and thinking: Re-vindicating culture in conceptual metaphor research. *Journal of Cognitive Semiotics, 5*(1–2), 268–290.

Green, M. M., & Igwe, G. E. (1963). *A descriptive grammar of Igbo.* Berlin: Akademie-Verlag.

Hare, G. (1991). Studying political slogans as communication. *Political Communication, 3*, 24–29.

Nnadi, I. C. (2010). A linguistic stylistic analysis of Chukwuemeka Ike's novels. [Unpublished doctoral dissertation]. University of Jos, Nigeria.

Ojekwe, G. I. (2016). Political advert campaigns and voting behavior: Akinwunmi Ambode's 2015 election campaign in Lagos State. *Journal of African Elections, 15*(2), 13–27. https://doi.org/10.20940/JAE/2016/v15i2a1

Saduov, R. (2018). The language of political slogans in 2016 Slovak parliamentary elections. *Studies in Applied Linguistics, 9*(2), 17–23.

Staugaite, I. (2014). Linguistic realization of rhetorical strategies in Barack Obama and Dalia Grybauskaite's political speeches. [Unpublished MA Thesis]. Lithuanian University of Educational Sciences, Lithuania.

Titus, O. S., & Bello, O. A. (2012). Musical forms in songs for political mobilization during 2011 general elections in Nigeria. *International Journal of Humanities and Social Science, 2*(13), 166–173.

CHAPTER 10

Performative sites of resistance: A challenge to oppression through artistic entertainment

Rachael Cofield

Florida State University, USA

Douglas L. Allen

Emporia State University, USA

Abstract

This chapter discusses how marginalized communities, specifically queer burlesque dancers of Metropolitan Studios and Black members of the Florida A&M University bands in the United States South, challenge societal oppressions by transforming entertainment spaces into places for projecting socio-political messaging and bringing into existence alternative, affirmative visions of society and place. These groups deploy the socio-cultural power of performance to project explicit political messaging (in the case of Metropolitan Studios, a queer burlesque group) and to implicitly challenge the racialization of space (in the case of FAMU's[1] band members). The authors use socio-spatial and performance theory to argue that entertainment, music, and performance are effective tools for societally marginalized communities to transform oppressive spaces into affirmative places that project alternative visions of society and place.

Keywords: Affirmative, burlesque, performance site, ephemerality, race, queer, marginalized communities

***

---

[1] Florida Agricultural and Mechanical University, USA.

Introduction

Events, marches, parades, and festivals often serve as tools of the oppressed to practice resistance, engage in solidarity, and find affirmation of one's life and ways of life. These events act as socially, culturally, and politically influential performances. Such performances evoke current embodied realities as well as express aspirational community goals and enact spatial visions. They instantiate and reinforce place, serving as a form of placemaking that makes new, more inclusive articulations of place possible. Those who might otherwise struggle to be seen and whose stories might be erased or contained by our largely white and heterosexual normative society, use these performances as spatial (counter) storytelling vehicles to resist oppressive narratives and amplify affirmative narratives. Albeit often fleeting, transient, and ephemeral, these places live on in the minds of those who attend and engage in them, becoming a powerful and useful resource well after the performances conclude.

This chapter provides two empirical examples to show this work in practice, and discusses how queer burlesque dancers use entertainment spaces to project explicit political messages and social messages of body positivity, and also how FAMU's Marching 100 and the FAMU wind symphony frame their performances around already existing racial politics. In particular, the FAMU band's 2015 performance at Carnegie Hall is seen by FAMU members as an implicit challenging of that space (and all concert spaces) as white spaces, instead transforming it into an affirmative space that projects Black excellence. The authors argue that both examples counter normative socio-spatial constructions and project alternative visions of a more inclusive, and just society. These examples show how entertainment/performance spaces are platforms for disseminating political messages, in addition to being socio-political constructs that are themselves challenged and transformed into more inclusive, just spaces.

Literature Review

In this section, the authors examine spatial theories undergirding their effort in assessing the political nature of performances by marginalized groups. First, we discuss place and how it is not simply a container but an active agent in the production of society. Then we discuss how performance is an important aspect of placemaking and storytelling that makes it possible to engage in crafting alternative visions of space and society through worldmaking. Finally, we end with an extended discussion of burlesque and how scholars have debated this performance style.

Space and Place

In this chapter, the authors conceptualize place as ever-evolving and reliant upon cultural flows between people and locations. Doreen Massey (1991) speaks out against seeing place as bounded, particularly when considering globalization in the modern era. She claims that the tendency to see space as contained is simply:

> A response to desire for fixity and for security of identity in the middle of all the movement and change. A "sense of place", of rootedness, can provide - in this form and on this interpretation - stability and a source of unproblematical identity (p. 26).

As such, space resists bounding, and place can never be condensed into a single sense of place. Instead, she is attentive to an increasingly global sense of place, where place becomes a nexus "constructed out of a particular constellation of social relations, meeting and weaving together at a particular locus" (Massey, 1991, p. 28). Together, these multiple senses of place, social relations, and global come together as an ever-changing process of making and re(making) place.

Unlike prior conceptualizations of space, which were largely seen as containers for political activity, recent theorizations have argued that it does not exist prior to identities and entities and their relations (Pierce et al., 2011; Allen et al., 2019). In addition, scholars have explicitly linked space and place to relations of socio-cultural belonging, a political process of crafting relationships, as not simply a stage on which political or cultural activity happens but an agent in the process of politics and culture. There is a temporal element to place as well. As place is processual and constantly remade through the humans that influence these re-makings, and the political notions that undergird these processes. Massey (2005) conceives of space as inherently tied to politics and conceptualizations of the future and the inherent political aims held within. She argues that space, like time, is open, and as such, filled with potential yet unknown. Space is instead a compilation of relations, ever-evolving, heterogenous, and open. It is this unsettled space that becomes ripe with potential for the future.

On a more practical level, other scholars have used Massey's (2005, p. 119) description of space as "'bundles' of space-time trajectories drawn together by individuals through cognitive and emotional processes" to examine the specific ways people engage in politics in place. Pierce, Martin, and Murphy (2011) determined that people create place, as a Masseyian nexus, in ways often related to local experience and political activism. They describe this process as placemaking, or "the set of social, political and material processes by which people iteratively create and recreate the experienced geographies in which they live" (p. 54). These places are agonistically negotiated, often through contestation and networks, and relational. In their work, they argue for a relational placemaking approach that can "focus analytical attention on the place / bundles drawn on by actors in the place-framing process in order to identify points of contention and commonality in the elements of the place /bundles experienced by actors on opposing sides of a conflict" (p. 60). This approach allows scholars to see places and placemaking as not simply a material phenomenon connected only to bounded territories, but a political and social process that binds together communities of people as much as it defines specific locations. In other words, placemaking is often about binding communities with similar visions of society and space together, which creates relations of belonging for some and can marginalize others by excluding their particular visions of place (Allen et al., 2019).

A conceptualization of place as multiple and of placemaking as an active process makes room to better examine actors and enactments in place that might otherwise remain invisible, especially those engagements by marginalized actors within society. Allen et al. (2019), for example, argue for the use of a relational place-making perspective when it comes to the study of Black geographies and argue that placemaking is a more viable means to examine different ways of worldmaking, particularly to highlight Black agency and placemaking. Jen Jack Gieseking (2020) also examines the placemaking practices of the urban lesbian and queer community, relating their activities to constellations, specifically making the astronomical connection of creating mental star charts. He argues that these constellations better capture the fleeting and alternative placemaking experience because this metaphor "invokes the resonance of place-making/moorings, including places no longer physically present but mentally and emotionally substantial" (p. 951). These star charts persist in the minds of those who experience them, often known only by those in the queer community.

Performance as Placemaking

Performance is integral to our discussion of the places created by different groups of performers, particularly in how it articulates the self to and with an audience. Hannah Rockwell (1996) focuses on how performances are embodied and filled with cultural meaning. She states that "Effective social performances *evoke, invite and compel* aesthetic engagement with social values expressed," and transform meaning through a relational engagement between different bodies (often that of performer and audience) (p. 67). Often, we perform our positions of subjectivity through bodily interaction. According to Rockwell, these subjectivities are mediated through the body and discursively merge and change due to difference. For instance, burlesque dancers might use this bodily connection to take control of space and change and punish/reward certain audience actions. Bodies perform culture, bringing to light various ideas, emotions, attitudes, and experiences all contingent upon positionality.

Aesthetic performances are a form of storytelling, or counter-storytelling, that bring into existence new inclusive and liberating worlds. Indeed, counter-storytelling has been a long-used strategy by marginalized groups to make visible their struggles, lives, and alternative visions of society and space (Solórzano and Yosso, 2002). According to Benjamin Shephard (2010, p. 12), such performances are a kind of play that "is understood as a resource that sustains, supports, and advances the aims of social movements." Performance allows for the development of different worlds, becoming a powerful form of political action that both can represent and undermine existing social structures (Rockwell, 1996). Terrie Waddell (2013) applies this sentiment to some burlesque performances, likening performers to trickster figures of legend that dwell in and flourish in the margins of society. These individuals often "traverse boundaries, remaining uncommitted to a sense of place, time or relationship" (Waddell, 2013, p. 101). Queer performances create realms that tell stories that leave "space for hybrids, freaks and un-beauties to thrive" (Sampatakakis, 2019, p. 265). These stories become liberatory for performer and audience alike as they present potential futures and inclusive ways of being.

For some, performance itself can become a part of placemaking, particularly for those that rely on ephemeral engagement, such as the Black and queer populations (see discussion below). Performance is particularly key to queer populations as resistance and personal freedom, especially if one considers temporary events such as PRIDE parades. This work specifically seeks to examine the means in which performance venues are ephemeral spaces that provide important political work. Marginalized groups often lack permanent physical locations to gather, necessitating explicitly ephemeral placemaking (Cofield, 2021). Much of this literature focuses on the lack of permanent queer locations. Stillwagon and Ghaziani (2019) push for a temporary turn to examining queer placemaking. They explore "queer pop-up" events, noting that even as events change venue "the effects on queer consciousness endure through cultural expressions like dance, gendered and genderless drag performances, relational support systems, elder care, and two-spirit empowerment" (p. 890). For them, ephemeral placemaking is a "performative outcome" that continues to influence the people who engage these spaces. Gieseking (2020) also acknowledges the productive flows of temporary place, describing how they serve as "constellations" in the minds of lesbian-queer populations as these groups make "sense of their lives between the spaces, people, and experiences available to them" (p. 942). These constellations, or ephemeral places, remain in their minds well after the interactions are over.

The worlds being performed may be ephemeral and constellation-like, but they are still important in the minds of those who experience them. As Massey (2005) states, "It is a world being made, and through relations, and there lies the politics" (p. 15). Space is not a static foregone conclusion, but one open to political possibility and intervention. We argue then, that it is not simply about the world as a cohesive and discrete unit, but instead about how people then create spatial worlds that represent the future they most desire. We extend this conversation by exploring explicitly ephemeral placemaking that is often necessary for the context of queer and BIPOC actors. The following section briefly covers the literature on the historical development of burlesque as it moves into the neo-burlesque discourses in our first case study.

Understanding Burlesque

Burlesque began as a type of nineteenth-century theatrical performance based upon, and often parodying or satirizing, historical or Romantic fantasy dramas. Early works encapsulated the themes of humor, gender, and daily life. And although these themes would eventually expand to include nudity and sexuality, such theatrics were utilized in classical theatre well before the strip tease was incorporated into the acts (Baldwin, 2004; Troxell, 2007). These performances were associated with the working class "leg shows" of the mid-1800s and were often associated with immoral behaviors. Several key figures spearheaded burlesque's entry into formal theatre settings, bringing working-class aesthetics with a more bourgeois audience. Laura Keene, a playwright and theater owner in the 1860s, began incorporating what was otherwise considered low-brow humor at the time into her theater to draw in a larger male audience. Shortly after, Adah Isaacs Menken took over the title role in Broadway's production of Lord Byron's *Mazeppa*, which featured a scene with a nude woman on horseback in the wilderness. Menken performed the stunt herself, wearing only a pink body stocking and a brief tunic that appeared as a blur to the audience, giving the illusion that she was completely naked. Not only did this rejuvenate interest in the play's otherwise failing run, it also brought out the style of "clothed nudity," another common theme of early burlesque. And although during the 1870s and 1930s burlesque was often merged with various vaudeville and carnival circuits, it would rise again to trendiness in the 1990s (Buszek, 1996).

Neo-burlesque, or the burlesque performances of the current time, encompasses many different styles and motivations. Claire Nally (2009) points to the distinctions between the mainstream or subcultural forms, each with their own vision of neo-burlesque. Mainstream neo-burlesque often focuses on and could be exemplified by a performer such as Dita von Teese, (also known as a retrolesque performer) who emphasizes traditional concepts of femininity through both costume and aesthetics without a critique about how such notions are themselves limiting of queer or non-white voices (Dahl, 2014). Nally (2009) focuses on the second type of neo-burlesque, which she refers to as subcultural or underground. This type of new burlesque seeks to force a shift in the audience, to rally behind the ugly or obscene, and most of all to critique what the audience might see on stage. There are also nerdlesque and queerlesque (though these are often academically understated) that tend to focus on the interweaving of parody, gender roles, sexuality, and popular culture (Sta kiewicz, 2017). These new performances have often had a specific intention to go beyond traditional forms of beauty by opening up space for different bodies (specifically fat and older-aged forms) and positionalities (race/physical ability) (Collard-Stokes, 2020; Ferreday, 2008; Giusti, 2012; Milbrodt, 2019). The focus on this chapter is on the subcultural form in the modern context, where nerd and queer are often engaged with each other to produce a specific lived experience that is brought to the stage in Atlanta, USA.

Feminist research has often debated whether these modes of dance were feminist or not anti-feminist (aka exploitative). Some compared it to sex work (although many burlesque dancers themselves would argue against that idea) or discussed how it (especially retro burlesque) reinforced harmful ideas about femininity. Ulrika Dahl (2014) brings in race analysis, arguing that this retro style often directly affirms whiteness. It is also notable that these are often apolitical examinations (rather, they considered them apolitical). More recently, scholars have turned to the idea of examining burlesque through a queer lens (Nally, 2009; Regehr, 2012; Siebler, 2015). The queer lens often focuses on the motivations behind dances, most often the idea of gender storytelling through bodily performances. Laura Winkiel (2005) talks about gender play as a longstanding theme in burlesque. She describes English suffragettes burlesque performance as a "combination of expressive sexuality and freedom from bourgeois restraint" that "created a threatening female figure." Annie Blanchette (2014) focuses not simply on gender, but the importance of time in framing how cultural norms of the past, present, and future may disrupt norms to create new forms of queer identity. However, many of these scholars speak most intentionally about breakdown of binary gender norms but with a focus on the inherent sexuality of performers.

In this chapter, the authors extend and build upon the above body of work, specifically in regard to spatiality and race, and argue that many of these works do not focus enough on the ways that performers (and their created performances) go beyond sexuality or sexual titillation. They often do not assess the inherent and explicit political messaging being practiced by some modern burlesque performers, nor do they contend with the spatiality inherent in performance venues. In her work, Sherril Dodds (2013) argues that we need to explore whether or not change occurs beyond the act of performance. This chapter shifts the focus of this question to ask instead a series of spatial questions such as – what happens in the site of the performance, what does the audience take with them, and who benefits from these kinds of ephemeral world makings. The authors argue that performances are a kind of placemaking that inherently transcend the stage. This placemaking is ephemeral and becomes durable within the psyches of the oppressed in the examples of Atlanta's Metropolitan Studios and FAMU's Marching 100.

Metropolitan Studios

Introduction and Background

This section examines the goals and attitudes of the performers in the Metropolitan Studios in East Atlanta, Georgia, USA. The research focus of one of the authors of this chapter is based on queer Atlanta, where there is an emergent queer spatial practice and fierce dedication to left-leaning political values. These values and practices create a particular progressive and transformative spatiality for those involved. The bar, stage, and audience work together to relationally create a transgressive and queer space that not only forecasts a more just world but brings that world into being for a temporary time. The authors provide details about the lack of permanent physical gathering spaces for queer persons in Atlanta, as well as rental locations for dance studios. To gather data for this section, one of the authors spent over one hundred hours of observation and conducted interviews with thirty-five out of forty study participants, all in a period of a four-month residency in Atlanta.

The Metropolitan Studios became an ephemeral gathering hub because of the historical context of Atlanta itself, wherein the former gay urban core was dispersed due to gentrification. Throughout the 1970s and 1980s, the urban core of Atlanta, particularly the Midtown gayborhood, flourished as a queer haven with low property values and a high renter population. Eventually, mass gentrification would push many, mostly lower-income queer persons, away to the surrounding metropolitan area. Mass displacement occurred around the time of the 1996 Olympics as the city officials sought to "clean up" the inner-city areas, transforming them into tourist-friendly and clean corporate environments. This would continue well into the present day. Without a dedicated "queer establishment" outside of the remaining gay bars most of the LGBTQ relied upon in-home or ephemeral gatherings, such as house parties or events such as the annual PRIDE parade or Dragoncon to flourish. Metropolitan Studios acted to fill this dearth of permanent dwellings.

Metropolitan Studios was established in 2016 by three queer women who sought to uplift marginalized communities by providing an accessible community space. Although they have moved from location to location (demonstrating the dispersed precarious nature of physical locations) the Metropolitan Studios is currently located in East Atlanta, close to the heart of the city and within one of the most heavily gentrified neighborhoods in the metro area. After finally getting their own location, they expanded upon their mission as not simply a burlesque school but instead providing a central location for women entrepreneurs, private event space for community artists, as well as a craft space and dance hall. Metropolitan Studios hosts various pop-ups, rehearsals, self-defense classes, and seminars for women-owned businesses, as well as posing classes for plus-size models.

Metropolitan Studios and their related burlesque shows were often cited as part of the queer community. Featured in a 2019 edition of *Q Magazine*, a queer Atlanta magazine, Metropolitan Studios owners and performers, state as their ultimate goal the idea of LGBTQ empowerment (Fleming, 2019). Talloolah Love, an owner and instructor, argues that burlesque allows performers the most freedom, as they are no longer being filtered and limited by scripts or the people in charge (who she describes as often being white cisgender and straight males). According to her, burlesque provides performers with a sense of autonomy, as they are free to express what they most wish to express. Talloolah considers grassroots burlesque as "about the politics of our naked (or almost naked) bodies telling our stories without that placated filter of the masses" (Fleming, 2019, p. 23). For performers like Talloolah, burlesque is about telling a queer story, even when that story is otherwise considered outside the heteronorm.

The need for space has always been well understood by the proponents of the studio itself. Through the use of language, Metropolitan Studios expresses an awareness of the need for safe space among participants, particularly in marginalized groups. Metropolitan Studios actively pushes progressive messages and are aware of how their political sentiments influence and contour the spaces they inhabit. Their goal is explicitly spatial, in that they are seeking to create inclusive and safe space. This is how they express this goal in their mission statement:

> Through identifying the importance of artistic self-expression, representation of marginalized communities, and the need for an inclusive and safe space for individuals; Metropolitan Studios was born. Celebrating diverse artists and makers, Metropolitan Studios is so much more than just a studio - it is an artistic haven.

This mission statement indicates that even the very creation of their dance studio acted as a response to the needs of the marginalized that otherwise may not have locations to gather. They wish to give voice to those whose viewpoints might otherwise be left out of the traditional burlesque community. What emerges is a particular set of spatial practices, where dancers and audience members form community ties and find validation in shared, temporary locations.

Metro Studios' Placemaking and Performances

These acts speak to the very bodily performative aspect of placemaking, wherein bodies actively pursue the act of transformative and transgressive space. Along these lines, another performer – Coco Rose – stated in *Q Magazine* (Fleming, 2019, p. 23) that burlesque cannot be oversimplified as "little more than glorified stripping" but that it is instead "about reclaiming society's objectification of women." For her own part, she seeks to demonstrate to the audience that she is not simply a person of color or sex worker or marketing gimmick, but "a black woman that has a story to tell who has embraced her sexuality, curves and taken her power back" (Fleming, 2019, p. 23). Burlesque, for Coco Rose, is about empowerment, about demonstrating her own power in a world that might otherwise be unjust. Again, the thread of storytelling emerges as well. For many such performers there is a bodily engagement with place (and the audiences therein) that explicitly tells a story about themselves in worlds, both real and imagined, often fantastical. These stories then become transgressive, taking audiences on a journey where they may experience an affective attachment along the way.

The Candybox Revue (CR), the burlesque dance group most often associated with Metropolitan Studios, specifically choreographs dances that are filled with contemporary political meaning. For instance, at the 2019 Americana Burlesque and Sideshow Festival the CR took inspiration from the recent #metoo movement. Their choreography has women in dingy white nightgowns, wearing rainbow shorts underneath, being grabbed by men in all black. The woman center stage (Roula Roulette) struggles to push them off as the other women on stage hide their faces, barely visible on the dark stage. She pushes forward, foisting the men off and raising a fist before being grabbed once more. Finally, she throws the men to the ground and continues her own dance. No amount of grabbing can stop the woman. Even as the men push her to the ground, she always manages to stumble away. A struggle is displayed, where the men eventually find themselves unable to control the feminine form in front of them. One by one, they are dismissed from the scene, sometimes gently, sometimes roughly, leaving only the women who then proceed to remove their dingy white garb, finally showing the rainbow shorts and pride-colored halter tops. As they do, the stage brightens and the audience finally clearly sees the faces of the women. The women smile and hug one another before joining hands and raising a fist as the scene closes out. The political messaging in this performance is clear – people that are femme-bodied often deal with various male figures holding them down.

The choice of venue is also a political one that involves considerations of participant safety. Bonnie Bodacious, a bisexual woman and member of the CR, explains that there are explicit discussions about creating and protecting queer spaces, especially when picking a venue. Although there are often limited choices in explicitly queer establishments, they make efforts to invite their community to locations where they can feel welcome. In many cases, they assess whether a location is acceptable for their particular community by discussing with the owners of the business itself. In this process, Bonnie explains that her organization tends to look for owners that are communicative and respectful. When owners do not give off the particular vibe the burlesque troupe is looking for, they do not waste time dealing with that establishment. Bonnie describes this as a process of "weeding out any place that is going to be explicitly queer-rejecting." For Bonnie, and those that attended burlesque shows, burlesque became a means of changing existing spaces into queer ones (personal interview, 24 July 2019). What is often explicit to the in-group of queers within the audience is often missed by those not within that group. Although not all burlesque is considered "queer" and not all performers are LGBTQ, several recent pushes within burlesque have contributed to a relatively strong queer community in the Atlanta scene coalescing around Metropolitan Studios.

The very act of performance becomes a political act tied inherently to space, particularly in regard to the creation of queer space. An important example of queer ephemeral placemaking occurs within the burlesque community as they change bar scenes themselves. Bonnie, both a queer woman and burlesque performer, describes the role of her revue (the Candybox Revue) in this process. She names the Red Light Café, a live music venue in Midtown, and Smith's Old Bar, another bar and music venue in downtown Atlanta as locations that are not explicitly queer unless their troupe are hosting an event. On discussing queerness, she says that "everywhere we go in masse becomes a queer inclusive space, and a pretty vocally queer and queer-inclusive space (personal interview, 24 July 2019)." This relates to their overt political goals but also on how a location can be queer in some moments and not-queer in other moments. When the burlesque troupe performs there, these locations become queer for a night as these dancers and their audience members 'take over' the bar.

Implicit Activism

Metropolitan Studios engages in various implicitly political actions, particularly when it comes to body positivity and inclusiveness. All throughout their website and events, there is a verbalized commitment to body acceptance. A prominent example is their logo, which displays many different women, all with diverse body types. Additionally, their classes state that they are for all body types and that they seek to promote an environment that helps participants feel good about their body. Statements owners and instructors indicate that all bodies are beautiful and hold within them the power to tell a story. These stories extend to the performers and dance students who come to terms with their own bodies, often having dealt with fatphobia or ageism in their daily lives.

Another thread of this body acceptance is that of affirming all women, including the LGBTQ spectrum. The studio offers the 'Sexify' class, a class that teaches sensual movement in dance that is specifically women-only. According to their website "Sexify is an LGBTQ+ affirming womxn's fitness class" that is intended to help those who do not identify as man/men to help feel attractive and confident.

Explicit Activism

Performers affiliated with Metropolitan Studios use their performances as a method of discussing topical political movements, to create a space, and to use the body to tell a story. Metropolitan Studios foregrounds "activism through art" in both their community engagement and burlesque performances, particularly through ensuring activist concerns directly influencing many of the dances. Often this does come out in the styling and choreography of the performance itself. In a 2019 show, the Candybox Revue dancers wear long-sleeved black shirts with such words as – babe, whore, object, bitch, girl, slut – until the end of the dance, where they remove their shirts to reveal shirts reading "human." Another example is from Bonnie Bodacious (personal interview, 24 July 2019) who described how she recently wore corporate logos all over her body and skin. As part of her act, she slowly undressed to remove these logos, thereby freeing herself from capitalist influences. Both examples reveal the ways in which overt leftist politics come out in their performances directly.

They serve as a hub for various political events in Atlanta. Importantly, they acted as a community hub during the Black Lives Matter protests occurring all over Atlanta in summer 2020. Propelled by the political urgency about black lives, Metropolitan Studios jumped into action, calling upon volunteers within their sphere to organize ride-sharing during the protests, as well as picking people up who might be in danger of wrongful arrests during police kettling. Throughout this time, they also served as a donation center through the various protests, including one at Freedom Park only a few minutes' walk from their current East Atlanta location. They also opened their studio to act as a childcare center, with babysitters who could watch the children of those going to protests. Their doors were also open to anyone stranded in need of crash space, a hot shower, food, water, as well as a place to charge their phone.

These activist efforts extend outside of the bars and entertainment venues as well, to the digital presence of the studio and to their efforts in the community. Metropolitan Studios, along with the Atlanta Theatre Artists for Justice, hosted an artist market and fundraiser seeking to "Paint Georgia Blue" in the 2020 runoff election and donated $1,500 to the Raphael Warnock and Jon Ossoff campaigns for the US Senate seats in Georgia, as well as to Daniel Blackman's campaign for the state's public service commission. As part of this event, they also had people on-site to sign up volunteers for the election. They also hosted various Dykes on Bikes meetings that discussed upcoming PRIDE Parade and biking activities. All these decisions about community engagement reinforce the idea that certain people (namely queer and PoC individuals) are welcome and accepted by the burlesque community. They seek to demonstrate the political orientation of the organizers and dancers. They reinforce the activist goals that are otherwise carried by the performers' bodies on stage.

Burlesque performers, and others spearheading queer place-making, demonstrate an awareness of the power their shows hold. It is a well-understood and active goal among participants, not simply virtual-signaling mission statements. This is reinforced by having not only a large number of LGBTQ-representing performers, but also in the events organized themselves. The performers of Metropolitan Studio are aware of their direct impact on spaces around them and intentionally utilize mobility to navigate different otherwise heteronormative venues.

Affirmative Racial Politics: FAMU Performances as Sites of Black Affirmation and Anti-Black Resistance

Like the queer performances of Metropolitan Studios, FAMU's band performances demonstrate how performances can transform entertainment and performance spaces and engage in subtle, but powerful, racial politics. This section analyses the socio-cultural politics of performances by bands in the FAMU Music Department and is grounded in over 800 hours of embedded observation and over 40 in-depth interviews conducted by the second author of this chapter.[2] These interviews explored faculty, student, and alumni understandings of their performances in relation to race and place, and they reveal how FAMU's performances, even though they are often not explicit about politics and race, nonetheless are intended to have an impact on how society understands Blackness and place. In addition, faculty, students, and alumni explained how the development of the FAMU bands and the construction of their performances are interconnected to historical and contemporary racial politics. FAMU's performances also demonstrate how cultural and racial politics influence the creation and development of entertainment and performance spaces, and how performances in these spaces, in turn, influence our understandings of cultural and racial politics.

---

[2] Names of students and alumni have been anonymized using pseudonyms chosen by the participants

FAMU is a public Historically Black College/University (HBCU) located in Tallahassee, Florida (USA), a mid-sized capital city that is home to both FAMU and a large Predominantly White Institution (PWI) Florida State University. One of FAMU's many claims to fame is the FAMU Marching 100, created and developed by Dr. William P. Foster in the 1940s. Under the baton of Dr. Foster, the Marching 100 and FAMU's associated concert bands gained national and international recognition for their high-performance standards and their unique style, which have become the standard across other HBCUs throughout the US. The Marching 100 has grown to become a major recruiting tool for FAMU and is often a kind of public ambassador for the school, representing the school in many high-profile functions. FAMU's bands have performed at presidential inaugurations, nationally televised events, and was even selected as the representative of the U.S.A. for France's 200th Bastille Day Parade in 1989. These performances often become sites to engage in subtle cultural and racial politics that challenge anti-Black stereotypes.

The rest of this section details FAMU performances as overt political sites of resistance, the intentional development of the FAMU Marching 100 as an organization for racial justice, and an analysis of how performances in 2015 by the FAMU Wind Symphony at Carnegie Hall in New York City and 2019 by the Marching 100 at the Tournament of Roses Parade in Pasadena, California continue this tradition into the present day through subtle, affirmational performance politics. Though some of these performances inspire more explicit political protest and participation, FAMU's band performances more often are subtle political performances that challenge anti-Black racism through a kind of affirmational, representational politics and claim space in historically and traditionally white coded music spaces.

Sites of Resistance: FAMU's Performances as Sites for overt Political Resistance

While their performances often intentionally shy away from overtly political stances or expressions, previous scholarship has demonstrated that their performances and style are themselves a kind of affirmative politics that expresses the inherent value of Black life and Black culture in the face of containment and erasure by white supremacy within society (Allen 2020; Allen and McCreary 2020). This is not to say that overt politics are not present in FAMU performances. Indeed, FAMU's performances are often sites of overt political activism and campaigning, even if these are not engaged in by the musicians themselves.

FAMU's pre-game performances provide opportunities to transform the entertainment space of the American football field and stadium into a site of political action and Black placemaking. Pre-Game performances before football games, for example, are organized differently at HBCUs than at PWIs. While nearly all bands perform the US National Anthem ("Star Spangled Banner") before games, HBCUs, like FAMU, often perform "Lift Every Voice and Sing", written by James Weldon Johnson and often referred to as the Black National Anthem, directly before playing the US National Anthem. This intentional organization of music illustrates what Du Bois (1903) called double consciousness, that is, the struggle to reconcile the experiences and identity of being both Black and American. This performance celebrates Blackness with the Black National Anthem while also asserting Black belonging in the American citizenry and body politic. The connection of these two musical pieces (not so) subtly put in tension Black communities belonging to an American nation with the historical and contemporary treatment of Black communities by that nation.

This performance is not only a subtle assertion of the double consciousness but also opens interesting opportunities for Black spectators to engage in overt political activism. During many of the performances the second author witnessed, for example, FAMU spectators took the opportunity to protest the US National Anthem in solidarity Colin Kaepernick, a professional football player that had been the target of anti-Black attacks for his own protest of kneeling during the pre-game singing of the US anthem. The unique performance style of playing the Black National Anthem followed immediately by the US National Anthem provided a site and opportunity to protest Black experiences of discrimination and anti-Black violence in the US. Spectators stood and sang along with the Black National Anthem as FAMU's Marching 100 played, but many immediately sat down or turned their back as the US National Anthem began (See Image 1). This transforms the entertainment space designed for football games and marching band performances into a space of political activism, a stage to protest anti-Black police brutality, to stand (or sit) in solidarity with Kaepernick against the white rage[3] backlash to his non-violent protest of kneeling during the US National Anthem, and to express Black experiences of racism in the US.

The simple, but deliberate and powerful, act of sitting during the US National Anthem after participating in the Black National Anthem asserts a Black vision of America, one that displays its anti-Black racism and one that protests the extrajudicial killing of Black men and women by the police, Kaepernick's original motivation. It turns the musical selection into a space of political and civil refusal for Black spectators. These spectators use their agency to refuse to participate in the civil religion of patriotically honoring a country where police

---

[3] Carol Anderson (2016, p. 4) has discussed white rage as a way to punish Blackness "that refuses to accept subjugation," a kind of white backlash (whitelash) that is often a subtle, non-violent way of changing the narrative away from social justice activism and avoiding accountability for anti-Black racism.

killings appear to continue unabated. Furthermore, the second author saw a marked increase over time in the number of spectators participating in these protests after Kaepernick began suffering further and further consequences for his non-violent act. While a number of spectators joined Kaepernick at the initial stage of his protests, the number significantly grew in the 2017 football season after the backlash (or whitelash) he received from Donald Trump and white communities across the country (Serwer, 2017). Additionally, this politics of refusal by Black spectators asserts a Black vision of place that seeks to highlight the experiences of anti-Black racism experienced by Black people in the US. It also seeks to unveil the white supremacy endemic in America; a white American nationalism that would rather ignore, erase from memory, and/or contain spatially and historically Black experiences of racism rather than acknowledge them.

FAMU performances also engage directly with elections and campaigning, becoming sites to encourage civic participation and even sites to highlight particular candidates. For example, as Florida elections were approaching in 2018 the FAMU Marching band staged a performance where they reminded people to vote by spelling out "VOTE" on the field. In another example, FAMU's Homecoming often includes politicians and people running for office as part of the festivities. These explicit election campaigning activities are so deeply intertwined with homecoming parade activities that they seem like a natural part of the parade, almost like a celebration of their candidacy or political status rather than electioneering. Indeed, many of these politicians are Black and alumni of FAMU itself. While the fans and spectators for the FAMU homecoming parade are mainly there to see the FAMU Marching 100 and the FAMU Marching 100 Alumni Band perform near the end of the parade, these campaign/celebration stops by politicians are important political activities that remind their constituents to vote and whom to vote for in the election. These political activities are often supplemented by voting suffrage activism. During homecoming, for example, the second author observed individuals canvassing for a petition to allow recently released individuals convicted of felonies to have their voting rights restored. In this sense, FAMU performance spaces, because of their ability to attract large numbers of the Black community to a single event, become premier sites to campaign and canvas for political purposes.

Being Part of the Difference: The Influence of Racial Politics on the Marching 100

Though members of FAMU bands rarely participate in outright political activities themselves, the bands and their performances were historically developed with intention and in direct response to racial politics within the US. Indeed, Dr. William P. Foster's decision to create a renowned, unique Marching Band and performance style at an HBCU developed through his own experiences with segregation and discrimination while getting his Bachelor of Music Education at the University of Kansas in the late 1930s and early 1940s. While enrolled at the university, he was routinely reminded of the dearth of Black band directors in the US. While in the dean's office Dr. Foster indicated he wanted to be a conductor and was promptly advised to "rethink that" because "there are no jobs for colored conductors" (Foster, 2016, p. 24). Dr. Foster marks this as the motivation to "develop a band that would be better than any white band in the country" in order to "disprove his [dean's] assertion" (p. 24). Thus, he created and developed at FAMU an energetic, unique performance style that was adopted across the country by HBCUs and has even been influential in many PWIs as well.

Dr. Foster noted that while the FAMU Marching 100 gained national recognition during the 1960s, the nation was in the midst of "years of turmoil and change" as civil rights activists fought against segregation and discrimination (Foster, 2016, p. 92). He described the Marching 100 as a "forerunner of the desired change" in the country and directly connected the Civil Rights Movement's fight against discrimination to the Marching 100's own goals and performances. While the Marching 100 was gaining in notoriety at this time, for example, Dr. Foster noted that to many white communities, the Marching 100 was still just another "Negro band" that "better know our place and stay in it" (p. 94). The Marching 100, in other words, in spite of its notoriety and fame, and despite their largely apolitical performances (explicitly at least) was still a target of the racial politics of white supremacy.

Thus, Dr. Foster positioned the band's performances as a response and even resistance to white racial politics during the Civil Rights era. Some of these were more explicit, such as the performances following President John F. Kennedy's 1963 assassination. Remembered by Dr. Foster as a leader that provided hope to Black communities, he and the FAMU band took President Kennedy's death hard and used their final two performances of that year as stages in which to remember and mourn the assassinated president. Most of the subsequent performances were more subtle about their engagement with racial politics. For example, following the 1968 assassination of Dr. Martin Luther King Jr., a prominent Black civil rights leader, Dr. Foster reflected upon Dr. King's values and his importance for Black people in the US: "He spoke for me. He marched for me. In the end he gave his life for me" (Foster, 2016, p. 95). Following Dr. King's death, Dr. Foster noted that "good people of all races stood together for justice" and to "make a difference in this country." Directly connecting the Marching 100's performances to this socio-political goal, Dr. Foster said he "wanted the 'Hundred' to be a part of that difference. I wanted my staff to work even harder. I wanted our performances to be even better than they had been" (Foster, 2016, p. 96).

This deliberate connection of FAMU performances to racial politics and discrimination has continued through all performances by the FAMU bands. In the face of deep segregation within Tallahassee and a long history of focusing the city's attention on FSU at the expense of FAMU, the Marching 100's performances provide moments of celebration that transform the city into a place that affirms FAMU and Black communities within the city. Students and Black residents of Tallahassee, in particular, view these performances as opportunities to challenge negative stereotypes about Black people and as sites from which to express Black excellence and Black culture (Allen, 2020; Allen & McCreary, 2020). Two examples demonstrate how FAMU's performances continue to maintain the elements of engagement in racial politics advocated by Dr. Foster. They are the FAMU's Wind Symphony performance at Carnegie Hall in New York City in 2015 and the Marching 100's selection and performance in the 2019 Tournament of Roses Parade in Pasadena, California. Both demonstrate how FAMU's performances are positioned as responses to anti-Black discrimination as well as a resistance to that discrimination through affirmative politics.

Tournament of Roses and Carnegie Hall Performance: Sites for Affirmative Racial Politics and Challenge to anti-Black Stereotypes

In 2019 the FAMU Marching 100 traveled across the country to represent FAMU, Tallahassee, and Florida in the Tournament of Roses Parade in Pasadena, California. This nationally televised event accentuated the Marching 100's return to high-profile music events on the national stage. This performance held a plethora of important meanings for Marching 100 alumni, the current staff, FAMU students, Marching 100 members, and the Tallahassee Black community as well. Indeed, this performance was infused with a heightened importance due to the incredible hard work and struggle the Marching 100 staff and students had endured since the Marching 100 was banned in 2011, following the national captivation with the hazing death of a Marching 100 drum major. Thus, this performance was widely seen as an opportunity to change negative narratives solidified in society about FAMU and the Marching 100, and to amplify an affirmative counter-narrative.

In 2011, following a performance at the Florida Classic in Orlando, Florida, Marching 100 Drum Major, Robert Champion, died from a hazing initiation. The event sent shockwaves throughout the HBCU band world, the Black music scene more broadly, and held national news reporters captivated for years. The fallout from this incident led to the resignation of FAMU President James H. Ammons and Marching 100 Director Dr. Julian White, along with much of the Marching 100 staff. These resignations, however, were not enough to completely save the program. The band was suspended for 22 months, and only after much debate and criticism allowed to restart activities in a limited fashion in 2013 (Montgomery, 2012). Slowly and deliberately, the new directors, Dr. Sylvester

Young and later Dr. Shelby Chipman, rebuilt the Marching 100 and its standard of excellence. It is in this context that the selection to perform in the 2019 Tournament of Roses Parade gained increased importance. Students and staff positioned this performance as an opportunity to return to their role as a leading HBCU and Marching band in the US.

Cognizant of the negative reputation the Marching 100 gained after the hazing incident, FAMU students expressed disappointment over it, and affirmed their commitment to countering the negative stereotypes that grew thereafter. Vanessa Thompson, for example, states the Black people are often stereotyped as "being more aggressive and...being thugs" (personal interview, 14 February 2018) and the hazing incident made that issue worse. Many students expressed that they felt that FAMU had become known lately only for the hazing incident and that it began to overshadow the positive work being done and the Black excellence being exhibited daily at the university and in the band. Just as they are trying to "move forward," Denzel, a FAMU M100 student, says, when you "pull up the Marching 100...the hazing incident is the first thing you are going to see" (personal interview, 10 November 2017). This consistent and durable narrative of hazing was important to counter for students and staff at FAMU as they prepared for the Tournament of Roses Parade.

Though FAMU Marching 100 members rarely said much publicly about using Pasadena as a site for asserting a counter-narrative, students privately and through in-group conversations frequently discussed the performance as an opportunity to change the narrative. "Doing these big performances," Denzel claimed, "can show progress that has been going on" and could be an opportunity to "get our name back" (personal interview, 10 November 2017). They saw it as an opportunity to demonstrate that they are still great musicians and part of a great marching band. It was a way to shift the narrative from hazing to music, to attempt to replace narratives centering Black suffering and violence surrounding the hazing incident with counter-narratives of Black excellence.

This example demonstrates how performances offer opportunities beyond the immediate site and entertainment value and are often influenced by cultural and racial politics that are not readily evident at first glance. To many that watched the Marching 100 in the Tournament of Roses Parade, it was a brilliant performance by an amazing (Black) marching band. For FAMU students and alumni, however, it was a performance infused with racial politics and context. Despite not explicitly naming those influences in their performance, the performance represents an attempt at a subtle affirmative politics that challenges anti-Black stereotypes by performing a counter-narrative of Black excellence.

Similarly, students expressed that their 2015 performance at Carnegie Hall in New York City was an important opportunity to demonstrate Black excellence and claim traditional sites of whiteness for Black musicians and Black representation in the classical/symphonic music world. While the Pasadena performance was largely centered on changing narratives around the FAMU Marching 100, students viewed their 2015 Carnegie Hall performance as more broadly challenging anti-Black stereotypes within the broader musician culture. Their selection and performance on the hallowed stage at Carnegie Hall, a crowning achievement for most musicians, was set within a broader racial context and historical stereotypes that students were, again, explicitly aware of as they discussed this performance. This is framed by Alex Franklin when he states: "Playing at Carnegie Hall is a big deal no matter what skin tone you are, but it's a bigger deal when it's us" (personal interview, 4 December 2017).

Symphonic/classical music has traditionally been positioned as an incredibly white aesthetic (Ross, 2020), a positioning that often obscures the contributions and participation of Black musicians. As Ross (2020) states, "classical music is a world in which Black people have seldom been allowed to play a leading role." Ultimately, he concludes that the symphonic/classical music world is "blindingly white, both in its history and its present" despite Black participation as listeners, musicians, and composers. This is a sentiment experienced by many Black musicians at FAMU as well. FAMU M100 student, Alex Franklin, for example, states that "music is definitely a white space…[especially] when you step inside of classical music" (personal interview, 4 December 2017). Students also discussed how this whiteness, particularly of symphonic music, is combined with a kind of Black containment to particular genres. "For African Americans…it feels like it's almost limited to rap, hip hop, R&B, jazz," says John Hudson (personal interview, 8 October 2017), and Bob spatialized this sentiment saying that "if it's not jazz settings like clubs or jazz festivals, there's not many doorways and not many opportunities for us to actually insert ourselves into those spaces" (personal interview, 30 November 2017).

This containment of Black musical participation, facilitated by Black erasure from symphonic spaces, creates representational gaps for young Black musicians. While FAMU students all express things like "music should be meant for everyone" (Carl Thanos, personal interview, 12 December 2017), they acknowledge that the reality is that music as a profession and music spaces are often incredibly white and unwelcoming to marginalized communities. "We always say that music is a universal language," says Alex, "but when someone else starts to speak it, we're looked at funny" (Alex Franklin, personal interview, 4 December 2017).

This marginalization plays out within concert spaces despite being in areas that are predominantly Black. Courtney Andrews, for example, discussed a time when she watched five different bands play in Atlanta and did not see a single Black oboe player, thus encouraging her to take up the instrument to add Black representation and be an inspiration for other young kids (Interview, 12 November 2017). Carl Thanos echoes this lack of representation, stating that "when you look at really good ensembles, you think of a Chicago Symphony Orchestra...and you rarely see African Americans in those ensembles" (personal interview, 12 December 2017), an observation that is supported by the fact that only one musician in the orchestra as of 2021 is Black. This lack of representation positions symphonic bands and stages known for classical / symphonic music as spaces of whiteness.

This is the context in which FAMU students understood their performance at Carnegie Hall, a premiere concert venue for symphonic performances. FAMU's selection and performance at Carnegie Hall, for FAMU students, challenged the whiteness of the symphonic musical world and claimed a traditionally white coded space for the purpose of Black excellence. You do not typically see "African Americans play on that kind of performance stage," Carl Thanos says, "but...I definitely see, you know, white people traditionally in those kind of settings" (personal interview, 12 December 2017). Vanessa Thompson helps frame this lack of representation as a whiteness problem rather than a Black musician ability issue. "I don't think we haven't been there previously because of talent" Vanessa explained, but "because it was typically white performance stage" (Vanessa Thompson, personal interview, 14 February 2018). This is not to say that Carnegie Hall only has white performers. On the contrary, many prominent Black performers like Billie Holliday, Louis Armstrong, Nina Simone, and Wynton Marsalis have performed there. It is that these performances are aberrations that prove the rule that, as Vanessa said, "it was a typically white performance stage."

Students, like Michael Johnson, framed their Carnegie performance as a way of challenging the anti-Black stereotypes that marginalize Black participation in symphonic performances. "There's a pride in getting to Carnegie Hall, in beating out your predominantly white competition" says Michael. "It's a way of saying we're undeniable" (personal interview, 30 November 2017). "It just shows how great we are," adds Osi Hernandez, "how we stand in without being swayed left or right by stereotypes or what people have to say" (personal interview, 2 February 2018). Courtney Andrews sums up this pride and purpose of the Carnegie Hall performance by stating that FAMU students like her take pride that their performance was "a step, a tiny step, but one step forward to people understanding that music is diversified" and that Black ensembles like the FAMU Wind Symphony are out here performing symphonic music at a high level (personal interview, 12 November 2017).

The FAMU Wind Symphony Performance at Carnegie Hall in 2015, then, was a performance intended by students to dispel anti-Black stereotypes perceived and experienced within the symphonic music world. It served as a way of challenging the white symphonic space and the Black containment of musical expression by defying that containment and claiming Carnegie Hall for the expression of Black musical excellence, at least for that temporary time. Students and staff were never explicit in public about the way their performance challenged anti-Black racism, but their comments and understanding of their performance demonstrate that it held an implicit racial and political message. They sought to affirm Black presence in the symphonic world and prominently claim a typically white space to inspire future generations of Black musicians.

With their performances in Pasadena and Carnegie, as well as numerous performances across Tallahassee, Florida every year, FAMU's various bands affirm Black presence and challenge anti-Black racism. They claim and transform entertainment spaces into spaces of resistance and affirmation. From the inception of the FAMU bands to contemporary performances, FAMU's students and staff continue a long, important legacy of engaging in cultural and racial politics through performance.

Conclusion

In this chapter, the authors examined the placemaking efforts of Atlanta's Metropolitan Studios and Tallahassee's Marching 100. Both groups struggled to find a place for themselves within the normative society (particularly white and heteronormative), and instead were forced to create their own ephemeral spaces. As they did, they often transformed normative sites into ones that reinforced the visions and political agendas of their given communities. For the Metropolitan Studios this occurred both in terms of how they designed performances with explicit and implicit messaging around body positivity, inclusion, and gender, and also in how they used their physical location to act as a prominent hub during the Black Lives Matter protests of 2020. Similarly, the FAMU Marching 100 intentionally addressed racial politics, and resisted white supremacy through the use of performances that highlighted counter-storytelling, albeit in a rather subtle manner. Inundated with negative narratives, Marching 100 members see their performances as re-branding the band with more positive press. In addition, the FAMU Wind Symphony's performance at Carnegie Hall is viewed by students as a claiming of the traditionally white space of the concert stage in order to amplify affirmative narratives of Blackness. These performances by Metropolitan Studios and the FAMU bands highlight the political potential of performances and performance spaces, and they foreground a sense of what a queer or Black world might look like, thus becoming potent cognitive realities for those in attendance.

The study of ephemeral performances that engage in remaking performance and entertainment spaces demonstrate how cultural politics (queer and racial) provide context for such performances. Whether explicit or implicit, these performances are direct challenges to oppressive articulations of space and society. They affirm the lives (and ways of life) of queer and racially marginalized communities. Such performances seek to project more affirmative counter-narratives into society and display more inclusive, justice-oriented articulations of space and performance.

Future studies looking at these issues can continue to expand upon the ways that marginalized communities resist oppression but also how these performances do not require particular incidents of oppression to be powerful statements of life. Black and queer performances, often, can simply be about finding joy in music and dance, and while such ostensibly apolitical performances are not directly intended to address marginalization, these performances continue to have importance for scholars and society.

References

Allen, A. (2020). Asserting a Black vision of race and place: Florida A&M University's homecoming as an affirmative, transgressive claim of place. *Geoforum, 111*, 62–72.

Allen, D., Lawhon, M., & Pierce, J. (2019). Placing race: On the resonance of place with black Geographies. *Progress in Human Geography, 43*(6), 1001–1019.

Allen, D., & McCreary, T. (2020). Performing Black life: The FAMU Marching 100 and the Black aesthetic politics of disruption, presence and affirmation. *Cultural Geographies, 28*(1), 41–55.

Anderson, C. (2016). *White Rage: The Unspoken Truth of Our Racial Divide*. New York: Bloomsbury Publishing.

Baldwin, M. *Burlesque and the New Bump-n-Grind*. Denver, CO: Speck Press, 2004.

Blanchette, A. (2014). Revisiting the "passée": history rewriting in the neo-burlesque community. *Consumption Markets & Culture, 17*(2), 158–184.

Buszek, M. (1996). Representing "Awarishness": Burlesque, Femininst Transgression, and the 19th-Century Pin-up. *The Drama Review, 43*(4), 141–162.

Cofield, R. 2021. Queer Urban Space Beyond the Gayborhood: Sexuality, Gentrification, and Displacement in Atlanta. [Doctoral dissertation, Florida State University]. ProQuest Dissertations Publishing.

Collard-Stokes, G. (2020). Recreational burlesque and the aging female body: challenging Perceptions. *Journal of Women & Aging*, 1–15. Online First. https://doi.org/10.1080/08952841.2020.1839319

Dahl, U. (2014). White gloves, feminist fists: race, nation and the feeling of 'vintage' in femme movements. *Gender, Place and Culture, 21*(5), 604–621.

Dodds, S. (2013). Embodied Transformations in Neo-Burlesque Striptease. *Dance Research Journal, 45*(3), 75–90.

du Bois, W. E. B. (1903). *The Souls of Black Folk: Modernity and Double Consciousness*. London: Verso.

Ferreday, D. (2008). 'Showing the girl': The new burlesque. *Feminist Theory*, 9(1), 47–65.

Fleming, M. (2019, February). Queer Burlesque: The Women of Metropolitan Studios Show Us How They Vamp. *Q Magazine Atlanta*, 2(14). https://issuu.com/projectqatlanta/docs/q_mag_v2i14_022119_issuu

Foster, W. P. (2016). *The Man Behind the Baton: The Maestro, The Law, The Legend*. Charleston, SC: Advantage.

Gieseking, J. J. (2020). Mapping lesbian and queer lines of desire: Constellations of queer urban space. *Environment and Planning D: Society and Space*, 38(5), 941–960.

Guisti, J. 2012. "Burlesque Female Behemoths": Transgressions of Fat, Femme Burlesque. [Unpublished doctoral dissertation]. University of Minnesota.

Massey, D. (1991). A Global Sense of Place. *Marxism Today*, 24–29.

Massey, D. (2005). *For space*. Thousand Oaks, CA: Sage.

Milbrodt, T. 2019. Sexy Like Us Expanding Notions of Disability and Sexuality Through Burlesque Performance. *Journal of Literary & Cultural Disability Studies* 13(4), 377–392.

Montgomery, B. (2012, November 10). Recounting the deadly hazing that destroyed FAMU band's reputation. *Tampa Bay Times*. https://www.tampabay.com/news/humaninterest/recounting-the-deadly-hazing-that-destroyed-famu-bands-reputation/1260765/

Montgomery, T. (2019). Sexy Like Us Expanding Notions of Disability and Sexuality Through Burlesque Performance. *Journal of Literary & Cultural Disability Studies*, 13(4), 377–392.

Nally, C. (2009). Grrrly hurly burly: neo-burlesque and the performance of gender. *Textual Practice*, 23(4), 621–643.

Pierce, J., Martin, D. G., & Murphy, J. T. (2011). Relational place-making: the networked politics of place. *Transactions of the Institute of British Geographers*, 36(1), 54–70.

Regehr, K. 2012. The Rise of Recreational Burlesque: Bumping and Grinding Towards Empowerment. *Sexuality & Culture* 16, 134-157.

Rockwell, H. (1996). An 'Other' Burlesque: Feminine Bodies and Irigaray's Performing Textuality. *Body & Society*, 2(1), 65–89.

Ross, A. (2020, September 21). Black Scholars Confront White Supremacy in Classical Music. *The New Yorker*. https://www.newyorker.com/magazine/2020/09/21/black-scholars-confront-white-supremacy-in-classical-music

Sampatakakis, G. (2019). Bodies of truth: The terrible beauty of queer performance. *Journal of Greek Media & Culture*, 4(2), 255–267.

Serwer, A. (2017, September 23). Trump's War of Words with Black Athletes. *The Atlantic*. https://www.theatlantic.com/politics/archive/2017/09/trump-urges-nfl-owners-to-fire-players-who-protest/540897/.

Siebler, K. 2015. What's so feminist about garters and bustiers? Neo-burlesque as post- feminist. *Journal of Gender Studies* 24(5), 561-573.

Shepard, B. (2010). *Queer Political Performance and Protest: Play, Pleasure, and Social Movement*. New York: Routledge.

Solórzano, G., & Yosso, T. J. (2002). "Critical Race Methodology: Counter-Storytelling as an Analytical Framework for Education Research. *Qualitative Inquiry*, 8(1), 23–44.

Staśkiewicz, J. (2017). The new burlesque as an example of double-simulacrum. *Forum Socjologiczne, 8*, 111–122.

Stillwagon, R., & Ghaziani, A. (2019). Queer Pop-Ups: A Cultural Innovation in Urban Life. *City & Community, 18*(3), 874–895.

Troxell, N.D. (2007). Feminist Perspectives on Liberation and Exploitation: A Phenomenological Study of Performance. [Unpublished Master's Thesis]. University of New Orleans, New Orleans, USA. https://scholarworks.uno.edu/td/614

Waddell, T. (2013). Trickster-Infused Burlesque: Gender Play in the Betwixt and Between. *Australasian Drama Studies, 63*, 96–109.

Winkiel, L. (2004). Suffrage Burlesque: Modernist Performance in Elizabeth Robin's "The Convert". *Modern Fiction Studies, 50*(3), 270–294.

CHAPTER 11
Chile's *Nueva Canción* and the Pinochet Regime: Censoring political messages in music

Kelly Grenier

University of Kentucky, USA

Abstract

How does music gain political power, and under what circumstances are regimes motivated to censor political music? What are the consequences of that censorship? This chapter explores these questions using archived interviews and lyrics from artists who were a part of Chile's Nueva Canción movement, tracing the history of the movement's development, censorship, and subsequent evolution. To explore the process of music becoming explicitly political, this chapter begins with the work of Violeta Parra and traces Nueva Canción's development from its origins until the democratically elected regime of Salvador Allende. The author then offers evidence that the censorship from the military dictatorship of Augusto Pinochet that deposed Allende could have been motivated by the facts that songs from this movement appeared to critique the regime, and because they called for collective action. Finally, the chapter discusses the fact that even as Nueva Canción musicians endured censorship, imprisonment, and exile, they continued to pursue their art, modifying it to persist and prevail in the face of a brutal dictatorship and, in some cases, continuing to challenge the regime openly.

Keywords: Cultural censorship, Latin America, dictatorship, Nueva Canción, music movement

***

Introduction

The Nueva Canción (New Song) was a Chilean music movement that faced severe censorship under the military dictatorship of President Augusto

Pinochet. Known for its use of folk instruments, rhythms and lyrics promoting social justice, the music became intertwined with a leftist political movement Chile that led to the election of socialist president Salvador Allende in 1970, who was ultimately overthrown by Pinochet in a military coup in 1973. With lyrics both critical of the status quo, particularly as it related to marginalized communities, and calling for collective action against social inequalities, the music caught the attention of officials in the Pinochet regime, with dire consequences for many of the artists. During the Pinochet regime, some artists remained in Chile where they faced censorship, jail, or death. Others went into exile, where they could continue making music.

Though a tragic and often brutal story, this case study of Chile's Nueva Canción offers many insights to those seeking to understand political messages in music. The movement demonstrates that music is a versatile feature of human social organization, evoking emotional responses that serve to orient individuals in social and temporal contexts that may become explicitly political. Censorship theories tell us that political regimes may become threatened either from critiques of the regime or by collective action against the regime. What the Nueva Canción demonstrates is how art forms such as music are in the distinct position to offer a mix of both threats simultaneously by the critical messages they communicate and their collective organizing power.

This chapter explores the political messaging in the Nueva Canción by asking three questions: Why and how does a musical genre develop explicitly political messages? When would a regime seek to censor such messages? What becomes of the messengers under censorship? Relying on primary sources, this chapter first uses the lyrics of songs from the Nueva Canción movement and then archived interviews with Nueva Canción artists to understand what features of the music and musicians lead to their censorship, and the impact of censorship on the subsequent political messages of the music. These primary sources help to provide insights into the evolution of the Nueva Canción movement. There are two types of messages in the songs; messages that are critical of social conditions, and messages calling for change. With the emergence of these messages, the music of the Nueva Canción became an effective and malleable political tool used by artists that posed a threat to the ruling powers. The regime reacted to this threat by censoring artists, which led those artists either away from political music or more deeply into it. The archived interviews used in this chapter explore the effects of politically motivated artistic censorship on this particular musical movement.

This chapter finds that the Nueva Canción was not expressly political in its origins. However, what politicized the movement appears to be a combination of factors: (a) giving a new voice to the traditional stories of the rural, indigenous, and marginalized people; (b) encouraging the people's collective identity and communicating the injustices they have faced. Once these injustices were named, the music provided more explicitly activist musicians with the medium and platform to politicize the issues. The music both encouraged action against the government and criticized the policies and practices of the regime. For these reasons, the music was censored, and the artists who were not put to death were forced to modify their roles. Some remained in Chile as curators of culture, and re-focused on the traditional elements of the music, in some cases offering more subtle political messages, while others fled to exile and continued to be politically active through songs abroad.

The Politicization of the Nueva Canción

Music is a versatile feature of human social organization. Through song, individuals may disclose and share collective memories, personal feelings, and other emotions as well as communicate an identity to both in-group members and outsiders. (Eyerman & Jamison, 1998). Through its rhythm, melody, and instruments, music communicates with its audience in multiple ways, linking to past experiences and assumptions. From lullabies and fables to anthems and epics, music allows human beings to decide who they are and how to communicate their expression. These songs then may become artifacts that individuals are later able to place in a social context as well as in their own cogitation. This is what makes listeners nostalgic, sad, happy, or even angry when hearing certain tunes (Turino, 2008). The Nueva Canción was a movement that articulated an identity for marginalized groups in Chile and carried that message across the world. It grew and changed over several decades, transforming into a movement that had personal and political consequences.

In 1950s Chile, a poet and visual artist named Violeta Parra gave birth to the "new song" simply by collecting the voices of her country. Violeta Parra was a poet and songwriter, and also a painter and fiber artist, who sought to capture her country's beauty through her talents in those media (Verba, 2013), but she is also rightly considered an oral historian. In early 1952, Parra journeyed around the Chilean countryside on foot, equipped with her tape recorder and guitar (Blau, 2020; Vetter, 2017). Travelling to small villages in the interior of the country, she spoke to the elders about their community's folklore (Cabezes, 1977). In the process of her rural and indigenous cultural preservation efforts, Parra also communicated with rural musicians known as *cantores*. These musicians helped Parra piece together stories and songs largely forgotten by modern Chilean society (Fairley, 1984). By finding and recording these pieces, Parra preserved these artistic artifacts for future generations and brought awareness of these traditions to Chile's urban centers. As such, Parra is largely credited as the mother of Nueva Canción for her preservation efforts and her own musical compositions informed by the social conditions she observed.

At that point in Chile's history, the world was embroiled in the Cold War which encouraged Western imperialism to extend into new spheres of influence. This expansion diminished pride in, and production of, local identities (Becerra, 1978; Jara, 1984). Radio, television, and cinema all featured American music, soap operas, and movies, respectively (Jara, 1984). Through their soft power, American arts were beginning to form the hegemonic culture for Chileans. This type of commercialism may be perceived as a form of inauthenticity and even destructive to the traditional music in the Chilean culture (Trilling, 2009). The music that began with Parra revived traditional instruments and rhythms, which allowed for the pieces to portray a Chilean identity that was deeply personal to the people of Chile. Violeta Parra's reinterpretation of folk melodies, songs, themes, and sounds was invaluable to the preservation and resurgence of a Chilean identity communicated through recording traditional melodies, instruments, and themes of Chile.

Andean woodwind instruments such as the zampoñas and quena, and the stringed charango, were used by the artists associated with the Nueva Canción movement. The instruments were chosen to enrich the work and experiment with sounds (Becerra, 1978). However, the lyrics of these songs were equally powerful in challenging imperialism. In her song, "Arauco Tiene Una Pena (*Arauco has a Sorrow*)," Parra sang about the indigenous people of Chile. In the lyrics, she describes the marginalization that occurred first from Spanish colonizers and then from the privileged classes within Chile.

While traditional instruments and musical elements were a part of the folklore that Parra recorded and helped to reinterpret, the artists who joined the movement used all available instruments as tools to create the sound, and evoke the feelings, they desired. While the Andean instruments such as the quena were employed, so too were non-native instruments such as the guitar. "Cultured" music, as it was called by the artists, was another major artistic influence on the development of the Nueva Canción (Becerra, 1978). Cultured music is a term that references the music from European heritage that was considered the ideal in society and thus, more accessible to the audiences because they too were familiar with it. Considered essential to a proper musical education, this music was a remnant of Spanish imperialism deeply embedded into the culture. Some of the artists in the movement incorporated their classical training into their new works, combining with indigenous music in a manner that complemented each other. Since a large part of the Nueva Canción was about exposing the injustices of imperialism, it appears to be an anomaly to see imperialistic forms of music as a part of the genre. But, the new imperialism coming from the West was different from the older Spanish imperialism that was by this time embedded in Chile's broader culture. As such, it could not be completely disentangled from the movement. Thus, while the Nueva Canción was critiquing historical and contemporary imperial structures, some of those same imperial structures were also embedded in the movement itself, because of the training and tastes of the musicians who came to be involved with the music. The messaging of the Nueva Canción allowed for two potentially contradictory artistic spaces to merge into one.

As the following quote demonstrates, for artists like Sergio Ortega, such a merge was unavoidable, as instruments did not belong to any culture, but to humanity as a whole:

Los instrumentos son patrimonio universal. Nosotros podíamos usar sin problemas la guitarra, un instrumento árabe-español; el arpa, un instrumento europeo; el piano, otro instrumento europeo. ¿Por qué no entonces todos los demás? Ahora bien: en la música no hay técnicas autóctonas. La música es el esfuerzo de millones de hombres de todos los tiempos y de todas las latitudes. El retraso de nuestra música durante todo un siglo se debe a este afán particular de creer que su contenido y su forma se contaminaban utilizando otros instrumentos «extranjeros» que los que ya ocupaban una plaza en la tradición. Pero ni siquiera el cultrún es chileno, porque la percusión no es un descubrimiento de Arauco, sino del hombre.	*The instruments are universal heritage. We could use the guitar without problems, an Arabic-Spanish instrument; the harp, a European instrument; the piano, another European instrument. Why not all of the others then? Now, in music there are no indigenous techniques. Music is the effort of millions of men and women of all times and from all latitudes. The delay of our music for a whole century is due to this particular eagerness to believe that its content and its form would be contaminated by using other "foreign" instruments than those that already occupied a place in the tradition. But not even the cultrún is Chilean, because percussion is not a discovery of Arauco, but of man.*

Sergio Ortega (Becerra, 1978)

The Nueva Canción maintained a delicate tension between preserving culture and expressing modern grievances with music that was both traditional and new. In the beginning, with the work of Parra, we see an artist who was creating an identity for marginalized groups by documenting hardships endured and elevating traditional cultural forms (Costa, 2017). This was an important foundation for the Nueva Canción movement—such an identity can serve as the basis for communicating ideas and ideals and encourage those who connect to that identity to address their hardships. Thus, while folklore was an important part of the development of the musical movement, the Nueva Canción was not explicitly defined by its connections to and expressions of folklore. The Nueva Canción is sometimes viewed as a type of neo-folklore or nationalistic music; indeed, if looking at the work of Parra, this conclusion seems valid. However, the music produced was highly experimental and did not align with these genres alone, which is why the music formed its own distinct genre (Becerra, 1978). The musical movement instead would go on to feature a wider range of political and cultural implications.

In 1957, Violeta Parra met Victor Jara. Jara was a musician, an artist, activist and, later, a professor of the State University of Technology in Santiago. Together Parra and Jara encouraged other artists to join the movement to preserve Chilean culture and, thanks to Jara's influence, to fight for the rights of the people. In her song, "La Carta (1971)," officially released posthumously, Violeta Parra sang about such themes when she described a person watching and lamenting her brother being arrested and dragged through the streets for having supported a strike. In this same song, Parra sings of the hunger and injustice found in the country. The themes in Parra's "La Carta" are a common line for the songs of the Nueva Canción. In his song "Plegaria a un Labrador (released posthumously in 1969)," for example, Victor Jara sings about being freed from the rulers who let the farmers live in poverty. His lyrics call for the workers to unite against people in power.

"La Carta (1971)" begins with the following stanzas:

Me mandaron una carta	They sent me a letter
por el correo temprano	by the post, this morning.
y en esa carta me dicen	In this letter they tell me that my brother is
que cayó preso mi hermano	in jail and that, merciless, they dragged him
y sin lástima con grillos	in chains by the street, yes.
por la calle lo arrastraron, si.	
La carta dice el motivo	The letter tells the reason.
que ha cometido Roberto	What Roberto has done.
haber apoyado el paro	He had supported the strike that is now
que ya se había resuelto	resolved.
si acaso esto es un motivo	Well, if that is the reason please take me to
presa también voy sargento, si.	jail too, sergeant, yes.

Plegaria a un Labrador (1969), by contrast, ends with the following:

Líbranos de aquel que nos domina	Deliver us from the one who dominates us
en la miseria.	in misery.
Tráenos tu reino de justicia	Bring us your kingdom of justice
e igualdad.	and equality.
Sopla como el viento la flor	The flower blows like the wind
de la quebrada.	of the ravine.
Limpia como el fuego	Clean like fire
el cañón de mi fusil.	the barrel of my rifle.
Hágase por fin tu voluntad	Your will be done at last
aquí en la tierra.	here in the earth.
Danos tu fuerza y tu valor	Give us your strength and your courage

al combatir.	when fighting.
Levántate y mírate las manos	Get up and look at your hands
para crecer estréchala a tu hermano.	to grow, shake it to your brother.
Juntos iremos unidos en la sangre	Together we will go united in blood
ahora y en la hora de nuestra muerte.	now and at the hour of our death.
Amén.	Amen.

Though the songs of Parra and Jara express a similar dissatisfaction and even a disgust with the current reality for the poor in the country, the difference in their messaging is stark. Parra is describing a person being punished for joining socialist movements but is lamenting, offering themselves up as a kind of passive martyr "...please take me to jail too, sergeant...". By contrast, Jara is encouraging the workers to rise up. Through the lyrics of these two pieces, we see how political messages are communicated through songs. Music is able to communicate values and ideals of both the individual and the larger society. It is able to communicate the realities lived by people to others who may not have the same experiences or confirm those realities to those who have.

We also see how those political messages feature critiques and can also serve as a call to collective action. Parra is illustrating an injustice and articulating the grief that is felt in her country during her life. The lyrics of the song further point to the fact that there is little to be done to solve the issues providing a critique that is almost fatalist. In contrast, Jara is describing a similar injustice, but is encouraging collective action to resolve it. When musicians advocate collective action, not only are they communicating to their audiences about a resonant issue, they are also encouraging a pathway forward. This may enable disaffected individuals to overcome coordination problems, as the song not only communicates that others feel the same way but also suggests undertaking action that individuals can be assured others who hear the song are also being encouraged to undertake.

When a singer is only documenting injustice, even injustice at the hands of the regime in power, but not encouraging action, his or her audience may not engage because they do not know if others will follow attempts to change the situation. A popular song advocating collective action, by contrast, when heard on the radio or sung along at a concert, can communicate that others not only feel the same, but are also willing to take action (McNeill, 1997). Music is particularly good at this kind of communication, because the message is repeated, which is an element of ritualistic behavior that facilitates further coordination (Chwe, 2013). Music is also an effective communication tool because messages are able to be concealed within the lyrics of a song. Violeta Parra used such lyrical devices in her song, "Mazúrquica Modérnica" (1966). This political song was able to communicate its message effectively through the use of jargon. Thus, music is able to communicate meaning to its audience in a variety of ways and express political thought without being overtly political.

Ultimately, Jara would have to continue spreading the messages of the Nueva Canción alone, as Violeta Parra, the internationally celebrated and beloved Mother of Folklore for the Chilean people, succumbed to the depression she had dealt with for most of her life, and died by suicide in 1967. Like Parra, Victor Jara also saw that one of the main problems that Chile faced was confronting imperialistic influences. He described these influences to his wife, Joan, in the following way:

> The cultural invasion is like a leafy tree which prevents us from seeing our own sun, sky and stars. Therefore in order to be able to see the sky above our heads, our task is to cut this tree off at the roots. US imperialism understands very well the magic of communication through music and persists in filling out young people with all sorts of commercial tripe. With professional expertise they have taken certain measures: first, the commercialization of so-called 'protest music'; second, the creation of 'idols' of protest music who obey the same rules and suffer from the same constraints as the other idols of the consumer music industry – they last a little while and then disappear. Meanwhile they are useful in neutralizing the innate spirit of rebellion of young people. The term 'pretest song' is no longer valid because it is ambiguous and has been misused. I prefer the term 'revolutionary song' (Jara, 1984, p. 121).

In this quote, we see Jara recognizing that art has the ability to both narrate and block other narratives from becoming hegemonic (Said, 2012). Jara would not allow the music of the movement to be neutralized through commercialization. Instead, he advanced the Nueva Canción beyond protest music and produced songs fit for a revolution. By the late sixties, Jara was writing revolutionary songs that were "no longer autobiographical but dealt much more with the general problems, task and objectives facing the peoples of Latin America – even though they were very often about individual human beings" (Jara, 1984, p. 174).

In order for the political messaging of the Nueva Canción to take hold, there needed to be an audience for Jara's revolutionary songs, and that audience needed to be receptive to his political messaging. During this time period, these revolutionary themes were finding popularity with the socially aware. This included students, unionists, rural workers, and the urban poor. The music was an integral part of these individuals' gatherings and the creation of their social networks (McSherry, 2017). The movement gained widespread recognition after the *First Festival of the New Chilean Song* organized by the Catholic University of Santiago in 1968. The concert's organizer, Ricardo García, chose to invite "protest" singers such as Victor Jara, Particio Manns, and Violeta's child, Angel

Parra. It is from this concert that the work that started with Parra and Jara came to be a recognized genre. The Nueva Canción would be the term used to describe the reinterpretation of traditional music (Mattern, 1996).

The political messaging in the music was not simply of Chilean nationalism or patriotism, the music of the movement told of class divisions and struggles and highlighted marginalized identities. Such themes connected the music of the Nueva Canción to the labor movement quite naturally. As time went on, the artists of the musical movement began to support political reform and the platforms of specific parties and individuals. Victor Jara, for example, brought the issues he presented in his songs to the political sphere, working to advocate for political change through supporting the early presidential bids of Salvador Allende and becoming involved with the socialist and communist parties of Chile (Anderson & Herr, 2007). This action cemented Nueva Canción's political messaging, linking the music with leftist political ideology and eventually gaining the attention of the subsequent right-wing military regime.

By the presidential campaign of 1970, several prominent musicians in the movement, including Victor Jara, were also involved in the Popular Unity party. Popular Unity was a leftist party that sought to transition the country to socialism. The main tenets of the party were the end of the domination of foreign capital in natural resource development, agrarian reform, and income redistribution to benefit the poorer classes (Caviedes et al., 2020). Nueva Canción artists supported the movement by composing songs to spread the messages to voters. The following is the song "Venceremos" written by Claudio Iturra and Sergio Ortega and served as presidential candidate Salvador Allende's campaign song (Morris, 1986):

Venceremos	From the deep crucible of the homeland
Desde el hondo crisol de la patria	The popular clamor rises,
Se levanta el clamor popular,	The new dawn is announced,
Ya se anuncia la nueva alborada,	All of Chile begins to sing.
Todo Chile comienza a cantar.	
Venceremos, venceremos,	We will overcome, we will overcome,
Mil cadenas habra que romper,	A thousand chains will have to be broken,
Venceremos, venceremos,	We will overcome, we will overcome,
La miseria (al fascismo) sabremos vencer.	We will know how to win misery (fascism).
Campesinos, soldados, mineros,	Peasants, soldiers, miners,
La mujer de la patria tambien,	The woman of the homeland too,
Estudiantes, empleados why obreros,	Students, employees and workers,
Cumpliremos con nuestro deber.	We will do our duty.
Sembraremos las tierras de gloria,	We will sow the lands of glory
Socialista sera el porvenir,	The future will be Socialist
Todos juntos haremos la historia,	Together we will make history
A cumplir, a cumplir, a cumplir.	To fulfill, to fulfill, to fulfill.

This song is a prime example of the themes present in the music of the Nueva Canción. In it, we see that the singer is suggesting that the "peasants, soldiers, miners...students, employees, and workers" will work together for a better Chile after breaking their chains that are holding back the society.

In 1970, Popular Unity candidate Salvador Allende won the election and served as Chile's first socialist president. Inti-Illimani an Andean band of university students who formed in 1967 and became one of the best know groups to emerge from the Nueva Canción, performed their politically charged songs for community and political gatherings. They supplemented the messaging of the Allende government through songs. In 1970, they even recorded an album called "Canto al Programa (*Sing of the Program*)" to detail the party's agenda after the election in accessible language and style (Morris, 1984). For example, the song "Vals de la Educacion Para Todos (Worth of Education for All)" outlined the new education policy. The following is an excerpt:

Para que los eduquen	For them to be educated
Obreros y campesinos	Workers and peasants
Tendrán mejores salarios	They will have better wages
Con este proceso lindo.	With this beautiful process.
Pero no hay que conformarse	But you don't have to settle
Sólo con los niños chicos	with education young children only
Porque ahora educaremos	Because now we will educate those
A los que son mayorcitos	who are older

In this song, the lyrics show Allende's plan for education as well as continued Nueva Canción themes. The song suggests that education will be available for all citizens and through education the people will be able to improve the life conditions they face.

Tracing the evolution of the Nueva Canción, we see its origins in Violeta Parra's cultural recordings of the indigenous and rural people of Chile's history. The songs she sang told the stories of their folklore and of class struggles and deprivation. These themes were picked up by other artists such as Victor Jara, Iturra, and Ortega, and augmented with more explicit calls to political action. Writing lyrics around the themes of poverty and injustice, and composing the accompaniment using traditional instruments and musical motifs familiar to the people, the artists of the Nueva Canción began a new genre that eventually communicated political identity and ideals through music. With lyrics of the songs communicating a marginalized identity and calling Chilean people to act, and popularizing events like music festivals, such communications took forms that also demonstrated the clear coordinating power of the musical movement. When the singers began to align themselves with the Popular Unity party, and that party won the 1970 general elections, the entire genre became associated with leftist political ideology. It is from these associations that we may begin to understand our next question: when would a regime seek to stop such messages?

Pinochet, censorship and the Nueva Canción

Music is fundamental to people's freedom of expression and has flourished in a multitude of cultures and contexts. At the same time, "throughout history it has been a source of fear and object of repression" for governments threatened by what their citizens might have to say (Street, 2012, p. 9). The questions then become when and why are regimes motivated to censor music? In the case of the censorship of the Nueva Canción, it appears as though Augusto Pinochet's military regime was threatened by both the implicit critique and collective organizing power contained in the music of the movement. As such, the regime used its military might to engage in a brutal censorship campaign, as soon as its military coup was underway.

During Allende's time as president, he endeavored to restructure the country to redistribute incomes and improve the conditions faced by the urban poor and peasants. These reforms, while supported by Allende's base and Nueva Canción musicians, were unpopular with key domestic and foreign political actors, specifically the Chilean middle class and the United States. Furthermore, during Allende's presidency, the country had multiple political factions that were difficult to control, including even some with similar leftist ideologies (Gorlinski, 2019).

As a result, on September 11, 1973, a military junta overthrew the Allende Regime and began to terrorize Chileans.

During the coup d'état, executed by army commander in chief, Augusto Pinochet, the national police jammed the telephone lines and closed the airports (O'Shaughnessy, 2013). The national police also blocked the streets and fired upon the presidential palace. An eyewitness account describes farmers headed into the city center to defend President Allende from the coup, but those farmers ultimately died at the hands of the national police (Sheehy, 2018) and Allende later died by suicide (Associated Press, 2011). The national police also herded students and professors, who were protesting and attempting to protect the State University of Technology, into the national stadium in the capital city. There, the protesters were detained without being arrested. Even as these events were unfolding, those under Pinochet's control also began a campaign of artistic censorship.

At the time of the coup d'état, the perpetrators burned large piles of books and media associated with leftist ideology in the streets. Upon seeing this, an onlooker was reported to have hidden his LPs of Nueva Canción musicians such as Andean bands Quilapayún and Inti-Illimani to prevent them from being destroyed (Sheehy, 2018). The Pinochet regime deployed the military to ban the music of the Nueva Canción from the radio and to confiscate and destroy recordings from stores and homes during the house-to-house searches that followed the coup d'état (Morris, 1986). They also made efforts to further extinguish the memory of the singers by destroying their master recordings (Rohter, 2002).

The Pinochet regime targeted musicians because of the viability of and the musicians' relationship with the now-opposition. As exiled singer Eduardo Carrasco explains:

| En la situación de Chile, la defensa de la música nacional llegó a tal grado de identificación con la lucha revolucionaria que en las primeras Semanas del negro penodo iniciado por el Gobierno fascista se llamó a una reunión a todos los folkloristas más destacados para informarles que ciertos instrumentos folklóricoscomo la quena y el charango quedaban prohibidos. Es decir, que para estos astutos militares el solo timbre de la música del Pueblo era Ya una manifestación de rebeldía revolucionaria | In the Chilean situation, the defense of national music reached such a degree of identification with the revolutionary struggle that in the first weeks of the black period initiated by the fascist government, a meeting was called to all the most prominent folklorists to inform them that certain folk instruments like the quena and the charango were forbidden. This means that for this 'astute' military men, even the sound of the music of the people was in itself a manifestation of revolutionary resistance |

This observation that traditional music was so closely associated with political opposition is borne out by a broader view of Pinochet's policies. Though the regime banned traditional instruments, there is no evidence that the Pinochet government was specifically opposed to indigenous cultures or objected to the fostering of a distinctive Chilean cultural identity. In fact, some Nueva Canción artists survived by shifting their focus to work on indigenous music, which the Pinochet junta continued to allow. The prohibition of certain instruments shows how successfully Nueva Canción had been able to connect political messaging and contemporary leftist ideology to traditional Chilean artistic expression through the Nueva Canción. By the time the Pinochet administration engaged in its censorship, the mere sound of these instruments would orient individuals toward the messages that the music of Nueva Canción normally projected.

After the coup d'état, censorship was further enforced through limitations placed on the press, radio, and television. Any new music had to have formal approval by the government (USIP, 2002). The only songs from the Nueva Canción movement that were allowed to play in public could not feature any overtly political themes. The only concerts that were permitted required song lyrics and a list of all performers be given to local police stations in advance. There were also lists of performers who were not allowed to appear on television or radio (Morris, 1986). The cultural censorship experienced during this period was so severe that it is referred to as a time of "agagón cultural" or cultural blackout (Morris, 1986).

In researching political censorship, scholars have identified two theories that explain why the state may censor its citizens. The first theory—the state critique theory—holds that the regime wishes to promote a hegemonic culture and diminish a plurality of voices that may critique it. By not allowing one group to communicate its traditions and values, the state automatically narrows the range of expression and limits opportunities for critique (Korpe, Reitov, & Cloonan, 2006). A state may also choose to censor to promote or create a hegemonic culture. To achieve this, regimes may decide to censor one group while openly promoting another (King, Pan, & Roberts, 2013).

The state critique theory of political censorship can be extended to understand music censorship. Music can provide a powerful channel to communicate political ideals. Through lyrics, individuals are able to voice their critiques of the state (Côté, 2011). These critiques are all the more powerful as they are memorized and internalized by the listener. A lone musician singing or playing a song critiquing the state is not likely to cause alarm. However, what begins as a soloist and a guitar can become a rallying cry of the disenfranchised and undermine the perceived legitimacy of the regime. For example, in Nazi Germany, international music as well as the music of minorities was prohibited in order to prevent a plurality of voices from being heard. These efforts were further augmented by the existence of an office producing German folksongs (Music in The Third Reich, 2020), seeking that musical power to produce a more homogenous Nazi culture.

The second theory regarding state censorship—the collective action potential theory—holds that regimes censor media to prevent collective action against the state (King, Pan, & Roberts, 2013). Individuals face several challenges turning their own objections to a political regime into action that might actually challenge the state. In making the decision to act, individuals may want to know that others feel the same grievances they feel. They might also want to know or gauge that if they choose to act on those feelings, they will not be alone in doing so. When individuals know that others feel the same way they do, and when individuals have information about others' willingness and plans to act, they are more likely to be able to overcome coordination problems and act on their concerns (De Mesquita, 2010). For example, when a newspaper or radio program reports on dissatisfaction, others are able to know that they are not alone with their dissatisfaction. Media further helps coordination through allowing individuals to communicate how and when to act. Thus, a state wanting to prevent collective action will find censorship an effective means of doing so.

This theory explaining a state's rationale to censor information can also be applied to music censorship. Through music's lyrics, individuals can communicate their dissatisfaction with the regime and the popularity of a given song or genre allows individuals to know that they are not alone in their critiques of the state. By virtue of its popularity, music may also allow individuals to understand that others are willing to act and, as a result, individuals may feel more empowered to assemble and act against the state. There is no clear scholarly understanding of which songs ultimately become protest songs. What constitutes a protest song changes through time. Groups select and rally behind message and motifs that they find compelling (Moore, 2013), and the messages in the music need do not to be overtly political to inspire political action. Instead, over time, the message may become a symbol to the people and to the regime. Once this process has occurred, however, the regime may be motivated to censor such music.

The music of the Nueva Canción was extremely important to the development of the left as it attracted "masses of people to political causes, popularizing radical-democratic and socialist political visions through their song, and inspiring broad sectors of society to fight for progressive social change (McSherry, 2016)." Indeed, the political themes in Nueva Canción were developing in a moment where the working class within Chile was becoming well organized with peasants and students, a factor that underscored the movement's collective action potential. When a song is calling for action and that message is reaching a primed audience, the regime may have good reason to fear the kind of action that could result (Jara, 1984).

Regardless of how the popularity of any genre or piece of music is measured, by sales or the number of venues where they were played, it was evident to the authorities that the music of the Nueva Canción movement contained leftist themes around which their listeners rallied and were willing to embark on actions detrimental to the administration. This did not go unnoticed by the agents of the Pinochet junta.

In order for censorship of music to be effective, it requires a great deal of enforcement. The regime must deal with the musicians who compose and perform them, the radio stations that air the tunes, the record stores that sell them, and the people who listen to, and can themselves reproduce, the music. Because of the censorship implementation and enforcement costs, it is understandable that the regime would only choose to take such action when it seems necessary for its survival. Thus, when musicians are promoting an ideology of the opposition or are suggesting that the citizens rise against the very forces that a regime represents, and that music is popular—resonating in particular with citizens with organizational capacity—a regime might decide censorship is worth the cost.

The Nueva Canción featured lyrics that could be construed as critical of the Pinochet regime (openly criticizing fascism, for example) and called for collective action against injustices observed. For example, in this verse of "El Pueblo Unido Jamás Será Vencido," by Quilapayún we see the themes that the Pinochet Regime worked hard to censor.

De pie cantar [luchar], el pueblo va a triunfar	Stand up to sing [fight], the people will conquer
Millones ya imponen la verdad;	Millions already impose the truth;
De acero son, ardiente batallón	They are made of steel, fiery battalion
Sus manos van llevando la justicia y la razón	Their hands carry justice and reason
Mujer, con fuego y con valor	Woman, with fire and with courage
Ya estás aquí junto al trabajador	You are already here with the worker
Y ahora el pueblo que se alza en la lucha	And now the people who rise up in the fight
Con voz de gigante gritando; adelante!	With a giant's voice screaming: go ahead!
El pueblo unido jamás será vencido!	The people united will never be defeated!

This song is an example of lyrics encouraging the workers to rise up and fight the state. To the Pinochet government, what was important and cause to censor this form of music was not about the size of the audience when it was played, nor the venue or channel used to air it, but the fear that the music was a call to arms against it. These features of the movement support both the state critique and collective action theories of censorship. It is difficult to determine which theory better applies to the Pinochet regime's censorship of Nueva Canción. Because music may both describe injustices and call for collective action simultaneously, it highlights how art may not fit the theoretical dichotomy that has been thus far used to understand political motivations for censorship. Instead, it suggests that certain media such as music may pose both threats of critique and collective action at once, which can help us understand why, beginning with the actions during the military coup d'état itself, the Pinochet regime undertook the costly and unpopular decision to censor, and implemented that choice with brutality and callousness. However, the censorship was also unevenly applied, as some musicians suffered extreme repression while others were largely untouched. By studying which musicians were forced into exile or killed and which were allowed to stay and perform in the next section of this chapter, we gain additional insights into the regime's implementation of censorship.

The fate of Victor Jara is an example of the most extreme form of censorship: murder of the artist. As a professor of the State University of Technology, Jara was among those protesting Pinochet's coup d'état who were detained at the stadium. Because he was an open advocate for the kind of change to the country's economic and political systems that Pinochet opposed, Jara knew that he would be a target of the military regime. However, he chose to stand at the university in solitary with the students and other faculty (Naddaff & Meedzan, n.d.). As the time that Jara and other protesters were kept inside the stadium stretched into several days, one of the guards was reported to have recognized him. Once recognized, Jara was singled out among the protestors, and tortured by the guards. Witnesses described the guards breaking Jara's hands and then taunting him to play his guitar. Jara, a man of peace and nonviolence, died by multiple gunshot wounds and his body was dumped outside the stadium.

While the story of Jara's death was infamous due to his popularity, he was not the only Nueva Canción musician murdered by the regime during Pinochet's rule. However, Jara's high-profile death sent a specific message to the musicians of the movement: that the regime did not welcome the messages expressed through the Nueva Canción. In his final days as a captive, Jara composed his final song perhaps anticipating his death and knowing what it would mean to the artistic community. Those who escaped the stadium wrote down the lyrics he sang which expressed how "hard it is to sing when I must sing of horror" (Tapscott, 1996). The death of Victor Jara left an imprint on the cultural memory of Chile. While his death served as a warning from the regime to other artists, it also showed the people of Chile the brutality, callousness, and inhumanity of the regime. As stated in her biography of Victor Jara's life, his wife wrote that his only crime was "awakening the consciousness of the Chilean people with his message of hope and social change (Jara, 1984, 1)." But, for a regime wishing to silence critiques and prevent collective action, this was indeed a crime.

The Pinochet regime left few options available to the artists. They could stay in the country, enduring censorship and risking being jailed or killed, or flee and live free in exile. Some of the artists from the Nueva Canción who stayed in Chile and accepted censorship restrictions include Eduardo Carrasco, Hans Stein, Luis Advis, Margot Loyola, the members of Santiago del Nuevo Extremo, Silvia Urbina, Kiko Alvarez, Tito Fernandez, and Carlos Isamitt Alarcón. These individuals vary in their contributions to the movement and popularity; however, each of the artists was associated with the movement in some fashion. Generally, those artists who remained in Chile were part of musical groups and created music that emphasized the indigenous roots of the movement instead of the political ties to the Nueva Canción. In order to prevent persecution, some of the artists such as Margot Loyola chose to refocus their work back to the movement's origins with Violeta Parra, and returned to documenting Chile's folklore heritage.

The artists who stayed and did not observe the regime's strict censorship rules were arrested and jailed. Over the course of the Pinochet administration, censorship was enforced by arresting and torturing around 130,000 members of the opposition. Musicians were among those whose lifestyles, as well as lives, were threatened the most. Mauricio Redolés was a singer, songwriter, and poet and was one of the musicians who was jailed even though his work was only tangentially related to the Nueva Canción movement. He served two years as a political prisoner in the Valparaiso prison (Chornik, 2014). Some artists still attempted to write from prison and managed to smuggle their work out to the public. The resulting songs are known as the Cantos Cautvos and have recently been collected by scholars to piece together the experience of being jailed during that time (Vulliamy, 2016). Because of the enforced censorship, a climate of insecurity and fear arose and those working in fields subject to censorship developed an attitude of self-censorship, a far more efficient means of control by the regime (USIP, 2002).

The artists who decided to leave their homeland appear to be primarily solo artists in the movement, but also included groups whose music had overt political themes. Some appear to have left due to direct relations to someone who was central to the leftist movement in the country. These individuals included Violeta Parra's children, Isabel and Ángel Parra, who composed and performed in exile. Additionally, Charo Cofre, Daniel Salinas, Eulogio Davalos, Hugo Arevalo, Inti-Illimani, Miguel Angel Cherubito, Patricio Castillo, Patricio Manns, Sergio Ortega, Osvaldo Rodriguez, Gabriela Pizarro, Héctro Pavez, Illapu, Julio Numhauser, Los Jaivas, Quilapayún, Rodolfo Parada, Max Berru, and Payo Grondona also fled Chile. These are arguably the most influential artists for the movement because their ideas were uncensored. Since they lived abroad, they were free to compose without fear of retribution. Their music was influential to audiences abroad and was well received. People in Europe, the United States, and other countries within Latin America were able to learn about the struggles faced by the people of Chile through the music of the Nueva Canción musicians in exile. Furthermore, when receiving broadcasts from abroad, the Pinochet government did not have the capabilities to censor the radio channels. Thus, producing works abroad became a strategy used by the artists to continue to perform and spread their message. It is from their archived interviews and songs that we may address the final question in this chapter: What became of the messengers?

How the *Nueva Canción* withstood Censorship

Even if there are some debates about the overall popularity of Nueva Canción music, not only was it undoubtedly popular among well-organized people who were politically active, it exerted a further influence by extending into and inspiring other artistic disciplines. The music was used to underscore films and dance performances, inspired visual artist to create work such as murals in cities, and its themes as well as songs were used in theatre performance. These collaborations are credited as occurring both because of the music's popularity as well as the connections among those in the artistic community in Chile. While these connections and influences undoubtedly further increased the perception that the Nueva Canción was a threat, they also allowed the movement to endure even the strictest of censorship rules. Using archived interviews from the artists performing during the cultural blackout, this final section looks at how some of the music was adjusted to make the political messages more subtle and acceptable to evade the attention of political elites in Chile, and how some artists continue their art more explicitly in exile.

Nueva Canción music after the Pinochet coup d'état is often referred to as the Canto Nuevo movement. While the former music was about fighting imperialism and spreading ideas of social justice, the Canto Nuevo movement provided a space for groups and artists to grieve Pinochet's brutal repression and censorship, and the systematic restriction on their expression. For the music produced in Chile that followed the coup's censorship and repression, the political messaging was deeply embedded in metaphor to protect the musicians, as the brutality of the regime's censorship had made clear the consequences for open political messaging. Obviously, the musicians who lived through this time of censorship were deeply affected by it, but had to be careful over how they expressed those feelings, for fear of more reprisal.

Despite all efforts to stamp out the political messaging in the music, it was still able to endure the censorship of the Pinochet regime, due to the symbolism of both the music's structure and the lyrics themselves. There remained a role for the artist both inside and outside of Chile. As Inti-Illimani, put it (Becerra, 1978):

Han nacido numerosos grupos, con formas propias de encauzar el canto, fuera y dentro de Chile. Vemos caminos nuevos en la poesía, fenómeno claro en el caso de las canciones que se hacen en Chile. La situación de nuestro país, el peso del fascismo, la vida bajo el fascismo, sin duda que están dando una dimensión al canto que antes no tenía. Hoy, cantar al derecho a vivir, a lo más	Numerous groups have been born, with their own ways of channeling the song, outside and inside Chile. We see new paths in poetry, a clear phenomenon in the case of songs that are made in Chile. The situation in our country, the weight of fascism, life under fascism, are undoubtedly giving a dimension to the song that it did not have before. Today, singing to the right

elemental, es una batalla desesperada, y la canción recoge todo esto. Inti-Illimani	to live, the most elemental, it is a desperate battle, and the song summarizes all of this. Inti-Illimani

From this quote, we can see that the art produced by the artists during this period were altered by the political climate after the coup d'état, but still had a very clear role. The composers of the Nueva Canción who remained and those who fled still continued to produce music that expressed the emotions of the oppressed and calling for social justice, even as they were responding to censorship.

Political messages and ideals were still held by each artist, but how each artist chose to express those ideas differed. After enduring censorship and threats, it is rational to expect that artists and their art would be impacted. The coup d'état left a lasting memory on the people of Chile both at home and abroad. As Angel Parra, son of Violeta Parra, describes, no one was left unscathed by the coup (Becerra, 1978):

El golpe militar ha influido en todos los chilenos, desde la derecha hasta la izquierda. Con mayor razón en un pintor, en un escritor, en un músico. Se nota en las canciones. En las mías y en las de otros compañeros; se nota en la violencia del lenguaje, en la decisión, los textos están profundamente marcados por 10s acontecimientos. La razón ya estaba dicha hace diez años atrás: nuestra Canción no es de salón, es una canción hecha de la vida diaria, de 10 que está pasando. ¿Cómo entonces no sentir la influencia del golpe? Angel Parra	The military coup has influenced all Chileans, from the right to the left. Even more so in a painter, a writer, a musician. It shows in the songs. In mine and in those of other comrades; It is evident in the violence of the language, in the decision, the lyrics are deeply defined by the events. The reason was already known ten years ago: our Song is not for fancy venues, it is a song made from daily life, from what is happening. How then not to feel the influence of the coup? Angel Parra

From this quote, we see further evidence that the political messaging in music was changed after the coup d'état, but the message was still very much present in the work that was being produced. As the musicians of the Nueva Canción had always done earlier, the songwriter expresses the stories of those who are being oppressed and silenced through music and amplifies those voices. Through lyrics, the influence of coup d'état and the subsequent dictatorship were processed by both performer and audience.

Those who had the most freedom to express political themes in their music were Nueva Canción artists who could not stay in Chile under Pinochet. Most of them fled to neighboring countries and Europe. This decision was pragmatic for both the safety of the artists and the preservation of the art. From exile, Nueva Canción artists continued to compose and record their songs. They continued to play for universities, unions, towns, and in smaller venues. To each eager audience, the musicians explained the social, historical, and economic significance of the pieces, effectively transporting the audience to a different space and time. Some of them would return to Chile after the fall of the Pinochet regime in 1990. That was after several years of separation from the culture they were trying desperately to protect and preserve. So, how did the musicians view their heavily censored artistic spaces, personal harassment and political messaging under the Pinochet dictatorship? This issue is explored below.

Charo Cofre and her husband Hugo Arevalo were among the artists that lived in exile. Both were independent singers and musicians who contributed to the Nueva Canción movement through continuing to play overtly political music. Before escaping the violence of the Pinochet regime, Hugo Arevalo worked as the director of programs for Teletrece, a popular national broadcasting station in Chile. At the time of the coup d'état, he was working on a project about the poet, Pablo Neruda, who was also communist party senator. After Arevalo was fired for this work, the couple decided to flee the country, to Italy via Argentina, for safety. In exile, they continued to compose and record. As Arevalo said (Arévalo et al, 1985):

| Las influencias vienen, por ahora, sólo de Chile. En primer lugar, el pueblo mismo y su canto, o sea, las cantoras campesinas y principalmente los poetas populares, tocadores de guitarrón y cantores de la zona de Puente Alto, de quienes he aprendido casi todo lo que sé y hago de música. | The influences come, for now, only from Chile. In the first place, the people themselves and their songs, that is, the peasant singers and mainly the popular poets, guitar players and singers from the Puente Alto area, from whom I have learned almost everything I know and do about music. |

Although they were living abroad, these artists remained connected to Chile through their music. For them, music not only provided a way of life and a way to process their own emotions, but also allowed the political messaging of the movement to continue. The artists took their role fighting the regime through song seriously. For some, the song was a sword to wield and destroy the forces that were trying to prevent freedom of expression. In this way, the music changed. It was no longer advocating for social justice and anti-imperialism. In the post-coup context, the same music took on a new meaning. Instead of the original political movement, supporting the emergence of a new Chilean version of socialism, in new compositions, there were more explicit themes of anti-fascism. Hugo Arevalo made this his life's purpose as he said (Arévalo et al., 1985):

De la simple intepretación de cantos folklóricos de recopilación y de la creación de canciones personales he pasado a una etapa de contribución con mi pequeña obra y mi canto a la lucha contra el fascismo. Mi creación está ahora, por lo tanto, orientada casi exclusivamente a golpear a la Junta	From the simple interpretation of compilation folk songs and the creation of personal songs, I have gone on to a stage of contribution with my humble work and my song to the fight against fascism. My creation is now, therefore, geared almost exclusively to criticize the Junta.

From interviews with the artists of the Nueva Canción living in exile, it is clear that the artists understood that the music they produced was inherently political. However, there was a general consensus among them that Nueva Canción was not unique in its political potential; that all cultural media could be used as a weapon to fight fascism. On one hand, Patricio Manns suggested that songs were arguably the strongest of the arts due to their ability to transmit a message and evoke emotion simultaneously (Becerra, 1978). This potential to fight fascism was part of the motivation to live in exile. Exile allowed artists to survive to continue creating expressions too powerful for words alone.

Mi opinión es formal: Debe haber dos tipos de canciones. Las que son difundidas para Chile y las que están destinadas a ser difundidas en el resto del mundo. Los programas de radio destinados al interior deben constituir un verdadero soporte espiritual e ideológico de la resistencia, y deben construirse no sólo con canciones de autores e intérpretes chilenos, sino hacer una selección de otras canciones que sirvan; solicitar la colabo- ración de autores e intérpretes extranjeros amigos. Patricio Manns	My opinion is formal: There must be two types of songs. Those that are broadcast for Chile and those that are destined to be broadcast in the rest of the world. Domestic Radio programs must constitute a true spiritual and ideological support for the resistance and must be built not only with songs by Chilean authors and interpreters, but also make a selection of other songs that serve; [the purpose of the ideological resistance] request the collaboration of friendly foreign authors and interpreters Patricio Manns

From this quote, we see something interesting identified by the artist: the role of the global audience. The world outside of Chile is not merely a safe haven for the artists to avoid the repressive regime. Instead, it is able to be a source of support and assistance for the artists fighting political oppression. The music produced abroad was often able to be more expressive and sorrowful, enumerating the grief the artists felt for the country they left behind. Those who composed abroad mostly kept their overall style the same and did not conform to their new local culture. While some of the songs from the initial movement would age and disappear, others would continue to be played as the artist continued to compose, waiting for the day they could safely return home.

However, like the artists who remained in the country performing, some exiled artists also modified their music to offer more subtle political messaging.

Quilapayún, one of the most popular bands during the Nueva Canción, continues to play and produce Canto Nuevo music. One of the original members, Eduardo Carrasco was interviewed on behalf of the band for a magazine in 1978. In it, he spoke about how their music continued, even in exile (Becerra, 1978).

En nuestra experiencia concreta de hoy día hay diversos ejemplos que muestran que no por el hecho de estar sometida a la más feroz represión de nuestra historia, la canción ha dejado de ser política. Es que en la situación actual de Chile nuestro pueblo ha inventado otro lenguaje, una manera de decir.las cosas sin decirlas, en la cual una mínima alusión habla más que cien discursos. Pero además este carácter político amplio que puede adoptar el arte lo hemos visto a lo largo de todos estos años en la la lucha por la revalorización del folklore, en la defensa de la Nueva Canción Chilena y en el redescubrimiento de la música indígena.	In our concrete experience today there are various examples that show that in spite of being subjected to tremendous repression in history, national and folkloric music has never ceased to be political. In our current Chilean situation, our people have invented another language, a way of saying things without saying them, in which the smallest allusion speaks louder than a hundred speeches. Additionally, the broad political character that art has adopted throughout all these years, is clearly visible in the struggle for the reassessing of folklore, the defense of the New Chilean Song and the rediscovery of indigenous music.
Lo que venimos diciendo no significa que subestimemos la canción que toma la consigna política e intenta responder a la circunstancia concreta y hablar el lenguaje que la situación exige. Pero es necesario reconocer sus límites y darse cuenta de que la función política de la música popular no se reduce a la acción de las marchas y de las canciones contingentes, por más importantes y necesarias que éstas sean Eduardo Carrasco	This does not mean that we underestimate the song explicitly political that takes on the politically relevant messages and attempts to respond to these in concrete circumstances, utilizing the necessary language that the situation demands. But it is necessary to recognize its limits and realize that the political function of popular music is not limited to the action of marches and contingent songs, however important and necessary they may be. Eduardo Carrasco

This view demonstrates how music can be political, even in very subtle ways. Through the choice of rhythms and melodies, music can link itself to another period or movement. Through lyrical symbolism, music can covertly express messages. Given the elements of music that Carrasco identifies with and sang, we understand why the Pinochet Regime censored the music of this period. It is not necessarily that the music was calling for collective action or that it was critiquing the regime, but that it had a latent potential to do both.

In his interview, Carrasco explained the challenges of producing art away from the source of inspiration of the song, the homeland. For Carrasco, the music was always political and always addressed an anti-imperialist struggle by re-discovering peasant songs and remembering indigenous music. Due to censorship, the band played music abroad, but the music had to change so that the message was able to be consumed by the foreign audience. Thus, the band tried to make the music universal and thereby more accessible to foreign audiences, but remarked that it further distanced them from their homeland because the themes were no longer clearly identifying with the Chilean people. Thus, we see that Nueva Canción artists in exile lived and produced their art amidst a series of tensions—free to express regime opposition more openly, but constrained in their ability to return home; they were able to access a broader audience that might offer political support to the people of Chile, but always risking a loss of connection with those very people as they sought more universal appeal and support for the movement.

Overall the Canto Nuevo or revised Nueva Canción music still expressed a love of the Chilean people, but now it expressed a hatred for fascism (Becerra, 1978). In Europe, the music was played on radio and television; the artists toured and performed in Europe. The receptive audiences were both political and apolitical. In some ways, the music itself was similar to what had always been played, but for most, the violence witnessed and endured by Chilean society influenced their work. The lyrics now reflected the pain felt by both the artist and community.

The Pinochet Regime ended in 1990 with the election of a new president. Some of the artists were able to return home before that time while others could not. Thanks to more subtle political messaging and the continued production of artists in exile, the Nueva Canción music continued through censorship and is still an active genre of music today. The music continues to be deeply cultural, carrying meanings from the initial movement and progressing through time with the needs of the people, and responding to the brutal repression of the military regime. While Chile was the birthplace of such a movement and the people who were a part of its creation experienced severe censorship, Chile was not the only country to experience expressed political discourse through music. Argentina, Brazil, Cuba, France, Nicaragua, Spain, and Uruguay all had a variation of people seeking to protect their cultural identity and critique their government through songs (Gorlinski, 2019).

The artists of this movement continued to produce music to the best of their abilities. Acting as curators of culture, the musicians who remained at home were able to preserve the parts of the movement they could and decide on the new directions of the movement within the confines of the repressive regime. Abroad, some played their same songs while others adjusted for the comfort and understanding of the audience. Some artists hid their themes through metaphor while others loudly declared their lyrics. Regardless, the music continued despite the regime's attempts at repressive censorship, showing a triumph of the art and the human spirit in the face of political oppression.

Conclusion

The Nueva Canción began from a single woman's efforts to record the songs found in the rural interior of Chile. Capturing these songs brought forth a marginalized identity, revealed frustrations of the working classes of Chile, and, over time, started to promote social justice. Social justice themes turned into political themes with the aid of more action-oriented artists, which then aligned with the growing leftist political movement and organizations in Chile. In this way, a musical genre developed a political message. When the Pinochet Regime seized power, it found the music threatening, and censored these songs that both critiqued the regime and suggested an intense potential to continue the collective action it had already inspired in the leftist political movement and Allende presidency.

Despite the censorship that Nueva Canción artists were subjected to, the music endured. Either individual artists hid the overt political messages in their compositions and highlighted the folkloric roots of the movement, or other individuals produced music abroad and continued more open political critiques and calls to action through international audiences and less monitored airways. Though the musicians of the Nueva Canción endured a long period of severe censorship, the songs they produced still continued to reach the people that desperately needed the messages they told, to let marginalized Chileans know that they were not alone in their struggles. As Violeta Parra sang:

Por suerte tengo guitarra	*Luckily, I have a guitar*
Para llorar mi dolor	*To cry my pain*

References

Anderson, G. L., & Herr, K. G. (Eds.). (2007). *Encyclopedia of activism and social justice*. Sage Publications.

Arévalo, H., Cofré, H., & Fuente, A. (1985, October 15). *Entrevista después de un exilio: Charo Cofré y Hugo Arévalo. Disponible en Memoria Chilena, Biblioteca Nacional de Chile.* http://www.memoriachilena.gob.cl/602/w3-article-75195.html

Associated Press. (2011, July 19). Chilean president Salvador Allende committed suicide, autopsy confirms. *The Guardian.* https://www.theguardian.com/world/2011/jul/20/salvador-allende-committed-suicide-autopsy

Becerra, G. (1978). Discusion Dobre la Musica Chilena. *Araucaria de Chile.* http://www.memoriachilena.gob.cl/602/w3-article-67662.html

Blau, J. A. (2020, September 30). Violeta Parra. In the *Encyclopædia Britannica*. Retrieved October 10, 2021 from https://www.britannica.com/biography/Violeta-Parra

Caviedes, C. (2020, December 29). Chile. In the Encyclopædia Britannica. Retrieved October 10 2021 from https://www.britannica.com/place/Chile

Chews, M. S. Y. (2013). *Rational ritual*. Princeton University Press.

Chornik, K. (2014, May 15). When Julio Iglesias played Pinochet's Prison. *The Guardian*. https://www.theguardian.com/music/2014/may/15/julio-iglesias-valparaiso-pinochet-chile

Côté, T. (2011). Popular musicians and their songs as threats to national security: A world perspective. *The Journal of Popular Culture, 44*(4), 732–754.

de Costa, E. M. (2017). The Sociopolitical Discourse of Violeta Parra and Víctor Jara-The Culture of People's Power: Giving Voice to Social Justice in Chile's New Song Movement. In U. Onyebadi (Ed.), *Music as a Platform for Political Communication* (pp. 109–126). Hershey, PA: IGI Global.

de Mesquita, E. B. (2010). Regime change and revolutionary entrepreneurs. *American Political Science Review, 104*(3), 446–466.

Eyerman, R., & Jamison, A. (1998). *Music and social movements: Mobilizing traditions in the twentieth century*. Cambridge University Press.

Jara, J. (1984). *An Unfinished Song: The Life of Victor Jara*. New York: Ticknor & Fields.

King, G., Pan, J., & Roberts, M. E. (2014). Reverse-engineering censorship in China: Randomized experimentation and participant observation. *Science, 345*(6199).

Korpe, M., Reitov, O., & Cloonan, M. (2006). Music censorship from Plato to the present. *Music and Manipulation: On the Social Uses and Social Control of Music, 1*, 239–263.

Mattern, M. S. (1966). *Acting in concert: Music, community and political action*. Rutgers University Press.

McNeill, W. H. (1995). *Keeping together in time*. Harvard University Press.

McSherry, J. P. (2016, March 14). The Chilean New Song Movement: Far More Than a Relic of the Past. *Social Justice*. http://www.socialjusticejournal.org/the-chilean-new-song-movement/

McSherry, J. P. (2017). The political impact of Chilean New Song in exile. *Latin American Perspectives, 44*(5), 13–29.

Moore, A. F. (2013). *Song means: Analysing and interpreting recorded popular song*. Ashgate Publishing, Ltd.

Morris, N. (1986).). Canto porque es necesario cantar: The New Song movement in Chile, 1973–1983. *Latin American Research Review, 21*(2), 117–136.

Music In The Third Reich. (2020, December 31). *Music and the Holocaust*. https://holocaustmusic.ort.org/politics-and-propaganda/third-reich/

Naddaff, A., & Meedzan, J. (n.d.). *Cultural Resistance Through Music: Nueva Canción in Chile*. https://www.forgingmemory.org/narrative/nueva-cancion-chile

O'Shaughnessy, H. (2013, September 7). Chilean coup: 40 years ago I watched Pinochet crush a democratic dream. *The Guardian*. https://www.theguardian.com/world/2013/sep/07/chile-coup-pinochet-allende.

Rohter, L. (2002, December 23).). A Voice Stilled by a Junta Now Lives Again. *New York Times*. https://www.nytimes.com/2002/12/23/arts/a-voice-stilled-by-a-junta-now-lives-again.html

Said, E. W. (2012). *Culture and imperialism*. Vintage.

Sheehy, D. (2018, September 10). *An Eyewitness Account of Pinochet's Coup 45 Years Ago*. https://www.smithsonianmag.com/smithsonian-institution/eyewitness-account-pinochets-coup-45-years-ago-180970241/

Street, J. (2013). *Music and politics*. John Wiley & Sons.

Tapscott, S. (1996). *Twentieth-century Latin American poetry: a bilingual anthology*. University of Texas Press.

Trilling, T. (2009). *Sincerity and authenticity*. Harvard University Press.

Turino, T. (2008). *Music as social life: The politics of participation*. University of Chicago Press.

USIP. (2002). *Report of the Chilean National Commission on Truth and Reconciliation*. United States Institute of Peace.

Verba, E. K. (2013). To Paris and Back: Violeta Parra's Transnational Performance of Authenticity. *The Americas, 70*(2), 269–302.

Vetter, M. A. (2017, June 8). Violeta Parra: Popular Educator [Conference session]. Adult Education Research Conference, Norman, OK, United States. https://newprairiepress.org/aerc/2017/papers/11

Vulliamy, E. (2016, December 2). Freedom Songs: Chile's sounds of resistance ring out again. *The Guardian*. https://www.theguardian.com/world/2016/dec/04/chile-pinochet-music-song-political-prisoners

CHAPTER 12

Zimbabwe: Music, performance, and political lyrics as "cure" for post *Bhalagwe*[1] trauma

Mphathisi Ndlovu
Stellenbosch University, South Africa

Khanyile Joseph Mlotshwa
University of KwaZulu-Natal, South Africa

Abstract

As a nation, Zimbabwe is still wounded and haunted by the historical injustices of the *Gukurahundi* massacre of nearly four decades ago, which left an estimated figure of over 20,000 people dead in Matabeleland and the Midlands provinces. *Gukurahundi* denotes the extermination of predominantly Ndebele people, masterminded by a government-sponsored military unit, from 1983 to 1987. Although these atrocities "ended" in 1987, the *Gukurahundi* remains a dark chapter in national politics and memory. The perpetrators of the heinous crimes were not prosecuted, and memories of the crimes remain repressed by the state. Using the case of Bongani Mncube, a musician and protest poet from Matabeleland, this chapter examines the role of music and poetry as subversive expressions and performances of the memories of the mass killings. An interview with Mncube and an analysis of his songs demonstrate that *Gukurahundi* survivors, as the subaltern, continue to use music and poetry to demand justice and truth, and to memorialize the victims of the state-sponsored murder.

---

[1] Bhalagwe was a notorious detention camp in Matobo district, Matabeleland South where thousands were detained, tortured, sexually assaulted and murdered by the Fifth Brigade and other state agents (Eppel, 2020, p. 260). As a "torture and death camp" (Eppel, 2020, p. 260), Bhalagwe symbolizes the horror and trauma of Gukurahundi.

Keywords: Representation, subaltern, voice, Matabeleland, Gukurahundi, Bongani Mncube, popular music

***

Introduction

In 1983, the Zimbabwean government deployed the Fifth Brigade, a counterinsurgency military force, to Matabeleland and the Midlands under the guise of quashing a "dissident" movement in these provinces. Soldiers of the Fifth Brigade went on to commit heinous crimes such as executions, sexual assaults, torture, enforced disappearances and detention of civilians (CCJP & LRF, 1997). The civilians were accused of aiding the "dissidents." The mass killings have come to be known as *Gukurahundi*, a Shona (an ethnic group in Zimbabwe) expression that means the "rain that washes away the chaff from the last harvest, before the spring rains" (CCJP & LRF, 1997, p. xiii). *Gukurahundi* massacres were carried out against predominantly Ndebele people. By the time the *Gukurahundi* genocide ended in 1987 with the signing of the Unity Accord between the ruling party, ZANU PF[2] and the opposition, ZAPU[3], at least 20,000 Ndebele-speaking civilians had been killed. The pogrom remains a dark chapter in national politics and memory (Mpofu, 2019a). The perpetrators of *Gukurahundi* are yet to be brought to justice for their crimes, as discourses on this past remain heavily guarded by the state. This chapter examines the role of music and musicians in communicating political messages in the aftermath of mass atrocities. The authors draw upon the case of Bongani Mncube, a musician and protest poet from Matabeleland, to examine the subversive nature of his musical performances in the context of *Gukurahundi*. Drawing upon theories of representation and the subaltern (Alcoff, 1991; Spivak, 1988), this chapter explores how *Gukurahundi* survivors are using music and poetry to memorialize the victims and demand justice.

Given the prevailing culture of impunity and forced forgetting, the survivors have been "forced to live with their silenced memories of horror and fear" (Eppel, 2004, p. 46). Various attempts by family members and communities to memorialize, exhume and rebury *Gukurahundi* victims have been thwarted by the government (Alexander, McGregor & Ranger, 2000; Eppel, 2020). Given that the killings remain a taboo topic (Mpofu, 2014), there is a struggle by the people of Matabeleland and Midlands to voice their traumatic experiences. Nonetheless, there are growing demands for truth, justice and commemoration for

---

[2] Zimbabwe African National Union Patriotic Front
[3] Zimbabwe African People's Union

Gukurahundi victims. There is a corpus of research that examines how new media technologies are enabling the subaltern communities to bear witness to the traumatic past events and subvert ZANU PF's hegemonic narratives (Mhlanga & Mpofu, 2014; Mpofu, 2015; Ndlovu, 2018a). Recent scholarship also focuses on the subversive nature of visual arts and theatre as *Gukurahundi* memory-making practices (Mlotshwa, 2019; Mpofu, 2019b). However, the key absence in this literature is the role of music and musicians in performing and mediating memories of *Gukurahundi* massacre.

Using the case of Bongani Mncube, a musician and protest poet from Matabeleland, this chapter examines his music and poetry as subversive expressions and performances of the memories of this unspeakable and unrepresentable pogrom. Drawing upon theories of representation (Alcoff, 1991; Spivak, 1988), the authors explore how *Gukurahundi* survivors are using music and poetry to demand justice, truth and commemoration for *Gukurahundi* victims. Given the "indignity" (Deleuze & Foucault, 1977, p. 209) of "speaking for others" (Alcoff, 1991, p. 23), the authors' interest is on how *Gukurahundi* surviving communities are using music as avenues of expression and speaking against the "power bloc" (Mano, 2007, p. 62). Popular music in Zimbabwe constitutes the "voice of the voiceless" as it communicates the daily lived experiences of the subaltern (Mano, 2007, p. 61). Protest songs are vehicles of "what is wrong in society" (Makina, 2009, p. 222). Critical Discourse Analysis (CDA) is employed as a method of analysing Mncube's randomly selected songs and poetry on *Gukurahundi*. Furthermore, a qualitative interview was completed with Mncube to make sense of the socio-political and historical contexts that shaped the ways in which he uses performing arts (music and poetry) to communicate messages on *Gukurahundi* historical injustices.

Bongani Mncube

Bongani Mncube is a South African-based Zimbabwean musician and poet. Born in 1977 in Plumtree (Matabeleland), Mncube self-identifies as an "activist" more than an "artist" (Matabeleland Broadcasting Corporation, 2020). His poetry and music articulate issues of "tribal imbalances, social decay, suppression of democracy in Zimbabwe and Africa" (Ncube, 2016). Mncube's popular songs include *Ngibhace ezizweni* (I am in exile), *War of peace, The soldier, Why Africa,* and *Wounded Nation*. As a young boy, he witnessed the *Gukurahundi* terror in his village. His grandfather and father were tortured by the government forces, and died from the result of the wounds (Matabeleland Broadcasting Corporation, 2020). After losing his grandfather who was the breadwinner, Mncube and his family struggled financially, and as a result, he could not proceed with his education. In 1995, he migrated to South Africa for greener pastures. Mncube's artistic work should be situated within the socio-historical and political contexts that have shaped his lived experiences and imaginations. As a musician and poet, Mncube uses art as a "political tool" to draw attention to the ills in society (Matabeleland Broadcasting Corporation, 2020). In this chapter, the authors focus on Mncube's musical performances that express *Gukurahundi* historical injustices.

Gukurahundi: A socio-historical context

Zimbabwe gained independence from colonial rule in 1980 after a protracted nationalist struggle. The Zimbabwe African National Union – Patriotic Front (ZANU PF) and the Zimbabwe African People's Union (ZAPU) were the dominant movements that spearheaded the nationalist cause. Although these two parties had a "national" outlook, the liberation struggle was characterized by ethnic fissures and animosities (Sithole, 1999). The 1963 "grand split" in the nationalist struggle reinforced ethnic animosities and cleavages (Ndlovu-Gatsheni, 2011, p. 36) as prominent nationalists defected from ZAPU and formed a splinter party, ZANU PF. Most of the leaders of the breakaway group like Robert Mugabe, Herbert Chitepo and Leopold Takawira were predominantly Shona-speakers. As a result, ZANU PF became "Shona-dominated" whilst ZAPU became synonymous with the Ndebele people (Ndlovu-Gatsheni, 2008, p. 44). The Shona people constitute the dominant ethnic group in the country whereas the Ndebele are a minority group. However, both Ndebeles and Shonas are not homogenous groupings, because there are sub-groups, sub-ethnicities and dialects that highlight the complex and contested nature of ethnic identities in the country (Ndlovu-Gatsheni, 2008).

During the liberation struggle, ZANU PF's recruitment was concentrated in Mashonaland provinces, an area inhabited, in the main, by the Shona people. The armed wing of ZANU PF was the Zimbabwe African National Liberation Army (ZANLA). ZAPU, on the other hand, concentrated its recruitment in Matabeleland, a region inhabited predominantly by the Ndebeles. The Zimbabwe People's Revolutionary Army (ZIPRA) was the military wing of ZAPU. Since the 1963 grand split, the history of these two liberation parties has become a "tale of ethnic politics and tribalism," hence "bringing more division than unity to the Ndebele and the Shona" (Ndlovu-Gatsheni, 2008, p. 44). The "tragic massacre" of ZIPRA guerrillas in 1976 at Morogoro and Mgagao trainings camps in Tanzania at the hands of ZANLA forces highlights the pre-independence tensions between these two armed forces (Chung, 2006, p. 147).

The ZANU PF party led by Robert Mugabe won the country's inaugural elections in 1980. A national army was formed comprising of ex-Rhodesian, ex-ZANLA and ex-ZIPRA forces. However, the new environment was characterized by clashes and tensions between the latter forces (Alexander, 1998; Eppel, 2004). Clashes that erupted at Entumbane (Matabeleland) pitting ex-ZIPRA against ex-

ZANLA forces in late 1980 were notable precursors to the Gukurahundi massacres (Alexander, 1998; Ndlovu-Gatsheni, 2008. In 1982, armed caches were "discovered" at a property owned by ZAPU (Alexander, 1998; Kriger, 2003). ZANU PF's response was to accuse ZAPU and its leader, Joshua Nkomo, of attempting to topple the government (Alexander, 1998). Some ex-ZIPRA combatants defected from the national army, and this group of deserters became branded as "dissidents" (Kriger, 2003, p. 30). The western parts of the country where "dissident" activities were taking place were largely inhabited by Ndebele-speaking people. The following table provides a timeline of events from the creation of Ndebele kingdom up to *Gukurahundi*.

Table 1.1: Chronology (1820 – 1987)

1820	Mzilikazi Khumalo, the founder of the Ndebele kingdom, breaks away from the Zulu kingdom. In 1840, Mzilikazi's group settles in Matabeleland, and the Ndebele kingdom is established.
1893 – 1894	Anglo-Ndebele War, or the First Matabele War, is fought against the British colonialists.
1896 – 1897	The First Umvukela/Chimurenga takes place. This was the Ndebele-Shona uprising against the British forces. The Ndebele and Shona forces are defeated.
1960s - 1979	Second Umvukela/Chimurenga. The Zimbabwe liberation struggle led mainly by ZAPU and ZANU PF. ZAPU was associated with the people in Matabeleland, and ZANU PF with those in Mashonaland.
1980	Zimbabwe gains independence, with ZANU PF winning the elections.
1982	Arms caches are "discovered" at a property owned by ZAPU. ZANU PF accuses ZAPU of plotting a coup. Former ZIPRA guerrillas desert the national army, citing persecution. This group is tagged dissidents by the government.
1983	ZANU PF deploys a North Korean trained Fifth Brigade to Matabeleland and Midlands provinces to suppress the "dissident" movement. The Fifth Brigade commit atrocities in Matabeleland and the Midlands, targeting civilians.
1987	The mass killings end in 1987 with the signing of the Unity Accord between ZANU PF and ZAPU.

In her study on dissident perspectives, Alexander (1998) highlights that the former ZIPRA guerrillas deserted the national army due to persecution and repression at the hands of the ZANLA military personnel. Despite disassociating himself and ZAPU from the "dissidents," Nkomo was accused by ZANU PF of engineering this insurgency movement to topple the government (Alexander, 1998; Phimister, 2009). Mugabe responded by deploying a North-Korean trained Fifth Brigade counter-insurgency unit to Matabeleland and Midlands to quell the "dissident" movement (Kriger, 2003; Lindgren, 2005). Led by Perrance Shiri, an ex-ZANLA guerrilla (Kriger, 2003, p. 31), this counter-insurgency unit operated outside the conventional military chain and reported directly to Mugabe (Alexander, 1998; Ndlovu-Gatsheni, 2003). The Fifth Brigade was dominated by Shona-speakers who were ex-ZANLA guerrillas (Ndlovu-Gatsheni, 2003, p. 17). This militia went to commit executions, abductions, torture, rapes and other atrocities that are detailed extensively in the Zimbabwe Catholic Commission for Justice and Peace (CCJP) and Legal Resources Foundation (LRF) Report (1997). From 1983, the Fifth Brigade "murdered and tortured thousands of civilians, burned hundreds of villages, and raped and pillaged entire communities" (Cameron, 2018, p. 5). Villagers were "burnt to death in huts" by the Fifth Brigade (Eppel, 2020, p. 265) and pregnant women "bayonetted to death" (Cameron, 2018, p. 5).

The brutalities were meted out on ZAPU members, former ZIPRA guerrillas and civilians in general for allegedly aiding the "dissidents" (Kriger, 2003; Phimister, 2009). Ethnic and political categories became conflated as the victims were told by the Fifth Brigade that they "were being punished because they were Ndebele" (Eppel, 2004, p. 45). Thus, Ndebeles were accused of supporting ZAPU, and therefore labelled "dissidents" (Eppel, 2020, p. 260). Cameron (2018, p. 5) also asserts that from the outset, it was evident that the "Fifth Brigade were not interested in seeking out dissidents and that their actual target was the Ndebele civilian population." Enos Nkala, a prominent Ndebele in ZANU PF, accused Nkomo of being a "self-appointed Ndebele king" and claimed that the dissidents were "Ndebeles who were calling for a second war of liberation" (Alexander, 1998, p. 153; Kriger, 2003, p. 76). Further, the Fifth Brigade evoked memories of the nineteenth century Ndebele raids on Shona people (Lindgren, 2005, p. 161) by modelling itself as a "Shona defence force" that came to "punish the Ndebele for their historical transgressions" (Ndlovu-Gatsheni, 2003, p. 25). However, other writers dismiss the ethnic factor by arguing that ZANU PF leaders wanted to establish a one-party state by dismantling ZAPU and its support base in Matabeleland (Rwafa, 2012; Vambe, 2012).

At Bhalagwe camp (Matabeleland South), thousands were detained, beaten, tortured and killed by the Fifth Brigade militia (Eppel, 2004). The bodies of some victims were thrown down in mine shafts (Eppel, 2004, p. 43). Some *Gukurahundi* victims were made to disappear and their fate remains unknown (Eppel, 2006; 2004). Although the violence ended with the signing of the Unity Accord between ZANU PF and ZAPU in 1987, the nation-state remains haunted by the unresolved crimes of *Gukurahundi* (Mpofu, 2015; Ndlovu-Gatsheni, 2003). The survivors were left with permanent physical scars such as "recurrent miscarriage, impotence, infertility and kidney damage," and also psychological trauma (Cameron, 2018, p. 6). Bhalagwe remains a contested memorial site as efforts by Matabeleland activists to commemorate *Gukurahundi* victims tend to be thwarted by state agents (Eppel, 2020, p. 277). Within the prevailing culture of impunity, open discussions on *Gukurahundi* tend to be tabooed by state officials (Mpofu, 2014; Ndlovu, 2018a). Mpofu's (2019a) and Ndlovu's (2018a) works explore the discourses of silence perpetuated by government officials in media spaces that seek to justify and downplay the *Gukurahundi* atrocities. Those calling for accountability and justice are threatened and intimidated by state agents (Eppel, 2020; Mpofu, 2015).

The new administration that toppled President Mugabe in what was arguably a coup d'état in 2017, sought to "project a democratic leadership" (Eppel, 2020, p. 272), and as a result, spaces opened up for Gukurahundi dialogue. In 2018, President Emmerson Mnangagwa who replaced his former boss, established a National Peace and Reconciliation Commission (NPRC) to address historical injustices such as *Gukurahundi*. However, the NPRC public meetings held in Bulawayo and Lupane were disrupted by Mthwakazi Republic Party (MRP) and Ibhetshu Likazulu activists who disputed the composition of the Commission leading the dialogue (Eppel, 2020, p. 273). Out of the nine NPRC members, seven are Shona-speakers (Eppel, 2020, p. 272). As a result, the NPRC commissioners are "conflated with the Shona-speaking perpetrators" of *Gukurahundi* atrocities (Eppel, 2020, p. 272). At the first public meeting held in Gwanda, the NPRC members were confronted by some participants, mostly second-generation survivors, who labelled the group a "commission of perpetrators" (Eppel, 2020, p. 272). Recently, Mnangagwa has been engaging with some civic groups under the banner of Matabeleland Collective to address the legacies of *Gukurahundi*. Nonetheless, these government initiatives have failed to provide any genuine process of dialogue, healing and reconciliation in the country. In such a deeply wounded and divided society, there is a need for a truth and reconciliation commission to heal the wounds of *Gukurahundi* (Ngwenya, 2018; Tshuma, 2019).

Identity and Memory Politics in post-*Gukurahundi*

At Joshua Nkomo's funeral in 1999, Robert Mugabe referred to *Gukurahundi* as a "moment of madness." In 2011, President Mnangagwa claimed that *Gukurahundi* was a "closed chapter" that was addressed by the Unity Accord (Ndlovu, 2018a, p. 281). Attempts by government officials to repress the *Gukurahundi* past were evident during President Mnangagwa's November 2017 inauguration speech when he urged citizens to "let bygones be bygones" (Mpofu, 2019a, p. 109). More recently, in 2019, Obert Mpofu, another ZANU PF official, echoed these sentiments that *Gukurahundi* was "resolved" and people had "moved on" (Mpofu, 2019). In 2020, Vice President Kembo Mohadi added his voice by accusing those raising the *Gukurahundi* issue of reopening old wounds and "dividing the nation" (*Herald*, 2020). Mohadi's rhetorical question, "Who has not wronged the other?" serves as an attempt to repress memories of the mass atrocities. Forced amnesia is imposed by ZANU PF officials in order to silence dissenting voices. Despite these attempts at repressing *Gukurahundi* memories, the demands for accountability, truth-telling, justice, and commemoration are intensifying among the current generation in Matabeleland (Eppel, 2020, p. 276; Mpofu, 2015). Memories of the *Gukurahundi* have been inherited by the children and grandchildren of the victims, who are now taking up "the struggle to voice this history" (Eppel, 2020, p. 272).

In spite of these denials and attempts at obfuscation of facts, the reality that must be acknowledged is that the Zimbabwean government has also made attempts to address the sordid past. An Organ for National Healing, Reconciliation and Integration was created under the Government of National Unity (2009 – 2013) to promote peace, reconciliation and healing (Mpofu, 2014). This power-sharing government included three political parties, namely, ZANU PF, MDC-T [4] and MDC[5]. Although the Organ for National Healing, Reconciliation and Integration generated hope of addressing the legacies of *Gukurahundi* and the 2008 post-election violence (Fontein, 2010, p. 440), it failed to make any progress towards promoting peace, reconciliation and healing (Mpofu, 2015, p. 84). In 2010, an artist, Owen Maseko, was arrested for his *Gukurahundi* paintings that were exhibited at an art gallery in Bulawayo (Ncube & Siziba, 2015, p. 3). For displaying the *Gukurahundi* paintings, Maseko was charged with "undermining the authority of the President" and "offending an ethnic group" (Eppel, 2020, p. 271). The following year, Moses Mzila-Ndlovu, a co-Minister of National Healing, Reconciliation and Integration, and Father Marko Mkandla, a Roman Catholic priest, were arrested for attending a *Gukurahundi* memorial service (Mpofu, 2015, p. 84).

Although writers such as Vambe (2012) claim that *Gukurahundi* victims have healed and "moved on," it is evident that the wounds are yet to heal (Eppel, 2004; Ngwenya, 2018). Vambe's (2012) work has been critiqued on ethical grounds (Ndlovu & Dube, 2014) and for perpetuating "forgetfulness and silences" (Mpofu, 2016). As the past hurts remain unhealed, memories of *Gukurahundi* are being evoked, reproduced and transmitted by Matabeleland pressure groups and secessionist movements in ways that seek to solidify a sense of Ndebele nationalism (Ndlovu, 2018b; Ndlovu-Gatsheni, 2008). More importantly, new digital technologies are transforming the ways in which aggrieved communities are publicly recalling and sharing testimonies on *Gukurahundi* (Mpofu, 2015; Ndlovu, 2017). Subaltern communities are using news websites such as *Newzimbabwe.com* (Mpofu, 2015) and email listservs (Mhlanga & Mpofu, 2017; 2014) to bear witness to the *Gukurahundi* atrocities. Ncube and Siziba's (2015) work demonstrate how the nation's "forgotten" past is remembered through fictional works and other artistic expressions. Mlotshwa (2019) focusses on subversive or protest art in Matabeleland that memorialized *Gukurahundi*. First, a theatre play titled *The Good President* produced by Cont Mhlanga's Amakhosi was stopped from running by the government in 2007 (Mlotshwa, 2019, p. 87). Second, a visual art exhibition on *Gukurahundi* was shut down in 2010 (Mlotshwa, 2019, p. 87). Further,

---

[4] The Movement for Democratic Change faction was led by Morgan Tsvangirai.
[5] The Movement for Democratic Change faction was led by Arthur Mutambara.

Tshuma and Ndlovu (2020) argue that the "buried memories" of *Gukurahundi* are being immortalised through photographs that are displayed and circulated on Zimbabwean news websites. These photographs reinforce the calls for justice and commemoration of *Gukurahundi* victims (Tshuma & Ndlovu, 2020). In addition, *Gukurahundi* memories are conjured up and transmitted on *Umthwakazireview* news website (Ndlovu, 2018b), email listservs (Mhlanga & Mpofu, 2014), and diasporic online platforms such as *Inkundla.net* (Moyo, 2009) in ways that promote Ndebele secessionist politics. Although the aforementioned scholarship focuses on the preservation of memories through digital media, much of this research has largely ignored the role of music and musicians in reproducing *Gukurahundi* memories.

Popular music as the "Voice of the Voiceless" in Zimbabwe

Popular music plays a role in mediating people's lived realities and reflecting the political goings-on in society. Political songs reflect the "social consciousness of the people at a given time in their history" (Makina, 2009, p. 222). Zimbabwean musicians such as Thomas Mapfumo produced songs that resonated with the nationalist struggle (Vambe, 2000, p. 77). Revolutionary songs galvanised the freedom fighters and masses against the colonial regime (Makina, 2009, p. 223). Solomon Skhuza and Fallen Heroes performed revolutionary songs as ZIPRA cadres (Nkabinde, 1992, p. 7). At independence, music was used to celebrate the birth of Zimbabwe (Makina, 2009; Vambe, 2000). In post-colonial Zimbabwe, Mapfumo produced songs such as *Corruption* which openly attacked the growing levels of corruption in government (Mano, 2007, p. 68). Given its subversive lyrics, the song "mysteriously" disappeared from the airwaves (Mano, 2007, p. 77). Another musician, Paul Matavire, produced songs that questioned the poverty that characterized post-colonial Zimbabwe (Vambe, 2000, p. 78). These musicians began a process of "soul-searching about the true meaning of independence" (Vambe, 2000, p. 79). In the early 1990s, the working class and the poor were hit hard by poverty caused by the effects of the government's Economic Structural Adjustment Programme (ESAP). Artists such as Lovemore Majaivana and Leonard Zhakata produced songs that reflected working-class consciousness and the struggles of the poor (Vambe, 2000, p. 80). Zhakata's *Mugove* (pay) song communicated the trials of the working class in the 1990s (Mano, 2007).

Mano (2007, p. 61) posits that in contexts where the "mass media are weak and opposition political parties are frail, music can serve as the voice of the voiceless by offering subtle avenues of expression." He adds that music can serve a journalistic function by communicating the "daily issues in ways that challenge the powerful and give a voice to the disadvantaged" (Mano, 2007, p. 61). Thus, music can be used to denounce the "mighty and powerful" by communicating "everyday life problems" that tend to be obscured and marginalised in mainstream media (Mano,

2007, p. 61). In other words, popular music can serve as the "voice of the voiceless" (Mano, 2007, p. 63). Mapfumo's Chimurenga Rebel album, released in 2001, articulated the deepening political and economic crises in the country such as human rights violations and bad governance (Mano, 2007). Oliver Mtukudzi's song *Wasakara* (accept that you are worn out) ridiculed the late former president Robert Mugabe for overstaying in power. Makina (2009) uses the case of a musician, Comrade Fatso, to examine the role of protest music in Zimbabwe. Manase (2009) explores the subversive performances of "urban grooves" genre in the country in post-2000 epoch. Urban grooves were a product of the collusion of artists and the government in "propagating an anti-Western imperialism campaign" (Manase, 2009, p. 56). Former government officials such as Professor Jonathan Moyo and Elliot Manyika were heavily involved in producing songs that articulated ZANU PF's nationalist discourses (Manase, 2009, p. 57). Manase (2009) identifies the ambivalent nature of the urban grooves by noting that some artists subverted ZANU PF's anti-colonial rhetoric. Thus, the "state-sponsored urban grooves artists were able to subvert the same government machinery of control and resist the local oppression propagated by the ZANU-PF government" (Manase, 2009, p. 61). Dube and Ncube (2019, p. 149) argue that Lovemore Majaivana's music serves as a "socio-political commentary" challenging the marginalisation of the Ndebele people in post-colonial Zimbabwe. Thus, Dube and Ncube (2019, p. 149) posit that the minority Ndebeles are using Majaivana's protest music for "counter-hegemonic purposes." They used CDA to analyse Majaivana's five songs that bemoan the marginalisation of the Ndebele people in Zimbabwe (Dube & Ncube, 2019, p. 155).

Conceptual Framework

From a constructivist approach, representation then is central to subjectivity and can be both empowering and disempowering. Webb (2009) posits that representation is central to everyday life in that "we live immersed in representation: it is how we understand our environments and each other" (p. 2). It is political in that "central to all its uses, and domains of use, are three questions: who is performing the representation; what does it mean; and what effects does it have?" (Webb, 2009, p. 2). Even after so much theorization and making sense of representation, it remains a complex and slippery concept. Following Spivak, Webb (2009) turns to German language that offers a nuanced discussion of Darstellung (making present), Vertretung (speaking for and standing in for), Wortvorstellung (representations of words), and Sach- or Dingvorstellung (representations of things) and allows fairly precise uses of the term (Webb, 2009, p. 7). For Prendergast, among other meanings, representation refers to "re-present, to make present again, in two interrelated ways, spatial and temporal" (2000, p. 4).

In his music, Mncube seeks to "re-present" the nation between Zambezi and Limpopo rivers. However, in the constructivist approach, representation is problematic in that it is one of the "master concepts of modernity" (Foucault, 1970, p. 51; Prendergast, 2000, p. 2). This was a time of Mastery when man became, "therefore, the subject and mastermind of history" (Alves, 2000, p. 488). As a time of Mastery, it involves such excesses as colonial and slavery-linked genocides. Black people were represented in certain ways that justified their enslavement and colonization. This is seen continuing into the present uses of representation such that Lloyd questions "the seemingly unyielding racism of the so-called liberal institutions," and asks, "how could institutions whose missions promised democratic inclusivity and enlightened inquiry remain in practice so resistant to the project of racial desegregation?" (2019, p. vii). Lloyd traces the racial regime of representation, genealogically, "from Enlightenment thinkers like Kant and Schiller to late modernist critics like Adorno and Benjamin" (Lloyd, 2019, p. viii).

Against the above backdrop, representation means the replacement of the subject with another subject where the first subject lacks a voice. Several scholars regard this form of representation as problematic and dehumanising. In the case of women and feminist theory, Alcoff (1991) referenced this as the problem of speaking on behalf of others. Deleuze & Foucault call it the indignity of speaking for others (1977, p. 205). In the light of what they see as marginalisation, one key problem has been that of being represented.

Methodology

This chapter takes a qualitative approach that seeks to provide "a detailed description and analysis of the quality, or the substance, of the human experience" (Marvasti, 2004, p. 7). The authors applied this method to Bongani Mncube's music, in order to explore and understand his experiences as a human being, an artist, and the people he represents in his music. Qualitative research locates the observer in the world consisting of "a set of interpretive, material practices that makes the world visible" (Denzin & Lincoln, 2005, p. 3). It puts emphasis on meaning-making (Merriam, 2009, p. 9). Music and poetry, as forms of art, are about making sense of the world and various phenomena in it. Art is also about meaning-making about the world around the artist.

To obtain data for this chapter, the authors first accessed the entire oeuvre of Mncube's work. As at the time of this study, Mncube had produced three albums, namely: *Inkulu Lendaba*, *War of Peace* and *Dear Brother*. Thereafter, the authors narrowed down the data to focus on the songs that have *Gukurahundi* as their theme. Consequently, the authors identified and used six of the artist's songs – a purposive sample, for in-depth examination, using the Critical Discourse Analysis (CDA) method.

The songs were analyzed alongside data from in-depth interviews with Mncube. Interviews are taken as conversations between researchers and people they believe can give them information that is germane to their work. The interview has also been described as "an inter change of views between two persons conversing about a theme of mutual interest" (Kvale, 1996, p. 2). It is "a conversation that has a structure and a purpose" (Kvale, 1996, p. 6). The qualitative and in-depth interview is a "construction site of knowledge" (Kvale, 1996, p. 2). In linguistics, discourse is considered as language in use; but a Foucauldian approach focuses on discourses as "ways of looking at the world, of constructing objects and concepts in certain ways" (Baker & McEnery, 2015, pp. 4–5). For Bednarek and Caple (2017), as much as discourses are language in use, they are also multimodal, combining two or more modalities such as visual and aural, and also multi-semiotic, that is combining two or more semiotics, that is, meaning-making systems such as image or language (p. 7).

Since this chapter is about both words, as in poetry, and music in the songs that accompany the poems, the material analyzed in this study is multimodal. Mcdonald (2003) notes that the concept of a discourse is complex and confusing. She defines it as "a system of communicative practices that are integrally related to wider social and cultural practices, and that help to construct specific frameworks of thinking" (p. 1). Mcdonald, however, points out that discourses can be contested, and are provisional, thus making them more of "a process of making meaning" (2003, p. 1). Mncube's poetry can be considered as raising counter-discourses as most of it challenges the hegemonic Zimbabwean discourses. Discourse analysis is therefore "language or image with its socio-cultural roots exposed and its socio-cultural effects revealed" (Mcdonald, 2003, p. 10). The authors examined Mncube's work within the context of marginalising the Ndebeles and other minority groups, Zimbabwean nationalism, migration and the diaspora as the artist works from South Africa in self-imposed exile.

Mncube, the focus of this chapter, is a Zimbabwean musician who uses his platform to communicate challenging political messages in the aftermath of *Gukurahundi* massacre. The critical discourse analysis method used in this study not only produces knowledge within socio-historical contexts, but is also enmeshed in power relations (Wodak, De Cillia, Reisigl & Liebhart, 2009, p. 7). It is also focused on what Richardson (2007, p. 23) called "language in use." In this regard, the method does not only unmask social inequalities and injustices that manifest through language, but also examines the ways in which relations of domination can be resisted and thwarted (Richardson, 2007, p. 26; Wodak et al., 2009, p. 8). Therefore, all instruments of critical discourse analysis, including historical perspective, discursive strategies, linguistic patterns and construction, and meaning-making, were used in the examination of six of Mncube's songs and interview used in this chapter.

Remembering the past and healing historical wounds through Music and Performance

The authors' interaction with Mncube suggests that his childhood experiences shaped his activism. *Gukurahundi* affected his family when he was in primary school. He has recollections of how his father and grandfather were victimized and tortured by the Fifth Brigade in 1984. His grandfather, who was the breadwinner, died two months after the torture. His father, who was already ill, died in 1987. As a result, Mncube could not proceed to secondary school. His efforts to get scholarships and bursaries were unfruitful. He had to migrate to South Africa in 1995 in search for greener pastures. Mncube regards his musical performances as shaped by the legacies of *Gukurahundi*. His songs and poetry are performed in Ndebele and English. In his song, *Sihamba nomhlaba*, Mncube laments about being vagabonds due to oppression and marginalisation in Zimbabwe:

> Sihamba nomhlaba, kodwa likhona izwe labo baba bethu
> Ngancitshwa ithuba lokufunda, qeda ngahlekwa kwathiwa angifundanga
>
> *We are vagabonds although we have a land of our forefathers.*
> *I was denied an opportunity to go to school, but now they are mocking me*
> *that I am not educated.*

The above song speaks about Mncube's own personal experiences as it is a lamentation of how *Gukurahundi* denied him an opportunity to proceed to secondary school. Further, his song is also a response to the dominant stereotype in Zimbabwe that people of Matabeleland are not educated. The former president, Robert Mugabe, once denigrated the Kalanga people (one of the sub-groups in Matabeleland) by claiming that they are not educated and are obsessed with migrating to South Africa. Mncube's song subverts this dominant stereotype by reminding his audiences about the legacies of *Gukurahundi*.

He uses music and poetry not only to commemorate and memorialize *Gukurahundi* victims, but also to call for social healing. His song "*Wounded nation*" expresses the pain and trauma experienced by *Gukurahundi* survivors:

> In the land between Limpopo and Zambezi there is a nation. A nation which has never tasted freedom since 1980.
>
> A nation whose gallant sons and daughters who fought for freedom they never enjoyed. A nation with thousands massacred and the world never said a word.

> A nation with children who watched helplessly while their parents were burnt to death. A nation with parents who were forced to dance on top of their children's graves.

The land between Limpopo and Zambezi is a description of Zimbabwe. Although the country gained independence in 1980, Mncube provides a counter-narrative that Zimbabweans are yet to taste freedom. He adds that the "world never said a word" when ZANU PF orchestrated the *Gukurahundi* massacres. In this context, the term "world" denotes Western communities. Mncube's perspective corroborates Cameron's (2018, p. 1) assertion that despite being aware of the atrocities in Matabeleland, the British government chose to adopt a policy of "wilful blindness." In addition, Mncube narrates and describes the atrocities that were committed by the Fifth Brigade. Transitivity such as "burnt to death" and "forced to dance on top of their children's graves" express the traumatic experiences of *Gukurahundi* victims. Research has shown that *Gukurahundi* survivors were forced by the Fifth Brigade to perform disrespectful activities such as dancing on top of the graves of the murdered (Eppel, 2006). The CCJP and LRF report (1997) provides chilling accounts of the killings and other human rights violations unleashed on civilians during the *Gukurahundi*. Mncube uses his music to communicate about these historical injustices and demand redress. In this vein, he depicts Zimbabwe as a "wounded nation" that needs healing:

> *We are a nation with scars and wounds which were never treated.*
> Siyisizwe esigeleza inyembezi ezingesulwa muntu
>
> *We are a nation with tears that are yet to be wiped way*

"Wounds" and "scars" are metaphors employed to signify the trauma and pain experienced by survivors of *Gukurahundi*. Mncube's song seeks to subvert the government's perspective that *Gukurahundi* is a closed chapter (Mpofu, 2019a; Ndlovu, 2018a). Notions of "closed chapter" and "let bygones be bygones" are discursive strategies that serve to silence and minimise discussions on *Gukurahundi* (Mpofu, 2019a; Ndlovu, 2018a). Given that the metaphors "scars" and "wounds" are reminders about the unresolved legacies of the atrocities, Mncube uses artistic expressions to bear witness to what Ferrandiz regards as the "wounds of history" (2006, p. 7). Mncube's song challenges Vambe's (2012) claim that *Gukurahundi* survivors have "moved on" with their lives.

A number of scholarly works (Eppel, 2014; 2006; 2004; Ngwenya, 2018; Tshuma, 2019) highlight the need to heal the festering wounds of *Gukurahundi*. Proper funeral rites were not performed for some of the *Gukurahundi* victims (Eppel, 2006; Fontein, 2010). In some instances, the remains of *Gukurahundi* victims were left in the open to be "scavenged by animals" (Eppel, 2006, p. 268).

As a result, surviving relatives are haunted by "angry and restless" spirits of the *Gukurahundi* deceased (Eppel, 2014, p. 49; 2006, p. 264). There is a belief amongst Ndebele communities that the "bones" of *Gukurahundi* victims that are "in the forest" need to be exhumed and reburied so that cultural customs are followed to appease the aggrieved spirits (Eppel, 2020, p. 266; 2006, p. 278). Mncube's music articulates such concerns raised by affected communities in Matabeleland.

In his *Wounded Nation* song, Mncube asserts that Ndebele people have become "*umhlambi kazelusile*" which means a "flock without a shepherd." He adds that Ndebele people are now "*imhambuma*" (vagabonds). Thus, the naming of Ndebele people as "vagabonds" and a "flock without a shepherd" serves to highlight how the experiences of migrants are intertwined with *Gukurahundi* atrocities. As a Zimbabwean artist based in South Africa, Mncube has first-hand experiences of the struggles of the migrant communities. Such experiences of Ndebele communities in the diaspora are intertwined with the legacies of *Gukurahundi*. Thus, "Gukurahundism" remains a reality through the experiences of the post-generation (Ndlovu, 2019, p. 187). There is a "generational ripple effect" that was caused by families losing breadwinners during the *Gukurahundi* (Ndlovu, 2019, p. 187). Due to a lack of economic opportunities, young people are forced to flee Zimbabwe as "economic migrants" (Ndlovu, 2019, p. 187). The song *Ngibhace ezizweni* (I am in exile) articulate a series of rhetorical questions posed by an artist in exile. These questions relate to the *Gukurahundi*:

> Lachithwa kwenzenjani igazi e Morogoro?
> Yabhalwa kutheni I Grand Plan?
> Kukhona okunuka santungwana ngendaba yama dissidents
> Yadalwa ngubani I moment of madness?
> Bangaki ababulawa yi Gukurahundi?
> Babotshwa yini abababulalayo?
> Sebabuya na abanyamalalayo?
> Abuthwa yini amathambo emigodini?
> Yasihlanganisa yini isizwe I Unity Accord?
> Ebalekela e Ngilandi wayewoneni u Mqabuko?
> Babotshwa nje badleni kabani u Dabengwa lo Masuku?
> Ngiphenduleni bakwethu angazi lutho ngibhace ezizweni
>
> *Why was the Grand Plan crafted?*
> *There is something amiss about the issue of dissidents.*
> *Who was responsible for this moment of madness?*
> *How many were massacred during the Gukurahundi?*
> *Were the perpetrators of Gukurahundi brought to justice?*
> *Have those who were disappeared during Gukurahundi returned?*

Were the bones of Gukurahundi victims collected from the disused mines?
Did the Unity Accord unite the nation?
What was Joshua Nkomo's crime when he fled to Britain?
Why were Dumiso Dabengwa and Lookout Masuku arrested?
I don't have answers to these questions, I am in exile.

The poetry to the song *Ngibhace ezizweni* anchors *Gukurahundi* in Zimbabwe's history and the politics of the country. It makes three key observations. First, it traces the genealogy of *Gukurahundi* in the Morogoro violence of 1976 and the Entumbane battles of 1980 between ZIPRA and ZANLA soldiers. Second, it makes it clear that *Gukurahundi* might have ended as a form of physical violence, but it continues to be alive in the marginalisation that sends a lot of young people, especially from Matabeleland, to South Africa. Third, the poetry makes a point that *Gukurahundi* as an ideology has extended from targeting the Ndebeles to focus on the whole country. The musician cites such human rights violations as Operation *Murambatsvina* of 2005 where people's houses were demolished by the government. By arguing that *ngibhace ezizweni* (I am a refugee hiding in foreign lands), Mncube effectively affirms his position, that is, his locus of enunciation, as out of the Zimbabwean nation. This then allows him to plead ignorance and therefore direct a series of rhetorical questions to Zimbabwe or those who consider themselves as Zimbabweans. As the song progresses and he brings up issues of migration, it becomes clear why Mncube feels he is out of the nation as far as Zimbabwe is concerned. Mncube is therefore exiled both physically and psychologically from Zimbabwe. These were the implications of *Gukurahundi*; it was not only physical violence but has had psychological implications.

Mncube raises the issue of the "Grand Plan" to bring attention to the legacies of *Gukurahundi*. There is a belief that *Gukurahundi* was a product of the 1979 document entitled "Grand Plan" purported to have been authored by Shona intellectuals within ZANU PF (Mpofu, 2019a, p. 123; Ngwenya, 2018, p. 28). This blueprint lays out plans for entrenching Shona domination and for oppressing and side-lining Ndebele people in the social, economic and political facets in Zimbabwe (Mpofu, 2019a, p. 123; Ndlovu-Gatsheni, 2011, p. 27).

Mncube's song delves deeper into the issue of *Gukurahundi* by posing a question regarding why this Grand Plan was crafted. In 1999, the late former President Mugabe described *Gukurahundi* as a "moment of madness." In response to Mugabe's rhetoric, Mncube calls for those responsible for this "madness" to be brought to justice. Given the culture of impunity and the fact that the perpetrators have not acknowledged the severity of their crimes, Mncube uses his music to communicate the legacies of *Gukurahundi*. He demands justice for *Gukurahundi* victims who were made to disappear and those whose bodies were thrown down in mine shafts (Eppel, 2004, p. 43). There is a call for the human remains of *Gukurahundi* victims to be exhumed and reburied as bones and graves occupy a central place in Zimbabwe (Eppel, 2006; Fontein, 2010). In the Ndebele belief system, for instance, proper funeral procedures have to be accomplished in order for the spirits of the dead to protect the family (Eppel, 2006). A traditional ceremony called *Umbuyiso* must be performed after the burial in order for the deceased to transition to the spiritual realm (Eppel, 2014). However, there are angry and unsettled spirits of *Gukurahundi* victims in Matabeleland which are haunting surviving relatives as proper funeral rites were not performed (Eppel, 2006). Further, Mncube questions the reasons for the victimisation of ZAPU leaders. Joshua Nkomo had to flee to Britain, whilst Dumiso Dabengwa and Lookout Masuku were incarcerated. Lastly, the song *Ngibhace ezizweni* ponders on whether the 1987 Unity Accord between ZANU PF and ZAPU has resulted to unity in the country. His argument is that Zimbabweans are wounded and the Unity Accord did not address these historical injustices.

Mncube's music: A Challenge to state-imposed Amnesia

Mncube's song on "let bygones be bygones" serves to highlight the challenges of forgiving the perpetrators of *Gukurahundi* who are still in power. He sang:

> Let bygones be bygones. Nangu umuntu efuna simxolele kodwa engafuni ukuxolisa
> Let bygones be bygones. Uthi sidlulise okwadlulayo yena esayenza okufanayo
> Uthi sixolele ababulali besaqhubeka besibulala
> Uthi sixolele abanenzondo bengakayeki ukusincindezela
>
> *Someone wants us to forgive him when he has not apologised*
> *He wants to forget the past when he has not changed his ways*
> *He wants us to forgive killers when they are still killing us*
> *He wants us to forgive the cruel people when they are still oppressing us*

In his inauguration speech in November 2017, President Mnangagwa, who is implicated in the *Gukurahundi* atrocities, appealed to the victims to "let bygones be bygones" and "move on" (Mpofu, 2019a, p. 108). In a context where memories of *Gukurahundi* are "suppressed and criminalised," the idea of "let bygones be bygones" can be construed as one of the mechanisms of "genocide silencing" (Mpofu, 2019a, p. 108). In such instances, discourses of forgiveness can be used to perpetuate state-imposed forgetting of events (Ndlovu, 2017). There are limits to forgiveness (Mayo, 2015) as there are instances where victims are pressured to "move on" (Minow, 1998, p. 15).

Mncube's song is a response to Mnangagwa and the state-imposed forgiveness. First, he argues that the victims cannot forgive perpetrators who are yet to apologise for their crimes. The perpetrators of *Gukurahundi* have not acknowledged their crimes and sought forgiveness from the victims. The closest the perpetrators came to apologising was in 1999 at Joshua Nkomo's funeral when former president Robert Mugabe described *Gukurahundi* as a "moment of madness." Through his music, Mncube calls on the perpetrators to acknowledge their crimes and apologise to the affected communities. Second, Mncube rebukes the government for demanding that the victims "move on" while it maintains its authoritarian nature. One of the challenges facing survivors of mass atrocity is not only to forgive perpetrators who are "unknown," but also those who are "unrepentant, or still a threat" (Mayo, 2015, p. 26). Mncube presents ZANU PF as "unrepentant" and a "threat," and thus argues that it is difficult for *Gukurahundi* survivors to forgive the perpetrators of violence. By depicting ZANU PF leaders as "killers" and "oppressors," Mncube reinforces the view that *Gukurahundi* victims cannot "forgive and forget" the past.

The topos of an unrepentant ZANU PF and the challenges of forgiveness are further developed in Mncube's song where he poses a series of questions:

Nangu umuntu efuna ukusiphekela ukudla ngebhodo ebeliphekela I poison lingageziswanga?
Nangu umuntu efuna ukusiqhawula ngezandla ezigcwele igazi labafowethu?
Umxolela kanjani umuntu ekunyathele engakasusi unyawo?
Sikhohlwa kanjani abanyamalalayo bengakatholakali?
Sikhohlwa kanjani amathambo awababulalwayo engakabuthwa?

Someone wants to cook food for us using a pot that had poison and has not been washed
Someone wants us to greet us with hands dripping with the blood of our brothers
How do you forgive someone who is still oppressing you?
How do we forget about Gukurahundi when those who were disappeared have not be located?
How do forget about Gukurahundi when the bones/remains of those who were killed have not been recovered and collected?

The artist uses metaphors such as "poison" and "blood" to signify the crimes and unrepentant nature of ZANU PF. The musician seems to be challenging Mnangagwa's government which is projecting itself as a "new dispensation" and asking affected communities to "let bygones be bygones." Mncube represents Mnangagwa and ZANU PF as unrepentant, hence not in a position to facilitate the national healing process. Mnangagwa's government has been advocating dialogue meetings with Matabeleland civil society groups to address the *Gukurahundi* issue. Given that Mnangagwa is implicated in the *Gukurahundi* pogrom, the artist is questioning his role in leading the national healing process. As such, the government's plans to conduct "fast-track" exhumations of *Gukurahundi* victims is being challenged by Matabeleland pressure groups who view the process as an attempt to obscure the crimes.

The song attests to the challenges of forgiving the perpetrators of *Gukurahundi* who have not shown remorse for their crimes. In post-conflict situations such as in Zimbabwe, survivors tend to be coerced to "forget" about the past for the sake of "national unity." Such official narratives reinforce and sustain amnesia and impunity. Mncube views forgiveness as conditioned by the wrongdoer's repentance. The topos of "bones" is a reminder of the unresolved *Gukurahundi* legacies as there is a call for the victims' remains to be exhumed and reburied. Memory activism centred on exhumations and reburials attest to the growing calls for the need to address the legacies of the atrocities. The struggles of the *Gukurahundi* survivors is evident in Mncube's rhetorical question: *umxolela kanjani umuntu ekunyathele engakasusi unyawo? (How do you forgive someone who is still oppressing you?)*. The rhetoric of forgiveness tends to be employed by perpetrators of *Gukurahundi* to entrench collective amnesia (Ndlovu, 2017). As such, the refusal by *Gukurahundi* survivors to forgive the perpetrators is presented in Mncube's song as what Brudholm (2006, p. 23) terms a "moral protest".

In the song, "*Ngibhace ezizweni*" Mncube poses the question: "*ikuliphi I khabothi I Dumbutshena report (where is the Dumbutshena report hidden?*" The Dumbutshena report which detailed the causes of the *Gukurahundi* was "never publicly released" by the government (Alexander, 1998, p. 155). The Chihambakwe report which also provides details on the *Gukurahundi* killings was never made public as well. Through his music, Mncube is challenging the state-imposed amnesia on the Matabeleland atrocities. Further, Mncube raises the problem of enforced disappearances in Matabeleland. A documentary titled *Missing Persons in Zimbabwe* was produced by the Centre for Innovation and Technology (CITE) and Habakkuk Trust. This documentary film describes the problem of enforced disappearances in Zimbabwe and its legacies. Eppel (2014; 2006) argues that funeral rituals could not be performed for those who disappeared. Her work on "bones in the forest" calls for exhumations and reburials in order to appease the angry spirits (Eppel, 2014). Mncube buttresses this perspective by asserting that *Gukurahundi* survivors cannot let bygones be bygones as long as exhumations and reburials of the dead have not been conducted. Other songs such as *Where did we go wrong*, and *Ngeke sikhohlwe* reinforce the subversive narratives on *Gukurahundi*.

Conclusion

This chapter explored the role of music in expressing and articulating memories of the *Gukurahundi* massacre in Zimbabwe. Using a case study of Bongani Mncube's songs, the authors examined the role of music as a tool for communicating political messages about historical injustices. Mncube's songs not only trace the genealogy of *Gukurahundi*, but also articulate the implications of these atrocities on the second generation. His musical performances can only be understood in relation to his social location as an artist from Matabeleland who is currently based in South Africa. Mncube articulates his migrant experiences and highlights how his music is intertwined with the legacies of *Gukurahundi*. His music touches on a myriad of issues related to *Gukurahundi* such as migrant experiences, forgiveness, social healing, reburials, exhumations, justice, and impunity. Through his music, Mncube speaks for *Gukurahundi* survivors who are demanding the perpetrators to acknowledge their crimes and be held accountable. He represents Zimbabwe as a wounded nation that is yet to come to terms with its traumatic past events.

The memories of *Gukurahundi* remain a contested terrain as cultural artefacts such as popular music play a key role in subverting the government's official narratives. Musical performances in the diaspora demonstrate the struggles of Matabeleland people to represent their repressed historical memories. Matabeleland artists in South Africa are using artistic expressions to not only articulate their experiences in the diaspora, but also to reflect on the political situation "back home." As such, popular music plays a counter-hegemonic role as it enables suppressed communities such as the people of Matabeleland to express their grievances against ZANU PF and demand justice for *Gukurahundi* victims. Mncube's songs touch on a number of topical issues in a post-genocide context as they represent the struggles of the people of Matabeleland in exhuming, reburying and commemorating *Gukurahundi* victims. In a Zimbabwean environment characterized by authoritarianism, and with *Gukurahundi* discussions being criminalised and dissenting voices stifled, the people of Matabeleland based in the diaspora are employing art to express their disenchantments against the prevailing condition. Thus, art enables the subaltern communities to freely express themselves.

Similar to diasporic news websites that provide counter-narratives to ZANU PF's discourses (Moyo, 2007), popular music is empowering the subaltern to "speak" about their painful histories. As noted by Mano (2007), popular music serves as a "voice of the voiceless." Unlike other forms of subversive art, such as a theatre play that was stopped from running by the government (Mlotshwa, 2019), and a visual art exhibition that was shut down by the state (Mpofu, 2019b), popular music enables the people of Matabeleland to circumvent censorship and state-imposed amnesia. With the advent of digital technologies, Mncube's songs are circulated through social media platforms such as Facebook, YouTube and WhatsApp. Literature on postmemory (Hirsch, 2012) shows how memories of the Holocaust are being inherited by the generation after. In the same vein, the second-generation survivors in Matabeleland are actively involved in attempts to commemorate and demand justice for *Gukurahundi* victims (Eppel, 2020).

There is no doubt that there is an emergence of counter-hegemonic voices that are demanding *Gukurahundi* redress. Digital spaces such as Facebook, WhatsApp and Twitter are enabling the subaltern to preserve and disseminate memories of the genocide. Additionally, the emergence of fictional works such as Tshuma's (2018) *House of Stone* also demonstrates efforts of the current generation in Matabeleland to keep the *Gukurahundi* memories alive. In his account as a Holocaust survivor, Elie Wiesel believes that witnesses have a "moral obligation to try to prevent the enemy from enjoying one last victory by allowing his crimes to be erased from human memory" (2006, p. viii). In a context where *Gukurahundi* discourses are repressed by the state, Mncube's music is redemptive as it enables survivors to challenge the status quo, and to also prevent the perpetrators from erasing their crimes from public memory.

References

Alcoff, L. (1991). The problem of speaking for others. Cultural Critique. *Cultural Critique, 20*, 5–12. https://doi.org/10.2307/1354221

Alexander, J. (1998). Dissident perspectives on Zimbabwe's post-independence war. *Africa: Journal of the International African Institute, 68*(2), 151–182.

Alexander, J., McGregor, J., & Ranger, T. (2000). *Violence and memory: One hundred years in the 'dark forests' of Matabeleland*. United Kingdom: James Currey.

Alves, J. A. L. (2000). The declaration of human rights in postmodernity. *The Declaration of Human Rights in Postmodernity, 22*, 478–500.

Baker, P., & McEnery, T. (2015). *Corpora and discourse studies: Integrating discourse and corpora*. Palgrave Macmillan.

Bednarek, M., & Caple, H. (2017). *The discourse of news values: How news organisations create newsworthiness*. Oxford University Press.

Brudholm, T. (2006). Revisiting resentments: Jean Amery and the dark side of forgiveness and reconciliation. *Journal of Human Rights, 5*, 7–26. https://doi.org/10.1080/14754830500519714

Cameron, H. (2018). The Matabeleland massacres: Britain's wilful blindness. *International History Review, 40*(1), 1–19. https://doi.org/10.1080/07075332.2017.1309561

CCJP (Catholic Commission for Justice and Peace) and LRF (Legal Resources Foundation). (1997). *Gukurahundi in Zimbabwe: A Report on the disturbances in Matabeleland and the Midlands, 1980–1988*. CCJP and LRF.

Chung, F. (2006). *Re-living the second Chimurenga. Memories from the liberation struggle in Zimbabwe*. Nordic Africa Institute.

Deleuze, G., & Foucault, M. (Eds.). (1977). Intellectuals and power. In *Language, counter memory, practice* (pp. 205–217). Cornell University Press.

Denzin, N. K., & Lincoln, Y. S. (2005). Introduction: The discipline and practice of qualitative research. In N. K. Denzin, & Y. S. Lincoln (Eds.), *The Sage handbook of qualitative research* (pp. 1-32). Sage.

Dube, V., & Ncube, B. J. (2019). Majaivana and protest music in Zimbabwe. A challenge to political hegemony and marginalization. In U. T. Onyebadi (Ed.), *Music and messaging in the African political arena* (pp. 149–165). Hershey, PA: IGI Global.

Eppel, S. (2004). The need for truth and reparation. In B. Raftopoulos & T. Savage (Eds.), *Zimbabwe: Injustice and political reconciliation* (pp. 43–62). Cape Town, South Africa: Institute for Justice and Reconciliation.

Eppel, S. (2006). "Healing the dead": Exhumation and reburial as a tool to truth-telling and reclaiming the past in rural Zimbabwe. In T. A. Borer (Ed.), *Telling the truths: Truth telling and peacebuilding in post-conflict societies* (pp. 259–288). University of Notre Dame Press.

Eppel, S. (2014). "Bones in the forest" in Matabeleland, Zimbabwe: Exhumations as a tool for transformation. *The International Journal of Transitional Justice, 8*, 404–428.

Eppel, S. (2020). How Shall We Talk of Bhalagwe? Remembering the Gukurahundi Era in Matabeleland, Zimbabwe. In K. Wale, P. Gobodo-Madikizela, & J. Prager (Eds.), *Post-conflict Hauntings: Transforming memories of historical trauma* (pp. 259–284). Palgrave Macmillan.

Ferrandiz, F. (2006). The return of Civil War ghosts. The ethnography of exhumations in contemporary Spain. *Anthropology Today, 22*(3), 7–12. https://doi.org/10.1111/j.1467-8322.2006.00437.x.

Fontein, J. (2010). Between tortured bodies and resurfacing bones: The politics of the dead in Zimbabwe. *Journal of Material Culture, 15*(4), 423–448. https://doi.org/10.1177/1359183510383105

Foucault, M. (1970). *The Order of Things*. London: Tavistock Publications.

Hirsch, M. (2012). *The generation of postmemory: Writing and visual culture after the Holocaust*. Columbia University Press.

Kriger, N. (2003). *Guerrilla veterans in post-war Zimbabwe: Symbolic and violent politics, 1980–1987*. Cambridge University Press.

Kvale, S. (1996). *Interviews: An introduction to qualitative research interviewing*. Sage.

Lindgren, B. (2005). Memories of violence: Recreation of ethnicity in post-colonial Zimbabwe. In *No peace no war: An anthropology of contemporary armed conflicts* (pp. 155–172). London: James Currey Ltd.

Lloyd, D. (2019). *Under representation: The racial regime of aesthetics*. Fordham University Press.

Makina, B. (2009). Re-thinking white narratives: Popular songs and protest discourse in post-colonial Zimbabwe. *Muziki, 6*(2), 221–231. https://doi.org/10.1080/18125980903250772

Manase, I. (2009). Zimbabwe urban grooves and their subversive performance practices. Social Dynamics. *Social Dynamics*, 56–67. https://doi.org/10.1080/02533950802666923

Mano, W. (2007). Popular music as journalism in Zimbabwe. Journalism Studies. *Journalism Studies, 8*(1), 61–78. https://doi.org/10.1080/14616700601056858

Marvasti, A. B. (2004). *Qualitative research in sociology: An introduction.* Sage.
Matabeleland Broadcasting Corporation. (2020, October 25). *Bongani Mncube Interview* [Video]. YouTube. https://www.youtube.com/watch?v=ub_XuEsMp_A
Mayo, M. (2015). *The limits of forgiveness. Case studies in the distortion of a biblical ideal.* Minneapolis, MN: Fortress Press.
Mcdonald, M. (2003). *Exploring media discourse.* London: Arnold.
Merriam, S. (2009). *Qualitative research: A guide to design and implementation.* Hoboken, NJ: Jossey-Bass.
Mhlanga, B. & Mpofu, M. (2014). The virtual parallax: Imaginations of Mthwakazi Nationalism – online discussions and calls for self-determination. In A. Solo (Ed.), *Handbook on research on political activism in the Information Age* (pp. 129–146). Hershey, PA: IGI Global.
Mhlanga, B., & Mpofu, M. (2017). On virtuality and the aesthetics of spectacle: Nationalist imaginations of Mthwakazi and its passions of semblance. *Critical Arts, 31*(1), 64–81. https://doi.org/10.1080/02560046.2017.1300925
Minow, M. (1998). *Between vengeance and forgiveness. Facing history after genocide and mass violence.* Beacon Press.
Mlotshwa, K. (2019). Matabeleland and the rulers' political sins: Defining subversive art in Zimbabwe. *Metacritic Journal for Comparative Studies and Theory, 5*(1), 77–95. https://doi.org/10.24193/mjcst.2019.7.04
Moyo, D. (2007). Alternative media, diasporas and the mediation of the Zimbabwean crisis. *Ecquid Novi: African Journalism Studies, 28*(1), 81–105. https://doi.org/10.1080/02560054.2007.9653360
Moyo, L. (2009). Constructing a home away from home: The internet, nostalgia and identity politics among Zimbabwean communities in Britain. *Journal of Global Mass Communications, 2*(1), 66–85.
Mpofu, O. (2019, July 21). Exploring the causes of Gukurahundi (part 2). *Sunday News* (Zimbabwe). https://www.sundaynews.co.zw/exploring-the-causes-of-gukurahundi-part-2/
Mpofu, S. (2014). Memory, national identity and freedom of expression in the Information Age: Discussing the taboo in the Zimbabwean public sphere. In A. Solo (Ed.), *Handbook on research on political activism in the Information Age* (pp. 114–128). Hershey, PA: IGI Global.
Mpofu, S. (2015). When the Subaltern Speaks: Citizen Journalism and Genocide 'Victims' Voices Online. *African Journalism Studies, 36*(4), 82–101. https://doi.org/10. 1080/23743670.2015.1119491
Mpofu, S. (2019a). Art as journalism in Zimbabwe. The case of Owen Maseko's banned Zimbabwean genocide exhibition. *Journalism Studies, 20*(1), 60–78. https://doi.org/10.1080/1461670X.2017.1358652
Mpofu, S. (2019b). For a nation to progress victims must 'move on': A case of Zimbabwe's social media discourses of Gukurahundi genocide silencing and resistance. *African Identities, 17*(2), 108–129. https://doi.org/10.1080/14725843.2019.1660618
Mpofu, W. (2016). Zimbabwe's Gukurahundi Genocide. Beyond the Forgetfulness and Silences of Coloniality. In M. Muchie, V. Gumede, S. Oloruntoba, & N. A. Check (Eds.), *Regenerating Africa: Bringing African Solutions to African Problems* (pp. 114–137). African Institute of South Africa.

Ncube, G., & Siziba, G. (2015). (Re)membering the nation's 'forgotten' past: Portrayals of Gukurahundi in Zimbabwean literature. *The Journal of Commonwealth Literature, 15*(2), 1–17. https://doi.org/10.1177/0021989415615646

Ncube, M. (2016, November 14). Jumbo show for Bongani, as protest poet releases DVD. *Bulawayo24 (Zimbabwe)*. https://bulawayo24.com/entertainment/music/99540

Ndlovu, I., & Dube, B. (2014). Response to Maurice T. Vambe's 'Zimbabwe genocide: Voices and perceptions from ordinary people in Matabeleland and the Midlands provinces, 30 years on.' *African Identities, 11*(4), 1–14. https://doi.org/10.1080/14725843.2013.842159

Ndlovu, M. (2017). Facing history in the aftermath of Gukurahundi atrocities: New media, memory and the discourses on forgiveness on selected Zimbabwean news websites. *Peace and Conflict Studies, 24*(2 Article 3). https://doi.org/10.46743/1082-7307/2017.1400

Ndlovu, M. (2018a). Gukurahundi, new media and the 'discourses of silence': The reproduction of the hegemonic narratives of the Matabeleland post-colonial violence on selected Zimbabwean news websites. *African Identities, 16*(3), 275–289. https://doi.org/10.1080/14725843.2018.1439726

Ndlovu, M. (2018b). New media and Ndebele Hiraeth: Memory, nostalgia and Ndebele nationalism on selected news websites. *African Journalism Studies, 39*(4), 109–130. https://doi.org/10.1080/23743670.2018.1535990

Ndlovu, N. (2019). *The Gukurahundi "genocide". Memory and justice in independent Zimbabwe.* [Unpublished doctoral dissertation]. University of Cape Town, South Africa.

Ndlovu-Gatsheni, S. (2003). The post-colonial state and civil-military relations in Matabeleland: Regional perceptions. In R. Williams, C. Gavin, & D. Abrahams (Eds.), *Ourselves to know: Civil-military relations and defence transformation in Southern Africa* (pp. 17–38). Institute of Security Studies.

Ndlovu-Gatsheni, S. (2008). Nation building in Zimbabwe, and the challenges of Ndebele Particularism. *African Journal of Conflict Resolution, 8*, 27–55. https://doi.org/10.4314/ajcr.v8i3.39430

Ndlovu-Gatsheni, S. (2011). *The Zimbabwean nation-state project: A historical diagnosis of identity and power-based conflicts in a post-colonial state.* Nordica African Institute.

Ngwenya, D. (2018). *Healing the wounds of Gukurahundi in Zimbabwe. A participatory action research project.* Springer.

Phimister, I. (2009). "Zimbabwe is mine": Mugabe, murder and Matabeleland. *Safundi: The Journal of South African and American Studies, 10*(4), 471–478. https://doi.org/10.1080/17533170903210996

Prendergast, C. (2000). *The triangle of representation.* Columbia University Press.

Richardson, J. E. (2007). *Analysing newspapers. An approach from critical discourse analysis.* Palgrave Macmillan.

Rwafa, U. (2012). Representations of Matabeleland and Midlands disturbances through the documentary film Gukurahundi: A moment of madness (2007). *African Identities, 10*(3), 313–327. https://doi.org/10.1080/14725843.2012.715458

Sithole, M. (1999). *Zimbabwe: Struggles Within the Struggle.* Rujeko Publishers.

Spivak, C. (1988). Can the subaltern speak? In C. Nelson & L. Grossberg (Eds.), *Marxism and the interpretation of culture* (pp. 271–313). MacMillan Education.

Tshuma, D. (2019). Healing the wounds of the past. Peacebuilding prospects for Zimbabwe. *Conflict Trends, 2*, 14–21.

Tshuma, L., & Ndlovu, M. (2020). Immortalizing 'buried memories' of Gukurahundi genocide through the voice of the visual. *Journal of Genocide Research.* https://doi.org/10.1080/14623528.2020.1850393

Tshuma, N. (2018). *House of stone.* W. W. Norton & Company.

Vambe, M. T. (2000). Popular songs and social realities in post-independence Zimbabwe. *African Studies Review, 43*(2), 73–86. https://doi.org/10.2307/524985

Vambe, M. T. (2012). Zimbabwe genocide: Voices and perceptions from ordinary people in Matabeleland and the Midlands provinces, 30 years on. *African Identities, 10*(3), 281–300. https://doi.org/10.1080/14725843.2012.715456

Webb, J. (2009). *Understanding representation.* Sage.

Wiesel, E. (2006). *Night. (Translated from the French by Marion Wiesel).* Hill and Wang.

Wodak, R., de Cillia, R., Reisigl, M., & Liebhart, K. (2009). *The discursive construction of national identity.* Edinburg University Press.

CONTRIBUTORS

Douglas L. Allen (he/him/his) is an Assistant Professor of Geography in the Department of Social Sciences, Sociology, and Criminology at Emporia State University, USA. He is an urban cultural geographer whose research focuses on music, performance, and place-making as community affirming practices of resisting racial injustice. His recent work on place-making, music/festival performance, and Black geographies, particularly with HBCUs (Historically Black Colleges/Universities), has been published in prominent journals such as *Progress in Human Geography, Antipode, Cultural Geographies,* and *Geoforum* as well as recent book chapters in *The Handbook of Urban Educational Leadership* and the *Routledge Handbook on Media Geographies*. Dr. Allen's future work seeks to expand his research on Black joy and place-making to further understand how they contribute to changing socio-spatial conditions for racially marginalized communities.

Rachael Cofield (they/them) holds a Ph.D. in Geography from Florida State University, USA. A queer geographer who generally examines the issues of gentrification and queer life in Atlanta, Georgia (USA), Dr. Cofield is particularly interested in investigating and writing about the lives of the more-than-gay populations that have been displaced out of the Midtown gayborhood in the Atlanta's urban core area. Dr. Cofield previously served as Chair of the AAG's Graduate Student Affinity Group and is currently the Secretary for the Study of the American South Specialty Group. Dr. Cofield teaches in the Geography and Anthropology Department, Kennesaw State University (USA), and enjoys traveling, LARPing, and 'so-bad-it's good' TV.

Rodelio Cruz Manacsa (Ph.D.) is an Associate Professor of Politics at the University of the South (Sewanee), working on the international rule of law and security, human rights, and comparative judicial politics. He obtained a Ph.D. in Political Science (*With Distinction*) from Vanderbilt University, an M.A. Degree (*Examined with Distinction*) from Vanderbilt University, and an Executive M.A. (*With Distinction*) from the Amsterdam School of International Relations (ASIR) at the University of Amsterdam. He was a Fulbright Scholar at Boston College and a European Union Scholar at the Amsterdam School of International Relations.

Henrique C. T. D'Onofrio has an MBA in Marketing from the Faculty São Luis, and a Bachelor in Social Communication with emphasis in Radio and Television from Armando Alvares Penteado Foundation. Mr. D'Onofrio was a musician, and a member of *Anti-tédio*, one of the first punk rock bands in the

Brazilian federal capital. It was an experience which gave him unique insights into the history of the music scene in Brasília in the early 1980s. Currently, he is a marketing management specialist and serves as an adviser to a number of financial institutions in Brazil. He can be reached at kikedonofrio@hotmail.com.

Marta Fernanda T. D'Onofrio earned a Bachelor's degree in Social Communication with emphasis in Publishing, from the University of São Paulo. Marta was immersed in the cultural movement known as "Rock de Brasília" and participated in a number of events in that context in the early years of punk rock music in Brazil. Later, having worked in the events area of the State Social Service of Industry, Marta was, for several years, a personal assistant to the famous Italian artist, Gaetano Miani, in his studio in São Paulo, and can reached at mfyada@gmail.com.

Silvio C. T. D'Onofrio holds a Ph.D. in Social History from the University of São Paulo, Brazil. Dr. D'Onofrio was an Associate Professor in the Department of Letters at the Regional University Center of Espírito Santo do Pinhal, Brazil. He currently heads REGIONEM, a research group dedicated to the study of material, intellectual and spiritual elements linked to the notions of space, area and region, based in São Paulo. Dr. D'Onofrio's peer-reviewed articles have appeared in journals such as *Stichproben: Vienna Journal of African Studies* (University of Vienna), *Journal of Comparative Studies* (Daugavpils University) and *Acervo: Revista do Arquivo Nacional* (Rio de Janeiro). He has also published 7 book chapters, the last one being in a book titled *Museums and the Working Class* (Routledge). He serves as a reviewer for international scientific publications that include *Messages, Sages and Ages - The Bukonivian Journal of Cultural Studies* (Ştefan cel Mare University, Romania); *New Trends in Social and Liberal Sciences* (University of Texas) and *Cambridge Scholars Publishing* (Newcastle Upon Tyne, UK). He can be reached at opeltrezero@gmail.com.

Lyombe Eko (Ph.D.) is a Professor of Media Law, Comparative & International Communication in the Department of Journalism and Creative Media, College of Media and Communication, Texas Tech University, Lubbock, TX – USA. He is the author of *The Charlie Hebdo Affair & Comparative Journalistic Cultures* (https://link.springer.com/book/10.1007%2F978-3-030-18079-9#authorsand affiliationsbook).

Cecilia Amaoge Eme is a Professor of Linguistics in the Department of Linguistics, Nnamdi Azikiwe University, Awka, Nigeria. She was the head of her department from 2009 to 2014, and holds a Ph.D. in Linguistics, with specialization in Phonetics and Phonology. Dr. Eme's professional resume includes serving as editor and reviewer of manuscripts for several journals in her discipline; a keynote speaker and lead paper presenter at local and international conferences. She is the author of 8 books and over 70 scholarly journal articles.

She had the privilege to be chosen to deliver the 27th Inaugural Lecture at her university. Dr. Eme's areas of research include Sociolinguistics, Psycholinguistics, Documentary Linguistics and Applied Linguistics. She is a member of many learned societies, including the Nigerian Academy of Letters, the Linguistic Association of Nigeria, Association of Phoneticians and Phonologists in Nigeria, and the West African Linguistic Society. Dr. Eme can be reached at ca.eme@unizik.edu.ng.

Kelly Grenier is a Ph.D. student of Political Science at the University of Kentucky, USA. She holds an MA degree in Security from Aberystwyth University (U.K.). Her latest research project examines regime type and institutional rationale to censor both culture and media, and the effects of such actions on citizens' political engagement in Africa, the Americas, and other parts of the world. She aims to contribute to the literature on political trust, expand understanding of civil society to include artistic spaces, and uncover more about how regimes try to stay in power. She can be reached at kelly.grenier@uky.edu.

Khanyile Joseph Mlotshwa is a Ph.D. candidate in Media and Cultural Studies at the University of Kwazulu-Natal (UKZN) in South Africa. He researches on articulations of the media, migration, the city and the representations of Black African subjectivity in post-apartheid South Africa. He has published parts of his work as journal articles and chapters in edited book collections.

Benjamin Ifeanyi Mmadike is a Professor of Linguistics with specialization in Syntax and Semantics, in the Department of Linguistics, Nnamdi Azikiwe University, Awka, Nigeria. He earned his Ph.D. from the University of Ibadan, Nigeria. Dr. Mmadike has a published book and over 60 scholarly articles in both local and international journals. He has supervised 5 Ph.D. dissertations and several MA theses. His research interests cut across such areas as morphology, stylistics and applied linguistics. He is a member of the Linguistic Association of Nigeria and the Association for Promoting Nigerian Languages and Culture. Dr. Mmadike can be reached at b.mmadike@unizik.edu.ng.

Kameika Murphy (Ph.D.) is an Atlantic World historian with expertise on the experiences of Afro-diasporic peoples across the Greater Caribbean. She is an Assistant Professor of Historical Studies at Stockton University, USA. Her research pays special attention to the military as a lens through which political agency and change can be understood in much broader contexts, beyond conflict and war. Dr. Murphy also works as a consultant on corporate social responsibility initiatives that surround the public humanities, especially as they relate to historical memory and messaging across various platforms. Dr. Murphy's most recent work addresses the issue of late 18th and early 19th centuries' Black Loyalist refugees and their contributions to Afro-Caribbean civil society.

Bhekinkosi Jakobe Ncube (Ph.D.) is a Global Excellence Stature Postdoctoral Fellow in the Department of Communication and Media Studies at the University of Johannesburg, South Africa. His research interests include identity politics, community media and ethnic minority media, music and political messaging, social media, and the implications of computational journalism. His Ph.D. was on the online constructions and contestations of ethnic identities. Bhekinkosi is also a lecturer at the National University of Science and Technology, Zimbabwe where he teaches journalism and media studies courses. Email: bhekijncube54@gmail.com.

Mphathisi Ndlovu is a Research Fellow in the Department of Journalism at Stellenbosch University (South Africa). He is also a lecturer in the Department of Journalism and Media Studies at the National University of Science and Technology (Zimbabwe). He has a Ph.D. in Journalism from Stellenbosch University (South Africa). Mphathisi also holds the Africa No Filter (ANF) academic fellowship. His research interests are in digital cultures, collective memory, and identity politics, and has published his work as book chapters and journal articles.

Uche Onyebadi is a Professor and Chair of the Journalism Department in the Bob Schieffer College of Communication, Texas Christian University. He also served as the Director of the School of Journalism, Southern Illinois University, Carbondale, IL (2014-2016). He holds a doctoral degree in journalism, with a specialization in political communication, from the University of Missouri, Columbia-Missouri, USA., and his research interests focus on political communication, media and politics, mass communication theory, media ethics, and international communication. His articles have appeared in communication journals such as the *Journal of Mass Media Ethics*; *Journal of Broadcasting & Electronic Media*; *International Communication Gazette*; *Journalism: Theory, Practice & Criticism*; *Media, War & Conflict*; *International Communication Research Journal*; *International Journal of Communication*; *Journal of International and Intercultural Communication*; *The Journal of Social Media in Society*; and *Humanities*. Dr. Onyebadi is the editor of the volumes, *Music as a Platform for Political Communication* (2017), *Music and Messaging in the African Political Arena* (2019), and *Multidisciplinary Issues Surrounding African Diasporas* (2020). His professional experience includes working as a journalist in Nigeria, in sports management and sport commentary on television in Kenya, as a Fulbright Specialist at BRAC University, Dhaka, Bangladesh (2012), and as a Visiting Professor, International Summer School at the University of International Business and Economics, Beijing, China (2017). Dr. Onyebadi is a 2018-2019 Fellow of the Institute for Diverse Leadership in Journalism and Mass Communication (USA), and the current editor of the *International Communication Research Journal*, a publication of the International Communication Division of the Association for Education in Journalism and Mass Communication (AEJMC), USA.

Zeny Sarabia-Panol (Ph.D.) is a professor and associate dean at Middle Tennessee State University's College of Media and Entertainment. She is a co-author of the book: *Corporate Social Responsibility, Public Relations, and Community Engagement* and has published several book chapters and journal articles. A former editor of the *International Communication Research Journal*, she now serves on its editorial board as well as the editorial boards of the *International Journal of Strategic Communication* and *Journalism and Mass Communication Educator*. She received her B.S. in Journalism from Silliman University, MA in Communication, University of the Philippines, and her doctorate from Oklahoma State University, USA.

Julia Schmidt-Pirro received her Ph.D. in Musicology from the Technische Universität Berlin, Germany, in 1999. She has taught courses at Georgia Southern University & Armstrong Atlantic State University (USA), including the Honors Class, "Music and Politics." She is the author of a book and several articles on European and American Avant-garde composers, including George Antheil, John Cage, and Mayako Kubo. Her co-authored article, "Employing Music in the Cause of Social Justice: Ruth Crawford and Zilphia Horton," was selected by the editors of *Voices: The Journal of New York Folklore* for republication in the edited volume, *New York State Folklife Reader: Diverse Voices* (2013).

N. Usha Rani (Ph.D.) is a professor emeritus, and current Senior Fellow in the Department of Journalism and Mass Communication, at the University of Mysore, Mysore, India. She is the founding Director of the Educational Multi Media Research Centre (EMMRC), established by the Indian University Grants Commission in the State of Karnataka, with a mandate to produce educational media products for students in higher education. Dr. Rani is a recipient of several international awards, including the Lifetime Achievement Award by the *Business World* media group and the prestigious *Nadoja Dr. Patil Puttappa* Press Award for her contribution to journalism education; the ICSSR International Fellowship to undertake Research at the UN, (Geneva, Switzerland); two American Fulbright Fellowships (1990-91 & 2006-07); the Canadian Advance Faculty Research Fellowship for conducting research at McGill University, Montreal, Canada; and two National awards for producing the best educational TV documentaries in India. She is the author of major professional books, including *Folk Media for Development; Educational Television in India: Challenges and Issues and Communication Research*, and a 15-volume book series on *Social Development and Medi: A case study of Karnataka*. She can be reached at usharani_mc@yahoo.co.in.

Archie W. Simpson (Ph.D.) was a teaching fellow in Politics and International Relations at the University of Bath (UK) until 2017. He previously taught at the University of Aberdeen, University of St Andrews, University of Stirling and University of Nottingham. He is a founding member of the Centre for Small State Studies at the University of Iceland and is on the international editorial board of the new journal, *Small States and Territories*. His main research interests are in small states, international security, grand strategy and European politics. He is the author of a forthcoming book, *A Theory of Disfunctionality* (Vernon Press).

Cherry-Ann Smart (Ph.D.) is a principal consultant at *Information Smart Consulting* (Jamaica), where she combines a love for research and writing by providing research consultancy and editorial services. She is best known for scholarly works about libraries and the information society and their impact on Caribbean citizens. Cherry-Ann is particularly interested in themes surrounding literacy, social justice, diversity, e-government, and cultural heritage. In addition to periodical teaching assignments and presentations, she also conducts workshops on information-related themes and serves on several Editorial Boards.

INDEX

A

Aborto Elétrico, 139, 148, 150, 151
Abraham, John, 177
Adoor Gopalakrishnan, 177
AEJMC, xiii
affirmative, 227, 228, 240, 244, 245, 248, 249
Afghanistan, x
Anti-tédio, 137, 150, 157, 158
APC, 207, 208, 211, 213
APGA, 207, 213
Aravindan, G., 177
Arevalo, Hugo, 272
artist, 190

B

Bangla rock band, 173
batuque de umbigada, 141
Baym, G., xxiii
Benegal, Shyam, 179, 180
Bengal famine, 170
Bhalagwe, 279
Black Baptist, 102
Bossa Nova, 144
Brasília, 137, 139, 145
Brasília punk rock bands, 159, 160
Brazil, 138, 146
Brazilian music, 137
Brazilian Punk Rock, 139
Buffalo Soldier, 98
burlesque, 227, 228, 230, 231, 232, 233, 234, 235, 236, 237, 238, 239, 249, 250, 251

C

campaign jingles, 208, 210, 212
campaign messages, 208
Canto Nuevo, 270
Capital Inicial, 155
Carnegie Hall, 228, 240, 244, 246, 247, 248
Carpini, M.D., xxiii
Chorinho, 140
Christensen & Haas, 164, 165
Christmas Rebellion, 89
civil rights, 33, 37, 42, 45, 56
classical music, 33, 34, 35, 36, 37, 38, 39, 40, 41, 44, 46, 47, 49, 50, 52, 53, 55, 56, 59
CNN, ix
collective action potential theory, 265
Communist Party of India, 166, 175
Complexos, 153, 155, 156
counter-propaganda, 188
critical discourse analysis, 290

D

defiance, 195
Democracy, ix
Denton and Woodward, xiii, xxiii

E

election, 208, 209, 211, 212
electorate, 207
ephemeral, 228, 231, 233, 234, 237, 248

epithet, 212
erotic agency, 91
Escola de Escândalo, 137, 150
Esthappan, 179

F

FAMU, 227, 228, 234, 239, 240, 241, 242, 243, 244, 245, 246, 247, 248, 249, 250
Fifth Brigade, 280, 283, 284, 292
forgiveness, 295
Foster, 240, 242, 243, 244, 250

G

Gandhism, 166
Garratt, J, xxiii
Ghatak, Ritwik, 168, 170, 181
Ghoraguli, Moheener, 173
Ghosh, Rituparno, 172
Giannetti, 164, 181
Gianos, 164, 181
Glissant, Édouard, 91
Gukurahundi, 279, 280, 286, 291, 292, 294, 295, 298
Gukurahundi atrocities, 285, 295
Gukurahundi massacres, 280, 292
Gukurahundi survivors, 280, 297, 298
Gukurahundi victims, 280, 292, 294, 296

H

Hall, Stuart, 90
hortative, 212
humanism, 174
hyperbole, 212

I

Ìgbà, 213
Ìgba kā ÷gbà, 213
imperative, 212
inclusive pronoun, 212
Islam, Rupam, 173
Ìyọ̀m, 214

J

Jamaica revolution, 89, 101, 102, 104, 106
Jara, Victor, 258
jingle, 207, 209, 210
Jon Stewart, xiv
Joshua Nkomo, 283, 285, 295

K

Karun, Shaji, 176
Kazmi, 168, 181
Koivukoski, J. & Ödmark, S., xiv, xxiii
Kuti, Fela Aníkúlápó, xiv

L

Lage Raho Munna Bhai, 166
LBGT movement, 172
Leab, 167, 181
leftists, 163
left-oriented films, 171
Legião Urbana, 139, 148, 150, 152
liberal films, 171
liberalism, 171
Locke, Alain, 33, 47, 49, 57, 59
Love, N. S., xxiii
Lundu, 140
Lyombe Eko, ix

M

Manns, Patricio, 273
Marching 100, 228, 234, 240, 241, 242, 243, 244, 245, 246, 248, 249
marginalized communities, 227, 234, 235, 246, 249, 305
Marian Anderson, 33, 34, 35, 37, 40, 43, 44, 45, 46, 55, 58
Marley, Bob, xiv, 92, 98, 103, 106, 107, 109
Marxism, 163, 164, 166, 175, 177
Marxist, 163, 171, 177, 181
mass culture, 165
Matabeleland, 279, 280, 286, 293, 294, 297, 298
Mbuli, Mzwakhe, 183
Metropolitan Studios, 227, 234, 235, 236, 237, 238, 239, 248, 250
military reggae, 100
Mncube, Bongani, 279, 280, 281, 289, 291, 294, 296, 297
    Bongani Mncube's music, 289
    Mncube's songs, 295, 298
Mobilization, 202
Modinha, 140
Moyo, Desire, 183
Moyoxide, 184
Mugabe, Robert, 282, 285
music, 187
music and entertainment, ix, x

N

Ndebele, 282, 284, 288, 290, 293, 294
Neorealism, 163, 168, 169, 175, 176, 179
New Generation cinema, 178
New Wave, 163, 164, 165, 168, 176, 177, 178
Nigeria, xviii

Nouvelle Vague, 169

O

Onyebadi, Uche, xiii
Over-the-Top (OTT), 173

P

Pakistan, x
parallelism, 212
Parra, Violeta, 255
Pather Panchali, 169, 170, 179
Paunksnis, 165, 180, 181
PDP, 207, 208, 211, 214, 215
Pelo telephone, 142
perpetrators of *Gukurahundi*, 297
persuasion, 207
Pinochet, Augusto, 263
Piravi, 176
placemaking, 228, 229, 230, 231, 232, 233, 236, 237, 240, 248
Plebe Rude, 149, 150, 152
political communication, xiii
political manifesto, 211
Political messages, ix, 178, 180, 184
political radicalism, 167
political satire, x
political songs, 188
politics, xi, 186, 207, 209
popular music, 281, 287, 298
Popular Unity Party, 261
presupposition, 212
propaganda, 187, 208, 210
protest music, 288
protest songs, 186
punk Rock, 138, 146
Punk Rock of Brasília, 148

Q

queer, 227, 228, 230, 231, 232, 233, 234, 235, 236, 237, 239, 248, 249, 250, 305
Quilapayún, 274

R

Rang De Basanti, 167
Rastafari, 87, 88, 89, 91, 92, 93, 94, 98, 101, 103, 106, 107, 110
Ray, Satyajit, 168, 169, 170, 171, 172, 181
realism, 164, 169, 170, 174, 175, 178, 179
representation, 288
resistance, 191
Revolta, 158
right wing party, 163
Rio de Janeiro, 141
Robeson, Paul, 33, 34, 35, 37, 38, 46, 54, 58, 59
Rock de Brasília, 137, 139
rule of three, 212

S

Samba, 142, 143
Samba-canção, 144
Semba, 141
Sen, Mrinal, 168, 169, 171, 179, 181
Sharpe, Sam, 102
Shona, 282
slogan, 207, 210
socialism, 165, 166
songs of terror, x
spirituals, 33, 34, 35, 37, 38, 39, 40, 41, 44, 46, 47, 48, 49, 50, 52, 54, 58
state critique theory, 265

Still, William Grant, 33, 34, 36, 48, 50, 56, 58, 59
Street, J., xxiii
subaltern, 175
syllable structure repair, 212

T

Texas Christian University, xiii
theater, xv
Third World Cinema, 176

U

ululation, 212
Umbigada, 141
Unbwogable, 186
United States, xiv

V

voice modulation, 212

W

Wanta, Wayne, xiii

Y

Youssef, Bassem Raafat Mohamed, xiv

Z

ZANU PF, 280, 282, 283, 292, 296, 298
ZAPU, 282, 283, 284
Zelensky, Volodymyr Oleksandrovych, xiv
Zimbabwe, ix, 183

Printed in the USA
CPSIA information can be obtained
at www.ICGtesting.com
LVHW062049250824
789227LV00001B/61